HISTORY

OF THE

WAR IN THE PENINSULA

AND IN THE

SOUTH OF FRANCE

FROM THE YEAR 1807 TO THE YEAR 1814

VOLUME V

HISTORY

OF THE

WAR IN THE PENINSULA

AND IN THE

SOUTH OF FRANCE,

FROM THE YEAR 1807 TO THE YEAR 1814.

BY

W. F. P. NAPIER, C.B.

COLONEL H. P. FORTY-THIRD REGIMENT,
MEMBER OF THE ROYAL SWEDISH ACADEMY OF MILITARY SCIENCES.

VOL. V.

CONSTABLE · LONDON

This edition first published in Great Britain 1993
by Constable and Company Limited
3 The Lanchesters, 162 Fulham Palace Road
London W6 9ER

Originally published in London in 1836
by Thomas and William Boone

ISBN 0 09 471880 6

Printed in Great Britain by
St Edmundsbury Press Ltd
Bury St Edmunds, Suffolk

TABLE OF CONTENTS.

BOOK XVII.

CHAPTER I.

CHAP. II.

TABLE OF CONTENTS.

BOOK XVIII.

CHAP. I.

CHAP. II.

TABLE OF CONTENTS.

TABLE OF CONTENTS.

CHAP. II.

TABLE OF CONTENTS.

BOOK XX.

CHAP. VIII.

LIST OF APPENDIX.

LIST OF THE PLATES,
To be placed together at Page 582

NOTICE.

1°. In the present volume will be found a plan of the Peninsula on a very small scale, yet sufficient to indicate the general range of operations. A large map would be enormously expensive without any correspondent advantages to the reader; and it would only be a repetition of errors, because there are no materials for an accurate plan. The small one now furnished, together with the sketches which I have drawn and published with each volume, and which are more accurate than might be supposed, will give a clear general notion of the operations. Those who desire to have more detailed information will find it in Lieutenant Godwyn's fine atlas of the battles in the Peninsula—a work undertaken by that officer with the sole view of forming a record of the glorious actions of the British army.

2°. Most of the manuscript authorities consulted for former volumes have been also consulted for this volume, and in addition the official correspondence of Lord William Bentinck; some notes by Lord Hill; the journal and correspondence of Sir Rufane Donkin; a journal of Colonel Oglander, twenty-sixth regiment; a memoir by Sir George Gipps, royal engineers; and a variety of communications by other officers. Lastly, authenticated copies of the official journals and correspondence of most of the marshals and generals who commanded armies in Spain. These were at my request supplied by the French War-office with a prompt liberality indicative of that military frankness and just pride which ought and does characterize the officers of Napoleon's army. The publication of this volume also enables me with convenience to produce additional authorities for former statements, while answering, as I now do, the attacks upon my work which have appeared in the " Life of Sir Thomas Picton," and in the " Quarterly Review."

HISTORY

OF THE

PENINSULAR WAR.

BOOK XVII.

CHAPTER I.

GREAT and surprising as the winter campaign had been, its importance was not understood, and therefore not duly appreciated by the English ministers. But the French generals saw with anxiety that lord Wellington, having snapped the heavy links of the chain which bound him to Lisbon, had acquired new bases of operation on the Guadiana, the Agueda, and the Douro, that he could now choose his own field of battle, and Spain would feel the tread of his conquering soldiers. Those soldiers with the confidence inspired by repeated successes, only demanded to be led forward, but their general had still to encounter political obstacles, raised by the governments he served.

In Spain, the leading men, neglecting the war at hand, were entirely occupied with intrigues, with the pernicious project of reducing their revolted colonies, or with their new constitution. In Por-

tugal, and in the Brazils, a jealous opposition to
the general on the part of the native authorities had
kept pace with the military successes. In England the cabinet, swayed by Mr. Perceval's narrow
policy, was still vacillating between its desire to
conquer and its fear of the expense. There also
the Whigs greedy of office and dexterous in parliamentary politics, deafened the country with their
clamours, while the people, deceived by both parties as to the nature of the war, and wondering
how the French should keep the field at all, were,
in common with the ministers, still doubtful, if their
commander was truly a great man or an impostor.

The struggle in the British cabinet having ended
with the resignation of lord Wellesley, the consequent
predominance of the Perceval faction, left small
hopes of a successful termination to the contest in
the Peninsula. Wellington had, however, carefully
abstained from political intrigues, and his brother's
retirement, although a subject of regret, did not affect
his own personal position; he was the General of
England, untrammelled, undegraded by factious ties,
and responsible to his country only for his actions.
The ministers might, he said, relinquish or continue
the war, they might supply his wants, or defraud
the hopes of the nation by their timorous economy,
his efforts must be proportioned to his means; if
the latter were great, so would be his actions,
under any circumstances he would do his best, yet
he was well assured the people of England would
not endure to forego triumph at the call of a nig-
gard parsimony. It was in this temper that he had
undertaken the siege of Badajos, in this temper he
had stormed it, and meanwhile political affairs in
England were brought to a crisis.

Lord Wellesley had made no secret of Mr. Perceval's mismanagement of the war, and the public mind being unsettled, the Whigs were invited by the Prince Regent, his year of restrictions having now expired, to join a new administration. But the heads of that faction would not share with Mr. Perceval, and he, master of the secrets relating to the detestable persecution of the Princess of Wales, was too powerful to be removed. However, on the 11th of May, Perceval was killed in the house of Commons, and this act, which was a horrible crime, but politically no misfortune either to England or the Peninsula, produced other negociations, upon a more enlarged scheme with regard both to parties and to the system of government. Personal feelings again prevailed. Lord Liverpool would not unite with lord Wellesley, the Grey and Grenville faction would not serve their country without having the disposal of all the household offices, and lord Moira, judging a discourtesy to the Prince Regent too high a price to pay for their adhesion, refused that condition. The materials of a new cabinet were therefore drawn from the dregs of the Tory faction, and lord Liverpool became prime minister.

It was unfortunate that a man of lord Wellesley's vigorous talent should have been rejected for lord Liverpool, but this remnant of a party being too weak to domineer, proved less mischievous with respect to the Peninsula than any of the preceding governments. There was no direct personal interest opposed to lord Wellington's wishes, and the military policy of the cabinet yielding by degrees to the attraction of his ascending genius, was finally absorbed in its meridian splendour. Many prac-

tical improvements had also been growing up in
the official departments, especially in that of war
and colonies, where colonel Bunbury, the under-
secretary, a man experienced in the wants of an
army on service, had reformed the incredible disorders which pervaded that department during the
first years of the contest. The result of the political crisis was therefore comparatively favourable
to the war in the Peninsula, the story of which
shall now be resumed.

It has been shewn how the danger of Gallicia,
and the negligence of the Portuguese and Spanish
authorities with reference to Almeida and Ciudad
Rodrigo, stopped the invasion of Andalusia, and
brought the allies back to Beira. But if Wellington,
pursuing his first plan, had overthrown Soult on
the banks of the Guadalquivir and destroyed the
French arsenal at Seville, his campaign would have
ranked amongst the most hardy and glorious that
ever graced a general ; and it is no slight proof of
the uncertainty of war, that combinations, so extensive and judicious, should have been marred by the
negligence of a few secondary authorities, at points
distant from the immediate scenes of action. The
English general had indeed under-estimated the
force opposed to him, both in the north and south ;
but the bravery of the allied troops, aided by the
moral power of their recent successes, would have
borne that error, and in all other particulars his
profound military judgment was manifest.

Yet to obtain a true notion of his views, the various
operations which he had foreseen and provided
against must be considered, inasmuch as they shew
the actual resources of the allies, the difficulty of
bringing them to bear with due concert, and the

propriety of looking to the general state of the war, previous to each of Wellington's great movements. For his calculations were constantly dependent upon the ill-judged operations of men, over whom he had little influence, and his successes, sudden, accidental, snatched from the midst of conflicting political circumstances, were as gems brought up from the turbulence of a whirlpool.

Castaños was captain-general of Gallicia, as well as of Estremadura, and when Ciudad Rodrigo fell, lord Wellington, expecting from his friendly feeling some efficient aid, had counselled him upon all the probable movements of the enemy during the siege of Badajos.

First. He supposed Marmont might march into Estremadura, either with or without the divisions of Souham and Bonnet. In either case, he advised that Abadia should enter Leon, and, according to his means, attack Astorga, Benavente, Zamora, and the other posts fortified by the enemy in that kingdom; and that Carlos d'España, Sanchez, Saornil, in fine all the partidas in Castile and the Asturias, and even Mendizabel, who was then in the Montaña St. Ander, should come to Abadia's assistance. He promised also that the regular Portuguese cavalry, under Silveira and Bacellar, should pass the Spanish frontier. Thus a force of not less than twenty-five thousand men would have been put in motion on the rear of Marmont, and a most powerful diversion effected in aid of the siege of Badajos and the invasion of Andalusia.

The next operation considered, was that of an invasion of Gallicia, by five divisions of the army of Portugal, the three other divisions, and the cavalry, then in the valley of the Tagus and about Bejar, being left to contend, in concert with Soult, for Badajos. To help Abadia to meet such an attack, Bacellar and Silveira had orders to harass the left flank and rear of the French, with both infantry and cavalry, as much as the nature of the case would admit, regard being had to the safety of their raw militia, and to their connection with the right flank of the Gallician army, whose retreat was to be by Orense.

Thirdly. The French might invade Portugal north of the Douro. Abadia was then to harass their right flank and rear, while the Portuguese opposed them in front; and whether they fell on Gallicia or Portugal, or Estremadura, Carlos d'España, and the Partidas, and Mendizabel, would have an open field in Leon and Castile.

Lastly, the operation which really happened was considered, and to meet it lord Wellington's arrangements were, as we have seen, calculated to cover the magazines on the Douro, and the Mondego, and to force the enemy to take the barren difficult line of country, through Lower Beira, towards Castelo Branco, while Abadia and the Guerilla chiefs entered Castile and Leon on his rear. Carlos d'España had also been ordered to break down the bridges on the Yeltes, and the Huebra, in front of Ciudad Rodrigo, and that of Barba de Puerco on the Agueda to the left of that fortress. Marmont would thus have been delayed two days, and the magazines both at Castelo Branco and Celorico saved by the near approach of the allied army.

España did none of these things, neither did Abadia nor Mendizabel operate in a manner to be felt by the enemy, and their remissness, added to the other faults noticed in former observations, entirely marred Wellington's defensive plan in the north, and brought him back to fight Marmont. And when that general had passed the Agueda in retreat, the allied army wanting the provisions which had been so foolishly sacrificed at Castelo Branco, was unable to follow; the distant magazines on the Douro and the Mondego were its only resource; then also it was found that Ciudad and Almeida were in want, and before those places could be furnished, and the intermediate magazines on the lines of communication restored, it was too late to march against Andalusia. For the harvest which ripens the beginning of June in that province and a fortnight later in Estremadura, would have enabled the army of Portugal to follow the allies march by march.

Now Marmont, as Napoleon repeatedly told him, had only to watch lord Wellington's movements, and a temporary absence from Castile would have cost him nothing of any consequence, because the army of the north would have protected the great communication with France. The advantages of greater means, and better arrangements for supply, on which Wellington had calculated, would thus have been lost, and moreover, the discontented state of the garrison of Ciudad Rodrigo, and the approach of a new battering train from France, rendered it dangerous to move far from that fortress. The invasion of Andalusia, judicious in April, would in the latter end of May have been a false movement; and the more so that Castaños having, like his predecessors, failed to bring forward the Gallician army, it was again made painfully evident, that in critical circumstances no aid could be obtained from that quarter.

Such being the impediments to an invasion of Andalusia, it behoved the English general to adopt some other scheme of offence more suitable to the altered state of affairs. He considered that as the harvest in Leon and Castile, that is to say, in the districts north of the Gredos and Gata mountains, was much later than in Estremadura and Andalusia, he should be enabled to preserve his commissariat advantages over the French in the field for a longer period in the north than in the south. And if he could strike a decisive blow against Marmont, he would relieve Andalusia as securely as by a direct attack, because Madrid would then fall, and Soult, being thus cut off from his communications with France, would fear to be hemmed in on all sides. Wherefore to make the duke of Ragusa fight a great battle, to calculate the chances, and prepare the means of success, became the immediate objects of lord Wellington's thoughts.

The French general might be forced to fight by a vigorous advance into Castile, but a happy result depended upon the relative skill of the generals, the number and goodness of the troops. Marmont's reputation was great, yet hitherto the essays had been in favour of the Englishman's talents. The British infantry was excellent, the cavalry well horsed, and more numerous than it had ever been. The French cavalry had been greatly reduced by drafts made for the Russian contest, by the separation of the army of the north from that of Portugal, and by frequent and harassing marches. Marmont could indeed be reinforced with horsemen from the army of the centre, and from the army of the north,

but his own cavalry was weak, and his artillery
badly horsed, whereas the allies' guns were well
and powerfully equipped. Every man in the British
army expected victory, and this was the time to
seek it, because, without pitched battles the French
could never be dispossessed of Spain, and they
were now comparatively weaker than they had
yet been, or were expected to be; for such was
the influence of Napoleon's stupendous genius,
that his complete success in Russia, and return
to the Peninsula with overwhelming forces, was
not doubted even by the British commander.
The time, therefore, being propitious, and the
chances favourable, it remained only to combine
the primary and secondary operations in such a
manner, that the French army of Portugal, should
find itself isolated for so long as would enable the
allies to force it singly into a general action. If the
combinations failed to obtain that great result, the
march of the French succouring corps, would nevertheless relieve various parts of Spain, giving
fresh opportunities to the Spaniards to raise new
obstacles, and it is never to be lost sight of, that
this principle was always the base of Wellington's
plans. Ever, while he could secure his final
retreat into the strong holds of Portugal without
a defeat, offensive operations, beyond the frontiers,
could not fail to hurt the French.

To effect the isolating of Marmont's army, the
first condition was to be as early in the field as the
rainy season would permit, and before the coming
harvest enabled the other French armies to move in
large bodies. But Marmont could avail himself,
successively, of the lines of the Tormes and the
Douro to protract the campaign until the ripening

of the harvest enabled reinforcements to join him, and hence the security of the allies' flanks and rear during the operations, and of their retreat, if overpowered, was to be previously looked to. Soult, burning to revenge the loss of Badajos, might attack Hill with superior numbers, or detach a force across the Tagus, which, in conjunction with the army of the centre, now directed by Jourdan, could advance upon Portugal by the valley of the Tagus, and so turn the right flank of the allied army in Castile. Boats and magazines supplied from Toledo and Madrid, were already being collected at the fort of Lugar Nueva, near Almaraz, and from hence, as from a place of arms, the French could move upon Coria, Placencia, and Castelo Branco, menacing Abrantes, Celorico, Ciudad Rodrigo, and Almeida, while detachments from the army of the north reinforced the army of Portugal. But to obviate this last danger Wellington had planned one of those enterprizes, which as they are successful, principally because of their exceeding boldness, are beheld with astonishment when achieved, and are attributed to madness when they fail.

SURPRISE OF ALMARAZ.

For a clear understanding of this event, the reader must call to mind, 1[o.] that the left bank of the Tagus, from Toledo to Almaraz, is lined with rugged mountains, the ways through which, impracticable for an army, are difficult even for small divisions; 2[o.] that from Almaraz to the frontier of Portugal, the banks, although more open, were still difficult, and the Tagus was only to be crossed at certain points, to which bad roads leading through the mountains descended. But from Almaraz to

Alcantara, all the bridges had been long ruined, and those of Arzobispo and Talavera, situated between Almaraz and Toledo, were of little value, because of the ruggedness of the mountains above spoken of. Soult's pontoon equipage had been captured in Badajos, and the only means of crossing the Tagus, possessed by the French, from Toledo to the frontier of Portugal, was a boat-bridge laid down at Almaraz by Marmont, and to secure which he had constructed three strong forts and a bridge head.

The first of these forts, called Ragusa, was a magazine, containing many stores and provisions, and it was, although not finished, ˙exceedingly strong, having a loopholed stone tower, twenty-five feet high within, and being flanked without by a field-work near the bridge.

On the left bank of the Tagus the bridge had a fortified head of masonry, which was again flanked by a redoubt, called Fort Napoleon, placed on a height a little in advance. This redoubt, though imperfectly constructed, inasmuch as a wide berm, in the middle of the scarp, offered a landing place to troops escalading the rampart, was yet strong because it contained a second interior defence or retrenchment, with a loopholed stone tower, a ditch, draw-bridge, and palisades.

These two forts, and the bridge-head, were armed with eighteen guns, and they were garrisoned by above a thousand men, which seemed sufficient to insure the command of the river; but the mountains on the left bank still precluded the passage of an army towards Lower Estremadura, save by the royal road to Truxillo, which road, at the distance of five miles from the river, passed over the rugged Mirabete

ridge, and to secure the summit of the mountain
the French had drawn another line of works,
across the throat of the pass. This line consisted of a large fortified house, connected by
smaller posts, with the ancient watch-tower of
Mirabete, which itself contained eight guns, and
was surrounded by a rampart twelve feet high.

If all these works and a road, which Marmont, following the traces of an ancient Roman way, was
now opening across the Gredos mountains had been
finished, the communication of the French, although
circuitous, would have been very good and secure.
Indeed Wellington fearing the accomplishment, intended to háve surprised the French at Almaraz
previous to the siege of Badajos, when the redoubts
were far from complete, but the Portuguese government neglected to furnish the means of tran-
sporting the artillery from Lisbon, and he was baffled. General Hill was now ordered to attempt it
with a force of six thousand men, including four
hundred cavalry, two field brigades of artillery, a
pontoon equipage, and a battering train of six iron
twenty-four pound howitzers.

The enterprize at all times difficult was become
one of extreme delicacy. When the army was
round Badajos, only the resistance of the forts themselves was to be looked for; now Foy's division of
the army of Portugal had returned to the valley of
the Tagus, and was in no manner fettered, and
d'Armagnac, with troops from the army of the centre,
occupied Talavera. Drouet also was, with eight or
nine thousand men of the army of the south, at
Hinojosa de Cordoba, his cavalry was on the road
See Plan,
No. 1.
to Medellin, he was nearer to Merida than
Hill was to Almaraz, he might intercept the latter's

retreat, and the king's orders were imperative that
he should hang upon the English army in Estremadura. Soult could also detach a corps from
Seville by St. Ollala to fall upon sir William Erskine, who was posted with the cavalry and the
remainder of Hill's infantry, near Almendralejo.
However lord Wellington placed general Graham
near Portalegre, with the first and sixth divisions,
and Cotton's cavalry, all of which had crossed the
Tagus for the occasion, and thus including Erskine's
corps, above twenty thousand men were ready to
protect Hill's enterprize.

1812.
May.
Joseph's
Correspon-
dence,
MSS.

Drouet by a rapid march might still interpose
between Hill and Erskine, and beat them in detail
before Graham could support them, wherefore the
English general made many other arrangements to
deceive the enemy. First, he chose the moment of
action when Soult having sent detachments in various
directions, to restore his communications in Andalusia, had marched himself with a division to Cadiz,
and was consequently unfavourably placed for a
sudden movement. Secondly, by rumours adroitly
spread, and by demonstrations with the Portuguese
militia of the Alemtejo, he caused the French to
believe that ten thousand men were moving down
the Guadiana, towards the Niebla, preparatory to the
invasion of Andalusia, a notion upheld by the assembling of so many troops under Graham, by the pushing
of cavalry parties towards the Morena, and by restoring the bridge at Merida, with the avowed intention
of sending Hill's battering and pontoon train,
which had been formed at Elvas, to Almendralejo.
Finally, many exploring officers, taking the roads
leading to the province of Cordoba, made ostenta-
tious inquiries about the French posts at Belalcazar

and other places, and thus every thing seemed to point at Andalusia.

The restoration of the bridge at Merida proving unexpectedly difficult, cost a fortnight's labour, for two arches having been destroyed the opening was above sixty feet wide, and large timber was scarce. Hill's march was thus dangerously delayed, but on the 12th of May, the repairs being effected and all else being ready, he quitted Almendralejo, passed the Guadiana, at Merida, with near six thousand men and twelve field-pieces, and joined his pontoons and battering-train. These last had come by the way of Montijo, and formed a considerable convoy, nearly fifty country carts, besides the guns and limber carriages, being employed to convey the pontoons, the ladders, and the ammunition for the howitzers.

The 13th the armament reached the Burdalo river on the road to Truxillo; the 14th it was at Villa Mesias; the 15th at Truxillo. Meanwhile, to mislead the enemy on the right bank of the Tagus the guerillas of the Guadalupe mountains made demonstrations at different points between Almaraz and Arzobispo, as if they were seeking a place to cast a bridge that Hill might join lord Wellington. General Foy was deceived by these operations, and though his spies at Truxillo had early informed him of the passage of the Guadiana by the allies, they led him to believe that Hill had fifteen thousand men, and that two brigades of cavalry were following in his rear; one report even stated that thirty thousand men had entered Truxillo, whereas there were less than six thousand of all arms.

Hill having reached Jaraicejo early on the 16th,

formed his troops in three columns, and made a night march, intending to attack by surprise and at the same moment, the tower of Mirabete, the fortified house in the pass, and the forts at the bridge of Almaraz. The left column, directed against the tower, was commanded by general Chowne. The centre column, with the dragoons and the artillery, moved by the royal road, under the command of general Long. The right column, composed of the 50th, 71st, and 92d regiments, under the direction of Hill in person, was intended to penetrate by the narrow and difficult way of La Cueva, and Roman Gordo against the forts at the bridge. But the day broke before any of the columns reached their destination, and all hopes of a surprise were extinguished. This untoward beginning was unavoidable on the part of the right and centre column, because of the bad roads; but it would appear that some negligence had retarded general Chowne's column, and that the castle of Mirabete might have been carried by assault before daylight.

The difficulty, great before, was now much increased. An attentive examination of the French defences convinced Hill that to reduce the works in the pass, he must incur more loss than was justifiable, and finish in such plight that he could not afterwards carry the forts at the bridge, which were the chief objects of his expedition. Yet it was only through the pass of Mirabete that the artillery could move against the bridge. In this dilemma, after losing the 17th and part of the 18th in fruitless attempts to discover some opening through which to reach the valley of Almaraz with his guns, he resolved to leave them on the Sierra with the

centre column, and to make a false attack upon
the tower with general Chowne's troops while he
himself, with the right column, secretly penetrated
by the scarcely practicable line of La Cueva and
Roman Gordo to the bridge, intent, with infantry
alone, to storm works which were defended by
eighteen pieces of artillery and powerful garrisons!

This resolution was even more hardy, and bold,
than it appears without a reference to the general
state of affairs.   Hill's march had been one of
secrecy, amidst various divisions of the enemy;
he was four days' journey distant from Merida,
which was his first point of retreat; he expected
that Drouet would be reinforced, and advance
towards Medellin, and hence, whether defeated or
victorious at Almaraz, that his own retreat would
be very dangerous; exceedingly so if defeated,
because his fine British troops could not be repulsed
with a small loss, and he should have to fall back
through a difficult country, with his best soldiers
dispirited by failure, and burthened with numbers of wounded men.   Then harassed on one
side by Drouet, pursued by Foy and D'Armagnac
on the other, he would have been exposed to the
greatest misfortunes, every slanderous tongue would
have been let loose on the rashness of attacking
impregnable forts, and a military career, hitherto
so glorious, might have terminated in shame.   But
general Hill being totally devoid of interested
ambition, was necessarily unshaken by such fears.

The troops remained concealed in their position
until the evening of the 18th, and then the general,
reinforcing his own column with the 6th Portuguese
regiment, a company of the 60th rifles, and the
artillery-men of the centre column, commenced

the descent of the valley. His design was to storm
Fort Napoleon before daylight, and the march was
less than six miles, but his utmost efforts could
only bring the head of the troops to the fort, a
little before daylight, the rear was still distant,
and it was doubtful if the scaling-ladders, which
had been cut in halves to thread the short narrow
turns in the precipitous descent, would serve for an
assault. Fortunately some small hills concealed
the head of the column from the enemy, and at that
moment general Chowne commenced the false attack
on the castle of Mirabete. Pillars of white smoke
rose on the lofty brow of the Sierra, the heavy
sound of artillery came rolling over the valley,
and the garrison of Fort Napoleon, crowding on
the ramparts, were anxiously gazing at these portentous signs of war, when, quick and loud, a
British shout broke on their ears, and the gallant
50th regiment, aided by a wing of the 71st, came
bounding over the nearest hills.

The French were surprised to see an enemy so
close while the Mirabete was still defended, yet
they were not unprepared, for a patrole of English
cavalry had been seen from the fort on the 17th
in the pass of Roman Gordo; and in the evening
of the 18th a woman of that village had carried
very exact information of Hill's numbers and intentions to Lugar Nueva. This intelligence had caused
the commandant Aubert to march in the night with
reinforcements to Fort Napoleon, which was therefore defended by six companies, including the 39th
French and the voltigeurs of a foreign regiment.
These troops were ready to fight, and when the
first shout was heard, turning their heads, they,
with a heavy fire of musketry and artillery, smote

the assailants in front, while the guns of Fort
Ragusa took them in flank from the opposite side
of the river; in a few moments, however, a rise
of ground, at the distance of only twenty yards
from the ramparts, covered the British from the
front fire, and general Howard, in person, leading
the foremost troops into the ditch, commenced the
escalade. The great breadth of the berm kept
off the ends of the shortened ladders from the
parapet, but the soldiers who first ascended, jumped
on to the berm itself, and drawing up the ladders planted them there, and thus, with a second
escalade, forced their way over the rampart; then,
closely fighting, friends and enemies went together
into the retrenchment round the stone tower. Colonel Aubert was wounded and taken, the tower was
not defended, and the garrison fled towards the
bridge-head, but the victorious troops would not
be shaken off, and entered that work also in one
confused mass with the fugitives, who continued
their flight over the bridge itself. Still the British
soldiers pushed their headlong charge, slaying the
hindmost, and they would have passed the river if
some of the boats had not been destroyed by stray
shots from the forts, which were now sharply can-
nonading each other, for the artillery-men had turned
the guns of Napoleon on Fort Ragusa.

Many of the French leaped into the water and
were drowned, but the greatest part were made
prisoners, and to the amazement of the conquerors,
the panic spread to the other side of the river;
the garrison of Fort Ragusa, although perfectly
safe, abandoned that fort also and fled with the
others along the road to Naval Moral. Some
grenadiers of the 92d immediately swam over and

brought back several boats, with which the bridge
was restored, and Fort Ragusa was gained. The
towers and other works were then destroyed,
the stores, ammunition, provisions, and boats
were burned in the course of the day, and in the
night the troops returned to the Sierra above,
carrying with them the colours of the foreign
regiment, and more than two hundred and fifty
prisoners, including a commandant and sixteen
other officers. The whole loss on the part of the
British was about one hundred and eighty men, and
one officer of artillery was killed by his own mine,
placed for the destruction of the tower; but the only
officer slain in the actual assault was captain Candler,
a brave man, who fell while leading the grenadiers
of the 50th on to the rampart of Fort Napoleon.

This daring attack was executed with a decision
similar to that with which it had been planned.
The first intention of general Hill was, to have
directed a part of his column against the bridge-
head, and so to have assailed both works together,
but when the difficulties of the road marred this
project, he attacked the nearest work with the leading troops, leaving the rear to follow as it could.
This rapidity was an essential cause of the success,
for Foy hearing on the 17th that the allies were
at Truxillo, had ordered D'Armagnac to reinforce
Lugar Nueva with a battalion, which being at Naval
Moral the 18th, might have entered Fort Ragusa early Foy's
Official
in the morning of the 19th; but instead of march- Correspondence,
ing before day-break, this battalion did not move MSS.
until eleven o'clock, and meeting the fugitives on
the road, caught the panic and returned.

The works at Mirabete being now cut off from
the right bank of the Tagus, general Hill was

preparing to reduce them with his heavy artillery,
when a report, from sir William Erskine, caused
him, in conformity with his instructions, to commence
a retreat on Merida, leaving Mirabete blockaded
by the guerillas of the neighbourhood. It appeared
that Soult, being at Chiclana, heard of the allies'
march the 19th, and then only desired Drouet to make
a diversion in Estremadura without losing his communication with Andalusia; for he did not perceive
the true object of the enterprize, and thinking he
had to check a movement, which the king told him
was made for the purpose of reinforcing Wellington in the north, resolved to enforce Hill's stay
in Estremadura. In this view he recalled his own
detachments from the Niebla, where they had just
dispersed a body of Spaniards at Castillejos, and
then forming a large division at Seville, he purposed to strengthen Drouet and enable him to fight
a battle. But that general, anticipating his orders,
had pushed an advanced guard of four thousand
men to Dom Benito the 17th, and his cavalry
patroles passing the Guadiana on the 18th had
scoured the roads to Miajadas and Merida, while
Lallemand's dragoons drove back the British outposts from Ribera, on the side of Zafra.

Confused by these demonstrations, sir William
Erskine immediately reported to Graham, and to
Hill, that Soult himself was in Estremadura with
his whole army, whereupon Graham came up to
Badajos, and Hill, fearful of being cut off, retired, as
I have said, from Mirabete on the 21st, and on the
26th reached Merida unmolested. Drouet then with-
drew his advanced guards, and Graham returned to
Castello de Vide. Notwithstanding this error Wel-
lington's precautions succeeded, for if Drouet had

been aware of Hill's real object, instead of making demonstrations with a part of his force, he would with the whole of his troops, more than ten thousand, have marched rapidly from Medellin to fall on the allies as they issued out of the passes of Truxillo, and before Erskine or Graham could come to their aid; whereas acting on the supposition that the intention was to cross the Tagus, his demonstrations merely hastened the retreat, and saved Mirabete. To meet Hill in the right place, would, however, have required very nice arrangements and great activity, as he could have made his retreat by the road of Caceres as well as by that of Merida.

Lord Wellington was greatly displeased that this false alarm, given by Erskine, should have rendered the success incomplete; yet he avoided any public expression of discontent, lest the enemy, who had no apparent interest in preserving the post of Mirabete, should be led to keep it, and so embarrass the allies when their operations required a restoration of the bridge of Almaraz. To the ministers however he complained, that his generals, stout in action, personally, as the poorest soldiers, were commonly so overwhelmed with the fear of responsibility when left to themselves, that the slightest movement of the enemy deprived them of their judgment, and they spread unnecessary alarm far and wide. But instead of expressing his surprise, he should rather have reflected on the cause of this weakness. Every British officer of rank knew, that without powerful interest, his future prospects, and his reputation for past services, would have withered together under the first blight of misfortune; that a selfish government would instantly offer him up, a victim to a misjudging public and a ribald press

with whom success is the only criterion of merit.
English generals are and must be prodigal of their
blood to gain a reputation, but they are necessarily
timid in command, when a single failure, even without a fault, consigns them to an old age of shame
and misery. It is however undeniable that sir
William Erskine was not an able officer.

On the other side the king was equally discontented with Soult, whose refusal to reinforce Drouet,
he thought had caused the loss of Almaraz, and he
affirmed that if Hill had been more enterprising,
the arsenal of Madrid might have fallen as well as
the depôt of Almaraz, for he thought that general
had brought up his whole corps instead of a division
only six thousand strong.

CHAPTER II.

WHILE the Anglo-British army was thus cleansing and strengthening its position on the frontier of Portugal, the progress of the war in other parts had not been so favourable to the common cause. It has already been shewn that Gallicia, in the latter part of 1811, suffered from discord, poverty, and ill success in the field; that an extraordinary contribution imposed upon the province, had been resisted by all classes, and especially at Coruña the seat of Government; finally that the army torn by faction was become hateful to the people. In this state of affairs Castaños having, at the desire of lord Wellington, assumed the command, removed the seat of Government to St. Jago, leaving the troops in the Bierzo under the marquis of Portazgo.

Prudent conduct and the personal influence of the new captain-general soothed the bitterness of faction, and stopped, or at least checked for the moment, many of the growing evils in Gallicia, and the regency at Cadiz assigned an army of sixty thousand men for that province. But the revenues were insufficient even to put the few troops already under arms in motion, and Castaños, although desirous to menace Astorga while Marmont was on the Agueda, could not, out of twenty-two thousand men, bring even one division into the field. Nevertheless, so strange a people are the Spaniards, that a second expedition against the colonies, having with it all the field-artillery just supplied by Eng-

land, would have sailed from Vigo but for the prompt
interference of sir Howard Douglas.

When Castaños saw the penury of his army, he
as usual looked to England for succour, at the same
time, however, both he and the Junta made unusual
exertions to equip their troops, and the condition
of the soldiers was generally ameliorated. But it
was upon the efforts of the Partidas that the British
agent chiefly relied. His system, with respect to
those bodies, has been before described, and it is
certain that under it, greater activity, more perfect
combination, more useful and better timed exertions, had marked their conduct, and their efforts
directed to the proper objects, were kept in some
subordination to the operations of the allies. This
was however so distasteful to the regular officers,
and to the predominant faction, always fearful of
the priestly influence over the allies, that sir Howard
was offered the command of six thousand troops to
detach him from the Guerilla system; and the Partidas of the northern provinces would now have
been entirely suppressed, from mere jealousy, by
the general government, if lord Wellington and sir
H. Wellesley had not strenuously supported the
views of Douglas which were based on the following state of affairs.

The French line of communication extending
from Salamanca to Irun, was never safe while the
Gallician and Asturian forces, the English squadrons, and the Partidas in the Montaña, in Biscay,
in the Rioja, and in the mountains of Burgos and
Leon, menaced it from both sides. The occupation
of the Asturias, the constant presence of a division
in the Montaña, the employment of a corps to
threaten Gallicia, and the great strength of the

army of the north, were all necessary consequences
of this weakness. But though the line of communication was thus laboriously maintained, the lines
of correspondence, in this peculiar war of paramount importance, were, in despite of numerous fortified posts, very insecure, and Napoleon was always
stimulating his generals to take advantage of each
period of inactivity, on the part of the British army,
to put down the partidas. He observed, that without English succours they could not remain in
arms, that the secret of their strength was to be
found on the coast, and that all the points, which
favoured any intercourse with vessels, should be
fortified. And at this time so anxious was he for the
security of his correspondence, that he desired, if necessary, the whole army of the north should be employed merely to scour the lines of communication.

In accordance with these views, Santona, the
most important point on the coast, had been rendered a strong post in the summer of 1811, and
then Castro, Portagalete at the mouth of the Bilbao See Plan,
No. 6.
river, Bermeo, Lesquito, and Guetaria, were by
degrees fortified. This completed the line eastward
from Santander to St. Sebastian, and all churches,
convents, and strong houses, situated near the mouths
of the creeks and rivers between those places were
entrenched. The partidas being thus constantly intercepted, while attempting to reach the coast, were
nearly effaced in the latter end of 1811, and a considerable part of the army of the north was, in consequence, rendered disposable for the aid of the army
of Portugal. But when Bonet, because of the
siege of Ciudad Rodrigo, evacuated the Asturias,
the French troops in the Montaña were again exposed to the enterprizes of the seventh army, which

had been immediately succoured by Douglas, and which, including guerillas, was said to be twenty-three thousand strong. Wherefore Napoleon had so early as March directed that the Asturias should be re-occupied, and one of Bonet's brigades, attached to the army of the north, rejoined him in consequence; but the pass of Pajares being choked with snow, Bonet, who was then on the Orbijo, neglected this order until the approach of finer weather.

In May, Marmont having returned from Portugal, the emperor's order was reiterated, and the French troops on the Orbijo, being augmented to fifteen thousand drew the attention of the Gallicians to that quarter, while Bonet, passing the mountains of Leon, with eight thousand men, re-occupied Oviedo, Grado, and Gihon, and established small posts communicating through the town of Leon, with the army of Portugal. Thus a new military line was established which interrupted the Gallicians' communications with the partidas, the chain of sea-port defences was continued to Gihon, a constant intercourse with France was maintained, and those convoys came safely by water, which otherwise would have had to travel by land escorted by many troops and in constant danger.

Meanwhile Marmont, having distributed his division in various parts of Leon, was harassed by the partidas, especially Porlier's, yet he proceeded diligently with the fortifying of Toro and Zamora, on the Douro, and converted three large convents at Salamanca into so many forts capable of sustaining a regular siege; the works of Astorga and Leon were likewise improved, and strong posts were established at Benavente, La Baneza, Castro-Contrigo, and intermediate points. The defensive lines of the

Tormes and the Douro were thus strengthened against the British general, and as four thousand men sufficed to keep the Gallician forces of the Bierzo and Puebla Senabria in check, the vast and fertile plains of Leon, called the *Tierras de Campos*, were secured for the French, and their detachments chased the bands from the open country.

Sir Howard Douglas observing the success of the enemy in cutting off the Partidas from the coast, and the advantage they derived from the water communication; considering also that, if lord Wellington should make any progress in the coming campaign, new lines of communication with the sea would be desirable, proposed, that a powerful squadron with a battalion of marines and a battery of artillery, should be secretly prepared for a littoral warfare on the Biscay coast. This suggestion was approved of, and sir Home Popham was sent from England, in May, with an armament, well provided with scaling ladders, arms, clothing, and ammunition for the Partidas, and all means to effect sudden disembarkations. But the ministers were never able to see the war in its true point of view, they were always desponding, or elated, and sanguine, beyond what reason warranted in either case. Popham was ordered not only to infest the coast but, if possible, to seize some point, and hold it permanently as an entrance into Biscay, by which the French positions might be turned, if, as in 1808, they were forced to adopt the line of the Ebro! Now at this period three hundred thousand French soldiers were in the Peninsula, one hundred and twenty thousand were in the northern provinces, and, without reckoning the army of the centre which could also be turned in that direction, nearly fifty thousand were expressly appropriated to the protection of this very line of communication, on which a thousand marines were to be permanently established, in expectation of the enemy being driven over the Ebro by a campaign which was not yet commenced !

While Marmont was in Beira, the activity of the seventh army, and of the Partidas, in the Montaña, was revived by the supplies which sir Howard Douglas, taking the opportunity of Bonet's absence, had transmitted to them through the Asturian ports. The ferocity of the leaders was remarkable. Mina's conduct was said to be very revolting ; and on the 16th of April the curate Merino coming from the mountains of Espinosa, to the forests between Aranda de Duero, and Hontorica Valdearados, took several hundred prisoners, and hanged sixty of them, in retaliation for three members of the local junta, who had been put to death by the French ; he executed the others also in the proportion of ten for each of his own soldiers who had been shot by the enemy. The ignorance and the excited passions of the Guerilla chiefs, may be pleaded in mitigation of their proceedings, but to the disgrace of England, these infamous executions by Merino were recorded with complacency, in the newspapers, and met with no public disapprobation.

There are occasions, when retaliation, applied to men of rank, may stop the progress of barbarity, yet the necessity should be clearly shewn, and the exercise restricted to such narrow limits, that no reasonable ground should be laid for counter-retaliation. Here, sixty innocent persons were deliberately butchered to revenge the death of three, and

no proof offered that even those three were slain contrary to the laws of war; and though it is not to be
doubted that the French committed many atrocities, some in wantonness, some in revenge, such
savage deeds as the curate's are inexcusable. What
would have been said if Washington had hanged
twenty English gentlemen, of family, in return for
the death of captain Handy; or if sir Henry Clinton had caused twenty American officers, to die,
for the execution of André? Like atrocities are,
however, the inevitable consequence of a Guerilla
system not subordinate to the regular government
of armies, and ultimately they recoil upon the
helpless people of the country, who cannot fly
from their enemies. When the French occupied a
district, famine often ensued, because to avoid distant forages they collected large stores of provisions from a small extent of country, and thus
the Guerilla system, while it harassed the French,
without starving them, both harassed and starved
the people. And many of the chiefs of bands,
besides their robberies, when they dared not otherwise revenge affronts or private feuds, would slay
some prisoners, or stragglers, so as to draw down
the vengeance of the French on an obnoxious
village, or district. This in return produced asso-
ciations of the people, for self defence in many
places, by which the enemy profited.

Soon after this exploit a large convoy having
marched from Burgos towards France, Merino
endeavoured to intercept it, and Mendizabel, who
notwithstanding his defeat by Bonet, had again
gathered twelve hundred cavalry, came from the
Liebana, and occupied the heights above Burgos.
The French immediately placed their baggage and

followers in the castle, and recalled the convoy,
whereupon the Spaniards, dispersing in bands,
destroyed the fortified posts of correspondence,
at Sasamon, and Gamonal, and then returned to
the Liebana. But Bonet had now re-occupied the
Asturias, the remnant of the Spanish force, in that
quarter, fled to Mendizabel, and the whole shifted
as they could in the hills. Meanwhile Mina displayed great energy. In February he repulsed an
attack near Lodosa, and having conveyed the prisoners taken at Huesca to the coast, returned to
Aragon and maintained a distant blockade of Zaragoza itself. In March he advanced, with a detachment, to Pina, and captured one of Suchet's convoys
going to Mequinenza; but having retired, with his
booty, to Robres, a village on the eastern slopes of
the Sierra de Alcubierre, he was there betrayed to
general Pannetier, who with a brigade of the
army of the Ebro, came so suddenly upon him
that he escaped death with great difficulty.

He reappeared in the Rioja, and although hotly
chased by troops from the army of the north,
escaped without much loss, and, having five thousand men, secretly gained the defiles of Navas
Tolosa, behind Vittoria, where on the 7th of April,
he defeated with great loss a Polish regiment,
which was escorting the enormous convoy that had
escaped the curate and Mendizabel at Burgos.
The booty consisted of treasure, Spanish prisoners,
baggage, followers of the army, and officers retiring to France. All the Spanish prisoners, four
hundred in number, were released and joined Mina,
and, it is said, that one million of francs fell into
his hands, besides the equipages, arms, stores, and
a quantity of church plate.

On the 28th he captured another convoy going
from Valencia to France, but general Abbé, who
had been recently made governor of Navarre, now
directed combined movements from Pampeluna,
Jacca, and Sangüesa, against him. And so vigorously did this general, who I have heard Mina
declare to be the most formidable of all his opponents, urge on the operations, that after a series
of actions, on the 25th, 26th, and 28th of May,
the Spanish chief, in bad plight, and with the
utmost difficulty, escaped by Los Arcos to Guardia,
in the Rioja. Marshal Victor seized this opportunity to pass into France, with the remains of
the convoy shattered on the 7th, and all the
bands in the north were discouraged. However,
Wellington's successes, and the confusion attending
upon the departure of so many French troops for
the Russian war, gave a powerful stimulus to the
partizan chiefs in other directions. The Empecinado, ranging the mountains of Cuenca and
Guadalaxara, pushed his parties close to Madrid;
Duran entered Soria, and raised a contribution in
the lower town; Villa Campa, Bassecour, and
Montijo, coming from the mountains of Albarracin,
occupied Molino and Orejuella, and invested Daroca; the Catalonian Gayan, taking post in the
vicinity of Belchite, made excursions to the very
gates of Zaragoza; the Frayle, haunting the moun- See Plan, No. 6.
tains of Alcañiz and the Sierra de Gudar, interrupted Suchet's lines of communication by Morella
and Teruel, and along the right bank of the Ebro
towards Tortoza. Finally, Gay and Miralles infested
the Garriga on the left bank.

It was to repress these bands that the army of
the Ebro, containing twenty thousand men, of

whom more than sixteen thousand were under arms, was formed by drafts from Suchet's army, and given to general Reille. That commander immediately repaired to Lerida, occupied Upper Aragon with his own division, placed Severoli's division between Lerida and Zaragoza, and general Frere's between Lerida, Barcelona, and Taragona; but his fourth division, under Palombini, marched direct from Valencia towards the districts of Soria and Calatayud, to form the link of communication between Suchet and Caffarelli. The latter now commanded the army of the north, but the imperial guards, with the exception of one division, had quitted Spain, and hence, including the government's and the reserve of Monthion, this army was reduced to forty-eight thousand under arms. The reserve at Bayonne was therefore increased to five thousand men, and Palombini was destined finally to reinforce Caffarelli, and even to march, if required, to the aid of Marmont in Leon. However the events of the war soon caused Reille to repair to Navarre, and broke up the army of the Ebro, wherefore it will be clearer to trace the operations of these divisions successively and separately, and in the order of the provinces towards which they were at first directed.

February. Palombini having left a brigade at the entrenched bridge of Teruel, relieved Daroca on the 23d of February, and then deceiving Villa Campa, Montijo, and Bassecour, who were waiting about the passes of Toralva to fall on his rear-guard, turned them by the Xiloca, and reached Calatayud. This effected, he fortified the convent of La Peña, which, as its name signifies, was a rocky eminence, commanding that city and forming a part of it.

But on the 4th of March, having placed his
baggage and artillery in this post, under a guard
of three hundred men, he dispersed his troops
to scour the country and to collect provisions,
and the partidas, seeing this, recommenced operations. Villa Campa cut off two companies at
Campillo on the 8th, and made a fruitless attempt
to destroy the Italian colonel Pisa at Ateca. Five
hundred men were sent against him, but he drew
them towards the mountains of Albarracin, and
destroyed them at Pozonhonda on the 28th;
then marching another way, he drove the Italians
from their posts of communication as far as the
town of Albarracin on the road to Teruel, nor
did he regain the mountains until Palombini
came up on his rear and killed some of his men.
The Italian general then changing his plan,
concentrated his division on the plains of Hused,
where he suffered some privations, but remained
unmolested until the 14th of April, when he again
marched to cooperate with Suchet in a combined
attempt to destroy Villa Campa. The Spanish
chief evaded both by passing over to the southern
slopes of the Albarracin mountains, and before
the Italians could return to Hused, Gayan, in
concert with the alcalde of Calatayud, had exploded a plot against the convent of La Peña.

Some of the Italian officers, including the commandant, having rashly accepted an invitation to a
feast, were sitting at table, when Gayan appeared on
a neighbouring height; the guests were immediately
seized, and many armed citizens ran up to surprise
the convent, and sixty soldiers were made prisoners,
or killed in the tumult below; but the historian,
Vacani, who had declined to attend the feast, made

a vigorous defence, and on the 1st of May general St. Pol and colonel Schiazzetti, coming from Hused, and Daroca, raised the siege. Schiazzetti marched in pursuit, and as his advanced guard was surprised at Mochales by a deceit of the alcalde, he slew the latter, whereupon the Spaniards killed the officers taken at the feast of Calatayud.

Gayan soon baffled his pursuers, and then moved by Medina Celi and Soria to Navarre, thinking to surprise a money convoy going to Burgos for the army of Portugal, but being followed on one side by a detachment from Hused, and met on the other by Caffarelli, he was driven again to the hills above Daroca. Here he renewed his operations in concert with Villa Campa and the Empecinado, who came up to Medina Celi, while Duran descended from the Moncayo hills, and this menacing union of bands induced Reille, in May, to detach general Paris, with a French regiment and a troop of hussars, to the aid of Palombini. Paris moved by Calatayud, while Palombini briskly interposing between Duran and Villa Campa, drove the one towards Albarracin and the other towards Soria; and in June, after various marches, the two French generals uniting, dislodged the Empecinado from Siguenza, chasing him so sharply that his band dispersed and fled to the Somosierra.

During these operations, Mina was pressed by Abbé, but Duran entering Tudela by surprise, destroyed the artillery parc, and carried off a battering train of six guns. Palombini was only a few marches from Madrid, and the king, alarmed by lord Wellington's preparations for opening the campaign, ordered him to join the army of the centre, but these orders were intercepted, and the Italian general retraced

his steps, to pursue Duran. He soon recovered the
guns taken at Tudela, and drove the Spanish chief
through the Rioja into the mountains beyond the
sources of the Duero ;   then collecting boats, he
would have passed the Ebro, for Caffarelli was
on the Arga, with a division of the army of the
north, and a brigade had been sent by Reille to
the Aragon river with the view of destroying
Mina. This chief, already defeated by Abbé, was
in great danger, when a duplicate of the king's orders
having reached Palombini, he immediately recommenced his march for the capital, which saved Mina.
Caffarelli returned to Vittoria, and the Italians
reaching Madrid the 21st of July, became a part
of the army of the centre, having marched one hundred and fifty miles in seven days without a halt.
Returning now to the other divisions of the army
of the Ebro, it is to be observed, that their movements being chiefly directed against the Catalans,
belong to the relation of that warfare.

OPERATIONS IN ARAGON AND CATALONIA.

After the battle of Altafulla, the fall of Penis SeeVol.IV
Book XV.
cola, and the arrival of Reille's first division on
the Ebro, Decaen, who had succeeded Macdonald
in Upper Catalonia, spread his troops along the
coast, with a view to cut off the communication
between the British navy and the interior, where
the Catalan army still held certain positions.

Lamarque, with a division of five thousand men, February.
first seized and fortified Mataro, and then driving
Milans from Blanes, occupied the intermediate
space, while detachments from Barcelona fortified
Moncada, Mongat, and Molino del Rey, thus
securing the plain of Barcelona on every side.

The line from Blanes to Cadagués, including
Canets, St. Filieu, Palamos, and other ports, was
strengthened, and placed under general Bearman.

General Clement was posted in the vicinity of
Gerona, to guard the interior French line of march
from Hostalrich to Figueras.

Tortoza, Mequinenza, and Taragona were garrisoned by detachments from Severoli's division,
which was quartered between Zaragoza and Lerida,
and in communication with Bourke's and Pannetier's
brigades of the first division of the army of reserve.

General Frere's division was on the communication between Aragon and Catalonia, and there was
a division under general Quesnel, composed partly
of national guards, in the Cerdaña. Finally there
was a moveable reserve, of six or eight thousand
men, with which Decaen himself marched from
place to place as occasion required; but the supreme command of Valencia, Aragon, and Catalonia was with Suchet.

The Catalans still possessed the strong holds of
Cardona, Busa, Sceu d'Urgel, and the Medas
islands, and they had ten thousand men in the
field. Lacy was at Cardona with Sarzfield's division, and some irregular forces; colonel Green was
organizing an experimental corps at Montserrat,
near which place Erolles was also quartered; Rovira
continued about the mountains of Olot; Juan Claros,
who occupied Arenis de Mar when the French were
not there, was now about the mountains of Hostalrich; Milans, Manso, and the Brigand Gros, being
driven from the coast line, kept the hills near
Manreza; Gay and Miralles were on the Ebro.
But the communication with the coast being cut off,
all these chiefs were in want of provisions and

stores, and the French were forming new roads
along the sea line, beyond the reach of the English
ship guns.

Lacy thus debarred of all access to the coast, feeding his troops with difficulty, and having a great number of prisoners and deserters to maintain in Cardona, and Busa, because Coupigny refused to receive them in the Balearic isles, Lacy, I say, disputing with the Junta, and the generals, and abhorred by the people, in his spleen desired captain Codrington to cannonade all the sea-coast towns in the possession of the French, saying he would give the inhabitants timely notice; but he did not do so, and when Codrington reluctantly opened his broadsides upon Mataro, many of the people were slain. The Catalans complained loudly of this cruel, injudicious operation, and hating Lacy, affected Erolles more than ever, and Capt. Codrington's papers, MSS. the former sent him with a few men to his native district of Talarn, ostensibly to raise recruits, and make a diversion in Aragon, but really to deprive him of his division and reduce his power.

The distress in the Catalan army now became so great, that Sarzfield was about to force his way to the coast, and embark his division to commence a littoral warfare, when Erolles having quickly raised and armed a new division entered Aragon, whereupon Sarzfield followed him. The baron having entered the valley of Venasque, advanced to Graus, menacing all the district between Fraga and Huesca; but those places were occupied by detachments from Bourke's brigade of the army of the Ebro, and at this moment Severoli arrived from Valencia, whereupon the Spaniards instead of faling back upon Venasque, retired up the valley of the Isabena, to some heights above Roda, a village on the confines of Aragon.

Erolles had not more than a thousand regular infantry, three guns, and two hundred cavalry, for he had left five hundred in the valley of Venasque, and Bourke knowing this, and encouraged by the vicinity of Severoli, followed hastily from Bena-varre, with about two thousand men of all arms, thinking Erolles would not stand before him. But the latter's position besides being very steep and rough in front, was secured on both flanks by precipices, beyond which, on the hills, all the partidas of the vicinity were gathered; he expected aid also from Sarzfield, and was obliged to abide a battle or lose the detachment left in the valley of Venasque. Bourke keeping two battalions in re-serve attacked with the third, but he met with a stubborn opposition, and after a long skirmish, in which he lost a hundred and fifty men, and Erolles a hundred, was beaten, and being wounded him-self, retreated to Monza, in great confusion. This combat was very honorable to Erolles, but it was exposed to doubt and ridicule, at the time, by the extravagance of his public despatch; for he affirmed, that his soldiers finding their muskets too hot, had made use of stones, and in this mixed mode of action had destroyed a thousand of the enemy!

Severoli now advanced, and Erolles being still un-supported by Sarzfield, retired to Talarn, whereupon the Italian general returned to Aragon. Meanwhile Lacy who had increased his forces, approached Cervera, while Sarzfield, accused by Erolles of having treacherously abandoned him, joined with

Gay and Miralles, occupying the hills about Taragona, and straitening that place for provisions.
Milans and Manso also uniting, captured a convoy
at Arenis de Mar, and the English squadron intercepted several vessels going to Barcelona.

Decaen observing this fresh commotion came
down from Gerona with his reserve. He relieved
Taragona on the 28th of April, and then marched
with three thousand men upon Lerida, but on the
way, hearing that Sarzfield was at Fuentes Rubino,
near Villa Franca, he took the road of Braffin and
Santa Coloma instead of Momblanch, and suddenly
turning to his right defeated the Spanish general,
and then continued his march by Cervera towards
Lerida. Lacy in great alarm immediately aban- May.
doned Lower Catalonia and concentrated Manso's,
Milans', Green's, and Sarzfield's divisions, in the
mountains of Olot, and as they were reduced in
numbers he reinforced them with select Somatenes,
called the Companies of Preferencia. After a time
however seeing that Decaen remained near Lerida,
he marched rapidly against the convent of Mataro,
with five thousand men and with good hope, for the
garrison consisted of only five hundred, the works
were not strong, and captain Codrington, who had
anchored off Mataro at Lacy's desire, lent some
ship guns; but his sailors were forced to drag them
to the point of attack, because Lacy and Green had, Capt. Cod-
in breach of their promise, neglected to provide _{papers,} rington's
means of transport. _{MSS.}

The wall of the convent gave way in a few hours,
but on the 5th, Lacy, hearing that Decaen was
coming to succour the place, broke up the siege
and buried the English guns without having any
communication with captain Codrington. The

French found these guns and carried them into the convent, yet Lacy, to cover his misconduct, said in the official gazette, that they were safely re-embarked.

After this disreputable transaction, Manso, who alone had behaved well, retired with Milans to Vich, Lacy went to Cardona, the French sent a large convoy into Barcelona, and the men of Erolles' ancient division were, to his great dis-content, turned over to Sarzfield, who took post near Molina del Rey, and remained there until the 5th of June, when a detachment from Barcelona drove him to the Campo de Taragona. On the 14th of the same month, Milans was defeated near Vich by a detachment from the Ampurdan, and being chased for several days suffered considerably. Lamarque followed Sarzfield into the Campo and defeated him again on the 24th, near Villa Nueva de Sitjes, and this time the Spanish general was wounded, yet made his way by Santa Coloma de Querault and Calaf to Cardona where he rejoined Lacy. Lamarque then joined Deacen in the plains of Lerida, where all the French moveable forces were now assembled, with a view to gather the harvest; a vital object to both parties, but it was attained by the French.

This with Lacy's flight from Mattaro, the several defeats of Milans, and Sarzfield, and the dis-content of Erolles, disturbed the whole prin-cipality; and the general disquietude was aug-mented by the increase of all the frauds and oppressions, which both the civil and military authorities under Lacy, practised with impunity. Every where there was a disinclination to serve in the regular army. The Somatene argued, that

while he should be an ill-used soldier, under a bad
general, his family would either become the victims
of French revenge or starve, because the pay of
the regular troops was too scanty, were it even
fairly issued, for his own subsistence; whereas,
remaining at home, and keeping his arms, he could
nourish his family by his labour, defend it from
straggling plunderers, and at the same time always
be ready to join the troops on great occasions. In
some districts the people, seeing that the army
could not protect them, refused to supply the partidas with food, unless upon contract not to molest
the French in their vicinity. The spirit of resistance would have entirely failed, if lord Wellington's successes at Ciudad and Badajos, and
the rumour that an English army was coming to
Catalonia, had not sustained the hopes of the
people.

Meanwhile the partidas in the north, being aided
by Popham's expedition, obliged Reille to remove
to Navarre, that Caffarelli might turn his whole
attention to the side of Biscay, and the Montaña.
Decaen then received charge of the Lower as well
as of the Upper Catalonia, which weakened his
position; and at the same time some confusion was
produced, by the arrival of French prefects and
councillors of state, to organize a civil administration. This measure, ostensibly to restrain military
licentiousness, had probably the ultimate object of
preparing Catalonia for an union with France,
because the Catalans who have peculiar customs
and a dialect of their own, scarcely call themselves
Spaniards. Although these events embarrassed
the French army, the progress of the invasion was
visible in the altered feelings of the people whose

BOOK
XVII.
———
1812.
July.
enthusiasm was stifled by the folly and corruption, with which their leaders aided the active hostility of the French.

The troops were reduced in number, distressed for provisions, and the soldiers deserted to the enemy, a thing till then unheard of in Catalonia, nay, the junta having come down to the coast were like to have been delivered up to the French, as a peace offering. The latter passed, even singly, from one part to the other, and the people of the sea-coast towns readily trafficked with the garrison of Barcelona, when neither money nor threats could prevail on them to supply the British squadron. Claros and Milans were charged with conniving at this traffic, and of exacting money for the landing of corn, when their own people and soldiers were starving. But to such a degree was patriotism overlaid by the love of gain, that the colonial produce, seized in Barcelona, and other parts, was sold, by the enemy, to French merchants, and the latter undertook both to carry it off, and pay with provisions on the spot, which they successfully executed by means of Spanish vessels, corruptly licensed for the occasion by Catalan authorities.

Codring-
ton's pa-
pers,MSS.

Meanwhile the people generally accused the junta of extreme indolence, and Lacy, of treachery ; and tyranny because of his arbitrary conduct in all things, but especially that after proclaiming a general rising, he had disarmed the Somatenes, and suppressed the independent bands. He had quarreled with the British naval officers, was the avowed enemy of Erolles, the secret calumniator of Sarzfield, and withal a man of no courage or enterprize in the field. Nor was the story of his previous life, calculated to check the bad opinion

generally entertained of him. It was said that,
being originally a Spanish officer, he was banished,
for an intrigue, to the Canaries, from whence he
deserted to the French, and again deserted to his
own countrymen, when the war of independence
broke out.

Under this man, the frauds, which characterize
the civil departments of all armies in the field,
became destructive, and the extent of the mischief
may be gathered from a single fact. Notwithstanding the enormous supplies granted by England, the Catalans paid nearly three millions ster-
ling, for the expense of the war, besides contributions in kind, and yet their soldiers were
always distressed for clothing, food, arms, and
ammunition.

This amount of specie might excite doubt, were
it not that here, as in Portugal, the quantity of
coin accumulated from the expenditure of the
armies and navies was immense. But gold is not
always the synonyme of power in war, or of hap-
piness in peace. Nothing could be more wretched
than Catalonia. Individually the people were exposed to all the licentiousness of war, collectively
to the robberies, and revenge, of both friends and
enemies. When they attempted to supply the
British vessels, the French menaced them with Codrington's pa-
death; when they yielded to such threats, the pers, MSS.
English ships menaced them with bombardment,
and plunder. All the roads were infested with
brigands, and in the hills large bands of people,
whose families and property had been destroyed,
watched for straggling Frenchmen and small
escorts, not to make war but to live on the booty ;
when this resource failed they plundered their own

BOOK
XVII.
————
1812.
July.

Codring-
ton's pa-
pers,MSS.

countrymen. While the land was thus harassed, the sea swarmed with privateers of all nations, differing from pirates only in name; and that no link in the chain of infamy, might be wanting, the merchants of Gibraltar, forced their smuggling trade at the ports, with a shameless disregard for the rights of the Spanish government. Catalonia seemed like some huge carcass, on which all manner of ravenous beasts, all obscene birds, and all reptiles had gathered to feed.

CHAPTER III.

OPERATIONS IN VALENCIA AND MURCIA.

SUCHET having recovered his health was again at the head of the troops, but the king's military authority was so irksome to him, that he despatched an officer to represent the inconvenience of it to the Emperor, previous to that monarch's departure for Russia. The answer in some degree restored his independence; he was desired to hold his troops concentrated, and move them in the manner most conducive to the interests of his own command. Hence, when Joseph, designing to act against lord Wellington in Estremadura, demanded the aid of one division, Suchet replied that he must then evacuate Valencia; and as the natural line of retreat for the French armies would, during the contemplated operations, be by the eastern provinces, it would be better to abandon Andalusia first! an answer calculated to convince Joseph that his authority in the field was still but a name.

Suchet, from a natural disposition towards order, and because his revenue from the fishery of the Albufera depended upon the tranquillity of the province, took infinite pains to confirm his power; and his mode of proceeding, at once prudent and firm, was wonderfully successful. Valencia, although one of the smallest provinces in Spain, and

not naturally fertile, was, from the industry of the
inhabitants, one of the richest.   Combining manufactures with agriculture, it possessed great resources, but they had been injured by the war,
without having been applied to its exigencies; and
the people expected that a bloody vengeance would
be taken for Calvo's murder of the French residents at
the commencement of the contest.   Their fears were
soon allayed : discipline was strictly preserved, and
Suchet, having suppressed the taxes imposed by
the Spanish government, substituted others, which,
being more equal, were less onerous.   To protect
the people from oppression in the collection, he
published in every corner his demands, authorising
resistance to contributions which were not named
in his list and demanded by the proper officers;
and he employed the native authorities, as he had
done in Aragon.   Thus, all impolitic restrictions
upon the industry and traffic of the country being
removed, the people found the government of the
invaders less oppressive than their own.

Napoleon, in expectation of Suchet's conquest, had
however imposed a war contribution, as a punishment for the death of the French residents, so heavy,
that his lieutenant imagined Valencia would be
quite unable to raise the sum ; yet the emperor,
who had calculated the Valencians' means by a
comparison with those of Aragon, would not rescind
the order.   And so exact was his judgement, that
Suchet, by accepting part payment, in kind, and
giving a discount for prompt liquidation, satisfied
this impost in one year, without much difficulty, and
the current expenses of the army were provided for
besides ; yet neither did the people suffer as in other
provinces, nor was their industry so cramped, nor

their property so injured, as under their own
government. Valencia therefore remained tranquil,
and, by contrast, the mischief of negligence and
disorder was made manifest.

The advantages derived from the conquest were
even extended to the province of Aragon, and to
the court of Joseph, for the contributions were
diminished in the former, and large sums were
remitted to the latter to meet Napoleon's grant of
one-fifth of the war contributions in favour of the
intrusive government. This prosperous state of
French affairs in Valencia was established also in the
face of an enemy daily increasing in strength. For
the regent, Abispal, had given Blake's command
to his own brother Joseph O'Donel, who collecting
the remains of the armies of Murcia and Valencia,
had raised new levies, and during Suchet's illness
formed a fresh army of twelve or fourteen thousand
men in the neighbourhood of Alicant. In the
Balearic Isles also Roche and Whittingham's divisions were declared ready to take the field, and
fifteen hundred British troops, commanded by
general Ross, arrived at Carthagena. To avoid
the fever there, these last remained on shipboard,
and were thus more menacing to the enemy than
on shore, because they seemed to be only awaiting
the arrival of a new army, which the French knew
to be coming from Sicily to the eastern coast of
Spain. And as the descent of this army was the
commencement of a remarkable episode in the
history of the Peninsular War, it is proper to give
an exact account of its origin and progress.

Sir John Stuart had been succeeded, in Sicily,
by lord William Bentinck, a man of resolution,
capacity, and spirit, just in his actions, and ab-

horring oppression, but of a sanguine, impetuous
disposition. Being resolved to ameliorate the condition of the Sicilian people, after surmounting
many difficulties, he removed the queen from
power, vested the direction of affairs in the crown
prince, obtained from the barons a renunciation of
their feudal privileges, and caused a representative
constitution to be proclaimed. Believing then that
the court was submissive because it was silent ;
that the barons would adhere to his system, because
it gave them the useful power of legislation, in lieu
of feudal privileges alloyed by ruinous expenses
and the degradation of courtiers ; because it gave
them the dignity of independence at the cost only
of maintaining the rights of the people and restoring the honour of their country :—believing
thus, he judged that the large British force hitherto
kept in Sicily, as much to overawe the court as
to oppose the enemy, might be dispensed with ;
and that the expected improvement of the Sicilian
army, and the attachment of the people to the new
political system, would permit ten thousand men
to be employed in aid of lord Wellington, or in
Italy. In January, therefore, he wrote of these
projects to the English ministers, and sent his
brother to lord Wellington to consult upon the best
mode of acting.

Such an opportune offer to create a diversion on
the left flank of the French armies was eagerly
accepted by Wellington, who immediately sent
engineers, artificers, and a battering train complete,
to aid the expected expedition. But lord William
Bentinck was soon made sensible, that in large com-
munities working constitutions are the offspring, and
not the generators, of national feelings and habits.

They cannot be built like cities in the desert, nor cast, as breakwaters, into the sea of public corruption, but gradually, and as the insect rocks come up from the depths of the ocean, they must arise, if they are to bear the storms of human passions.

The Sicilian court opposed lord William with falsehood and intrigue, the constitution was secretly thwarted by the barons, the Neapolitan army, a body composed of foreigners of all nations, was diligently augmented, with a view to overawe both the English and the people; the revenues and the subsidy were alike misapplied, and the native Sicilian army, despised and neglected, was incapable of service. Finally, instead of going to Spain himself, with ten thousand good troops, lord William could only send a subordinate general with six thousand—British, Germans, Calabrese, Swiss, and Sicilians; the British and Germans only, being either morally or militarily well organised. To these, however, Roche's and Whittingham's levies, represented to be twelve or fourteen thousand strong, were added, the Spanish government having placed them at the disposition of general Maitland, the commander of the expedition. Thus, in May, twenty thousand men were supposed ready for a descent on Catalonia, to which quarter lord Wellington recommended they should proceed.

But now other objects were presented to lord William Bentinck's sanguine mind. The Austrian government, while treating with Napoleon, was secretly encouraging insurrections in Italy, Croatia, Dalmatia, the Venetian states, the Tyrol, and Switzerland. English, as well as Austrian agents, were active to organise a vast conspiracy against

the French emperor, and there was a desire, especially on the part of England, to create a kingdom for one of the Austrian archdukes.   Murat
was discontented with France, the Montenegrins
were in arms on the Adriatic coast, and the prospect
of a descent upon Italy in unison with the wishes
of the people, appeared so promising to lord
William Bentinck, that supposing himself to have
a discretionary power, he stopped the expedition
to Catalonia, reasoning thus.

" In Spain, only six thousand middling troops can
be employed on a secondary operation, and for a limited period, whereas twelve thousand British soldiers,
and six thousand men composing the Neapolitan
army of Sicily, can land in Italy, a grand theatre,
where success will most efficaciously assist Spain.
The obnoxious Neapolitan force being thus removed,
the native Sicilian army can be organised, and the
new constitution established with more certainty."
The time, also, he thought critical for Italy, not
so for Spain, which would suffer but a temporary
deprivation, seeing that failure in Italy would not
preclude after aid to Spain.

Impressed with these notions, which, it must
be confessed, were both plausible and grand, he
permitted the expedition, already embarked, to sail
for Palma in Sardinia, and Mahon in Minorca, yet
merely as a blind, because, from those places, he
could easily direct the troops against Italy, and
meanwhile they menaced the French in Spain.
But the conception of vast and daring enterprises,
even the execution of them up to a certain point,
is not very uncommon, they fail only by a little!
that little is, however, the essence of genius, the
phial of wit, which, held to Orlando's nostril,

changed him from a frantic giant to a perfect
commander.

It was in the consideration of such nice points
of military policy that lord Wellington's solid
judgement was always advantageously displayed.
Neither the greatness of this project nor the apparent facility of execution weighed with him. He
thought the recovery of Italy by the power of the
British arms would be a glorious, and might be
a feasible exploit, but it was only in prospect,
Spain was the better field, the war in the Peninsula
existed ; years had been devoted to the establishment of a solid base there, and experience
had proved that the chance of victory was not
imaginary. England could not support two armies.
The principle of concentration of power on an important point was as applicable here as on a field
of battle, and although Italy might be the more
vital point, it would be advisable to continue the
war already established in Spain: nay it would
be better to give up Spain, and direct the whole
power of England against Italy, rather than undertake double operations, on such an extensive
scale, at a moment when the means necessary to
sustain one were so scanty.

The ministers, apparently convinced by this
reasoning, forbad lord William Bentinck to proceed,
and they expressed their discontent at his conduct.
Nevertheless their former instructions had unques-
tionably conferred on him a discretionary power
to act in Italy, and so completely had he been
misled by their previous despatches, that besides
delaying the expedition to Spain, he had placed
twelve hundred men under admiral Fremantle, to
assist the Montenegrins. And he was actually

entangled in a negotiation with the Russian admiral, Greig, relative to the march of a Russian army; a march planned, as it would appear, without the knowledge of the Russian court, and which, from the wildness of its conception and the mischief it would probably have effected, deserves notice.

While the Russian war was still uncertain, admiral Tchtchagoff, who commanded sixty thousand men on the Danube, proposed to march with them, through Bosnia and the ancient Epirus, to the mouths of the Cattaro, and, there embarking, to commence the impending contest with France in Italy. He was, however, without resources, and expecting to arrive in a starving and miserable condition on the Adriatic, demanded, through admiral Greig, then commanding a squadron in the Mediterranean, that lord William Bentinck should be ready to supply him with fresh arms, ammunition, and provisions, and to aid him with an auxiliary force. That nobleman saw at a glance the absurdity of this scheme, but he was falsely informed that Tchtchagoff, trusting to his good will, had already commenced the march; and thus he had only to choose between aiding an ally, whose force, if it arrived at all, and was supplied by England, would help his own project, or permit it, to avoid perishing, to ravage Italy, and so change the people of that country from secret friends into deadly enemies. It would be foreign to this history to consider what effect the absence of Tchtchagoff's army during the Russian campaign would have had upon Napoleon's operations, but this was the very force whose march to the Beresina afterwards obliged the emperor to abandon Smolensko, and continue the retreat to Warsaw.

It was in the midst of these affairs, that the
English minister's imperative orders to look only to the coast of Spain arrived. The negociation with the Russians was immediately stopped, the project of landing in Italy was relinquished, and the expedition, already sent to the Adriatic, was recalled. Meanwhile the descent on Catalonia had been delayed, and as a knowledge of its destination, had reached Suchet through the French minister of war, and through the rumours rife amongst the Spaniards, all his preparations to meet it were matured. Nor was this the only mischief produced by the English minister's want of clear views and decided system of policy. Lord William Bentinck had been empowered to raise money on bills for his own exigences, and being desirous to form a military chest for his project in Italy, he had invaded lord Wellington's money markets. With infinite trouble and difficulty that general had just opened a source of supply at the rate of five shillings and four-pence, to five shillings and eight-pence the dollar, when lord William Bentinck's agents offering six shillings and eight-pence, swept four millions from the markets, and thus, as shall be hereafter shewn, seriously embarrassed lord Wellington's operations in the field.

This unhappy commencement of the Sicilian expedition led to other errors, and its arrival on the coast of Spain, did not take place, until after the campaign in Castile had commenced ; but as its proceedings connected the warfare of Valencia immediately with that of Catalonia, and the whole with lord Wellington's operations, they cannot be properly treated of in this place. It is, however, worthy of observation, how an illiberal and factious policy, inevitably recoils upon its authors.

In 1807 sir John Moore, with that sagacity and manliness which distinguished his career through life, had informed the ministers, that no hope of a successful attack on the French in Italy, could be entertained while the British army upheld the tyrannical system of the dissolute and treacherous Neapolitan court in Sicily. And as no change for the better could be expected while the queen was allowed to govern, he proposed, that the British cabinet should either relinquish Sicily, or, assuming the entire controul of the island, seize the queen and send her to her native Austria. This he judged to be the first step necessary to render the large British army in Sicily available for the field, because the Sicilian people could then be justly governed, and thus only could the organization of an effective native force attached to England, and fitted to offer freedom to Italy be effected.

He spoke not of constitutions but of justice to the people, and hence his proposal was rejected as a matter of Jacobinism. Mr. Drummond, the English plenipotentiary, even betrayed it to the queen, a woman not without magnanimity, yet so capable of bloody deeds, that, in 1810, she secretly proposed to Napoleon the perpetration of a second Sicilian vespers upon the English. The emperor, detesting such guilt, only answered by throwing her agent into prison, yet the traces of the conspiracy were detected by the British authorities in 1811; and in 1812 lord William Bentinck was forced to seize the government, in the manner before recommended by Moore, and did finally

expel the queen by force. But because these measures were not resorted to in time, he was now,
with an army of from twenty-five to thirty thousand men, sixteen thousand of which were British,
only able to detach a mixed force of six thousand
to aid lord Wellington. And at the same time the
oppression of Ireland required that sixty thousand
fine soldiers should remain idle at home, while
France, with a Russian war on hand, was able to
overmatch the allies in Spain. Bad government is
a scourge with a double thong !

CHAPTER IV.

OPERATIONS IN ANDALUSIA AND ESTRE-
MADURA.

BOOK
XVII.

1812.
April.

A SHORT time previous to Hill's enterprize against Almaraz, Soult, after driving Ballesteros from the Ronda, and restoring the communication with Grenada, sent three thousand men into the Niebla ; partly to interrupt the march of some Spaniards coming from Cadiz to garrison Badajos, partly to menace Penne Villemur and Morillo, who still lingered on the Odiel against the wishes of Wellington. The French arguments were more effectual. Those generals immediately filed along the frontier of Portugal towards Estremadura, they were hastily followed by the Spanish troops sent from Cadiz, and the militia of the Algarves were called out, to defend the Portuguese frontier. Soult then remained on the defensive, for he expected the advance of lord Wellington, which the approach of so many troops, the seeming reluctance of the Spaniards to quit the Niebla, the landing of fresh men from Cadiz at Ayamonte, and the false rumours purposely set afloat by the British general seemed to render certain. Nor did the surprize of Almaraz, which he thought to be aimed at the army of the south and not against the army of Portugal, alter his views.

The great advantage which lord Wellington had
gained by the fall of Ciudad Rodrigo and Badajos
was now very clearly illustrated ; for, as he could
at will advance either against the north or the south
or the centre, the French generals in each quarter
expected him, and they were anxious that the
others should regulate their movements accordingly.
None would help the other, and the secret plans
of all were paralyzed until it was seen on which
side the thunderbolt would fall. This was of most
consequence in the south, for Soult's plans were
vast, dangerous, and ripe for execution.

After the fall of Badajos he judged it unwise to
persevere in pushing a head of troops, into Estremadura, while his rear and flanks were exposed to
attacks from Cadiz, Gibraltar, and Murcia; but it
was essential, he thought, to crush Ballesteros
before his forces should be increased, and this was
not to be effected, while that general could flee to
Gibraltar on the one side, and Tarifa on the other.
Whereupon Soult had resolved first to reduce
Tarifa, with a view to the ruin of Ballesteros, and
then to lay siege to Carthagena and Alicant, and
he only awaited the development of Wellington's
menacing demonstrations against Andalusia to commence his own operations. Great and difficult his
plan was, yet profoundly calculated to effect his
main object, which was to establish his base so
firmly in Andalusia that, maugre the forces in Cadiz
and the Isla, he might safely enter upon and follow
up regular offensive operations in Estremadura and
against Portugal, instead of the partial uncertain
expeditions hitherto adopted. In fine, he designed
to make lord Wellington feel that there was a
powerful army within a few marches of Lisbon.

Thinking that Carthagena and Tarifa, and even Alicant must fall, with the aid of Suchet, which he expected, or that the siege of the first would bring down Hill's corps, and all the disposable Spanish troops to save it, he desired that the army of Portugal, and the army of the centre, should operate so as to keep lord Wellington employed north of the Tagus. He could then by himself carry on the sieges he contemplated, and yet leave a force under Drouet on the edge of Estremadura, strong enough to oblige Hill to operate in the direction of Carthagena instead of Seville. And if this should happen as he expected, he proposed suddenly to concentrate all his finely organized and experienced troops, force on a general battle, and, if victorious, the preparations being made before hand, to follow up the blow by a rapid march upon Portugal, and so enter Lisbon; or by bringing Wellington in all haste to the defence of that capital, confine the war, while Napoleon was in Russia, to a corner of the Peninsula.

This great project was strictly in the spirit of the emperor's instructions. For that consummate commander had desired his lieutenants to make lord Wellington feel that his enemies were not passively defensive. He had urged them to press the allies close on each flank, and he had endeavoured to make Marmont understand that, although there was no object to be attained by entering the north-east of Portugal, and fighting a general battle on ground favourable to lord Wellington, it was contrary to all military principles, to withdraw several days' march from the allies' outposts, and by such a timid defensive system, to give the English general the power of choosing when

and where to strike.   Now the loss of Badajos,
and the difficulty of maintaining a defensive war
against the increasing forces of the allies in the
south of Andalusia, rendered it extremely onerous
for Soult to press Wellington's flank in Estremadura ; and it was therefore a profound modification
of the emperor's views, to urge the king and Marmont to active operation in the north, while he
besieged Tarifa and Carthagena, keeping his army
in mass ready for a sudden stroke in the field,
if fortune brought the occasion, and if otherwise,
sure of fixing a solid base for future operations
against Portugal.

The duke of Dalmatia wished to have commenced
his operations by the siege of Tarifa in May, when
Wellington's return to Beira had relieved him from
the fear of an immediate invasion of Andalusia, but
the failure of the harvest in 1811 and the continual
movements during the winter, had so reduced his
magazines, both of provisions and ammunition, that
he could not undertake the operation until the new
harvest was ripe, and fresh convoys had replenished
his exhausted stores.   His soldiers were already on
short allowance, and famine raged amongst the
people of the country.   Meanwhile his agents in
Morocco had so firmly re-established the French
interests there, that the emperor refused all supplies
to the British, and even fitted out a squadron to
insure obedience to his orders.   To counteract this
mischief, the Gibraltar merchant, Viali, who had
been employed in the early part of the war by sir
Hew Dalrymple, was sent by sir Henry Wellesley
with a mission to the court of Fez, which failed,
and it was said from the intrigues of the notorious
Charmilly who was then at Tangier, and being con-

nected by marriage with the English consul there, unsuspected: indeed from a mean hatred to sir John Moore, there were not wanting persons in power who endeavoured still to uphold this man.

So far every thing promised well for Soult's plans, and he earnestly demanded that all his detachments, and sufficient reinforcements, together with artillery, officers, money, and convoys of ammunition should be sent to him for the siege of Carthagena. Pending their arrival, to divert the attention of the allies, he repaired to Port St. Mary where the French had, from the circumstances of the war in Estremadura, been a long time inactive. He brought down with him a number of the Villantroy mortars, and having collected about thirty gunboats in the Trocadero canal, commenced a serious bombardment of Cadiz on the 16th of May. While thus engaged, a sudden landing from English vessels was effected on the Grenada coast, Almeria was abandoned by the French, the people rose along the sea line, and general Frere, advancing from Murcia, entrenched himself in the position of Venta de Bahul, on the eastern frontier of Grenada. He was indeed surprised and beaten with loss, and the insurrection on the coast was soon quelled, but these things delayed the march of the reinforcements intended for Drouet; meanwhile Hill surprised Almaraz, and Ballesteros, whose forces had subsisted during the winter and spring, upon the stores of Gibraltar, advanced against Conroux's division then in observation at Bornos on the Guadalete.

This Spanish general caused equal anxiety to Soult and to Wellington, because his proceedings involved one of those intricate knots, by which the important parts of both their operations were fastened. Lord Wellington judged, that, while a large CHAP.
IV. and increasing corps which could be aided by a disembarkation of five or six thousand men from 1812.
May. the Isla de Leon, menaced the blockade of Cadiz and the communications between Seville and Grenada, Soult must keep a considerable body in observation, and consequently, Hill would be a match for the French in Estremadura. But the efficacy of this diversion, depended upon avoiding battles, seeing that if Ballesteros' army was crushed, the French, reinforced in Estremadura, could drive Hill over the Tagus, which would inevitably bring Wellington himself to his succour. Soult was for the same reason as earnest to bring the Spanish general to action, as Wellington was to prevent a battle, and Ballesteros, a man of infinite arrogance, despised both. Having obtained money and supplies from Gibraltar to replace the expenditure of his former excursion against Seville, he marched with eight thousand men against Conroux, and that Frenchman, aware of his intention, induced him, by an appearance of fear, to attack an entrenched camp in a disorderly manner. On the 1st of June the battle took place, and Conroux issuing forth unexpectedly killed or took fifteen hundred Spaniards, and drove the rest to the hills, from whence they retreated to San Roque. How this victory was felt in Estremadura shall now be shewn.

The loss of Almaraz had put all the French corps in movement. A division of Marmont's army crossed the Gredos mountains, to replace Foy in the valley of the Tagus, and the latter general, passing that river by the bridge of Arzobispo moved through the mountains of Guadalupe, and succoured the garrison of Mirabete on the 26th of May. When

he retired the partidas of the Guadalupe renewed
the blockade, and Hill, now strongly reinforced by
lord Wellington, advanced to Zafra, whereupon
Drouet, unable to meet him, fell back to Azagua.
Hill, wishing to protect the gathering of the harvest, then detached Penne Villemur's horsemen,
from Llerena on the right flank, and general Slade,
with the third dragoon guards and the royals,
from Llera on the left flank ; General Lallemande,
having a like object, came forward with two regiments of French dragoons, on the side of Valencia
de las Torres, whereupon Hill, hoping to cut him off,
placed Slade's dragoons in a wood with directions to await further orders. Slade hearing that
Lallemand was so near, and no wise superior to
himself in numbers, forgot his orders, advanced
and drove the French cavalry with loss beyond the
defile of Maquilla, a distance of eight miles ; and
through the pass also the British rashly galloped in
pursuit, the general riding in the foremost ranks,
and the supports joining tumultuously in the charge.

But in the plain beyond stood Lallemand with
his reserves well in hand. He broke the disorderly
English mass thus rushing on him, killed or wounded forty-eight men, pursued the rest for six miles,
recovered all his own prisoners, and took more than
a hundred, including two officers, from his adversary ; and the like bitter results will generally attend
what is called " *dashing*" in war, which in other
words means courage without prudence. Two days
after this event the Austrian Strenowitz, whose exploits have been before noticed, marched with fifty
men of the same regiments, to fetch off some of the
English prisoners who had been left, by the French,
under a slender guard in the village of Maquilla.

Eighty of the enemy met him on the march, yet by fine management he overthrew him, and losing only one man himself, killed many French, executed his mission, and returned with an officer and twenty other prisoners.

Such was the state of affairs, when the defeat of Ballesteros at Bornoz, enabled Soult to reinforce Drouet, with Barois's division of infantry and two divisions of cavalry ; they marched across the Morena, but for reasons, to be hereafter mentioned, by the royal road of St. Ollala, a line of direction which obliged Drouet to make a flank march by his left towards Llerena to form his junction with them. It was effected on the 18th, and the allies then fell back gradually towards Albuera, where being joined by four Portuguese regiments from Badajos, and by the fifth Spanish army, Hill formed a line of battle furnishing twenty thousand infantry, two thousand five hundred cavalry, and twenty-four guns.

Drouet had only twenty-one thousand men, of which three thousand were cavalry, with eighteen pieces of artillery ; the allies were therefore the most numerous, but the French army was better composed, and battle seemed inevitable, for both generals had discretionary orders. However the French cavalry did not advance further than Almendralejo, and Hill who had shewn himself so daring at Aroyo Molino and Almaraz, now, with an uncommon mastery of ambition, refrained from an action which promised him unbounded fame, simply because he was uncertain whether the state of lord Wellington's operations in Castile, then in full progress, would warrant one. His recent exploits had been so splendid that a great battle gained at this time would, with the assistance of envious malice, have placed his reputation on a level with Wellington's. Yet he was habituated to command, and his adversary's talents were moderate, his forbearance must therefore be taken as a proof of the purest patriotism.

Early in July the French cavalry entered Almendralejo and Santa Marta, cut off two hundred Spanish horsemen, and surprised a small British cavalry post; Hill who had then received fresh instructions, and was eager to fight, quickly drove them with loss from both places. Drouet immediately concentrated his forces and retired to La Granja, and was followed by the allies, but the account of the transactions in Andalusia and Estremadura must be here closed, because those which followed belong to the general combinations. And as the causes of these last movements, and their effects upon the general campaign, are of an intricate nature, to avoid confusion the explanation of them is reserved for another place: meanwhile I will endeavour to describe that political chaos, amidst which Wellington's army appeared as the ark amongst the meeting clouds and rising waters of the deluge.

CHAPTER V.

POLITICAL SITUATION OF FRANCE.

THE unmatched power of Napoleon's genius was ⟨CHAP.⟩
now being displayed in a wonderful manner. His ⟨V.⟩
interest, his inclination, and his expectation were ⟨1812.⟩
alike opposed to a war with Russia, but Alexander
and himself, each hoping that a menacing display
of strength would reduce the other to negotiation,
advanced, step by step, until blows could no longer
be avoided. Napoleon, a man capable of sincere
friendship, had relied too much and too long on
the existence of a like feeling in the Russian emperor ; and misled, perhaps, by the sentiment of
his own energy, did not sufficiently allow for the
daring intrigues of a court, where secret combinations of the nobles formed the real governing
power.

That the cabinet of Petersburgh should be, more
than ordinarily subject to such combinations at
this period, was the necessary consequence of the
greatness of the interests involved in the treaties
of Tilsit and Erfurth ; the continental system
had so deeply injured the fortunes of the Russian
noblemen, that their sovereign's authority in support
of it was as nothing. During the Austrian war
of 1809, when Alexander was yet warm from
Napoleon's society at Erfurth, the aid given to

France was a mockery, and a desire to join a northern confederation against Napoleon was even then
scarcely concealed at St. Petersburgh, where the
French ambassador was coldly treated. The royal
family of Prussia were, it is true, at the same time,
mortified by a reception which inclined them to side
with France, against the wishes of their people and
their ministers, but in Russia, Romanzow alone
was averse to choose that moment to declare against
Napoleon. And this was so certain that Austria,
anticipating the explosion, was only undecided
whether the king of Prussia should be punished
or the people rewarded, whether she herself should
befriend or plunder the Prussian monarchy.

At that time also, the Russian naval commander,
in the Adriatic, being ordered to sail to Ancona
for the purpose of convoying Marmont's troops
from Dalmatia to Italy, refused, on the plea
that his ships were not sea-worthy; yet secretly
he informed the governor of Trieste that they
would be in excellent order to assist an Austrian
corps against the French! Admiral Tchtchagoff's
strange project of marching upon Italy from
Bucharest has been already noticed, and it is
remarkable that this expedition was to be conducted
upon popular principles, the interests of the Sicilian court being to be made subservient to the wishes
of the people. At a later period, in 1812, admiral
Grieg proposed to place an auxiliary Russian army
under either Wellington or lord William Bentinck,
and it was accepted; but when the Russian ambassador in London was applied to upon the subject,
he unequivocally declared that the emperor knew
nothing of the matter!

With a court so situated, angry negotiations

once commenced rendered war inevitable, and the
more especially that the Russian cabinet, which had
long determined on hostilities though undecided
as to the time of drawing the sword, was well
aware of the secret designs and proceedings of
Austria in Italy, and of Murat's discontent. The
Hollanders were known to desire independence,
and the deep hatred which the people of Prussia
bore to the French was a matter of notoriety.
Bernadotte, who very early had resolved to cast
down the ladder by which he rose, was the secret
adviser of these practices against Napoleon's power
in Italy, and he was also in communication with
the Spaniards. Thus Napoleon, having a war in
Spain which required three hundred thousand
men to keep in a balanced state, was forced, by
resistless circumstances, into another and more
formidable contest in the distant north, when the
whole of Europe was prepared to rise upon his
lines of communication, and when his extensive
sea-frontier was exposed to the all-powerful navy
of Great Britain.

A conqueror's march to Moscow, amidst such
dangers, was a design more vast, more hardy, more
astounding than ever before entered the imagination
of man; yet it was achieved, and solely by the force
of his genius. For having organised two hundred
thousand French soldiers, as a pretorian guard, he
stepped resolutely into the heart of Germany, and
monarchs and nations bent submissively before him;
secret hostility ceased, and, with the exception of
Bernadotte, the crowned and anointed plotters quitted
their work to follow his chariot-wheels. Dresden
saw the ancient story of the King of Kings renewed
in his person; and the two hundred thousand French

soldiers arrived on the Niemen in company with
two hundred thousand allies. On that river four
hundred thousand troops, I have seen the imperial
returns, were assembled by this wonderful man, all
disciplined warriors, and, notwithstanding their
different national feelings, all proud of the unmatched genius of their leader. Yet, even in that
hour of dizzy elevation, Napoleon, deeply sensible
of the inherent weakness of a throne unhallowed
by time, described by one emphatic phrase the delicacy of his political situation. During the passage
of the Niemen, twelve thousand cuirassiers, whose
burnished armour flashed in the sun while their
cries of salutation pealed in unison with the
thunder of the horses' feet, were passing like a
foaming torrent towards the river, when Napoleon
turned and thus addressed Gouvion St. Cyr, whose
republican principles were well known,

" No monarch ever had such an army ?"

" No, sire."

" The French are a fine people; they deserve
more liberty, and they shall have it, but, St. Cyr,
no liberty of the press! That army, mighty as it
is, could not resist the songs of Paris!"

Such, then, was the nature of Napoleon's power
that success alone could sustain it; success which
depended as much upon others' exertions as upon
his own stupendous genius, for Russia was far
distant from Spain. It is said, I know not upon
what authority, that he at one moment, had resolved
to concentrate all the French troops in the Peninsula
behind the Ebro during this expedition to Russia,
but the capture of Blake's force at Valencia changed
his views. Of this design there are no traces in
the movements of his armies, nor in the captured

papers of the king, and there are some indications

of a contrary design; for at that period several foreign agents were detected examining the lines of Torres Vedras, and on a Frenchman, who killed himself when arrested in the Brazils, were found papers proving a mission for the same object. Neither is it easy to discern the advantage of thus crowding three hundred thousand men on a narrow slip of ground, where they must have been fed from France, already overburthened with the expenses of the Russian war; and this when they were numerous enough, if rightly handled, to have maintained themselves on the resources of Spain, and near the Portuguese frontier for a year at least.

To have given up all the Peninsula, west of the Ebro, would have been productive of no benefit, save what might have accrued from the jealousy which the Spaniards already displayed towards their allies; but if that jealousy, as was probable, had forced the British general away, he could have carried his army to Italy, or have formed in Germany the nucleus of a great northern confederation on the emperor's rear. Portugal was therefore, in truth, the point of all Europe in which the British strength was least dangerous to Napoleon during the invasion of Russia; moreover, an immediate war with that empire was not a certain event previous to the capture of Valencia. Napoleon was undoubtedly anxious to avoid it while the Spanish contest continued; yet, with a far-reaching European policy, in which his English adversaries were deficient, he foresaw and desired to check the growing strength of that fearful and wicked power which now menaces the civilised world.

The proposal for peace which he made to England

before his departure for the Niemen is another circumstance where his object seems to have been misrepresented. It was called a device to reconcile the French to the Russian war; but they were as eager for that war as he could wish them to be, and it is more probable that it sprung from a secret misgiving, a prophetic sentiment of the consequent power of Russia, lifted, as she then would be towards universal tyranny, by the very arm which he had raised to restrain her. The ostensible ground of his quarrel with the emperor Alexander was the continental system; yet, in this proposal for peace, he offered to acknowledge the house of Braganza in Portugal, the house of Bourbon in Sicily, and to withdraw his army from the Peninsula, if England would join him in guaranteeing the crown of Spain to Joseph, together with a constitution to be arranged by a national Cortes. This was a virtual renunciation of the continental system for the sake of peace with England; and a proposal which obviated the charge of aiming at universal dominion, seeing that Austria, Spain, Portugal, and England would have retained their full strength, and the limits of his empire would have been fixed. The offer was made also at a time when the emperor was certainly more powerful than he had ever yet been, when Portugal was, by the avowal of Wellington himself, far from secure, and Spain quite exhausted. At peace with England, Napoleon could easily have restored the Polish nation, and Russia would have been repressed. Now, Poland has fallen, and Russia stalks in the plenitude of her barbarous tyranny.

Political state of England.—The new administration, despised by the country, was not the less

powerful in parliament; its domestic proceedings
were therefore characterised by all the corruption
and tyranny of Mr. Pitt's system, without his re-
deeming genius. The press was persecuted with
malignant ferocity, and the government sought to
corrupt all that it could not trample upon. Repeated successes had rendered the particular contest
in the Peninsula popular with the ardent spirits of
the nation, and war-prices passed for glory with
the merchants, land-owners, and tradesmen; but
as the price of food augmented faster than the
price of labour, the poorer people suffered, they
rejoiced, indeed, at their country's triumphs because
the sound of victory is always pleasing to warlike
ears, but they were discontented. Meanwhile all
thinking men, who were not biassed by factions,
or dazzled by military splendour, perceived in the
enormous expenses incurred to repress the democratic principle, and in the consequent transfer of
property, the sure foundation of future reaction and
revolution. The distresses of the working classes
had already produced partial insurrections, and the
nation at large was beginning to perceive that
the governing powers, whether representative or
executive, were rapacious usurpers of the people's
rights; a perception quickened by malignant pro-
secutions, by the insolent extravagance with which
the public money was lavished on the family of
Mr. Perceval, and by the general profusion at
home, while lord Wellesley declared that the war
languished for want of sustenance abroad.

Napoleon's continental system, although in the
nature of a sumptuary law, which the desires of
men will never suffer to exist long in vigour, was
yet so efficient, that the British government was

forced to encourage, and protect, illicit trading, to the great detriment of mercantile morality. The island of Heligoland was the chief point of deposit for this commerce, and either by trading energy, or by the connivance of continental governments, the emperor's system was continually baffled; nevertheless its effects will not quickly pass away; it pressed sorely upon the manufacturers at the time, and by giving rise to rival establishments on the continent, has awakened in Germany a commercial spirit by no means favourable to England's manufacturing superiority.

But ultimate consequences were never considered by the British ministers; the immediate object was to procure money, and by virtually making banknotes a legal tender, they secured unlimited means at home, through the medium of loans and taxes, which the corruption of the parliament, insured to them, and which, by a reaction, insured the corruption of the parliament. This resource failed abroad. They could, and did, send to all the allies of England, enormous supplies in kind, because to do so, was, in the way of contracts, an essential part of the system of corruption at home; a system aptly described, as bribing one-half of the nation with the money of the other half, in order to misgovern both. Specie was however only to be had in comparatively small quantities, and at a premium so exorbitant, that even the most reckless politician trembled for the ultimate consequences.

The foreign policy of the government was very simple, namely, to bribe all powers to war down France. Hence to Russia every thing, save specie, was granted; and hence also, amicable relations with Sweden were immediately re-established, and

the more readily that this power had lent herself
to the violation of the continental system by permitting the entry of British goods at Stralsund ;
but wherever wisdom, or skill, was required,
the English minister's resources failed altogether.
With respect to Sicily, Spain, and Portugal, this
truth was notorious ; and to preserve the political
support of the trading interests at home, a degrading and deceitful policy, quite opposed to the
spirit of lord Wellington's counsels, was followed
in regard to the revolted Spanish colonies.

The short-sighted injustice of the system was however most glaring with regard to the United States
of America. Mutual complaints, the dregs of the
war of independence, had long characterised the intercourse between the British and American governments, and these discontents were turned into extreme hatred by the progress of the war with France.
The British government in 1806 proclaimed, contrary to the law of nations, a blockade of the
French coast, which could not be enforced. Napoleon, in return, issued the celebrated decrees of
Berlin and Milan, which produced the no less celebrated orders in council. The commerce of all
neutrals was thus extinguished by the arrogance
of the belligerents ; but the latter very soon finding
that their mutual convenience required some re-
laxation of mutual violence, granted licenses to
each other's ships, and by this scandalous evasion
of their own policy, caused the whole of the evil
to fall upon the neutral, who was yet called the
friend of both parties.

The Americans, unwilling to go to war with two
such powerful states, were yet resolved not to sub-

1812.

mit to the tyranny of either; but the injustice of
the English government was the most direct, and
extended in its operations, and it was rendered
infinitely more bitter by the violence used towards
the seamen of the United States : not less than six
thousand sailors, it was said, were taken from merchant vessels on the high seas, and forced to serve
in the British men-of-war.   Wherefore, after first
passing retaliatory, or rather warning acts, called the
non-intercourse, non-importation, and embargo acts,
the Americans finally declared war, at the moment
when the British government, alarmed at the consequences of their own injustice, had just rescinded the orders in council.

18th June,
1812.

The immediate effects of these proceedings on
the contest in the Peninsula, shall be noticed in
another place, but the ultimate effects on England's prosperity have not yet been unfolded.
The struggle prematurely told the secret of
American strength, and it has drawn the attention
of the world to a people, who, notwithstanding
the curse of black slavery which clings to them,
adding the most horrible ferocity to the peculiar
baseness of their mercantile spirit, and rendering
their republican vanity ridiculous, do in their
general government uphold civil institutions, which
have startled the crazy despotisms of Europe.

Political state of Spain.—Bad government is more
hurtful than direct war; the ravages of the last are
soon repaired, and the public mind is often purified,
and advanced, by the trial of adversity, but the
evils, springing from the former, seem interminable.
In the Isla de Leon the unseemly currents of folly,
although less raging than before, continued to

break open new channels and yet abandoned none
of the old. The intrigues of the princess Carlotta
were unremitted, and though the danger of provoking the populace of Cadiz, restrained and
frightened her advocates in the Cortez, she opposed the English diplomacy, with reiterated, and
not quite unfounded accusations, that the revolt
of the colonies was being perfidiously fostered
by Great Britain :—a charge well calculated to
lower the influence of England, especially in
regard to the scheme of mediation, which being
revived in April by lord Castlereagh, was received by the Spaniards with outward coldness,
and a secret resolution to reject it altogether ; nor
were they in any want of reasons to justify their
proceedings.

This mediation had been commenced by lord
Wellesley, when the quarrel between the mother
country and the colonies was yet capable of
adjustment ; it was now renewed when it could
not succeed. English commissioners were appointed to carry it into execution, the duke of Infantado was to join them on the part of Spain, and
at first Mr. Stuart was to have formed part of the
commission, Mr. Sydenham being to succeed him
at Lisbon, but finally he remained in Portugal and
Mr. Sydenham was attached to the commission,
whose composition he thus described.

" I do not understand a word of the Spanish
language, I am unacquainted with the Spanish
character, I know very little of Old Spain, and
I am quite ignorant of the state of the colonies,
yet I am part of a commission composed of men
of different professions, views, habits, feelings, and
opinions. The mediation proposed is at least a

year too late, it has been forced upon the government of Old Spain, I have no confidence in the
ministers who employ me, and I am fully persuaded that they have not the slightest confidence
in me."

The first essential object was to have Bardaxi's
secret article, which required England to join Old
Spain if the mediation failed, withdrawn; but as
this could not be done without the consent of the
Cortez, the publicity thus given would have ruined
the credit of the mediation with the colonists.
Nor would the distrust of the latter have been unfounded, for though lord Wellesley had offered the
guarantee of Great Britain to any arrangement
made under her mediation, his successors would
not do so!

" They empower us," said Mr. Sydenham, " to
negociate and sign a treaty but will not guarantee
the execution of it! My opinion is, that the
formal signature of a treaty by plenipotentiaries is
in itself a solemn guarantee, if there is good faith
and fair dealing in the transaction; and I believe
that this opinion will be confirmed by the authority
of every writer on the law of nations. But this is
certainly not the doctrine of our present ministers,
they make a broad distinction between the rati-
fication of a treaty and the intention of seeing it
duly observed."

The failure of such a scheme was inevitable.
The Spaniards wanted the commissioners to go first
to the Caraccas, where the revolt being full blown,
nothing could be effected; the British government
insisted that they should go to Mexico, where the
dispute had not yet been pushed to extremities.
After much useless diplomacy, which continued

until the end of the year, the negociation, as Mr.
Sydenham had predicted, proved abortive.

In March the new constitution of Spain had been
solemnly adopted, and a decree settling the succession of the crown was promulgated. The infant
Francisco de Paula, the queen of Etruria, and
their respective descendants were excluded from
the succession, which was to fall first to the princess Carlotta if the infant don Carlos failed of
heirs, then to the hereditary princess of the Two
Sicilies, and so on, the empress of France and her
descendants being especially excluded. This ex-
hibition of popular power, under the pretext of
baffling Napoleon's schemes, struck at the principle of legitimacy. And when the extraordinary
Cortez decided that the ordinary Cortez, which
ought to assemble every year, should not be con-
voked until October 1813, and thus secured to
itself a tenure of power for two years instead of
one, the discontent increased both at Cadiz and in
the provinces, and a close connection was kept up
between the malcontents and the Portuguese government, which was then the strong hold of arbitrary
power in the Peninsula.

The local junta of Estremadura adopted Carlotta's
claims, in their whole extent, and communicated on
the subject, at first secretly with the Portuguese
regency, and then more openly with Mr. Stuart.
Their scheme was to remove all the acting provin-
cial authorities, and to replace them with persons
acknowledging Carlotta's sovereignty; they even
declared that they would abide by the new constitution, only so far as it acknowledged what they
called legitimate power, in other words, the princess
was to be sole regent. Nevertheless this party

was not influenced by Carlotta's intrigues, for they would not join her agents in any outcry against the British; they acted upon the simple principle of opposing the encroachments of democracy, and they desired to know how England would view their proceedings. The other provinces received the new constitution coldly, and the Biscayens angrily rejected it as opposed to their ancient privileges. In this state of public feeling, the abolition of the Inquisition, a design now openly agitated, offered a point around which all the clergy, and all that the clergy could influence, gathered against the Cortes, which was also weakened by its own factions; yet the republicans gained strength, and they were encouraged by the new constitution established in Sicily, which also alarmed their opponents, and the fear and distrust extended to the government of Portugal.

However amidst all the varying subjects of interest the insane project of reducing the colonies by force, remained a favourite with all parties; nor was it in relation to the colonies only, that these men, who were demanding aid from other nations, in the names of freedom, justice, and humanity, proved themselves to be devoid of those attributes themselves. " The humane object of the abolition of the slave-trade has been frustrated," said lord Castlereagh, " because not only Spanish subjects but Spanish public officers and governors, in various parts of the Spanish colonies, are instrumental to, and accomplices in the crimes of the contraband slave-traders of Great Britain and America, furnishing them with flags, papers, and solemn documents to entitle them to the privileges of Spanish cruizers, and to represent their property as Spanish."

With respect to the war in Spain itself, all manner of mischief was abroad. The regular cavalry had been entirely destroyed, and when, with the secret permission of their own government, some distinguished Austrian officers, proffered their services to the regency, to restore that arm, they were repelled. Nearly all the field artillery had been lost in action, the arsenals at Cadiz were quite exhausted, and most of the heavy guns on the works of the Isla were rendered unserviceable by constant and useless firing; the stores of shot were diminished in an alarming manner, no sums were appropriated to the support of the founderies, and when the British artillery officers made formal representations of this dangerous state of affairs, it only produced a demand of money from England to put the founderies into activity. To crown the whole, Abadia, recalled from Gallicia, at the express desire of sir Henry Wellesley because of his bad conduct, was now made minister of war.

In Ceuta, notwithstanding the presence of a small British force, the Spanish garrison, the galley slaves, and the prisoners of war who were allowed to range at large, joined in a plan for delivering that place to the Moors; not from a treacherous disposition in the two first, but to save themselves from starving, a catastrophe which was only staved off by frequent assistance from the magazines of Gibraltar. Ceuta might have been easily acquired by England at this period, in exchange for the debt due by Spain, and general Campbell urged it to lord Liverpool, but he rejected the proposal, fearing to awaken popular jealousy. The notion, however, came originally from the people themselves, and that jealousy which lord Liverpool feared, was already in full activity, being only another name for the democratic spirit rising in opposition to the aristocratic principle upon which England afforded her assistance to the Peninsula.

The foreign policy of Spain was not less absurd than their home policy, but it was necessarily contracted. Castro, the envoy at Lisbon, who was agreeable both to the Portuguese and British authorities, was removed, and Bardaxi, who was opposed to both, substituted. This Bardaxi had been just before sent on a special mission to Stockholm, to arrange a treaty with that court, and he was referred to Russia for his answer, so completely subservient was Bernadotte to the czar. One point however was characteristically discussed by the Swedish prince and the Spanish envoy. Bardaxi demanded assistance in troops, and Bernadotte in reply asked for a subsidy, which was promised without hesitation, but security for the payment being desired, the negociation instantly dropped! A treaty of alliance was however concluded between Spain and Russia, in July, and while Bardaxi was thus pretending to subsidize Sweden, the unceasing solicitations of his own government had extorted from England a grant of one million of money, together with arms and clothing for one hundred thousand men, in return for which five thousand Spaniards were to be enlisted for the British ranks.

To raise Spanish corps had long been a favourite project with many English officers, general Graham had deigned to offer his services, and great advantages were anticipated by those who still believed in Spanish heroism. Joseph was even disquieted, for the Catalans had formally demanded such assistance, and a like feeling was now expressed in other places, yet when it came to the proof only two or three hundred starving Spaniards of the poorest condition enlisted; they were recruited principally by the light division, were taught with care and placed with English comrades, yet the experiment failed, they did not make good soldiers. Meanwhile the regency demanded and obtained from England, arms, clothing, and equipments for ten thousand cavalry, though they had scarce five hundred regular horsemen to arm at the time, and had just rejected the aid of the Austrian officers in the organization of new corps. Thus the supplies granted by Great Britain continued to be embezzled or wasted; and with the exception of a trifling amelioration in the state of Carlos d'Españas' corps effected by the direct interposition of Wellington, no public benefit seemed likely at first to accrue from the subsidy, for every branch of administration in Spain, whether civil or military, foreign or domestic, was cankered to the core. The public mischief was become portentous.

Ferdinand living in tranquillity at Valençay was so averse to encounter any dangers for the recovery of his throne, that he rejected all offers of assistance to escape. Kolli and the brothers Sagas had been alike disregarded. The councellor Sobral, who while in secret correspondence with the allies, had so long lived at Victor's head-quarters, and had travelled with that marshal to France, now proposed to carry the prince off, and he also was baffled as his predecessors had been. Ferdinand would listen to no proposal save through Escoiquez, who lived at some distance, and Sobral who judged this man one not to be trusted, immediately made his way to

Lisbon, fearful of being betrayed by the prince to whose succour he had come.

Meanwhile Joseph was advancing towards the political conquest of the country, and spoke with ostentation, of assembling a cortes in his own interests ; but this was to cover a secret intercourse with the cortes in the Isla de Leon where his partizans called " *Afrancesados* " were increasing : for many of the democratic party, seeing that the gulf which separated them from the clergy, and from England, could never be closed, and that the bad system of government, deprived them of the people's support, were willing to treat with the intrusive monarch as one whose principles were more in unison with their own. Joseph secretly offered to adopt the new constitution, with some modifications, and as many of the cortes were inclined to accept his terms, the British policy was on the eve of suffering a signal defeat, when Wellington's iron arm again fixed the destiny of the Peninsula.

CHAPTER VI.

POLITICAL STATE OF PORTUGAL.

THE internal condition of this country was not improved. The government, composed of civilians, was unable, as well as unwilling to stimulate the branches of administration connected with military affairs, and the complaints of the army, reaching the Brazils, drew reprimands from the prince; but instead of meeting the evil with suitable laws, he only increased Beresford's authority, which was already sufficiently great. Thus while the foreigner's power augmented, the native authorities were degraded in the eyes of the people; and as their influence to do good dwindled, their ill-will increased, and their power of mischief was not lessened, because they still formed the intermediate link between the military commander and the subordinate authorities. Hence what with the passive patriotism of the people, the abuses of the government, and the double dealing at the Brazils, the extraordinary energy of lord Wellington and Mr. Stuart was counterbalanced.

The latter had foreseen that the regent's concessions at the time of Borel's arrest would produce but a momentary effect in Portugal, and all the intrigues at Rio Janeiro revived when lord Wellesley disgusted with Perceval's incapacity, had quitted the British cabinet. But previous to that event, Mr. Sydenham, whose mission to Portugal has been noticed, had so strongly represented the evil effects of lord Strangford's conduct, that lord Wellesley would have immediately dismissed him, if Mr. Sydenham, who was offered the situation, had not refused to profit from the effects of his own report. It was then judged proper to send lord Louvaine with the rank of ambassador, and he was to touch at Lisbon and consult with lord Wellington whether to press the prince's return to Portugal, or insist upon a change in the regency; meanwhile a confidential agent, despatched direct to Rio Janeiro, was to keep lord Strangford in the strict line of his instructions until the ambassador arrived.

But lord Louvaine was on bad terms with his uncle, the duke of Northumberland, a zealous friend to lord Strangford; and for a government, conducted on the principle of corruption, the discontent of a nobleman, possessing powerful parliamentary influence, was necessarily of more consequence than the success of the war in the Peninsula. Ere a fit successor to lord Strangford could be found, the prince regent of Portugal acceded to lord Wellington's demands, and it was then judged expedient to await the effect of this change of policy. Meanwhile the dissensions, which led to the change of ministry arose, and occupied the attention of the English cabinet to the exclusion of all other affairs. Thus lord Strangford's career was for some time uncontrolled, yet after several severe rebukes from lord Wellington and Mr. Stuart, it was at last arrested, by a conviction that his tenure of place depended upon their will.

However, prior to this salutary check on the Bra-

zilian intrigues, lord Wellesley had so far intimidated
the prince regent of Portugal, that besides assenting
to the reforms, he despatched Mr. De Lemos from Rio
Janeiro, furnished with authority for Beresford to
act despotically in all things connected with the
administration of the army. Moreover lord Wellington was empowered to dismiss Principal Souza
from the regency; and lord Castlereagh, following
up his predecessor's policy on this head, insisted
that all the obnoxious members of the regency
should be set aside and others appointed. And these
blows at the power of the Souza faction, were accompanied by the death of Linhares, the head of
the family, an event which paralyzed the court of
Rio Janeiro for a considerable time; nevertheless
the Souzas were still so strong, that Domingo Souza,
now Count of Funchal, was appointed prime minister, although he retained his situation as ambassador
to the English court, and continued to reside in
London.

Lord Wellington, whose long experience of Indian
intrigues rendered him the fittest person possible to
deal with the exactions, and political cunning of a
people who so much resemble Asiatics, now opposed
the removal of the obnoxious members from the
regency. He would not even dismiss the Principal
Souza; for with a refined policy he argued, that the
opposition to his measures arose, as much from the
national, as from the individual character of the
Portuguese authorities, several of whom were under
the displeasure of their own court, and consequently
dependent upon the British power, for support
against their enemies. There were amongst them
also, persons of great ability, and hence no beneficial change could be expected, because the influ-

ence already gained would be lost with new men. The latter would have the same faults, with less talent, and less dependence on the British power, and the dismissed ministers would become active enemies. The patriarch would go to Oporto, where his power to do mischief would be greatly increased, and Principal Souza would then be made patriarch. It was indeed very desirable to drive this man, whose absurdity was so great as to create a suspicion of insanity, from the regency, but he could neither be persuaded, nor forced, to quit Portugal. His dismissal had been extorted from the prince by the power of the British government, he would therefore maintain his secret influence over the civil administration, he would be considered a martyr to foreign influence, which would increase his popularity, and his power would be augmented by the sanctity of his character as patriarch. Very little advantage could then be derived from a change, and any reform would be attributed to the English influence, against which the numerous interests, involved in the preservation of abuses, would instantly combine with active enmity.

On the other hand, the government of Portugal had never yet laid the real nature of the war fairly before the people. The latter had been deceived, flattered, cajoled, their prowess in the field extolled beyond reason, and the enemy spoken of contemptuously; but the resources of the nation, which essentially consisted neither in its armies, nor in its revenue, nor in its boasting, but in the sacrificing of all interests to the prosecution of the contest, had never been vigorously used to meet the emergencies of the war. The regency had neither appealed to the patriotism of the population nor yet enforced sacri-

fices, by measures, which were absolutely necessary, because as the English general honestly observed, no people would ever voluntarily bear such
enormous, though necessary burthens; strong laws
and heavy penalties could alone insure obedience.
The Portuguese government relied upon England,
and her subsidies, and resisted all measures which
could render their natural resources more available.
Their subordinates on the same principle executed
corruptly and vexatiously, or evaded, the military
regulations, and the chief supporters of all this mischief were the Principal and his faction.

Thus dragged by opposing forces, and environed
with difficulties, Wellington took a middle course.
That is, he strove by reproaches and by redoubled
activity, to stimulate the patriotism of the authorities; he desired the British ministers at Lisbon, and
at Rio Janeiro, to paint the dangerous state of Portugal in vivid colours, and to urge the prince regent
in the strongest manner, to enforce the reform of
those gross abuses, which in the taxes, in the customs, in the general expenditure, and in the execution of orders by the inferior magistrates, were
withering the strength of the nation. At the same
time, amidst the turmoil of his duties in the field,
sometimes actually from the field of battle itself, he
transmitted memoirs upon the nature of these different evils, and the remedies for them; memoirs which
will attest to the latest posterity the greatness and
vigour of his capacity.

These efforts, aided by the suspension of the
subsidy, produced partial reforms, yet the natural
weakness of character and obstinacy of the prince
regent, were insurmountable obstacles to any general or permanent cure; the first defect rendered

him the tool of the court intriguers, and the second was to be warily dealt with, lest some dogged conduct should oblige Wellington to put his often repeated threat, of abandoning the country, into execution. The success of the contest was in fact of more importance to England, than to Portugal, and this occult knot could neither be untied nor cut; the difficulty could with appliances be lessened, but might not be swept away; hence the British general involved in ceaseless disputes, and suffering hourly mortifications, the least of which would have broken the spirit of an ordinary man, had to struggle as he could to victory.

Viewing the contest as one of life or death to Portugal, he desired to make the whole political economy of the state a simple provision for the war, and when thwarted, his reproaches were as bitter as they were just; nevertheless, the men to whom they were addressed, were not devoid of merit. In after times, while complaining that he could find no persons of talent in Spain, he admitted that amongst the Portuguese, Redondo possessed both probity and ability, that Nogueira was a statesman of capacity equal to the discussion of great questions, and that no sovereign in Europe had a better public servant than Forjas. Even the restless Principal disinterestedly prosecuted measures, for forcing the clergy to pay their just share of the imposts. But greatness of mind, on great occasions, is a rare quality. Most of the Portuguese considered the sacrifices demanded, a sharper ill than submission, and it was impossible to unite entire obedience to the will of the British authorities, with an energetic, original spirit, in the native government. The Souza faction was always violent and foolish;

the milder opposition of the three gentlemen, above
mentioned, was excusable.   Lord Wellington, a
foreigner, was serving his own country, pleasing his
own government, and forwarding his own fortune,
final success was sure to send him to England, re-
splendent with glory, and beyond the reach of Portuguese ill-will. The native authorities had no
such prospects. Their exertions brought little of
personal fame, they were disliked by their own
prince, hated by his favourites, and they feared to
excite the enmity of the people, by a vigour, which,
being unpleasing to their sovereign, would inevitably draw evil upon themselves; from the French if
the invasion succeeded, from their own court if the
independence of the country should be ultimately
obtained.

But thus much conceded, for the sake of justice,
it is yet to be affirmed, with truth, that the conduct
of the Portuguese and Brazilian governments was
always unwise, often base. Notwithstanding the
prince's concessions, it was scarcely possible to remedy any abuses. The Lisbon government substi-
tuting evasive for active opposition, baffled Wellington and Stuart, by proposing inadequate laws,
or by suffering the execution of effectual measures
to be neglected with impunity; and the treaty of
commerce with England always supplied them a
source of dispute, partly from its natural difficulties, partly from their own bad faith. The general's
labours were thus multiplied not abated by his new
powers, and in measuring these labours, it is to be
noted, so entirely did Portugal depend upon England, that Wellington instead of drawing provisions
for his army from the country, in a manner fed the
whole nation, and was often forced to keep the army

magazines low, that the people might live. This is proved by the importation of rice, flour, beef, and pork from America, which increased, each year of the war, in a surprising manner, the price keeping pace with the quantity, while the importation of dried fish, the ordinary food of the Portuguese, decreased.

In 1808 the supply of flour and wheat, from New York, was sixty thousand barrels. In 1811 six hundred thousand; in 1813, between seven and eight hundred thousand. Ireland, England, Egypt, Barbary, Sicily, the Brazils, parts of Spain, and even France, also contributed to the consumption, which greatly exceeded the natural means of Portugal; English treasure therefore either directly or indirectly, furnished the nation as well as the armies.

The peace revenue of Portugal, including the Brazils, the colonies, and the islands, even in the most flourishing periods, had never exceeded thirty-six millions of cruzada novas; but in 1811, although Portugal alone raised twenty-five millions, this sum, added to the British subsidy, fell very short of the actual expenditure; yet economy was opposed by the local government, the prince was continually creating useless offices for his favourites, and encouraging law-suits and appeals to Rio Janeiro. The troops and fortresses were neglected, although the military branches of expense amounted to more than three-fourths of the whole receipts; and though Mr. Stuart engaged that England either by treaty or tribute would keep the Algerines quiet, he could not obtain the suppression of the Portuguese navy, which always fled from the barbarians. It was not until the middle of the year 1812, when admiral

Berkeley, whose proceedings had at times produced
considerable inconvenience, was recalled, that Mr.
Stuart, with the aid of admiral Martin, who succeeded Berkeley, without a seat in the regency,
effected this naval reform.

The government, rather than adopt the measures
suggested by Wellington, such as keeping up the
credit of the paper-money, by regular payments
of the interest, the fair and general collection of
the " Decima," and the repression of abuses in
the custom-house, in the arsenal, and in the militia,
always more costly than the line, projected the
issuing of fresh paper, and endeavoured, by unworthy stock-jobbing schemes, to evade instead of
meeting the difficulties of the times. To check
their folly the general withheld the subsidy, and
refused to receive their depreciated paper into the
military chest ; but neither did this vigorous proceeding produce more than a momentary return
to honesty, and meanwhile, the working people
were so cruelly oppressed that they would not
labour for the public, except under the direction
of British officers. Force alone could overcome
their repugnance and force was employed, not to
forward the defence of the country, but to meet
particular interests and to support abuses. Such
also was the general baseness of the Fidalgos, that
even the charitable aid of money, received from
England, was shamefully and greedily claimed
by the rich, who insisted, that it was a donation
to all and to be equally divided.

Confusion and injustice prevailed every where,
and Wellington's energies were squandered on
vexatious details ; at one time he was remonstrating
against the oppression of the working people, and

devising remedies for local abuses; at another
superintending the application of the English
charities, and arranging the measures necessary to
revive agriculture in the devastated districts; at
all times endeavouring to reform the general administration, and in no case was he supported. Never
during the war did he find an appeal to the patriotism of the Portuguese government answered frankly;
never did he propose a measure which was accepted
without difficulties. This opposition was at times
carried to such a ridiculous extent, that when some
Portuguese nobles in the French service took refuge
with the curate Merino, and desired from their
own government, a promise of safety, to which
they were really entitled, the regency refused to
give that assurance; nor would they publish an
amnesty, which the English general desired for
the sake of justice and from policy also, because
valuable information as to the French army, could
have been thus obtained. The authorities would
neither say yes! nor no! and when general Pam-
plona applied to Wellington personally for some
assurance, the latter could only answer that in
like cases Mascarheñas had been hanged and
Sabugal rewarded!

To force a change in the whole spirit, and action
of the government, seemed to some, the only remedy for the distemperature of the time; but this
might have produced anarchy, and would have
given countenance to the democratic spirit, contrary to the general policy of the British government. Wellington therefore desired rather to have
the prince regent at Lisbon, or the Azores, whence
his authority might, under the influence of England, be more directly used to enforce salutary

regulations; he however considered it essential that
Carlotta, whose intrigues were incessant, should
not be with him, and, she on the other hand,
laboured to come back without the prince, who
was prevented from moving, by continued disturbances in the Brazils. Mr. Stuart, then despairing
of good, proposed the establishment of a military
government at once, but Wellington would not
agree, although the mischief afloat clogged every
wheel of the military machine.

A law of king Sebastian, which obliged all
gentlemen holding land to take arms was now
revived, but desertion, which had commenced with
the first appointment of British officers, increased;
and so many persons sailed away in British vessels
of war, to evade military service in their own
country, that an edict was published to prevent
the practice. Beresford checked the desertion for
a moment, by condemning deserters to hard labour,
and offering rewards to the country people to
deliver them up; yet griping want renewed the
evil at the commencement of the campaign, and
the terrible severity of condemning nineteen at
once to death, did not repress it. The cavalry,
which had been at all times very inefficient, was
now nearly ruined, the men were become faint-
hearted, the breed of horses almost extinct, and
shameful peculations amongst the officers increased
the mischief: one guilty colonel was broke and his
uniform stripped from his shoulders in the public
square at Lisbon. However these examples produced fear and astonishment rather than correction,
the misery of the troops continued, and the army,
although by the care of Beresford it was again

augmented to more than thirty thousand men under arms, declined in moral character and spirit.

To govern armies in the field, is at all times a great and difficult matter; and in this contest the operations were so intimately connected with the civil administration of Portugal, Spain, and the Brazils, and the contest, being one of principles, so affected the policy of every nation of the civilised world, that unprecedented difficulties sprung up in the way of the general, and the ordinary frauds and embarrassments of war were greatly augmented. Napoleon's continental system joined to his financial measures, which were quite opposed to debt and paper money, increased the pernicious effects of the English bank restriction; specie was abundant in France, but had nearly disappeared from England; it was only to be obtained from abroad, and at an incredible expense. The few markets left for British manufactures, and colonial produce, did not always make returns in the articles necessary for the war, and gold, absolutely indispensable in certain quantities, was only supplied, and this entirely from the incapacity of the English ministers, in the proportion of one sixth of what was required, by an army which professed to pay for every thing. Hence continual efforts, on the part of the government, to force markets, hence a depreciation of value both in goods and bills; hence also a continual struggle, on the part of the general, to sustain a contest, dependant on the fluctuation of such a precarious system. Dependant also it was upon the prudence of three governments, one of which had just pushed its colonies to rebellion, when the French armies were in possession of four-fifths of the mother country; another was hourly raising up obstacles to its own defence though the enemy had just been driven from the capital; and the third was forcing a war with America, its greatest and surest market, when by commerce alone it could hope to sustain the struggle in the Peninsula.

The failure of the preceding year's harvest all over Europe had rendered the supply of Portugal very difficult. Little grain was to be obtained in any country of the north of Europe accessible to the British, and the necessity of paying in hard money rendered even that slight resource null. Sicily and Malta were thrown for subsistence upon Africa, where colonial produce was indeed available for commerce, yet the quantity of grain to be had there, was small, and the capricious nature of the barbarians rendered the intercourse precarious. In December 1811 there was only two months' consumption of corn in Portugal for the population, although the magazines of the army contained more than three. To America therefore it was necessary to look. Now in 1810 Mr. Stuart had given treasury bills to the house of Sampayo for the purchase of American corn; but the disputes between England and the United States, the depreciation of English bills, from the quantity in the market, together with the expiration of the American bank charter, had prevented Sampayo from completing his commission, nevertheless, although the increasing bitterness of the disputes with America discouraged a renewal of this plan, some more bills were now given to the English minister at Washington, with directions to purchase corn, and consign it to Sampayo, to resell in Portugal as before, for the benefit of the military chest. Other bills were also sent to the Brazils, to purchase rice, and all the consuls in the Mediterranean were desired to encourage the exportation of grain and the importation of colonial produce. In this manner, despite of the English ministers' incapacity, lord Wellington found resources to feed the population, to recover some of the specie expended by the army, and to maintain the war. But as the year advanced, the Non-intercourse-Act of Congress, which had caused a serious drain of specie from Portugal, was followed by an embargo for ninety days, and then famine, which already afflicted parts of Spain, menaced Portugal.

Mr. Stuart knew of this embargo before the speculators did, and sent his agents orders to buy up with hard cash, at a certain price, a quantity of grain which had lately arrived at Gibraltar. He could only forestall the speculators by a few days, the cost soon rose beyond his means in specie, yet the new harvest being nearly ripe, this prompt effort sufficed for the occasion, and happily so, for the American declaration of war followed, and American privateers were to take the place of American flour-ships. But as ruin seemed to approach, Stuart's energy redoubled. His agents seeking for grain in all parts of the world, discovered that in the Brazils a sufficient quantity might be obtained in exchange for English manufactures, to secure Portugal from absolute famine; and to protect this traffic, and to preserve that with the United States, he persuaded the regency to declare the neutrality of Portugal, and to interdict the sale of prizes within its waters. He also, at Wellington's desire, besought the English admiralty to reinforce the squadron in the Tagus, and to keep cruisers at particular stations. Finally he pressed the financial reforms in Portugal with the utmost vigour and with some success. His efforts were, however, strangely counteracted from quarters least expected. The English consul, in the Western Isles, with incredible presumption, publicly excited the Islanders to war with America, when Mr. Stuart's efforts were directed to prevent such a calamity; the Admiralty neglecting to station cruisers in the proper places, left the American privateers free to range along the Portuguese and African coast; and the cupidity of English merchants broke down the credit of the English commissariat paper-money, which was the chief medium of exchange on the immediate theatre of war.

This paper had arisen from a simple military regulation. Lord Wellington, on first assuming the command in 1809, found that all persons, gave their own vouchers in payment for provisions, whereupon he proclaimed, that none save commissaries should thus act; and that all local accounts should be paid within one month, in ready money, if it was in the chest, if not, with bills on the commissary-general. These bills soon became numerous, because of the scarcity of specie, yet their value did not sink, because they enabled those who had really furnished supplies, to prove their debts without the trouble of following the head-quarters; and they had an advantage over receipts, inasmuch as they distinctly pointed out the person who was to pay; they were also in accord with the customs of the country, for the people were used to receive government bills. The possessors were paid in rotation, whenever there

was money; the small holders, who were the real
furnishers of the army first, the speculators last, a
regulation by which justice and the credit of the
paper were alike consulted.

In 1812, this paper sunk twenty per cent., from
the sordid practices of English mercantile houses
whose agents secretly depreciated its credit and
then purchased it; and in this dishonesty they
were aided by some of the commissariat, notwithstanding the vigilant probity of the chief commissary. Sums, as low as ten pence, payable in
Lisbon, I have myself seen in the hands of poor
country people on the frontiers. By these infamous
proceedings the poorer dealers were ruined or forced
to raise their prices, which hurt their sales and
contracted the markets to the detriment of the
soldiers; and there was much danger, that the
people generally, would thus discover the mode
of getting cash for bills by submitting to high
discounts, which would soon have rendered the
contest too costly to continue. But the resources
of lord Wellington and Mr. Stuart were not exhausted. They contrived to preserve the neutrality
of Portugal, and by means of licenses continued
to have importations of American flour, until the
end of the war; a very fine stroke of policy, for
this flour was paid for with English goods, and
resold at a considerable profit for specie which
went to the military chest. They were less successful in supporting the credit of the Portuguese
government paper; bad faith, and the necessities
of the native commissariat, which now caused an
extraordinary issue, combined to lower its credit.

The conde de Funchal, Mr. Villiers, and Mr. Vansittart proposed a bank, and other schemes, such

as a loan of one million and a half from the English
treasury, which shall be treated more at length in
another place. But lord Wellington ridiculing the
fallacy of a government, with revenues unequal to its
expenditure, borrowing from a government which
was unable to find specie sufficient to sustain the
war, remarked, that the money could not be realised
in the Portuguese treasury, or it must be realised at
the expense of a military chest, whose hollow sound
already mocked the soldiers' shout of victory.
Again therefore he demanded the reform of abuses,
and offered to take all the responsibility and odium
upon himself, certain that the exigences of the
war could be thus met, and the most vexatious
imposts upon the poor abolished; neither did he
fail to point out in detail the grounds of this conviction. His reasoning made as little impression
upon Funchal, as it had done upon Linhares;
money was no where to be had, and the general,
after being forced to become a trader himself, now
tolerated, for the sake of the resources it furnished,
a contraband commerce, which he discovered Soult
to have established with English merchants at
Lisbon, exchanging the quicksilver of Almaden
for colonial produce ; and he was still to find in
his own personal resources, the means of beating
the enemy, in despite of the matchless follies of
the governments he served. He did so, but complained that it was a hard task.

BOOK XVIII.

CHAPTER I.

BOOK XVIII.

1812.
May.

In the foregoing book, the political state of the belligerents, and those great chains, which bound the war in the Peninsula to the policy of the American as well as to the European nations, have been shewn; the minor events of the war have also been narrated, and the point where the decisive struggle was to be made has been indicated; thus nought remains to tell, save the particular preparations of each adverse general ere the noble armies were dashed together in the shock of battle.

Nearly three hundred thousand French still trampled upon Spain, above two hundred and forty thousand were with the eagles, and so successful had the plan of raising native soldiers proved, that forty thousand Spaniards well organized marched under the king's banners.

In May the distribution of this immense army, which however according to the French custom included officers and persons of all kinds attached to the forces, was as follows :—

Appendix, No. 1. Section 1.

Seventy-six thousand, of which sixty thousand were with the eagles, composed the armies of Catalonia and Aragon, under Suchet, and they occupied Valencia, and the provinces whose name they bore.

Forty-nine thousand men, of which thirty-eight thousand were with the eagles, composed the army of the north, under Caffarelli, and were distributed on the grand line of communication, from St. Sebastian to Burgos ; but of this army two divisions of infantry and one of cavalry with artillery, were destined to reinforce Marmont.

Nineteen thousand, of which seventeen thousand were with the eagles, composed the army of the centre, occupying a variety of posts in a circle round the capital, and having a division in La Mancha.

Sixty-three thousand, of which fifty-six thousand were with the eagles, composed the army of the south, under Soult, occupying Andalusia and a part of Estremadura; but some of these troops were detained in distant governments by other generals.

The army of Portugal, under Marmont, consisted of seventy thousand men, fifty-two thousand being with the eagles, and a reinforcement of twelve thousand men were in march to join this army from France. Marmont occupied Leon, part of Old Castile, and the Asturias, having his front upon the Tormes, and a division watching Gallicia.

The numerous Spanish *juramentados* were principally employed in Andalusia and with the army of the centre, and the experience of Ocaña, of Badajos, and many other places, proved that for the intrusive monarch, they fought with more vigour than their countrymen did against him.

In March Joseph had been appointed commander-in-chief of all the French armies, but the generals, as usual, resisted his authority. Dorsenne denied it altogether, Caffarelli, who succeeded Dorsenne, disputed even his civil power in the governments of

BOOK
XVIII.
———
1812.
May.
The king's
correspon-
dence cap-
tured at
Vittoria.

the north, Suchet evaded his orders, Marmont neglected them, and Soult firmly opposed his injudicious military plans.   The king was distressed for
money, and he complained that Marmont's army
had consumed or plundered in three months, the
whole resources of the province of Toledo and the
district of Talavera, whereby Madrid and the army
of the centre were famished.   Marmont retorted by
complaints of the wasteful extravagance of the
king's military administration in the capital.   Thus
dissensions were generated when the most absolute
union was required.

After the fall of Badajos Joseph judged that the
allies would soon move, either against Marmont in
Castile, against himself by the valley of the Tagus,
or against Soult in Andalusia.   In the first case he
designed to aid Marmont, with the divisions of the
north, with the army of the centre, and with fifteen
thousand men to be drawn from the army of the
south.   In the second case to draw the army of
Portugal and a portion of the army of the south
into the valley of the Tagus, while the divisions
from the army of the north entered Leon.   In the
third case, the half of Marmont's army reinforced by
a division of the army of the centre, was to pass the
Tagus at Arzobispo and follow the allies.   But the
army of the centre was not ready to take the field,
and Wellington knew it, Marmont's complaint was
just ; waste and confusion prevailed at Madrid, and
there was so little military vigour that the Empecinado, with other partida chiefs, pushed their excursions to the very gates of that capital.

Joseph finally ordered Suchet to reinforce the army
of the centre, and then calling up the Italian division
of Palombini from the army of the Ebro, directed

Soult to keep Drouet, with one-third of the army of
the south, so far advanced in Estremadura as to
have direct communication with general Trielhard
in the valley of the Tagus; and he especially ordered that Drouet should pass that river if Hill
passed it. It was necessary, he said, to follow the
English army, and fight it with advantage of numbers, to do which required a strict co-operation of
the three armies Drouet's corps being the pivot.
Meanwhile Marmont and Soult being each convinced, that the English general would invade their
separate provinces, desired that the king would so
view the coming contest, and oblige the other to
regulate his movements thereby. The former complained, that having to observe the Gallicians, and
occupy the Asturias, his forces were disseminated,
and he asked for reinforcements to chase the partidas, who impeded the gathering of provisions in
Castile and Leon. But the king, who over-rated the
importance of Madrid, designed rather to draw more
troops round the capital; and he entirely disapproved of Soult besieging Tarifa and Carthagena,
arguing that if Drouet was not ready to pass the
Tagus, the whole of the allies could unite on the
right bank, and penetrate without opposition to the
capital, or that lord Wellington would concentrate
to overwhelm Marmont.

The duke of Dalmatia would not suffer Drouet to
stir, and Joseph, whose jealousy had been excited
by the marshal's power in Andalusia, threatened to
deprive him of his command. The inflexible duke
replied that the king had already virtually done so
by sending orders direct to Drouet, that he was
ready to resign, but he would not commit a gross
military error. Drouet could scarcely arrive in

Joseph's
correspon-
dence cap
tured at
Vittoria,
MSS.

time to help Marmont, and would be too weak for
the protection of Madrid, but his absence would
ruin Andalusia, because the allies whose force in
Estremadura was very considerable could in five
marches reach Seville and take it on the sixth;
then communicating with the fleets at Cadiz they
would change their line of operations without loss,
and unite with thirty thousand other troops, British
and Spanish, who were at Gibraltar, in the Isla, in
the Niebla, on the side of Murcia, and under Ballesteros in the Ronda. A new army might also come
from the ocean, and Drouet, once beyond the Tagus
could not return to Andalusia in less than twelve
days; Marmont could scarcely come there in a
month; the force under his own immediate command was spread all over Andalusia, if collected it
would not furnish thirty thousand sabres and bayonets, exclusive of Drouet, and the evacuation of the
province would be unavoidable.

The French misfortunes, he said, had invariably
arisen from not acting in large masses, and the
army of Portugal, by spreading too much to its
right, would ruin this campaign as it had ruined
the preceding one. " Marmont should leave one or
two divisions on the Tormes, and place the rest of
his army in position, on both sides of the pass of
Baños, the left near Placentia, and the right, extending towards Somosierra, which could be occupied by a detachment. Lord Wellington could not
then advance by the valley of the Tagus without
lending his left flank; nor to the Tormes without
lending his right flank. Neither could he attack
Marmont with effect, because the latter could easily
concentrate, and according to the nature of the
attack secure his retreat by the valley of the Tagus,

or by the province of Avila, while the two divisions

on the Tormes reinforced by two others from the
army of the north would act on the allies' flank."
For these reasons Soult would not permit Drouet to
quit Estremadura, yet he promised to reinforce him
and so to press Hill, that Graham whom he supposed still at Portalegre, should be obliged to bring
up the first and sixth divisions. In fine he promised that a powerful body of the allies should be
forced to remain in Estremadura, or Hill would be
defeated and Badajos invested. This dispute raged
during May and the beginning of June, and meanwhile the English general well acquainted from
the intercepted letters with these dissensions, made
his arrangements, so as to confirm each general in
his own peculiar views.

Soult was the more easily deceived, because he had
obtained a Gibraltar newspaper, in which, so negligent was the Portuguese government, lord Wellington's secret despatches to Forjas containing an account of his army and of his first designs against
the south were printed, and it must be remembered
that the plan of invading Andalusia was only relinquished about the middle of May. Hill's exploit
at Almaraz menaced the north and south alike, but
that general had adroitly spread a report, that his
object was to gain time for the invasion of Andalusia, and all Wellington's demonstrations were calculated to aid this artifice and impose upon Soult.
Graham indeed returned to Beira with the first and
sixth divisions and Cotton's cavalry; but as Hill
was. at the same time reinforced, and Graham's
march sudden and secret, the enemy were again
deceived in all quarters. For Marmont and the
king, reckoning the number of divisions, thought

the bulk of the allies was in the north, and did not
discover that Hill's corps had been nearly doubled
in numbers though his division seemed the same,
while Soult not immediately aware of Graham's departure, found Hill more than a match for Drouet,
and still expected the allies in Andalusia.

Drouet willing rather to obey the king than
Soult, drew towards Medellin in June, but Soult, as
we have seen, sent the reinforcements from Seville,
by the road of Monasterio, and thus obliged him to
come back. Then followed those movements and
counter-movements in Estremadura, which have
been already related, each side being desirous of
keeping a great number of their adversaries in that
province. Soult's judgment was thus made manifest, for Drouet could only have crossed the Tagus
with peril to Andalusia, whereas, without endanger-
ing that province, he now made such a powerful
diversion for Marmont, that Wellington's army in
the north was reduced below the army of Portugal,
and much below what the latter could be raised to,
by detachments from the armies of the north, and
of the centre. However in the beginning of June,
while the French generals were still disputing, lord
Wellington's dispositions were completed, he had
established at last an extensive system of gaining intelligence all over Spain, and as his campaign
was one which posterity will delight to study, it is
fitting to shew very exactly the foundation on which
the operations rested.

His political and military reasons for seeking a
battle have been before shewn, but this design was
always conditional; he would fight on advantage,
but he would risk nothing beyond the usual chances
of combat. While Portugal was his, every movement,

which obliged the enemy to concentrate was an advantage, and his operations were ever in subservience to this vital condition. His whole force amounted to nearly ninety thousand men, of which about six thousand were in Cadiz, but the Walcheren expedition was still to be atoned for: the sick were so numerous amongst the regiments which had served there, that only thirty-two thousand or a little more than half of the British soldiers, were under arms. This number, with twenty-four thousand Portuguese, made fifty-six thousand sabres and bayonets in the field; and it is to be remembered that now and at all times the Portuguese infantry were mixed with the British either by brigades or regiments; wherefore in speaking of English divisions in battle the Portuguese battalions are always included, and it is to their praise, that their fighting was such as to justify the use of the general term.

The troops were organized in the following manner.

Two thousand cavalry and fifteen thousand infantry, with twenty-four guns, were under Hill, who had also the aid of four garrison Portuguese regiments, and of the fifth Spanish army. Twelve hundred Portuguese cavalry were in the Tras Os Montes, under general D'Urban, and about three thousand five hundred British cavalry and thirty-six thousand infantry, with fifty-four guns, were under Wellington's immediate command, which was now enlarged by three thousand five hundred Spaniards, infantry and cavalry, under Carlos D'España and Julian Sanchez.

The bridge of Almaraz had been destroyed to lengthen the French lateral communications, and

Wellington now ordered the bridge of Alcantara
to be repaired to shorten his own. The breach
in that stupendous structure was ninety feet wide,
and one hundred and fifty feet above the water line.
Yet the fertile genius of colonel Sturgeon furnished
the means of passing this chasm, with heavy artillery, and without the enemy being aware of the
preparations made until the moment of execution.
In the arsenal of Elvas he secretly prepared a net-
work of strong ropes, after a fashion which permitted
it to be carried in parts, and with the beams,
planking, and other materials it was transported
to Alcantara on seventeen carriages. Straining
beams were then fixed in the masonry, on each
side of the broken arch, cables were stretched across
the chasm, the net-work was drawn over, tarpaulin
blinds were placed at each side, and the heaviest
guns passed in safety. This remarkable feat procured a new, and short, internal line of communication, along good roads, while the enemy, by the
destruction of the bridge at Almaraz, was thrown
upon a long external line, and very bad roads.

Hill's corps was thus suddenly brought a fortnight's march nearer to Wellington, than Drouet
was to Marmont, if both marched as armies with
artillery; but there was still a heavy drag upon
the English general's operations. He had drawn
so largely upon Portugal for means of transport,
that agriculture was seriously embarrassed, and
yet his subsistence was not secured for more than
a few marches beyond the Agueda. To remedy
this he set sailors and workmen to remove obstruc-
tions in the Douro and the Tagus; the latter,
which in Philip the Second's time had been navigable from Toledo to Lisbon, was opened to Mal-

pica, not far from Alcantara, and the Douro was
opened as high as Barca de Alba, below which
it ceases to be a Spanish river. The whole land
transport of the interior of Portugal was thus relieved ; the magazines were brought up the Tagus,
close to the new line of communication by Alcantara,
on one side ; on the other, the country vessels
conveyed povisions to the mouth of the Douro, and
that river then served to within a short distance
of Almeida, Ciudad Rodrigo, and Salamanca. Still
danger was to be apprehended from the American
privateers along the coast, which the Admiralty
neglected; and the navigation of the Douro was
suddenly suspended by the overheated zeal of a
commissary, who being thwarted by the delays
of the boatmen, issued, of his own authority, an
edict, establishing regulations, and pronouncing
pains and penalties upon all those who did not
conform to them. The river was immediately
abandoned by the craft, and the government endeavoured by a formal protest, to give political
importance to this affair, which was peculiarly
vexatious, inasmuch as the boatmen were already
so averse to passing the old points of navigation,
that very severe measures were necessary to oblige
them to do so.

When this matter was arranged, Wellington had
still to dread that if his operations led him far into
Spain, the subsistence of his army would be insecure ; for there were many objects of absolute
necessity, especially meat, which could not be
procured except with ready money, and not only
was he unfurnished of specie, but his hopes of
obtaining it were nearly extinguished, by the sweep
lord William Bentinck had made in the Mediterra-

nean money market : moreover the English ministers
chose this period of difficulty to interfere, and in
an ignorant and injurious manner, with his mode
of issuing bills to supply his necessities.   His
resolution to advance could not be shaken, yet
before crossing the Agueda, having described his
plan of campaign to lord Liverpool, he finished in
these remarkable words.

" I am not insensible to losses and risks, nor
am I blind to the disadvantages under which I
undertake this operation. My friends in Castile, and
I believe no officer ever had better, assure me that
we shall not want provisions even before the harvest
will be reaped ; that there exist concealed granaries
which shall be opened to us, and that if we can
pay for a part, credit will be given to us for the
remainder, and they have long given me hopes that
we should be able to borrow money in Castile
upon British securities.   In case we should be
able to maintain ourselves in Castile, the general
action and its results being delayed by the enemy's
manœuvres, which I think not improbable, I have
in contemplation other resources for drawing supplies from the country, and I shall have at all
events our own magazines at Almeida and Ciudad
Rodrigo.   *But with all these prospects I cannot
reflect without shuddering upon the probability that
we shall be distressed ; nor upon the consequences
which may result from our wanting money in the
interior of Spain.*"

In the contemplated operations lord Wellington
did not fail to look both to his own and to his
enemy's flanks.   His right was secured by the
destruction of the forts, the stores, and boats at
Almaraz ; for the valley of the Tagus was exhausted

of provisions, and full of cross rivers which required a pontoon train to pass if the French should
menace Portugal seriously in that line : moreover
he caused the fortress of Monte Santos, which
covered the Portuguese frontier between the Tagus
and Ciudad Rodrigo to be put into a state of
defence, and the restoration of Alcantara gave Hill
the power of quickly interfering. On the other
side if Marmont, strengthened by Caffarelli's
division, should operate strongly against the allies'
left, a retreat was open either upon Ciudad Rodrigo,
or across the mountains into the valley of the Tagus.
Such were his arrangements for his own interior
line of operations, and to menace his enemy's flanks
his measures embraced the whole Peninsula.

1⁰· He directed Silveira and D'Urban, who were
on the frontier of Tras os Montes, to file along the
Douro, menace the enemy's right flank and rear,
and form a link of connection with the Gallician
army, with which Castaños promised to besiege
Astorga, as soon as the Anglo-Portuguese should
appear on the Tormes. Meanwhile sir Home Popham's expedition was to commence its operations,
in concert with the seventh Spanish army, on the
coast of Biscay and so draw Caffarelli's divisions
from the succour of Marmont.

2⁰· To hinder Suchet from reinforcing the king,
or making a movement towards Andalusia, the Sicilian expedition was to menace Catalonia and Valencia, in concert with the Murcian army.

3⁰· To prevent Soult overwhelming Hill, Wellington trusted, 1⁰· to the garrison of Gibraltar, and
to the Anglo-Portuguese and Spanish troops, in the
Isla de Leon ; 2⁰· to insurrections in the kingdom
of Cordoba, where Echevaria going from Cadiz, by

the way of Ayamonte, with three hundred officers,
was to organize the Partidas of that district, as
Mendizabel had done those of the northern parts;
$3^{o.}$ to Ballesteros's army, but he ever dreaded the
rashness of this general, who might be crushed in a
moment, which would have endangered Hill and
rendered any success in the north nugatory.

It was this fear of Ballesteros's rashness that
caused Wellington to keep so strong a corps in
Estremadura, and hence Soult's resolution to prevent Drouet from quitting Estremadura, even though
Hill should cross the Tagus, was wise and military.
For though Drouet would undoubtedly have given
the king and Marmont a vast superiority in Castile,
the general advantage would have remained with
Wellington. Hill could at any time have misled
Drouet by crossing the bridge of Alcantara, and returning again, when Drouet had passed the bridge
of Toledo or Arzobispo. The French general's
march would then have led to nothing, for either
Hill could have joined Wellington, by a shorter
line, and Soult, wanting numbers, could not have
taken advantage of his absence from Estremadura;
or Wellington could have retired within the Portuguese frontier, rendering Drouet's movement to
Castile a pure loss; or reinforcing Hill by the
bridge of Alcantara, he could have gained a fortnight's march and overwhelmed Soult in Andalusia.
The great error of the king's plan was that it depended upon exact co-operation amongst persons
who jealous of each other were far from obedient to
himself, and whose marches it was scarcely possible to time justly; because the armies were separated by a great extent of country and their lines of
communication were external long and difficult,

while their enemy was acting on internal short and easy lines. Moreover the French correspondence, continually intercepted by the Partidas, was brought to Wellington, and the knowledge thus gained by one side and lost by the other caused the timely reinforcing of Hill in Estremadura, and the keeping of Palombini's Italian division from Madrid for three weeks ; an event which in the sequel proved of vital consequence, inasmuch as it prevented the army of the centre moving until after the crisis of the campaign had passed.

Hill's exploit at Almaraz, and the disorderly state of the army of the centre, having in a manner isolated the army of Portugal, the importance of Gallicia and the Asturias, with respect to the projected operations of lord Wellington, was greatly increased. For the Gallicians could either act in Castile upon the rear of Marmont, and so weaken the line of defence on the Douro ; or, marching through the Asturias, spread insurrection along the coast to the Montaña de Santander and there join the seventh army. Hence the necessity of keeping Bonet in the Asturias, and watching the Gallician passes, was become imperative, and Marmont, following Napoleon's instructions, had fortified the different posts in Castile, but his army was too widely spread, and, as Soult observed, was extended to its right instead of concentrating on the left near Baños.

The duke of Ragusa had resolved to adopt the Tormes and Douro, as his lines of defence, and never doubting that he was the object of attack, watched the augmentation of Wellington's forces and magazines with the utmost anxiety. He had collected considerable magazines himself, and the king had formed others for him at Talavera and Segovia, yet he did not approach the Agueda, but continued to occupy a vast extent of country for the convenience of feeding them until June. When he heard of the restoration of the bridge of Alcantara, and of magazines being formed at Caceres, he observed that the latter would be on the left of the Guadiana if Andalusia were the object; and although not well placed for an army acting against himself, were admirably placed for an army which having fought in Castile should afterwards operate against Madrid, because they could be transported at once to the right of the Tagus by Alcantara, and could be secured by removing the temporary restorations. Wherefore, judging that Hill would immediately rejoin Wellington, to aid in the battle, that, with a prophetic feeling he observed, would be fought near the Tormes, he desired Caffarelli to put the divisions of the army of the north in movement; and he prayed the king to have guns, and a pontoon train sent from Madrid that Drouet might pass at Almaraz and join him by the Puerto Pico.

Joseph immediately renewed his orders to Soult, and to Caffarelli, but he only sent two small boats to Almaraz; and Marmont, seeing the allied army suddenly concentrated on the Agueda, recalled Foy from the valley of the Tagus, and Bonet from the Asturias. His first design was to assemble the army at Medina del Campo, Valladolid, Valdesillas, Toro, Zamora, and Salamanca, leaving two battalions and a brigade of dragoons at Benavente to observe the Gallicians. Thus the bulk of the troops would line the Duero, while two divisions formed an advanced guard, on the Tormes, and the whole could be concentrated in five days. His ultimate object was to hold the Tormes until Wellington's whole army was

See Plan,
No. 3.

on that river, then to assemble his own troops on the
Duero, and act so as to favour the defence of the forts
at Salamanca until reinforcements from the north
should enable him to drive the allies again within
the Portuguese frontier; and he warned Caffarelli
that the forts could not hold out more than fifteen
days after they should be abandoned by the French
army.

Marmont was a man to be feared. He possessed
quickness of apprehension and courage, moral and
physical, scientific acquirements, experience of
war, and great facility in the moving of troops; he
was strong of body, in the flower of life, eager for
glory, and although neither a great nor a fortunate
commander, such a one as might bear the test of
fire. His army was weak in cavalry but admirably
organized, for he had laboured with successful diligence, to restore that discipline which had been so
much shaken by the misfortunes of Massena's campaign, and by the unceasing operations from the
battle of Fuentes Onoro to the last retreat from Beira.
Upon this subject a digression must be allowed, because it has been often affirmed, that the bad conduct
of the French in the Peninsula, was encouraged by
their leaders, was unmatched in wickedness, and peculiar to the nation. Such assertions springing from
morbid national antipathies it is the duty of the historian to correct. All troops will behave ill, when ill-
governed, but the best commanders cannot at times
prevent the perpetration of the most frightful mischief; and this truth, so important to the welfare of
nations, may be proved with respect to the Peninsular
war, by the avowal of the generals on either side, and
by their endeavours to arrest the evils which they de-
plored. When Dorsenne returned from his expedition

BOOK
XVIII.
———
1812.
May.
Intercept-
ed French
papers,
MSS.

against Gallicia, in the latter end of 1811, he reproached his soldiers in the following terms. "The
fields have been devastated and houses have been
burned ; these excesses are unworthy of the French
soldier, they pierce the hearts of the most devoted
and friendly of the Spaniards, they are revolting to
honest men, and embarrass the provisioning of the
army. The general-in-chief sees them with sorrow,
and orders ; that besides a permanent court-martial,
there shall be at the head-quarters of each division,
of every arm, a military commission which shall
try the following crimes, and on conviction, sentence
to death, without appeal ; execution to be done on
the spot, in presence of the troops.

" 1$^{o\cdot}$ Quitting a post to pillage. 2$^{o\cdot}$ Desertion
of all kinds. 3$^{o\cdot}$ Disobedience in face of the enemy.
4$^{o\cdot}$ Insubordination of all kinds. 5$^{o\cdot}$ Marauding of
all kinds. 6$^{o\cdot}$ Pillage of all kinds.

" *All persons military or others, shall be considered
as pillagers, who quit their post or their ranks to enter
houses, &c. or who use violence to obtain from the inhabitants more than they are legally entitled to.*

" *All persons shall be considered deserters who
shall be found without a passport beyond the advanced
posts, and frequent patroles day and night shall be sent
to arrest all persons beyond the outposts.*

" *Before the enemy when in camp or cantonments
roll-calls shall take place every hour, and all persons
absent without leave twice running shall be counted
deserters and judged as such. The servants and sutlers of the camp are amenable to this as well as the
soldier.*"

This order Marmont, after reproaching his troops
for like excesses, renewed with the following addi-
tions.

" *Considering that the disorders of the army have arrived at the highest degree, and require the most vigorous measures of repression, it is ordered,*

" *1°· All non-commissioned officers and soldiers found a quarter of a league from their quarters, camp, or post without leave, shall be judged pillagers and tried by the military commission.*

" *2°· The gens d'armes shall examine the baggage of all sutlers and followers and shall seize all effects that appear to be pillaged, and shall burn what will burn, and bring the gold and silver to the paymaster-general under a ' procès verbal,' and all persons whose effects have been seized as pillage to the amount of one hundred livres shall be sent to the military commission, and on conviction suffer death.*

" *3°· All officers who shall not take proper measures to repress disorders under their command shall be sent in arrest to head-quarters there to be judged."*

Then appointing the number of baggage animals to each company, upon a scale which coincides in a remarkable manner with the allowances in the British army, Marmont directed the overplus to be seized and delivered, under a legal process, to the nearest villages, ordering the provost-general to look to the execution each day, and report thereon. Finally, he clothed the provost-general with all the powers of the military commissions ; and proof was soon given that his orders were not mere threats, for two captains were arrested for trial, and a soldier of the twenty-sixth regiment was condemned to death by one of the provisional commissions for stealing church vessels.

Such was the conduct of the French, and touching the conduct of the English, lord Wellington, in the same month, wrote thus to lord Liverpool.

" *The outrages committed by the British soldiers,
belonging to this army, have become so enormous, and
they have produced an effect on the minds of the people
of the country, so injurious to the cause, and likely to
be so dangerous to the army itself, that I request
your Lordship's early attention to the subject.   I am
sensible that the best measures to be adopted on this
subject are those of prevention, and I believe there
are few officers who have paid more attention to the
subject than I have done, and I have been so far successful, as that few outrages are committed by the
soldiers who are with their regiments, after the regiments have been a short time in this country.*"

" *But in the extended system on which we are acting, small detachments of soldiers must be marched
long distances, through the country, either as escorts,
or returning from being escorts to prisoners, or
coming from hospitals, &c. and notwithstanding that
these detachments are never allowed to march, except-
ing under the command of an officer or more, in proportion to its size, and that every precaution is taken
to provide for the regularity of their subsistence,
there is no instance of the march of one of these
detachments that outrages of every description are not
committed, and I am sorry to say with impunity.*"

" *The guard-rooms are therefore crowded with
prisoners, and the offences of which they have been
guilty remain unpunished, to the destruction of the
discipline of the army, and to the injury of the reputation of the country for justice.   I have thought it
proper to lay these circumstances before your lordship.   I am about to move the army further forward
into Spain, and I assure your lordship, that I have
not a friend in that country, who has not written to
me in dread of the consequences, which must result to*

*the army, and to the cause from a continuance of
these disgraceful irregularities, which I declare I
have it not in my power to prevent."*

To this should have been added, the insubordination, and the evil passions, awakened by the un-
checked plunder of Ciudad Rodrigo and Badajos.
But long had the English general complained of
the bad discipline of his army, and the following
extracts, from a letter dated a few months later,
shew that his distrust at the present time was not
ill-founded. After observing that the constitutions
of the soldiers were so much shaken from disorders
acquired by their service at Walcheren, or by their
own irregularities, that a British army was almost a
moving hospital, more than one-third or about
twenty thousand men being sick, or attending upon
the sick, he thus describes their conduct.

" *The disorders which these soldiers have, are of a
very trifling description, they are considered to render
them incapable of serving with their regiments, but
they certainly do not incapacitate them from committing outrages of all descriptions on their passage
through the country, and in the last movements of the
hospitals the soldiers have not only plundered the inhabitants of their property, but the hospital stores
which moved with the hospitals, and have sold the
plunder. And all these outrages are committed with
impunity, no proof can be brought on oath before a
court-martial that any individual has committed an
outrage, and the soldiers of the army are becoming
little better than a band of robbers."* " *I have carried the establishment and authority of the provost-
marshal as far as either will go ; there are at this
moment not less than one provost-marshal and nine-*

*teen assistant provost-marshals, attached to the several
divisions of cavalry and infantry and to the hospital
stations, to preserve order, but this establishment is
not sufficient, and I have not the means of increasing
it."*

The principal remedies he proposed, were the
admitting less rigorous proof of guilt, before courts
martial; the forming a military police, *such as the
French, and other armies possessed;* the enforcing
more attention on the part of the officers to their
duties; the increasing the pay and responsibility of
the non-commissioned officers, and the throwing
upon them the chief care of the discipline. But in
treating this part of the subject he broached an
opinion which can scarcely be sustained even by
his authority. Assuming, somewhat unjustly, that
the officers of his army were, from consciousness of
like demerit, generally too lenient in their sentences
on each other for neglect of duty, he says, " I am
inclined to entertain the opinion that in the British
army duties of inspection and control over the conduct and habits of the soldiers, the performance of
which by somebody is the only effectual check to
disorder and all its consequences, are imposed upon
the subaltern officers of regiments, which duties
British officers, being of the class of gentlemen in
society, and being required to appear as such, have
never performed *and which they will never perform.*
It is very necessary, however, that the duties should
be performed by somebody, and for this reason, and
having observed the advantage derived in the
guards, from the respectable body of non-commissioned officers in those regiments, who perform all
the duties required from subalterns in the marching

regiments, I had suggested to your lordship the ex-
pediency of increasing the pay of the non-commissioned officers in the army."

Now it is a strange assumption, that a gentleman
necessarily neglects his duty to his country. When
well taught, which was not always the case, gentlemen by birth generally performed their duties in
the Peninsula more conscientiously than others,
and the experience of every commanding officer
will bear out the assertion. If the non-commissioned officers could do all the duties of subaltern
officers, why should the country bear the useless
expense of the latter? But in truth the system of
the guards produced rather a medium goodness,
than a superior excellence; the system of sir John
Moore, founded upon the principle, that the officers
should thoroughly know, and be responsible for the
discipline of their soldiers, better bore the test of
experience. All the British regiments of the light
division were formed in the camps of Shorn-Cliff
by that most accomplished commander; very many
of the other acknowledged good regiments of the
army had been instructed by him in Sicily; and
wherever an officer, formed under Moore, obtained
a regiment, whether British or Portuguese, that
regiment was distinguished in this war for its discipline and enduring qualities; courage was common
to all.

CHAPTER II.

CAMPAIGN OF 1812.

BOOK
XVIII.

1812.
June.

See Plan,
No. 2.

On the 13th of June, the periodic rains having ceased, and the field magazines being completed, Wellington passed the Agueda and marched towards the Tormes in four columns, one of which was composed of the Spanish troops. The 16th he reached the Valmusa stream, within six miles of Salamanca, and drove a French detachment across the Tormes. All the bridges, save that of Salamanca which was defended by the forts, had been destroyed, and there was a garrison in the castle of Alba de Tormes, but the 17th the allies passed the river above and below the town, by the deep fords of Santa Marta and Los Cantos, and general Henry Clinton invested the forts the same day with the sixth division. Marmont, with two divisions, and some cavalry, retired to Fuente el Sauco, on the road of Toro, followed by an advanced guard of the allies; Salamanca instantly became a scene of rejoicing, the houses were illuminated, and the people shouting, singing, and weeping for joy, gave Wellington their welcome while his army took a position on the mountain of San Cristoval about five miles in advance.

SIEGE OF THE FORTS AT SALAMANCA.

Jones's
Sieges.

Four eighteen-pounders had followed the army from Almeida, three twenty-four pound howitzers were furnished by the field artillery, and the batter-

ing train used by Hill at Almaraz, had passed the
bridge of Alcantara the 11th. These were the
means of offence, but the strength of the forts had
been under-rated; they contained eight hundred
men, and it was said that thirteen convents and
twenty-two colleges had been destroyed in their
construction. San Vincente, so called from the large
convent it enclosed, was the key-fort. Situated on
a perpendicular cliff overhanging the Tormes, and
irregular in form, but well flanked, it was separated by a deep ravine from the other forts, which
were called St. Cajetano and La Merced. These
were also on high ground, smaller than San Vincente, and of a square form, but with bomb-proofs,
and deep ditches, having perpendicular scarps and
counterscarps.

In the night of the 17th colonel Burgoyne, the
engineer directing the siege, commenced a battery,
for eight guns, at the distance of two hundred and
fifty yards from the main wall of Vincente, and as
the ruins of the destroyed convents rendered it
impossible to excavate, earth was brought from a
distance; but the moon was up, the night short,
the enemy's fire of musketry heavy, the workmen
of the sixth division were inexperienced, and at
daybreak the battery was still imperfect. Meanwhile
an attempt had been made to attach the miner
secretly to the counterscarp, and when the vigilance
of a trained dog baffled this design, the enemy's
picquet was driven in, and the attempt openly
made, yet it was rendered vain by a plunging fire
from the top of the convent.

On the 18th eight hundred Germans, placed in
the ruins, mastered all the enemy's fire save that
from loop-holes, and colonel May, who directed

the artillery service, then placed two field-pieces
on a neighbouring convent, called San Bernardo,
overlooking the fort, however these guns could not
silence the French artillery.

In the night, the first battery was armed, covering
for two field-pieces as a counter-battery was raised
a little to its right, and a second breaching battery
for two howitzers, was constructed on the Cajetano
side of the ravine.

At daybreak on the 19th seven guns opened,
and at nine o'clock the wall of the convent was
cut away to the level of the counterscarp. The
second breaching battery, which saw lower down
the scarp, then commenced its fire ; but the iron
howitzers proved unmeet battering ordnance, and
the enemy's musketry being entirely directed on
this point, because the first battery, to save ammunition, had ceased firing, brought down a captain
and more than twenty gunners. The howitzers
did not injure the wall, ammunition was scarce,
and as the enemy could easily cut off the breach
in the night, the fire ceased.

The 20th at mid-day, colonel Dickson arrived
with the iron howitzers from Elvas, and the second
battery being then reinforced with additional pieces,
revived its fire, against a re-entering angle of the
convent a little beyond the former breach. The
wall here was soon broken through, and in an
instant a huge cantle of the convent, with its roof,
went to the ground, crushing many of the garrison
and laying bare the inside of the building: carcasses
were immediately thrown into the opening, to burn
the convent, but the enemy undauntedly maintained
their ground and extinguished the flames. A
lieutenant and fifteen gunners were lost this day,

on the side of the besiegers, and the ammunition being nearly gone, the attack was suspended until fresh stores could come up from Almeida.

During the progress of this siege, the general aspect of affairs had materially changed on both sides. Lord Wellington had been deceived as to the strength of the forts, and intercepted returns of the armies of the south and of Portugal now shewed to him, that they also were far stronger than he had expected; at the same time he heard of Ballesteros's defeat at Bornos, and of Slade's unfortunate cavalry action of Llera. He had calculated that Bonet would not quit the Asturias, and that general was in full march for Leon, Caffarelli also was preparing to reinforce Marmont, and thus the brilliant prospect of the campaign was suddenly clouded. But on the other hand Bonet had unexpectedly relinquished the Asturias after six days' occupation; three thousand Gallicians were in that province and in communication with the seventh army, and the maritime expedition under Popham had sailed for the coast of Biscay.

Neither was the king's situation agreeable. The Partidas intercepted his despatches so surely, that it was the 19th ere Marmont's letter announcing Wellington's advance, and saying that Hill also was in march for the north reached Madrid. Soult detained Drouet, Suchet refused to send more than one brigade towards Madrid, and Caffarelli, disturbed that Palombini should march upon the capital instead of Burgos, kept back the divisions promised to Marmont. Something was however gained in vigour, for the king, no longer depending upon the assistance of the distant armies, gave orders to blow up Mirabete and abandon La Mancha

on one side, and the forts of Somosierra and Buitrago
on the other, with a view to unite the army of the
centre.

A detachment of eight hundred men under
colonel Noizet, employed to destroy Buitrago, was
attacked on his return by the Empecinado with
three thousand, but Noizet, an able officer, defeated him and reached Madrid with little loss.
Palombini's march was then hastened, and imperative
orders directed Soult to send ten thousand men to
Toledo. The garrison of Segovia was reinforced
to preserve one of the communications with
Marmont, that marshal was informed of Hill's true
position, and the king advised him to give battle
to Wellington, for he supposed the latter to have
only eighteen thousand English troops; but he had
twenty-four thousand, and had yet left Hill so
strong that he desired him to fight Drouet if occasion required.

Meanwhile Marmont, who had remained in person
at Fuente el Sauco, united there, on the 20th, four
divisions of infantry and a brigade of cavalry,
furnishing about twenty-five thousand men of all
arms, with which he marched to the succour of
the forts. His approach over an open country was
descried at a considerable distance, and a brigade
of the fifth division was immediately called off from
the siege, the battering train was sent across the
Tormes, and the army, which was in bivouac on the
Salamanca side of St. Christoval, formed in order
of battle on the top. This position of Christoval
was about four miles long, and rather concave, the
ascent in front steep, and tangled with hollow roads
and stone enclosures, belonging to the villages, but
the summit was broad, even, and covered with ripe

corn; the right was flanked by the Upper Tormes, and the left dipped into the country bordering the Lower Tormes, for in passing Salamanca, that river makes a sweep round the back of the position. The infantry, the heavy cavalry, and the guns crowned the summit of the mountain, but the light cavalry fell back from the front to the low country on the left, where there was a small stream and a marshy flat. The villages of Villares and Monte Rubio were behind the left of the position; the village of Cabrerizos marked the extreme right, though the hill still trended up the river. The villages of Christoval, Castillanos, and Moresco, were nearly in a line, along the foot of the heights in front, the last was somewhat within the allies' ground, and nothing could be stronger than the position, which completely commanded all the country for many miles; but the heat was excessive and there was neither shade, nor fuel to cook with, nor water nearer than the Tormes.

About five o'clock in the evening the enemy's horsemen approached, pointing towards the left of the position, as if to turn it by the Lower Tormes, whereupon the British light cavalry made a short forward movement and a partial charge took place; but the French opened six guns, and the British retired to their own ground near Monte Rubio and Villares. The light division which was held in reserve, immediately closed towards the left of the position until the French cavalry halted and then returned to the centre. Meanwhile the main body of the enemy bore, in one dark volume, against the right, and halting at the very foot of the position, sent a flight of shells on to the lofty summit; nor did this fire cease until after dark, when the

See Plan,
No. 3.

French general, after driving back all the outposts, obtained possession of Moresco, and established himself behind that village and Castellanos within gun-shot of the allies.

The English general slept that night on the ground, amongst the troops, and at the first streak of light the armies were again under arms. Nevertheless, though some signals were interchanged between Marmont and the forts, both sides were quiet until towards evening, when Wellington detached the sixty-eighth regiment from the line, to drive the French from Moresco. This attack, made with vigour, succeeded, but the troops being recalled just as day-light failed, a body of French coming unperceived through the standing corn, broke into the village as the British were collecting their posts from the different avenues, and did considerable execution. In the skirmish an officer of the sixty-eighth, named Mackay, being suddenly surrounded, refused to surrender, and singly fighting against a multitude, received more wounds than the human frame was thought capable of sustaining, yet he still lives to shew his honourable scars.

On the 22d three divisions, and a brigade of cavalry joined Marmont, who having now nearly forty thousand men in hand, extended his left and seized a part of the height in advance of the allies' right wing, from whence he could discern the whole of their order of battle, and attack their right on even terms. However general Graham advancing with the seventh division dislodged this French detachment with a sharp skirmish before it could be formidably reinforced, and that night Marmont withdrew from his dangerous position to some heights about six miles in his rear.

It was thought that the French general's tempestuous advance to Moresco with such an inferior force, on the evening of the 20th, should have been his ruin. Lord Wellington saw clearly enough the false position of his enemy, but he argued, that if Marmont came up to fight, it was better to defend a very strong position, than to descend and combat in the plain, seeing that the inferiority of force was not such as to insure the result of the battle being decisive of the campaign ; and in case of failure, a retreat across the Tormes would have been very difficult. To this may be added, that during the first evening there was some confusion amongst the allies, before the troops of the different nations could form their order of battle. Moreover, as the descent of the mountain towards the enemy was by no means easy, because of the walls and avenues, and the two villages, which covered the French front, it is probable that Marmont, who had plenty of guns and whose troops were in perfect order ahd extremely ready of movement, could have evaded the action, until night. This reasoning, however, will not hold good on the 21st. The allies, whose infantry was a third more and their cavalry three times as numerous and much better mounted than the French, might have been poured down by all the roads passing over the position at daybreak ; then Marmont turned on both flanks and followed vehemently, could never have made his retreat to the Douro through the open country ; but on the 22d, when the French general had received his other divisions, the chances were no longer the same.

Marmont's new position was skilfully chosen ;

BOOK
XVIII.

1812.
June.
See Plan,
No. 3.

one flank rested on Cabeza Vellosa, the other at Huerta, the centre was at Aldea Rubia.   He thus refused his right and abandoned the road of Toro to the allies, but he covered the road of Tordesillas, and commanded the fort of Huerta with his left ; and he could in a moment pass the Tormes, and operate by the left bank to communicate with the forts. Wellington made corresponding dispositions, closing up his left towards Moresco, and pushing the light division along the salient part of his position to Aldea Lengua, where it overhung a ford, which was how- ever scarcely practicable at this period.   General Graham with two divisions was placed at the fords of Santa Marta, and the heavy German cavalry under general Bock crossed the Tormes to watch the ford of Huerta.   By this disposition the allies covered Salamanca, and could operate on either side of the Tormes on a shorter line than the French could operate.

The 23d the two armies again remained tranquil, but at break of day on the 24th some dropping pistol-shots, and now and then a shout, came faintly from the mist which covered the lower ground beyond the river ; the heavy sound of artillery succeeded, and the hissing of the bullets as they cut through the thickened atmosphere, plainly told that the French were over the Tormes. After a time the fog cleared up, and the German horsemen were seen in close and beautiful order, retiring before twelve thousand French infantry, who in battle array were marching steadily on- wards.   At intervals, twenty guns, ranged in front, would start forwards and send their bullets whistling and tearing up the ground beneath the Germans, while scattered parties of light cavalry, scouting

out, capped all the hills in succession, and peering
abroad, gave signals to the main body. Wellington immediately sent Graham across the river
by the fords of Santa Marta with the first and seventh divisions and Le Marchant's brigade of English
cavalry ; then concentrating the rest of the army
between Cabrerizos and Moresco, he awaited the
progress of Marmont's operation.

Bock continued his retreat in the same fine and
equable order, regardless alike of the cannonade
and of the light horsemen on his flanks, until the
enemy's scouts had gained a height above Calvarisa
Abaxo, from whence, at the distance of three miles,
they for the first time, perceived Graham's twelve
thousand men, and eighteen guns, ranged on an
order of battle, perpendicular to the Tormes.
From the same point also Wellington's heavy
columns were to be seen, clustering on the height
above the fords of Santa Marta, and the light
division was descried at Aldea Lengua, ready
either to advance against the French troops left
on the position of Aldea Rubia, or to pass the river
to the aid of Graham. This apparition made the
French general aware of his error, whereupon hastily facing about, and repassing the Tormes he
resumed his former ground.

Wellington's defensive dispositions on this occasion were very skilful, but it would appear that
unwilling to stir before the forts fell, he had again
refused the advantage of the moment ; for it is not to
be supposed that he misjudged the occasion, since the
whole theatre of operation was distinctly seen from
St. Christoval, and he had passed many hours in earnest observation ; his faculties were indeed so fresh
and vigorous, that after the day's work he wrote a

detailed memoir upon the proposal for establishing
a bank in Portugal, treating that and other financial
schemes in all their bearings, with a master hand.
Against the weight of his authority, therefore, any
criticism must be advanced.

Marmont had the easiest passage over the Tormes,
namely, that by the ford of Huerta; the allies had
the greatest number of passages and the shortest
line of operations. Hence if Graham had been
ordered vigorously to attack the French troops on
the left bank, they must have been driven upon
the single ford of Huerta, if not reinforced from
See Plan,
No. 2. the heights of Aldea Rubia. But the allies could
also have been reinforced by the fords of Santa
Marta and those of Cabrerizos, and even by that
of Aldea Lengua, although it was not good at
this early season. A partial victory would then
have been achieved, or a general battle would have
been brought on, when the French troops would
have been disadvantageously cooped up in the
loop of the Tormes and without means of escaping
if defeated. Again, it is not easy to see how the
French general could have avoided a serious defeat
if Wellington had moved with all the troops on
the right bank, against the divisions left on the hill
of Aldea Rubia; for the French army would then
have been separated, one part on the hither, one on
the further bank of the Tormes. It was said at the
time that Marmont hoped to draw the whole
of the allies across the river, when he would
have seized the position of Christoval, raised the
siege and maintained the line of the Tormes. It may
however be doubted that he expected Wellington
to commit so gross an error. It is more likely that
holding his own army to be the quickest of move-

ment, his object was to separate the allies' force
in the hopes of gaining some partial advantage to
enable him to communicate with his forts, which
were now in great danger.

When the French retired to the heights at Aldea
Rubia on the night of the 23d, the heavy guns
had been already brought to the right of the Tormes,
and a third battery, to breach San Cajetano, was
armed with four pieces, but the line of fire being
oblique, the practice, at four hundred and fifty
yards, only beat down the parapet and knocked
away the palisades. Time was however of vital
importance, the escalade of that fort and La Merced
was ordered, and the attack commenced at ten
o'clock, but in half an hour failed with a loss
of one hundred and twenty men and officers. The
wounded were brought off the next day under
truce and the enemy had all the credit of the fight,
yet the death of general Bowes must ever be admired. That gallant man, whose rank might have
excused his leading so small a force, being wounded
early, was having his hurt dressed when he heard
that the troops were yielding, and returning to the
combat fell.

The siege was now perforce suspended for want
of ammunition, and the guns were sent across the
river, but were immediately brought back in consequence of Marmont having crossed to the left
bank. Certain works were meanwhile pushed forward to cut off the communication between the
forts and otherwise to straiten them, and the miner
was attached to the cliff on which La Merced stood.
The final success was not however influenced by
these operations, and they need no further notice.

The 26th ammunition arrived from Almeida, the

second and third batteries were re-armed, the field-pieces were again placed in the convent of San Bernardo, and the iron howitzers, throwing hot shot, set the convent of San Vincente on fire in several places. The garrison again extinguished the flames, and this balanced combat continued during the night, but on the morning of the 27th the fire of both batteries being redoubled, the convent of San Vincente was in a blaze, the breach of San Cajetano was improved, a fresh storming party assembled, and the white flag waved from Cajetano. A negociation ensued, but lord Wellington, judging it an artifice to gain time, gave orders for the assault; then the forts fell, for San Cajetano scarcely fired a shot, and the flames raged so violently at San Vincente that no opposition could be made.

Seven hundred prisoners, thirty pieces of artillery, provisions, arms, and clothing, and a secure passage over the Tormes, were the immediate fruits of this capture, which was not the less prized, that the breaches were found to be more formidable than those at Ciudad Rodrigo. The success of a storm would have been very doubtful if the garrison could have gained time to extinguish the flames in the convent of San Vincente, and as it was the allies had ninety killed; their whole loss since the passage of the Tormes was nearly five hundred men and officers, of which one hundred and sixty men with fifty horses, fell outside Salamanca, the rest in the siege.

Marmont had allotted fifteen days as the term of resistance for these forts, but from the facility with which San Vincente caught fire, five would have been too many if ammunition had not failed.

His calculation was therefore false. He would

however have fought on the 23d, when his force was united, had he not on the 22d received intelligence from Caffarelli, that a powerful body of infantry, with twenty-two guns and all the cavalry of the north, were actually in march to join him. It was this which induced him to occupy the heights of Villa Rubia, on that day, to avoid a premature action, but on the evening of the 26th the signals, from the forts, having indicated that they could still hold out three days, Marmont, from fresh intelligence, no longer expected Caffarelli's troops, and resolved to give battle on the 28th. The fall of the forts, which was made known to him on the evening of the 27th, changed this determination, the reasons for fighting on such disadvantageous ground no longer existed, and hence, withdrawing his garrison from the castle of Alba de Tormes, he retreated during the night towards the Duero, by the roads of Tordesillas and Toro.

Wellington ordered the works both at Alba and the forts of Salamanca to be destroyed, and following the enemy by easy marches, encamped on the Guarena the 30th. The next day he reached the Trabancos, his advanced guard being at Nava del Rey. On the 2d he passed the Zapardiel in two columns, the right marching by Medina del Campo, the left following the advanced guard towards Rueda. From this place the French rear guard was cannonaded and driven upon the main body, which was filing over the bridge of Tordesillas. Some were killed and some made prisoners, not many, but there was great confusion, and a heavy disaster would have befallen the French if the English general had not been deceived by false

information, that they had broken the bridge the
night before.   For as he knew by intercepted
letters that Marmont intended to take a position
near Tordesillas, this report made him suppose
the enemy was already over the Duero, and hence
he had spread his troops, and was not in sufficient
force to attack during the passage of the river.

Marmont, who had fortified posts at Zamora and
Toro, and had broken the bridges at those places
and at Puente Duero and Tudela, preserving only
that of Tordesillas, now took a position on the
right of the Duero.   His left was at Simancas
on the Pisuerga, which was unfordable, and the
bridges at that place and Valladolid, were commanded by fortified posts.   His centre was at
Tordesillas, and very numerous, and his right was
on some heights opposite to Pollos.   Wellington
indeed caused the third division to seize the ford
at the last place which gave him a command of
the river, because there was a plain between it
and the enemy's heights, but the ford itself was
difficult and insufficient for passing the whole army.
Head-quarters were therefore fixed at Rueda, and
the forces were disposed in a compact form, the
head placed in opposition to the ford of Pollos
and the bridge of Tordesillas, the rear occupying
Medina del Campo and other points on the Zapardiel and Trabancos rivers, ready to oppose the
enemy if he should break out from the Valladolid
side.   Marmont's line of defence, measured from
Valladolid to Zamora, was sixty miles; from Simancas
to Toro above thirty, but the actual line of occupation was not above twelve ; the bend of the river
gave him the chord, the allies the arc, and the
fords were few and difficult.   The advantage was

therefore on the side of the enemy, but to understand the true position of the contending generals
it is necessary to know the secondary coincident
operations.

While the armies were in presence at Salamanca,
Silveira had filed up the Duero, to the Esla river,
menacing the French communications with Benavente. D'Urban's horsemen had passed the Duero
below Zamora on the 25th and cut off all intercourse
between the French army and that place; but when
Marmont fell back from Aldea Rubia, D'Urban recrossed the Duero at Fresno de la Ribera to avoid
being crushed, yet immediately afterwards advanced
beyond Toro to Castromonte, behind the right wing
of the enemy's new position. It was part of Wellington's plan, that Castaños, after establishing the
siege of Astorga, should come down by Benavente
with the remainder of his army, and place himself in
communication with Silveira. This operation, without disarranging the siege of Astorga, would have
placed twelve or fifteen thousand men, infantry,
cavalry, and artillery, behind the Esla, and with
secure lines of retreat; consequently able to check
all the enemy's foraging parties, and reduce him
to live upon his fixed magazines, which were
scanty. The usual Spanish procrastination defeated
this plan.

Castaños, by the help of the succours received
from England, had assembled fifteen thousand men
at Ponteferada, under the command of Santocildes,
but he pretended that he had no battering guns
until sir Howard Douglas actually pointed them
out in the arsenal of Ferrol, and shewed him how
to convey them to the frontier. Then Santocildes
moved, though slowly, and when Bonet's retreat

from the Asturias was known, eleven thousand men
invested Astorga, and four thousand others marched
to Benavente, but not until Marmont had called
his detachment in from that place. The Spanish
battering train only reached Villa Franca del Bierzo
on the 1st of July. However the Guerilla chief,
Marquinez, appeared about Palencia, and the other
Partidas of Castile acting on a line from Leon to
Segovia, intercepted Marmont's correspondence with
the king. Thus the immense tract called the
Campo de Tierras was secured for the subsistence
of the Gallician army ; and to the surprise of the
allies, who had so often heard of the enemy's
terrible devastations that they expected to find
Castile a desert, those vast plains, and undulating
hills, were covered with ripe corn or fruitful vines,
and the villages bore few marks of the ravages
of war.

While the main body of the Gallicians was still
at Ponte Ferrada, a separate division had passed
along the coast road into the Asturias, and in concert with part of the seventh army had harassed
Bonet's retreat from that kingdom; the French
general indeed forced his way by the eastern passes,
and taking post the 30th of June at Reynosa and
Aguilar del Campo, chased the neighbouring bands
away, but this movement was one of the great
errors of the campaign. Napoleon and Wellington
felt alike the importance of holding the Asturias at
this period. The one had ordered that they should
be retained, the other had calculated that such
would be the case, and the judgment of both was
quickly made manifest. For the Gallicians, who
would not have dared to quit the Bierzo if Bonet
had menaced their province by Lugo, or by the

King's pa-
pers cap-
tured at
Vittoria,
MSS.

Welling-
ton's de-
spatches,
MSS.

shore line, invested Astorga the moment he quitted the Asturias. And the Partidas of the north, who had been completely depressed by Mina's defeat, recovering courage, now moved towards the coast, where Popham's expedition, which had sailed on the 18th of June from Coruña, soon appeared, a formidable spectacle, for there were five sail of the line, with many frigates and brigs, in all twenty ships of war.

The port of Lesquito was immediately attacked on the sea-bord by this squadron, on the land side by the Pastor, and when captain Bouverie got a gun up to breach the convent the Spanish chief assaulted but was repulsed; however the garrison, two hundred and fifty strong, surrendered to the squadron the 22d, and on the two following days Bermeo and Plencia fell. The Partidas failed to appear at Guetaria, but Castro and Portagalete, in the Bilbao river, were attacked the 6th of July, in concert with Longa, and though the latter was rebuffed at Bilbao the squadron took Castro. The enemy recovered some of their posts on the 10th, and on the 19th the attempt on Guetaria being renewed, Mina and Pastor came down to co-operate, but a French column beat those chiefs, and drove the British seamen to their vessels, with the loss of thirty men and two guns.

It was the opinion of general Carrol who accompanied this expedition, that the plan of operations was ill-arranged, but the local successes merit no attention, the great object of distracting the enemy was obtained. Caffarelli heard at one and the same time, that Palombini's division had been called to Madrid; that Bonet had abandoned the Asturias; that a Gallician division had entered that province;

that a powerful English fleet, containing troops,
was on the coast, and acting in concert with all the
Partidas of the north; that the seventh army was
menacing Burgos, and that the whole country was
in commotion. Trembling for his own districts he
instantly arrested the march of the divisions destined for Marmont; and although the king, who saw
very clearly the real object of the maritime expedition, reiterated the orders to march upon Segovia or
Cuellar, with a view to reinforce either the army of
the centre or the army of Portugal, Caffarelli delayed obedience until the 13th of July, and then
sent but eighteen hundred cavalry, with twenty
guns.

Thus Bonet's movement which only brought a
reinforcement of six thousand infantry to Marmont,
kept away Caffarelli's reserves, which were twelve
thousand of all arms, uncovered the whole of the
great French line of communication, and caused the
siege of Astorga to be commenced. And while Bonet
was in march by Palencia and Valladolid to the
position of Tordesillas, the king heard of Marmont's
retreat from the Tormes, and that an English column
menaced Arevalo ; wherefore not being ready to move
with the army of the centre, and fearing for Avila,
he withdrew the garrison from that place, and thus
lost his direct line of correspondence with the army
of Portugal, because Segovia was environed by the
Partidas. In this state of affairs neither Wellington nor Marmont had reason to fight upon the
Duero. The latter because his position was so
strong he could safely wait for Bonet's and Caffarelli's
troops, and meanwhile the king could operate against
the allies' communications. The former because he
could not attack the French, except at great disad-

vantage; for the fords of the Duero were little
known, and that of Pollos was very deep. To pass
the river there, and form within gun-shot of the
enemy's left, without other combinations, promised
nothing but defeat, and the staff-officers, sent to
examine the course of the river, reported that the
advantage of ground was entirely on the enemy's
side, except at Castro Nuño, half-way between
Pollos and Toro.

While the enemy commanded the bridge at Tordesillas, no attempt to force the passage of the river
could be safe, seeing that Marmont might fall on
the allies' front and rear if the operation was within
his reach; and if beyond his reach, that is to say
near Zamora, he could cut their communication
with Ciudad Rodrigo and yet preserve his own with
Caffarelli and with the king. Wellington therefore
resolved to wait until the fords should become lower,
or the combined operations of the Gallicians and
Partidas, should oblige the enemy, either to detach
men, or to dislodge altogether for want of provisions. In this view he urged Santocildes to press
the siege of Astorga vigorously and to send every
man he could spare down the Esla; and an intercepted letter gave hopes that Astorga would surrender on the 7th, yet this seems to have been a
device to keep the Gallicians in that quarter for it
was in no danger. Santocildes, expecting its fall,
would not detach men, but the vicinity of D'Urban's
cavalry, which remained at Castromonte, so incommoded the French right, that Foy marched to drive
them beyond the Esla. General Pakenham however crossed the ford of Pollos, with some of the
third division, which quickly brought Foy back, and
Marmont then endeavoured to augment the number

and efficiency of his cavalry, by taking a thousand
horses from the infantry officers and the sutlers.

On the 8th Bonet arrived, and the French marshal immediately extending his right to Toro, commenced repairing the bridge there. Wellington, in
like manner, stretched his left to the Guarena, yet
kept his centre still on the Trabancos, and his right
at Rueda, with posts near Tordesillas and the ford
of Pollos. In this situation the armies remained for
some days. Generals Graham and Picton went to
England in bad health, and the principal powder
magazine at Salamanca exploded with hurt to
many, but no other events worth recording occurred.
The weather was very fine, the country rich, and
the troops received their rations regularly; wine
was so plentiful, that it was hard to keep the soldiers sober; the caves of Rueda, either natural or
cut in the rock below the surface of the earth, were
so immense and so well stocked, that the drunkards
of two armies failed to make any very sensible
diminution in the quantity. Many men of both
sides perished in that labyrinth, and on both sides
also, the soldiers, passing the Duero in groups, held
amicable intercourse, conversing of the battles that
were yet to be fought; the camps on the banks of
the Duero seemed at times to belong to one army,
so difficult is it to make brave men hate each other.

To the officers of the allies all looked prosperous,
their only anxiety was to receive the signal of
battle, their only discontent, that it was delayed;
and many amongst them murmured that the French
had been permitted to retreat from Christoval. Had
Wellington been finally forced back to Portugal his
reputation would have been grievously assailed by
his own people, for the majority, peering through

their misty politics, saw Paris in dim perspective, and overlooked the enormous French armies that were close at hand. Meanwhile their general's mind was filled with care and mortification, and all cross and evil circumstances seemed to combine against him.

The mediation for the Spanish colonies had just failed at Cadiz, under such circumstances, as left no doubt that the English influence was powerless and the French influence visibly increasing in the Cortez. Soult had twenty-seven gun-boats in the Trocadero canal, shells were cast day and night into the city, and the people were alarmed; two thousand French had marched from Santa Mary to Seville, apparently to reinforce Drouet in Estremadura; Echevaria had effected nothing in the kingdom of Cordoba, and a French division was assembling at Bornos, to attack Ballesteros, whose rashness, inviting destruction, might alone put an end to the campaign in Leon and bring Wellington back to the Tagus. In the north of Spain also affairs appeared equally gloomy, Mina's defeats, and their influence upon the other Partidas, were positively known, but the effect of Popham's operations was unknown, or at least doubtful. Bonet's division had certainly arrived, and the Gallicians who had done nothing at Astorga were already in want of ammunition. In Castile the activity of the Partidas instead of increasing, had diminished after Wellington crossed the Tormes, and the chiefs seemed inclined to leave the burthen of the war entirely to their allies. Nor was this feeling confined to them. It had been arranged, that new corps, especially of cavalry, should be raised, as the enemy receded in this campaign, and the necessary clothing

and equipments, supplied by England, were placed
at the disposal of lord Wellington, who to avoid the
burthen of carriage had directed them to Coruña;
yet now, when Leon and the Asturias were in a
manner recovered, no man would serve voluntarily.
There was great enthusiasm, in words, there had
always been so, but the fighting men were not increased, and even the *juramentados*, many of whom
deserted at this time from the king, well clothed
and soldier-like men, refused to enter the English
ranks.

Now also came the news that lord William Bentinck's plans were altered, and the intercepted despatches shewed that the king had again ordered
Drouet to pass the Tagus, but Soult's resistance to
this order was not known. Wellington therefore at
the same moment, saw Marmont's army increase,
heard that the king's army, reinforced by Drouet,
was on the point of taking the field; that the troops
from Sicily, upon whose operations he depended to
keep all the army of Aragon in the eastern part of
Spain, and even to turn the king's attention that
way, were to be sent to Italy; and that two millions
of dollars, which he hoped to have obtained at
Gibraltar, had been swept off by lord William Bentinck for this Italian expedition, which thus at once
deprived him of men and money! The latter was
the most serious blow, the promised remittances
from England had not arrived, and as the insuffi-
ciency of land-carriage rendered it nearly impossible
to feed the army even on the Duero, to venture
further into Spain without money would be akin to
madness. From Gallicia, where no credit was
given, came the supply of meat, a stoppage there
would have made the war itself stop, and no greater

error had been committed by the enemy, than delaying to conquer Gallicia, which could many times
have been done.

To meet the increasing exigences for money, the
English general had, for one resource, obtained a
credit of half a million from the Treasury to answer
certain certificates, or notes of hand, which his
Spanish correspondents promised to get cashed; but
of this resource he was now suddenly deprived by
the English ministers, who objected to the irregular
form of the certificates, because he, with his usual
sagacity, had adapted them to the habits of the
people he was to deal with. Meanwhile his troops
were four, his staff six, his muleteers nearly twelve
months in arrears of pay, and he was in debt every
where, and for every thing. The Portuguese
government had become very clamorous for the
subsidy, Mr. Stuart acknowledged that their distress
was very great, and the desertion from the Portuguese army, which augmented in an alarming manner, and seemed rather to be increased than repressed by severity, sufficiently proved their misery.
The personal resources of Wellington alone enabled
the army to maintain its forward position, for he
had, to a certain extent, carried his commercial speculations into Gallicia, as well as Portugal; and he
had persuaded the Spanish authorities in Castile to
give up a part of their revenue in kind to the army,
receiving bills on the British embassy at Cadiz in
return. But the situation of affairs may be best
learned from the mouths of the generals.

" The arrears of the army are certainly getting
to an alarming pitch, and if it is suffered to increase,
we cannot go on : we have only here two brigades
of infantry, fed by our own commissariat, and we

are now reduced to one of them having barely bread
for this day, and the commissary has not a farthing
of money. I know not how we shall get on!"

Such were Beresford's words on the 8th of July,
and on the 15th Wellington wrote even more forcibly.

" I have never," said he, " been in such distress
as at present, and some serious misfortune must
happen, if the government do not attend seriously
to the subject, and supply us regularly with money.
The arrears and distresses of the Portuguse government, are a joke to ours, and if our credit was not
better than theirs, we should certainly starve. As
it is, if we don't find means to pay our bills for
butcher's meat there will be an end to the war at
once."

Thus stript as it were to the skin, the English
general thought once more to hide his nakedness in
the mountains of Portugal, when Marmont, proud
of his own unripened skill, and perhaps, from the
experience of San Cristoval, undervaluing his adversary's tactics, desirous also, it was said, to gain
a victory without the presence of a king, Marmont,
pushed on by fate, madly broke the chain which
restrained his enemy's strength.

CHAPTER III.

When Wellington found by the intercepted letters, that the king's orders for Drouet to cross the Tagus, were reiterated, and imperative, he directed Hill to detach troops, in the same proportion. And as this reinforcement, coming by the way of Alcantara, could reach the Duero as soon as Drouet could reach Madrid, he hoped still to maintain the Tormes, if not the Duero, notwithstanding the king's power; for some money, long expected from England, had at last arrived in Oporto, and he thought the Gallicians, maugre their inertness, must soon be felt by the enemy. Moreover the harvest on the ground, however abundant, could not long feed the French multitudes, if Drouet and the king should together join Marmont. Nevertheless, fearing the action of Joseph's cavalry, he ordered D'Urban's horsemen to join the army on the Duero. But to understand the remarkable movements which were now about to commence, the reader must bear in mind, that the French army, from its peculiar organization, could, while the ground harvest lasted, operate without any regard to lines of communication; it had supports on all sides and procured its food every where, for the troops were taught to reap the standing corn, and grind it themselves if their cavalry could not seize flour in the villages. This organization approaching the ancient Roman military perfection, gave them

CHAP. III.

1812. July.

great advantages; in the field it baffled the irregular, and threw the regular force of the allies,
entirely upon the defensive; because when the
flanks were turned, a retreat only could save the
communications, and the French offered no point,
for retaliation in kind. Wherefore, with a force
composed of four different nations, Wellington was
to execute the most difficult evolutions, in an open
country, his chances of success being to arise only
from the casual errors of his adversary, who was an
able general, who knew the country perfectly, and
was at the head of an army, brave, excellently disciplined, and of one nation. The game would have
been quite unequal if the English general had not
been so strong in cavalry.

FRENCH PASSAGE OF THE DUERO.

In the course of the 15th and 16th Marmont,
who had previously made several deceptive movements, concentrated his beautiful and gallant army
between Toro and the Hornija river; and intercepted letters, the reports of deserters, and the talk
of the peasants had for several days assigned the
former place as his point of passage. On the morning of the 16th the English exploring officers, passing the Duero near Tordesillas, found only the
garrison there, and in the evening the reports
stated, that two French divisions had already
passed the repaired bridge of Toro. Wellington
united his centre and left at Canizal on the Guarena during the night, intending to attack those
who had passed at Toro; but as he had still some
doubts of the enemy's real object, he caused sir
Stapleton Cotton to halt on the Trabancos with the
right wing, composed of the fourth and light divi-

sions and Anson's cavalry. Meanwhile Marmont,
recalling his troops from the left bank of the Duero,
returned to Tordesillas and Pollos, passed that river
at those points and occupied Nava del Rey, where
his whole army was concentrated in the evening of
the 17th, some of his divisions having marched
above forty miles, and some above fifty miles, without a halt. The English cavalry posts being thus
driven over the Trabancos, advice of the enemy's
movement was sent to lord Wellington, but he was
then near Toro, it was midnight ere it reached
him, and the troops, under Cotton, remained near
Castrejon behind the Trabancos during the night
of the 17th without orders, exposed, in a bad See plan No. 3.
position, to the attack of the whole French army.
Wellington hastened to their aid in person, and he
ordered Bock's, Le Marchant's, and Alten's brigades
of cavalry, to follow him to Alaejos, and the fifth
division to take post at Torrecilla de la Orden six
miles in rear of Castrejon.

At daybreak Cotton's outposts were again driven
in by the enemy, and the bulk of his cavalry with a
troop of horse artillery immediately formed in front
of the two infantry divisions, which were drawn up,
the fourth division on the left, the light division on
the right, but at a considerable distance from each
other and separated by a wide ravine. The country
was open and hilly, like the downs of England, with
here and there water-gulleys, dry hollows, and bold
naked heads of land, and behind the most prominent
of these last, on the other side of the Trabancos, lay
the whole French army. Cotton however, seeing
only horsemen, pushed his cavalry again towards the
river, advancing cautiously by his right along some
high table-land, and his troops were soon lost to the

view of the infantry, for the morning fog was thick
on the stream, and at first nothing could be descried
beyond. But very soon the deep tones of artillery
shook the ground, the sharp ring of musketry was
heard in the mist, and the forty-third regiment was
hastily brought through Castrejon to support the
advancing cavalry; for besides the ravine which
separated the fourth from the light division, there
was another ravine with a marshy bottom, between the cavalry and infantry, and the village of
Castrejon was the only good point of passage.

The cannonade now became heavy, and the spectacle surprisingly beautiful, for the lighter smoke
and mist, curling up in fantastic pillars, formed a
huge and glittering dome tinged of many colours
by the rising sun; and through the grosser vapour
below, the restless horsemen were seen or lost as
the fume thickened from the rapid play of the
artillery, while the bluff head of land, beyond the
Trabancos, covered with French troops, appeared,
by an optical deception close at hand, dilated to
the size of a mountain, and crowned with gigantic
soldiers, who were continually breaking off and
sliding down into the fight. Suddenly a dismounted cavalry officer stalked from the midst of
the smoke towards the line of infantry; his gait
was peculiarly rigid, and he appeared to hold a
bloody handkerchief to his heart, but that which
seemed a cloth, was a broad and dreadful wound;
a bullet had entirely effaced the flesh from his left
shoulder and from his breast, and had carried away
part of his ribs, his heart was bared, and its movement plainly discerned. It was a piteous and yet
a noble sight, for his countenance though ghastly
was firm, his step scarcely indicated weakness, and

his voice never faltered. This unyielding man's name was Williams ; he died a short distance from the field of battle, and it was said, in the arms of his son, a youth of fourteen, who had followed his father to the Peninsula in hopes of obtaining a commission, for they were not in affluent circumstances.

General Cotton maintained this exposed position with skill and resolution, from daylight until seven o'clock, at which time Wellington arrived, in company with Beresford, and proceeded to examine the enemy's movements. The time was critical, and the two English generals were like to have been slain together by a body of French cavalry, not very numerous, which breaking away from the multitude on the head of land beyond the Trabancos, came galloping at full speed across the valley. It was for a moment thought they were deserting, but with headlong course they mounted the table-land on which Cotton's left wing was posted, and drove a whole line of British cavalry skirmishers back in confusion. The reserves indeed soon came up from Alaejos, and these furious swordsmen being scattered in all directions were in turn driven away or cut down, but meanwhile thirty or forty, led by a noble officer, had brought up their right shoulders, and came over the edge of the table-land above the hollow which separated the British wings at the instant when Wellington and Beresford arrived on the same slope. There were some infantry picquets in the bottom, and higher up, near the French, were two guns covered by a squadron of light cavalry which was disposed in perfect order. When the French officer saw this squadron, he reined in his horse with difficulty, and his troopers gathered in a con-

fused body round him as if to retreat. They
seemed lost men, for the British instantly charged,
but with a shout the gallant fellows soused down
upon the squadron, and the latter turning, galloped through the guns; then the whole mass,
friends and enemies, went like a whirlwind to the
bottom, carrying away lord Wellington, and the other
generals, who with drawn swords and some difficulty,
got clear of the tumult. The French horsemen were
now quite exhausted, and a reserve squadron of
heavy dragoons coming in cut most of them to
pieces; yet their invincible leader, assaulted by three
enemies at once, struck one dead from his horse, and
with surprising exertions saved himself from the
others, though they rode hewing at him on each
side for a quarter of a mile.

While this charge was being executed, Marmont,
who had ascertained that a part only of Wellington's army was before him, crossed the Trabancos in two columns, and passing by Alaejos,
turned the left of the allies, marching straight upon
the Guarena. The British retired by Torecilla de
la Orden, the fifth division being in one column on
the left, the fourth division on the right as they
retreated, and the light division on an intermediate
line and nearer to the enemy. The cavalry were
on the flanks and rear, the air was extremely
sultry, the dust rose in clouds, and the close order
of the troops rendered it very oppressive, but
the military spectacle was exceedingly strange and
grand. For then were seen the hostile columns of
infantry, only half musket-shot from each other,
marching impetuously towards a common goal,
the officers on each side pointing forwards with
their swords, or touching their caps, and waving

their hands in courtesy, while the German cavalry, huge men, on huge horses, rode between in a close compact body as if to prevent a collision. At times the loud tones of command, to hasten the march, were heard passing from the front to the rear, and now and then the rushing sound of bullets came sweeping over the columns whose violent pace was continually accelerated.

Thus moving for ten miles, yet keeping the most perfect order, both parties approached the Guarena, and the enemy seeing that the light division, although more in their power than the others, were yet outstripping them in the march, increased the fire of their guns and menaced an attack with infantry. But the German cavalry instantly drew close round, the column plunged suddenly into a hollow dip of ground on the left which offered the means of baffling the enemy's aim, and ten minutes after the head of the division was in the stream of the Guarena between Osmo and Castrillo. The fifth division entered the river at the same time but higher up on the left, and the fourth division passed it on the right. The soldiers of the light division, tormented with thirst, yet long used to their enemy's mode of warfare, drunk as they marched, and the soldiers of the fifth division stopped in the river for only a few moments, but on the instant forty French guns gathered on the heights above sent a tempest of bullets amongst them. So nicely timed was the operation.

The Guarena, flowing from four distinct sources which are united below Castrillo, offered a very strong line of defence, and Marmont, hoping to carry it in the first confusion of the passage, and so seize the table-land of Vallesa, had brought up all his artillery to the front; and to distract the allies' attention he had directed Clausel to push the head of the right column over the river at Castrillo, at the same time. But Wellington expecting him at Vallesa from the first, had ordered the other divisions of his army, originally assembled at Canizal, to cross one of the upper branches of the river; and they reached the table-land of Vallesa, before Marmont's infantry, oppressed by the extreme heat and rapidity of the march, could muster in strength to attempt the passage of the other branch. Clausel, however, sent Carier's brigade of cavalry across the Guarena at Castrillo and supported it with a column of infantry; and the fourth division had just gained the heights above Canizal, after passing the stream, when Carier's horsemen entered the valley on their left, and the infantry in one column menaced their front. The sedgy banks of the river would have been difficult to force in face of an enemy, but Victor Alten though a very bold man in action, was slow to seize an advantage, and suffered the French cavalry to cross and form in considerable numbers without opposition; he assailed them too late and by successive squadrons instead of by regiments, and the result was unfavourable at first. The fourteenth and the German hussars were hard-pressed, the third dragoons came up in support, but they were immediately driven back again by the fire of some French infantry, the fight waxed hot with the others, and many fell, but finally general Carier was wounded and taken, and the French retired. During this cavalry action the twenty-seventh and fortieth regiments coming down the hill, broke

the enemy's infantry with an impetuous bayonet
charge, and Alten's horsemen being then disengaged
sabred some of the fugitives.

This combat cost the French who had advanced
too far without support, a general and five hundred
soldiers; but Marmont, though baffled at Vallesa,
and beaten at Castrillo, concentrated his army at the
latter place in such a manner as to hold both banks
of the Guarena. Whereupon Wellington recalled his
troops from Vallesa; and as the whole loss of the
allies during the previous operations was not more
than six hundred, nor that of the French more than
eight hundred, and that both sides were highly
excited, the day still young, and the positions
although strong, open, and within cannon shot, a
battle was expected. Marmont's troops had however
been marching for two days and nights incessantly,
and Wellington's plan did not admit of fighting
unless forced to it in defence, or under such circumstances, as would enable him to crush his
opponent, and yet keep the field afterwards against
the king.

By this series of signal operations, the French
general had passed a great river, taken the initiatory movement, surprised the right wing of the
allies, and pushed it back above ten miles. Yet
these advantages are to be traced to the peculiari-
ties of the English general's situation which have
been already noticed, and Wellington's tactical
skill was manifested by the extricating of his
troops from their dangerous position at Castrejon
without loss, and without being forced to fight a battle. He however appears to have erred in extending
his troops to the right when he first reached the
Duero, for seeing that Marmont could at pleasure

pass that river and turn his flanks, he should have
remained concentrated on the Guarena, and only
pushed cavalry posts to the line of the Duero above
Toro. Neither should he have risked his right
wing so far from his main body from the evening
of the 16th to the morning of the 18th. He could
scarcely have brought it off without severe loss, if
Marmont had been stronger in cavalry, and instead
of pushing forwards at once to the Guarena had
attacked him on the march. On the other hand the
security of the French general's movements, from
the Trabancos to the Guarena, depended entirely on
their rapidity; for as his columns crossed the open
country on a line parallel to the march of the allies, a simple wheel by companies to the right
would have formed the latter in order of battle on
his flank while the four divisions already on the
Guarena could have met them in front.

But it was on the 16th that the French general
failed in the most glaring manner. His intent was,
by menacing the communication with Salamanca
and Ciudad Rodrigo, to force the allies back, and
strike some decisive blow during their retreat.
Now on the evening of the 16th he had passed the
Duero at Toro, gained a day's march, and was
then actually nearer to Salamanca than the allies
were; and had he persisted in his movement Wellington must have fought him to disadvantage or have
given up Salamanca, and passed the Tormes at
Huerta to regain the communication with Ciudad
Rodrigo. This advantage Marmont relinquished,
to make a forced march of eighty miles in forty-
eight hours, and to risk the execution of a variety of
nice and difficult evolutions, in which he lost
above a thousand men by the sword or by fatigue,

and finally found his adversary on the 18th still facing him in the very position which he had turned on the evening of the 16th !

On the 19th the armies maintained their respective ground in quiet until the evening, when Marmont concentrated his troops in one mass on his left near the village of Tarazona, and Wellington, fearing for his right, again passed the second branch of the Guarena, at Vallesa, and El Olmo, and took post on the table-land above those villages. The light division, being in front, advanced to the edge of the table-land, overlooking the enemy's main body which was at rest round the bivouac fires; yet the picquets would have been quietly posted, if Sir Stapleton Cotton coming up at the moment, had not ordered captain Ross to turn his battery of six-pounders upon a group of French officers. At the first shot the enemy seemed surprised, at the second their gunners run to their pieces, and in a few moments a reply from twelve eight-pounders shewed the folly of provoking a useless combat. An artillery officer was wounded in the head, several of the British soldiers fell in different parts of the line, one shot swept away a whole section of Portuguese, and finally the division was obliged to withdraw several hundred yards in a mortifying manner to avoid a great and unnecessary effusion of blood.

The allies being now formed in two lines on the table-land of Vallesa offered a fair though not an easy field to the enemy; Wellington expected a battle the next day, because the range of heights which he occupied, trended backwards to the Tormes on the shortest line; and as he had thrown a Spanish garrison into the castle of Alba de

Tormes, he thought Marmont could not turn his
right, or if he attempted it, that he would be
shouldered off the Tormes at the ford of Huerta. He
was mistaken. The French general was more perfectly acquainted with the ground and proved that
he could move an army with wonderful facility.

On the 20th at day-break instead of crossing
the Guarena to dispute the high land of Vallesa,
Marmont marched rapidly in several columns, covered by a powerful rear guard, up the river to
Canta la Piedra, and crossed the stream there, though
the banks were difficult, before any disposition
could be made to oppose him. He thus turned the
right flank of the allies and gained a new range of
hills trending towards the Tormes, and parallel to
those leading from Vallesa. Wellington immediately
made a corresponding movement. Then commenced an evolution similar to that of the 18th, but
on a greater scale both as to numbers and length of
way. The allies moving in two lines of battle
within musket-shot of the French endeavoured to
gain upon and cross their march at Cantalpino;
the guns on both sides again exchanged their
rough salutations as the accidents of ground favoured their play; and again the officers, like gallant gentlemen who bore no malice and knew no
fear, made their military recognitions, while the
horsemen on each side watched with eager eyes, for
an opening to charge; but the French general
moving his army as one man along the crest of the
heights, preserved the lead he had taken, and made
no mistake.

At Cantalpino it became evident that the allies
were outflanked, and all this time Marmont had so
skilfully managed his troops that he furnished no

opportunity even for a partial attack. Wellington therefore fell off a little and made towards the heights of Cabeça Vellosa and Aldea Rubia, intending to halt there while the sixth division and Alten's cavalry, forcing their march, seized Aldea Lengua and secured the position of Christoval. But he made no effort to seize the ford of Huerta, for his own march had been long and the French had passed over nearly twice as much ground, wherefore he thought they would not attempt to reach the Tormes that day. However when night approached, although his second line had got possession of the heights of Vellosa, his first line was heaped up without much order in the low ground between that place and Hornillos; the French army crowned all the summit of the opposite hills, and their fires, stretching in a half circle from Villaruela to Babila Fuente, shewed that they commanded the ford of Huerta. They could even have attacked the allies with great advantage had there been light for the battle. The English general immediately ordered the bivouac fires to be made, but filed the troops off in succession with the greatest celerity towards Vellosa and Aldea Rubia, and during the movement the Portuguese cavalry, coming in from the front, were mistaken for French and lost some men by cannon-shot ere they were recognised.

Wellington was deeply disquieted at the unexpected result of this day's operations which had been entirely to the advantage of the French general. Marmont had shewn himself perfectly acquainted with the country, had outflanked and outmarched the allies, had gained the command of the Tormes, and as his junction with the king's army was thus secured he might fight or wait for reinforcements or continue his operations as it seemed good to himself. But the scope of Wellington's campaign was hourly being more restricted. His reasons for avoiding a battle except at advantage, were stronger than before, because Caffarelli's cavalry was known to be in march, and the army of the centre was on the point of taking the field; hence though he should fight and gain a victory, unless it was decisive, his object would not be advanced. That object was to deliver the Peninsula, which could only be done by a long course of solid operations incompatible with sudden and rash strokes unauthorized by any thing but hope; wherefore yielding to the force of circumstances, he prepared to return to Portugal and abide his time; yet with a bitter spirit, which was not soothed by the recollection, that he had refused the opportunity of fighting to advantage, exactly one month before and upon the very hills he now occupied. Nevertheless that stedfast temper, which then prevented him from seizing an adventitious chance, would not now let him yield to fortune more than she could ravish from him : he still hoped to give the lion's stroke, and resolved to cover Salamanca and the communication with Ciudad Rodrigo to the last moment. A letter stating his inability to hold his ground was however sent to Castaños, but it was intercepted by Marmont, who exultingly pushed forwards without regard to the king's movements ; and it is curious that Joseph afterwards

King's
correspon-
dence,
MSS.
imagined this to have been a subtlety of Wellington's to draw the French general into a premature battle.

On the 21st while the allies occupied the old position of Christoval, the French threw a garri-

son into Alba de Tormes, from whence the Spaniards
had been withdrawn by Carlos D'España, without
the knowledge of the English general. Marmont
then passed the Tormes, by the fords between Alba
and Huerta, and moving up the valley of Mache-
chuco encamped behind Calvariza Ariba, at the
edge of a forest which extended from the river to
that place. Wellington also passed the Tormes in
the course of the evening by the bridges, and by the
fords of Santa Marta and Aldea Lengua ; but the
third division and D'Urban's cavalry remained on the
right bank, and entrenched themselves at Cabrerizos,
lest the French, who had left a division on the
heights of Babila Fuente, should recross the Tormes in the night and overwhelm them.

It was late when the light division descended the
rough side of the Aldea Lengua mountain to cross
the river, and the night came suddenly down,
with more than common darkness, for a storm, that
common precursor of a battle in the Peninsula, was
at hand. Torrents of rain deepened the ford, the
water foamed and dashed with encreasing violence,
the thunder was frequent and deafening, and the
lightning passed in sheets of fire close over the
column, or played upon the points of the bayonets.
One flash falling amongst the fifth dragoon guards,
near Santa Marta, killed many men and horses,
while hundreds of frightened animals breaking
loose from their piquet ropes, and galloping wildly
about, were supposed to be the enemy's cavalry
charging in the darkness, and indeed some of their
patroles were at hand ; but to a military eye there
was nothing more imposing than the close and
beautiful order in which the soldiers of that noble
light division, were seen by the fiery gleams to step

from the river to the bank and pursue their march amidst this astounding turmoil, defying alike the storm and the enemy.

The position now taken by the allies was nearly the same as that occupied by general Graham a month before, when the forts of Salamanca were invested. The left wing rested in the low ground on the Tormes, near Santa Marta, having a cavalry post in front towards Calvariza de Abaxo. The right wing extended along a range of heights which ended also in low ground, near the village of Arapiles, and this line being perpendicular to the course of the Tormes from Huerta to Salamanca, and parallel to its course from Alba to Huerta, covered Salamanca. But the enemy extending his left along the edge of the forest, still menaced the See Plan 3. line of communication with Ciudad Rodrigo; and in the night advice came that general Chauvel, with near two thousand of Caffarelli's horsemen, and twenty guns, had actually reached Pollos on the 20th, and would join Marmont the 22nd or 23rd. Hence Wellington, feeling that he must now perforce retreat to Ciudad Rodrigo, and fearing that the French cavalry thus reinforced would hamper his movements, determined, unless the enemy attacked him, or committed some flagrant fault, to retire before Chauvel's horsemen could arrive.

At day-break on the 22nd, Marmont who had called the troops at Babila Fuente over the Tormes, by the ford of Encina, brought Bonet's and Maucune's divisions up from the forest and took possession of the ridge of Calvariza de Ariba; he also occupied in advance of it a wooded height on which was an old chapel called Nuestra Señora de la Pena. But at a little distance from his left, and from the

English right, stood a pair of solitary hills, called
the *Two Arapiles*, about half cannon-shot from each
other; steep and savagely rugged they were, and
the possession of them would have enabled the
French general to form his army across Wellington's
right, and thus bring on a battle with every disadvantage to the allies, confined, as the latter would
have been, between the French army and the
Tormes. These hills were neglected by the English
general until a staff officer, who had observed the
enemy's detachments stealing towards them, first informed Beresford, and afterwards Wellington of the
fact. The former thought it was of no consequence,
but the latter immediately sent the seventh Caçadores
to seize the most distant of the rocks, and then a combat occurred similar to that which happened between
Cæsar and Afranius at Lerida; for the French seeing the allies' detachment approaching, broke their
own ranks, and running without order to the encounter gained the first Arapiles and kept it, but
were repulsed in an endeavour to seize the second.
This skirmish was followed by one at Nuestra
Señora de la Pena, which was also assailed by a
detachment of the seventh division, and so far successfully, that half that height was gained; yet the
enemy kept the other half, and Victor Alten, flanking the attack with a squadron of German hussars,
lost some men and was himself wounded by a
musket-shot.

The result of the dispute for the Arapiles
rendered a retreat difficult to the allies during day-
light; for though the rock gained by the English
was a fortress in the way of the French army,
Marmont, by extending his left, and by gathering a
force behind his own Arapiles, could still frame a

dangerous battle and pounce upon the allies during
their movement.   Wherefore Wellington immediately extended his right into the low ground, placing
the light companies of the guards in the village of
Arapiles, and the fourth division, with exception of
the twenty-seventh regiment, which remained at the
rock, on a gentle ridge behind them.   The fifth and
sixth divisions he gathered in one mass upon the internal slope of the English Arapiles, where from the
hollow nature of the ground they were quite hidden
from the enemy; and during these movements a
sharp cannonade was exchanged from the tops of
those frowning hills, on whose crowning rocks the
two generals sat like ravenous vultures watching
for their quarry.

Marmont's project was not yet developed; his
troops coming from Babila Fuente were still in the
forest, and some miles off; he had only two divisions
close up, and the occupation of Calvariza Ariba,
and Nuestra Señora de la Pena, was a daring
defensive measure to cover the formation of his
army.   The occupation of the Arapiles was however
a start forward, for an advantage to be afterwards
turned to profit, and seemed to fix the operations
on the left of the Tormes.   Wellington, therefore,
brought up the first and the light divisions to confront
the enemy's troops on the height of Calvariza Ariba;
and then calling the third division and D'Urban's
cavalry over the river, by the fords of Santa Marta,
he posted them in a wood near Aldea Tejada,
entirely refused to the enemy and unseen by him,
yet in a situation to secure the main road to Ciudad
Rodrigo.   Thus the position of the allies was suddenly reversed; the left rested on the English
Arapiles, the right on Aldea Tejada; that which

was the rear became the front, and the interval between the third and the fourth division was occupied by Bradford's Portuguese infantry, by the
Spaniards, and by the British cavalry.

This ground had several breaks and hollows, so
that few of these troops could be viewed by the
enemy, and those which were, seemed, both from
their movement and from their position, to be
pointing to the Ciudad Rodigo road as in retreat.
The commissariat and baggage had also been
ordered to the rear, the dust of their march was
plainly to be seen many miles off, and hence
there was nothing in the relative position of the
armies, save their proximity, to indicate an approaching battle. Such a state of affairs could not
last long. About twelve o'clock Marmont, fearing
that the important bearing of the French Arapiles on
Wellington's retreat would induce the latter to drive
him thence, hastily brought up Foy's and Ferey's
divisions in support, placing, the first, with some
guns, on a wooded height between the Arapiles
and Nuestra Señora de la Pena, the second, and
Boyer's dragoons, behind Foy on the ridge of Calvariza de Ariba. Nor was this fear ill-founded, for
the English general, thinking that he could not
safely retreat in daylight without possessing both
Arapiles, had actually issued orders for the seventh
division to attack the French, but perceiving the
approach of more troops, gave counter-orders lest
he should bring on the battle disadvantageously.
He judged it better to wait for new events, being
certain that at night he could make his retreat good,
and wishing rather that Marmont should attack him
in his now strong position.

The French troops coming from Babila Fuente

had not yet reached the edge of the forest, when
Marmont, seeing that the allies would not attack,
and fearing that they would retreat before his own
dispositions were completed, ordered Thomieres'
division, covered by fifty guns and supported by the
light cavalry, to menace the Ciudad Rodrigo road.
He also hastened the march of his other divisions,
designing, when Wellington should move in opposition to Thomieres, to fall upon him, by the village
of Arapiles, with six divisions of infantry and
Boyer's dragoons, which last, he now put in march
to take fresh ground on the left of the Arapiles
rocks, leaving only one regiment of cavalry, to guard
Foy's right flank at Calvariza.

In these new circumstances, the positions of the
two armies embraced an oval basin formed by
different ranges of hills, that rose like an amphi-
theatre of which the Arapiles rocks might be considered the door-posts. This basin was about
a mile broad from north to south, and more than
two miles long from east to west. The northern
and western half formed the allies' position, which
extended from the English Arapiles on the left
to Aldea Tejada on the right. The eastern heights
were held by the French right, and their left, consisting of Thomieres' division with the artillery and
light cavalry, was now moving along the southern
side of the basin; but the march was wide and
loose, there was a long space between Thomieres'
and the divisions, which, coming from the edge of
the forest were destined to form the centre, and
there was a longer space between him and the divisions about the Arapiles. Nevertheless, the mass
of artillery placed on his right flank was very imposing, and opened its fire grandly, taking ground

to the left by guns, in succession, as the infantry moved on; and these last marched eagerly,
continually contracting their distance from the
allies, and bringing up their left shoulders as if to
envelope Wellington's position and embrace it with
fire. At this time also, Bonet's troops, one regiment
of which held the French Arapiles, carried the village of that name, and although soon driven from the
greatest part of it again, maintained a fierce struggle.

Marmont's first arrangements had occupied several hours, yet as they gave no positive indica-
tion of his designs, Wellington ceasing to watch
him, had retired from the Arapiles. But at three
o'clock, a report reached him that the French left
was in motion and pointing towards the Ciudad
Rodrigo road; then starting up he repaired to the
high ground, and observed their movements for some
time, with a stern contentment, for their left wing
was entirely separated from the centre. The fault
was flagrant, and he fixed it with the stroke of a
thunder-bolt. A few orders issued from his lips
like the incantations of a wizard, and suddenly the
dark mass of troops which covered the English
Arapiles, was seemingly possessed by some mighty
spirit, and rushing violently down the interior slope
of the mountain, entered the great basin amidst a
storm of bullets which seemed to shear away the
whole surface of the earth over which the soldiers
moved. The fifth division instantly formed on the
right of the fourth, connecting the latter with
Bradford's Portuguese, who hastened forward at the
same time from the right of the army, and the heavy
cavalry galloping up on the right of Bradford, closed
this front of battle. The sixth and seventh divisions
flanked on the right by Anson's light cavalry, which

had now moved from the Arapiles, were ranged at half cannon-shot in a second line, which was prolonged by the Spaniards in the direction of the third division ; and this last, reinforced by two squadrons of the fourteenth dragoons, and by D'Urban's Portuguese horsemen, formed the extreme right of the army. Behind all, on the highest ground, the first and light divisions and Pack's Portuguese were disposed in heavy masses as a reserve.

When this grand disposition was completed, the third division and its attendant horsemen, the whole formed in four columns and flanked on the left by twelve guns, received orders to cross the enemy's line of march. The remainder of the first line, including the main body of the cavalry was directed to advance whenever the attack of the third division should be developed ; and as the fourth division must in this forward movement necessarily lend its flank to the enemy's troops stationed on the French Arapiles, Pack's brigade was commanded to assail that rock the moment the left of the British line should pass it. Thus, after long coiling and winding, the armies came together, and drawing up their huge trains like angry serpents mingled in deadly strife.

BATTLE OF SALAMANCA.

Marmont, from the top of the French Arapiles, saw the country beneath him suddenly covered with enemies at a moment when he was in the act of making a complicated evolution, and when, by the rash advance of his left, his troops were separated into three parts, each at too great a distance to assist the other, and those nearest the enemy neither strong enough to hold their ground, nor aware of what they had to encounter. The third division was, however, still hidden from him by the western heights, and he hoped that the tempest of bullets under which the British line was moving in the basin beneath, would check it until he could bring up his reserve divisions, and by the village of Arapiles fall on what was now the left of the allies' position. But even this, his only resource for saving the battle, was weak, for on that point there were still the first and light divisions and Pack's brigade, forming a mass of twelve thousand troops with thirty pieces of artillery; the village itself was well disputed, and the English Arapiles rock stood out as a strong bastion of defence. However, the French general, nothing daunted, despatched officer after officer, some to hasten up the troops from the forest, others to stop the progress of his left wing, and with a sanguine expectation still looked for the victory until he saw Pakenham with the third division shoot like a meteor across Thomieres' path; then pride and hope alike died within him, and desperately he was hurrying in person to that fatal point, when an exploding shell stretched him on the earth with a broken arm and two deep wounds in his side. Confusion ensued and the troops distracted by ill-judged orders and counterorders knew not where to move, who to fight or who to avoid.

It was about five o'clock when Pakenham fell upon Thomieres, and it was at the instant when that general, the head of whose column had gained an open isolated hill at the extremity of the southern range of heights, expected to see the allies, in full retreat towards the Ciudad Rodrigo road, closely followed by Marmont from the Arapiles. The

counter-stroke was terrible! Two batteries of artillery placed on the summit of the western heights
suddenly took his troops in flank, and Pakenham's
massive columns supported by cavalry, were coming
on full in his front, while two-thirds of his own
division, lengthened out and unconnected, were still
behind in a wood where they could hear, but could
not see the storm which was now bursting. From
the chief to the lowest soldier all felt that they were
lost, and in an instant Pakenham the most frank and
gallant of men commenced the battle.

The British columns formed lines as they
marched, and the French gunners standing up manfully for the honour of their country, sent showers of
grape into the advancing masses, while a crowd of
light troops poured in a fire of musketry, under
cover of which the main body endeavoured to display a front. But bearing onwards through the
skirmishers with the might of a giant, Pakenham
broke the half-formed lines into fragments, and sent
the whole in confusion upon the advancing supports;
one only officer, with unyielding spirit, remained by
the artillery; standing alone he fired the last gun at
the distance of a few yards, but whether he lived
or there died could not be seen for the smoke.
Some squadrons of light cavalry fell on the right
of the third division, but the fifth regiment repulsed
them, and then D'Urban's Portuguese horsemen, reinforced by two squadrons of the fourteenth dragoons
under Felton Harvey, gained the enemy's flank. The
Oporto regiment, led by the English Major Watson,
instantly charged the French infantry, yet vainly,
Watson fell deeply wounded and his men retired.

Pakenham continued his tempestuous course
against the remainder of Thomieres' troops, which

were now arrayed on the wooded heights behind the first hill, yet imperfectly, and offering two fronts the one opposed to the third division and its attendant horsemen, the other to the fifth division, to Bradford's brigade and the main body of cavalry and artillery, all of which were now moving in one great line across the basin. Meanwhile Bonet's troops having failed at the village of Arapiles were sharply engaged with the fourth division, Maucune kept his menacing position behind the French Arapiles, and as Clauzel's division had come up from the forest, the connection of the centre and left was in some measure restored; two divisions were however still in the rear, and Boyer's dragoons were in march from Calvariza Ariba. Thomieres had been killed, and Bonet, who succeeded Marmont, had been disabled, hence more confusion; but the command of the army devolved on Clauzel, and he was of a capacity to sustain this terrible crisis.

The fourth and fifth divisions, and Bradford's brigade, were now hotly engaged and steadily gaining ground; the heavy cavalry, Anson's light dragoons and Bull's troop of artillery were advancing at a trot on Pakenham's left; and on that general's right D'Urban's horsemen overlapped the enemy. Thus in less than half an hour, and before an order of battle had even been formed by the French, their commander-in-chief and two other generals had fallen, and the left of their army was turned, thrown into confusion and enveloped. Clauzel's division had indeed joined Thomieres', and a front had been spread on the southern heights, but it was loose and unfit to resist; for the troops were, some in double lines, some in columns, some in squares; a powerful sun shone full in their eyes, the light soil, stirred up

by the trampling of men and horses, and driven forward by a breeze, which arose in the west at the
moment of attack, came full upon them mingled
with smoke in such stifling clouds, that scarcely
able to breathe and quite unable to see, their fire
was given at random.

In this situation, while Pakenham, bearing onward
with a conquering violence, was closing on their
flank and the fifth division advancing with a storm
of fire on their front, the interval between the two
attacks was suddenly filled with a whirling cloud of
dust, which moving swiftly forward carried within
its womb the trampling sound of a charging multitude. As it passed the left of the third division
Le Marchant's heavy horsemen flanked by Anson's
light cavalry, broke forth from it at full speed, and
the next instant twelve hundred French infantry
though formed in several lines were trampled down
with a terrible clamour and disturbance. Be-
wildered and blinded, they cast away their arms
and run through the openings of the British squadrons stooping and demanding quarter, while the dragoons, big men and on big horses, rode onwards
smiting with their long glittering swords in uncon-
troulable power, and the third division followed at
speed, shouting as the French masses fell in succession before this dreadful charge.

Nor were these valiant swordsmen yet exhausted.
Their own general, Le Marchant, and many officers
had fallen, but Cotton and all his staff was at their
head, and with ranks confused, and blended together in one mass, still galloping forward they
sustained from a fresh column an irregular stream
of fire which emptied a hundred saddles; yet
with fine courage, and downright force, the sur-

vivors broke through this the third and strongest
body of men that had encountered them, and lord
Edward Somerset, continuing his course at the
head of one squadron, with a happy perseverance
captured five guns. The French left was entirely
broken, more than two thousand prisoners were
taken, the French light horsemen abandoned that
part of the field, and Thomieres' division no longer
existed as a military body. Anson's cavalry which
had passed quite over the hill and had suffered
little in the charge, was now joined by D'Urban's
troopers, and took the place of Le Marchant's exhausted men ; the heavy German dragoons followed
in reserve, and with the third and fifth divisions and
the guns, formed one formidable line, two miles in
advance of where Pakenham had first attacked ; and
that impetuous officer with unmitigated strength
still pressed forward spreading terror and disorder
on the enemy's left.

While these signal events, which occupied about
forty minutes, were passing on the allies' right, a
terrible battle raged in the centre. For when the
first shock of the third division had been observed
from the Arapiles, the fourth division, moving in a
line with the fifth, had passed the village of that
name under a prodigious cannonade, and vigourously driving Bonet's troops backwards, step by
step, to the southern and eastern heights, obliged
them to mingle with Clauzel's and with Thomieres'
broken remains. When the combatants had passed
the French Arapiles, which was about the time of
Le Marchant's charge, Pack's Portuguese assailed
that rock, and the front of battle was thus completely defined, because Foy's division was now exchanging a distant cannonade with the first and

light divisions.   However Bonet's troops, notwithstanding Marmont's fall, and the loss of their own
general, fought strongly, and Clauzel made a surprising effort, beyond all men's expectations, to
restore the battle.   Already a great change was
visible.   Ferey's division drawn off from the height
of Calvaraza Ariba arrived in the centre behind
Bonet's men ; the light cavalry, Boyer's dragoons,
and two divisions of infantry, from the forest, were
also united there, and on this mass of fresh men,
Clauzel rallied the remnants of his own and Thomieres' division.   Thus by an able movement,
Sarrut's, Brennier's, and Ferey's unbroken troops,
supported by the whole of the cavalry, were so
disposed as to cover the line of retreat to Alba de
Tormes, while Maucune's division was still in mass
behind the French Arapiles, and Foy's remained
untouched on the right.

But Clauzel, not content with having brought
the separated part of his army together and in a
condition to·effect a retreat, attempted to stem the
tide of victory in the very fulness of its strength
and roughness.   His hopes were founded on a misfortune which had befallen general Pack ; for that
officer ascending the French Arapiles in one heavy
column, had driven back the enemy's skirmishers
and was within thirty yards of the summit, believing himself victorious, when suddenly the French
reserves leaped forward from the rocks upon his
front, and upon his left flank.   The hostile masses
closed, there was a thick cloud of smoke, a shout,
a stream of fire, and the side of the hill was covered
to the very bottom with the dead the wounded
and the flying Portuguese, who were scoffed at for
this failure without any justice ; no troops could

have withstood that crash upon such steep ground, and the propriety of attacking the hill at all seems very questionable. The result went nigh to shake the whole battle. For the fourth division had just then reached the southern ridge of the basin, and one of the best regiments in the service was actually on the summit when twelve hundred fresh adversaries, arrayed on the reverse slope, charged up hill; and as the British fire was straggling and ineffectual, because the soldiers were breathless and disordered by the previous fighting, the French who came up resolutely and without firing won the crest. They were even pursuing down the other side when two regiments placed in line below, checked them with a destructive volley.

This vigorous counter-blow took place at the moment when Pack's defeat permitted Maucune, who was no longer in pain for the Arapiles hill, to menace the left flank and rear of the fourth division, but the left wing of the fortieth regiment immediately wheeled about and with a rough charge cleared the rear. Maucune would not engage himself more deeply at that time, but general Ferey's troops pressed vigorously against the front of the fourth division, and Brennier did the same by the first line of the fifth division, Boyer's dragoons also came on rapidly, and the allies being outflanked and overmatched lost ground. Fiercely and fast the French followed and the fight once more raged in the basin below. General Cole had before this fallen deeply wounded, and Leith had the same fortune, but Beresford promptly drew Spry's Portuguese brigade from the second line of the fifth division and thus flanked the advancing columns of the

enemy; yet he also fell desperately wounded, and
Boyer's dragoons then came freely into action be-
cause Anson's cavalry had been checked after Le
Marchant's charge by a heavy fire of artillery.

The crisis of the battle had now arrived and the
victory was for the general who had the strongest
reserves in hand. Wellington, who was seen that
day at every point of the field exactly when his
presence was most required, immediately brought
up from the second line, the sixth division, and its
charge was rough, strong, and successful. Nevertheless the struggle was no slight one. The men
of general Hulse's brigade, which was on the left,
went down by hundreds, and the sixty-first and
eleventh regiments won their way desperately and
through such a fire, as British soldiers only, can
sustain. Some of Boyer's dragoons also breaking in
between the fifth and sixth divisions slew many
men, and caused some disorder in the fifty-third;
but that brave regiment lost no ground, nor did
Clauzel's impetuous counter-attack avail at any
point, after the first burst, against the steady courage of the allies. The southern ridge was regained,
the French general Menne was severely, and general Ferey, mortally wounded, Clauzel himself was
hurt, and the reserve of Boyer's dragoons coming
on at a canter were met and broken by the fire of
Hulse's noble brigade. Then the changing current
of the fight once more set for the British. The
third division continued to outflank the enemy's left,
Maucune abandoned the French Arapiles, Foy retired from the ridge of Calvariza, and the allied
host righting itself as a gallant ship after a sudden
gust, again bore onwards in blood and gloom, for
though the air, purified by the storm of the night

before, was peculiarly clear, one vast cloud of smoke and dust rolled along the basin, and within it was the battle with all its sights and sounds of terror.

When the English general had thus restored the fight in the centre, he directed the commander of the first division to push between Foy and the rest of the French army, which would have rendered it impossible for the latter to rally or escape; but this order was not executed, and Foy's and Maucune's divisions were skilfully used by Clauzel to protect the retreat. The first, posted on undulating ground and flanked by some squadrons of dragoons, covered the roads to the fords of Huerta and Encina; the second, reinforced with fifteen guns, was placed on a steep ridge in front of the forest, covering the road to Alba de Tormes; and behind this ridge, the rest of the army, then falling back in disorder before the third, fifth, and sixth divisions, took refuge. Wellington immediately sent the light division, formed in two lines and flanked by some squadrons of dragoons, against Foy; and he supported them by the first division in columns, flanked on the right by two brigades of the fourth division which he had drawn off from the centre when the sixth division restored the fight. The seventh division and the Spaniards followed in reserve, the country was covered with troops, and a new army seemed to have risen out of the earth.

Foy throwing out a cloud of skirmishers retired slowly by wings, turning and firing heavily from every rise of ground upon the light division, which marched steadily forward without returning a shot, save by its skirmishers; for three miles the march was under this musketry, which was occasionally thickened by a can-

nonade, and yet very few men were lost, because
the French aim was baffled, partly by the twilight,
partly by the even order and rapid gliding of the
lines. But the French general Desgraviers was
killed, and the flanking brigades from the fourth division having now penetrated between Maucune and
Foy, it seemed difficult for the latter to extricate his
troops 'from the action ; nevertheless he did it and
with great dexterity. For having increased his skirmishers on the last defensible ridge, along the foot
of which run a marshy stream, he redoubled his fire
of musketry, and made a menacing demonstration
with his horsemen just as the darkness fell ; the
British guns immediately opened their fire, a squadron of dragoons galloped forwards from the left,
the infantry, crossing the marshy stream, with an
impetuous pace hastened to the summit of the hill,
and a rough shock seemed at hand, but there
was no longer an enemy ; the main body of the
French had gone into the thick forest on their own
left during the firing, and the skirmishers fled
swiftly after, covered by the smoke and by the
darkness.

Meanwhile Maucune maintained a noble battle.
He was outflanked and outnumbered, but the safety
of the French army depended on his courage ; he
knew it, and Pakenham, marking his bold demeanour, advised Clinton, who was immediately in his
front, not to assail him until the third division
should have turned his left. Nevertheless the sixth
division was soon plunged afresh into action under
great disadvanatge, for after being kept by its
commander a long time without reason, close
under Maucune's batteries which ploughed heavily
through the ranks, it was suddenly directed by a

staff officer to attack the hill. Assisted by a brigade
of the fourth division, the troops then rushed up, and
in the darkness of the night the fire shewed from afar
how the battle went. On the side of the British a
sheet of flame was seen, sometimes advancing with
an even front, sometimes pricking forth in spear
heads, now falling back in waving lines, and anon
darting upwards in one vast pyramid, the apex of
which often approached yet never gained the actual
summit of the mountain; but the French musketry,
rapid as lightning, sparkled along the brow of the
height with unvarying fulness, and with what destructive effects the dark gaps and changing shapes of
the adverse fire showed too plainly. Yet when Pakenham had again turned the enemy's left, and Foy's
division had glided into the forest, Maucune's task
was completed, the effulgent crest of the ridge became black and silent, and the whole French army
vanished as it were in the darkness.

Meanwhile Wellington, who was with the leading
regiment of the light division, continued to advance
towards the ford of Huerta leaving the forest to his
right, for he thought the Spanish garrison was still
in the castle of Alba de Tormes, and that the enemy
must of necessity be found in a confused mass at
the fords. It was for this final stroke that he had
so skilfully strengthened his left wing, nor was he
diverted from his aim by marching through standing corn where no enemy could have preceded him;
nor by Foy's retreat into the forest, because it pointed
towards the fords of Encina and Gonzalo, which
that general might be endeavouring to gain,
and the right wing of the allies would find
him there. A squadron of French dragoons also
burst hastily from the forest in front of the advanc-

ing troops, soon after dark, and firing their pistols
passed at full gallop towards the ford of Huerta,
thus indicating great confusion in the defeated
army, and confirming the notion that its retreat was
in that direction.   Had the castle of Alba been
held, the French could not have carried off a third
of their army, nor would they have been in much
better plight if Carlos D'España, who soon discovered his error in withdrawing the garrison, had
informed Wellington of the fact ; but he suppressed
it and suffered the colonel who had only obeyed
his orders to be censured ; the left wing therefore
continued their march to the ford without meeting
any enemy, and, the night being far spent, were
there halted ; the right wing, exhausted by long
fighting, had ceased to pursue after the action with
Maucune, and thus the French gained Alba unmolested ; but the action did not terminate without
two remarkable accidents.   While riding close behind the forty-third regiment, Wellington was struck
in the thigh by a spent musket-ball, which passed
through his holster; and the night picquets had
just been set at Huerta, when Sir Stapleton Cotton,
who had gone to the ford and returned a different
road, was shot through the arm by a Portuguese
sentinel whose challenge he had disregarded.
These were the last events of this famous battle, in
which the skill of the general was worthily seconded
by troops whose ardour may be appreciated by the
following anecdotes.

Captain Brotherton of the fourteenth dragoons,
fighting on the 18th at the Guarena, amongst
the foremost, as he was always wont to do, had a
sword thrust quite through his side, yet on the 22d he
was again on horseback, and being denied leave to

remain in that condition with his own regiment,
secretly joined Pack's Portuguese in an undress,
and was again hurt in the unfortunate charge at the
Arapiles. Such were the officers. A man of the
forty-third, one by no means distinguished above
his comrades, was shot through the middle of the
thigh, and lost his shoes in passing the marshy
stream; but refusing to quit the fight, he limped
under fire in rear of his regiment, and with naked
feet, and streaming of blood from his wound, he
marched for several miles over a country covered
with sharp stones. Such were the soldiers, and
the devotion of a woman was not wanting to the
illustration of this great day.

The wife of colonel Dalbiac, an English lady of a
gentle disposition and possessing a very delicate
frame, had braved the dangers, and endured the
privations of two campaigns, with the patient forti-
tude which belongs only to her sex; and in this
battle, forgetful of every thing but that strong
affection which had so long supported her, she
rode deep amidst the enemy's fire, trembling yet
irresistibly impelled forwards by feelings more im-
perious than horror, more piercing than the fear of
death.

CHAPTER IV.

During the few hours of darkness, which succeeded the cessation of the battle, Clauzel had with
a wonderful diligence, passed the Tormes by the
narrow bridge of Alba and the fords below it, and
at day-light was in full retreat upon Peneranda,
covered by an organized rear-guard. Wellington
also, having brought up the German dragoons and
Anson's cavalry to the front, crossed the river with
his left wing at day-light, and moving up the
stream, came about ten o'clock upon the French
rear which was winding without much order along
the Almar, a small stream at the foot of a height
near the village of La Serna. He launched his
cavalry against them, and the French squadrons,
flying from Anson's troopers towards their own left,
abandoned three battalions of infantry, who in separate columns were making up a hollow slope on
their right, hoping to gain the crest of the heights
before the cavalry could fall on. The two foremost
did reach the higher ground and there formed
squares, general Foy being in the one, and general Chemineau in the other; but the last regiment
when half-way up, seeing Bock's dragoons galloping hard on, faced about and being still in column
commenced a disorderly fire. The two squares already formed above, also plied their muskets with
far greater effect ; and as the Germans, after crossing

the Almar stream, had to pass a turn of narrow
road, and then to clear some rough ground before
they could range their squadrons on a charging
front, the troopers dropt fast under the fire.
By two's, by three's, by ten's, by twenties they
fell, but the rest keeping together, surmounted
the difficulties of the ground, and hurtling on the
column went clean through it ; then the squares
above retreated and several hundred prisoners were
made by these able and daring horsemen.

This charge had been successful even to wonder, the joyous victors standing in the midst of
their captives and of thousands of admiring friends
seemed invincible ; yet those who witnessed the
scene, nay the actors themselves remained with the
conviction of this military truth, that cavalry are
not able to cope with veteran infantry save by surprize. The hill of La Serna offered a frightful
spectacle of the power of the musket, that queen of
weapons, and the track of the Germans was marked
by their huge bodies. A few minutes only had the
combat lasted and above a hundred had fallen;
fifty-one were killed outright; and in several places
man and horse had died simultaneously, and so suddenly, that falling together on their sides they
appeared still alive, the horse's legs stretched out as
in movement, the rider's feet in the stirrup, his
bridle in hand, the sword raised to strike, and the
large hat fastened under the chin, giving to the
grim, but undistorted countenance, a supernatural
and terrible expression.

When the French main body found their rear-
guard attacked, they turned to its succour, but
seeing the light division coming up recommenced
the retreat and were followed to Nava de Sotroval.

Near that place Chauvel's horsemen joined them from the Duero, and covered the rear with such a resolute countenance that the allied cavalry, reduced in numbers and fatigued with continual fighting, did not choose to meddle again. Thus Clauzel carried his army clear off without further loss, and with such celerity, that his head-quarters were that night at Flores de Avila forty miles from the field of battle. After remaining a few hours there he crossed the Zapardiel, and would have halted the 24th, but the allied cavalry entered Cisla, and the march was then continued to Arevalo. This was a wonderful retreat, and the line was chosen with judgment, for Wellington naturally expected the French army would have made for Tordesillas instead of the Adaja. The pursuit was however somewhat slack, for on the very night of the action, the British left wing, being quite fresh, could have ascended the Tormes and reached the Almar before day-light, or, passing at Huerta, have marched by Ventosa to Peneranda; but the vigorous following of a beaten enemy was never a prominent characteristic of Lord Wellington's campaigns in the Peninsula.

The 25th the allied army halted on the Zapardiel, and Adaja rivers, to let the commissariat, which had been sent to the rear the morning of the battle, come up. Meanwhile the king having quitted Madrid with fourteen thousand men on the 21st reached the Adaja and pushed his cavalry towards SeePlan3. Fontiveros; he was at Blasco Sancho the 24th, within a few hours' march of Arevalo, and consequently able to effect a junction with Clauzel, yet he did not hurry his march, for he knew only of the advance upon Salamanca not of the defeat, and

having sent many messengers to inform Marmont of CHAP. IV.
his approach, concluded that general would await
his arrival. The next day he received letters from 1812. July.
the duke of Ragusa and Clauzel, dated Arevalo, King's correspon-
describing the battle, and telling him that the de- dence, MSS.'
feated army must pass the Duero immediately to
save the depôt of Valladolid, and to establish new
communications with the army of the north. Those
generals promised however to halt behind that river,
if possible, until the king could receive reinforcements from Suchet and Soult.

Joseph by a rapid movement upon Arevalo could
still have effected a junction, but he immediately
made a forced march to Espinar, leaving in Blasco
Sancho two officers and twenty-seven troopers, who
were surprised and made prisoners on the evening
of the 25th by a corporal's patrole ; Clauzel at the
same time marched upon Valladolid, by Olmedo,
thus abandoning Zamora, Toro, and Tordesillas,
with their garrisons, to the allies. Wellington immediately brought Santo Cildes, who was now upon
the Esla with eight thousand Gallicians, to the right
bank of the Duero, across which river he communicated by Castro Nuño with the left of the allies
which was then upon the Zapardiel.

The 27th the British whose march had become
more circumspect from the vicinity of the king's
army entered Olmedo. At this place, general
Ferrey had died of his wounds, and the Spaniards
tearing his body from the grave were going to mu-
tilate it, when the soldiers of the light division who
had so often fought against this brave man rescued
his corpse, remade his grave and heaped rocks upon
it for more security, though with little need ; for the
Spaniards, with whom the sentiment of honor is

always strong when not stifled by the violence of their passions, applauded the action.

On the 26th Clauzel, finding the pursuit had slackened, sent Colonel Fabvier to advise the king of it, and then sending his own right wing across the Duero, by the ford near Boecillo, to cover the evacuation of Valladolid, marched with the other wing towards the bridge of Tudela; he remained however still on the left bank, in the hope that Fabvier's mission would bring the king back. Joseph who had already passed the Puerta de Guadarama immediately repassed it without delay and made a flank movement to Segovia, which he reached the 27th, and pushed his cavalry to Santa Maria de Nieva. Here he remained until the 31st expecting Clauzel would join him, for he resolved not to quit his hold of the passes over the Guadarama, nor to abandon his communication with Valencia and Andalusia. But Wellington brought Santo Cildes over the Duero to the Zapardiel, and crossing the Eresma and Ciga rivers himself, with the first and light divisions and the cavalry, had obliged Clauzel to retire over the Duero in the night of the 29th; and the next day the French general whose army was very much discouraged, fearing that Wellington would gain Aranda and Lerma while the Gallicians seized Dueñas and Torquemada, retreated in three columns by the valleys of the Arlanza, the Duero and the Esquiva towards Burgos.

The English general entered Valladolid amidst the rejoicings of the people and there captured seventeen pieces of artillery, considerable stores, and eight hundred sick and wounded men ; three hundred other prisoners were taken by the Partida chief Marquinez, and a large French convoy intended for Andalusia returned to Burgos. While the left wing of the allies pursued the enemy up the Arlanza, Wellington, marching with the right wing against the king, reached Cuellar the 1st of August; on the same day the garrison of Tordesillas surrendered to the Gallicians, and Joseph having first dismantled the castle of Segovia and raised a contribution of money and church plate retreated through the Puerta de Guadarama, leaving a rear-guard of cavalry which escaped by the Ildefonso pass on the approach of the allied horsemen. Thus the army of the centre was irrevocably separated from the army of Portugal, the operations against the latter were terminated, and new combinations were made conformable to the altered state of affairs; but to understand these it is necessary to look at the transactions in other parts of the Peninsula.

Welling-
ton's des-
patch.

In Estremadura, after Drouet's retreat to Azagua, Hill placed a strong division at Merida ready to cross the Tagus, but no military event occurred until the 24th of July, when general Lallemand, with three regiments of cavalry pushed back some Portuguese horsemen from Ribera to Villa Franca. He was attacked in front by general Long, while general Slade menaced his left, but he succeeded in repassing the defile of Ribera; Long then turned him by both flanks, and aided by Lefebre's horse artillery, drove him with the loss of fifty men and many horses upon Llera, a distance of twenty miles. Drouet, desirous to retaliate, immediately executed a flank march towards Merida, and Hill fearing for his detachments there made a corresponding movement, whereupon the French general returned to the Serena; but though he received

See Chap.
IV. Book
XVIII.

BOOK
XVIII.
————
1812.
August.
Intercep-
ted corres-
pondence.

positive orders from Soult to give battle no action
followed and the affairs of that part of the Peninsula remained balanced.

In Andalusia, Ballesteros surprised colonel Beau-
vais, at Ossuna, took three hundred prisoners and
destroyed the French dépôt there. After this he
moved against Malaga, and was opposed by general Laval in front, while general Villatte, detached
from the blockade of Cadiz, cut off his retreat to
San Roque. The road to Murcia was still open to
him, but his rashness, though of less consequence
since the battle of Salamanca, gave Wellington
great disquietude, and the more so that Joseph
O'Donel had just sustained a serious defeat near Alicant. This disaster, which shall be described in a
more fitting place, was however in some measure
counterbalanced by the information, that the revived
expedition from Sicily had reached Majorca,
where it had been reinforced by Whittingham's division, and by the stores and guns sent from Portugal to Gibraltar. It was known also, that in the
northern provinces Popham's armament had drawn
all Caffarelli's troops to the coast, and although the
littoral warfare was not followed up the French
were in confusion and the diversion complete.

In Castile the siege of Astorga still lingered,
but the division of Santo Cildes, seven thousand
strong, was in communication with Wellington,
Silveira's militia were on the Duero, Clauzel had
retreated to Burgos, and the king joined by two
thousand men from Suchet's army, could concentrate twenty thousand to dispute the passes of the
Guadarama. Hence Wellington, having nothing
immediate to fear from Soult, nor from the army
of Portugal, nor from the army of the north, nor

from Suchet, menaced as that marshal was by the
Sicilian expedition, resolved to attack the king in
preference to following Clauzel. The latter general
could not be pursued without exposing Salamanca
and the Gallicians to Joseph, who was strong in
cavalry ; but the monarch could be assailed without
risking much in other quarters, seeing that Clauzel
could not be very soon ready to renew the campaign,
and it was expected Castaños would reduce Astorga
in a few days which would give eight thousand additional men to the field army. Moreover a strong
British division could be spared to cooperate with
Santo Cildes, Silveira, and the Partidas, in the watching of the beaten army of Portugal while Wellington
gave the king a blow in the field, or forced him to
abandon Madrid ; and it appeared probable that the
moral effect of regaining the capital would excite
the Spaniards' energy every where, and would prevent Soult from attacking Hill. If he did attack
him, the allies by choosing this line of operations,
would be at hand to give succour.

These reasons being weighed, Wellington posted
general Clinton at Cuellar with the sixth division,
which he increased to eight thousand men by the
addition of some sickly regiments and by Anson's
cavalry ; Santo Cildes also was put in communication
with him, and the Partidas of Marquinez, Saornil,
and El Principe agreed to act with Anson on a
prescribed plan. Thus exclusive of Silveira's militia, and of the Gallicians about Astorga, eighteen
thousand men were left on the Duero, and the English general was still able to march against Joseph
with twenty-eight thousand old troops, exclusive of
Carlos D'España's Spaniards. He had also assurance from lord Castlereagh, that a considerable

sum in hard money, to be followed by other remittances, had been sent from England, a circumstance of the utmost importance because grain could be purchased in Spain at one third the cost of bringing it up from Portugal.

Meanwhile the king, who had regained Madrid, expecting to hear that ten thousand of the army of the south were at Toledo, received letters from Soult positively refusing to send that detachment; and from Clausel, saying that the army of Portugal was in full retreat to Burgos. This retreat he regarded as a breach of faith, because Clausel had promised to hold the line of the Duero if Wellington marched upon Madrid; but Joseph was unable to appreciate Wellington's military combinations; he did not perceive, that, taking advantage of his central position, the English general, before he marched against Madrid, had forced Clausel to abandon the Duero to seek some safe and distant point to re-organize his army. Nor was the king's perception of his own situation much clearer. He had the choice of several lines of operations; that is, he might defend the passes of the Guadarama while his court and enormous convoys evacuated Madrid and marched either upon Zaragoza, Valencia or Andalusia; or he might retire, army and convoy together, in one of those directions.

Rejecting the defence of the passes, lest the allies should then march by their right to the Tagus, and so intercept his communication with the south, he resolved to direct his march towards the Morena, and he had from Segovia sent Soult orders to evacuate Andalusia and meet him on the frontier of La Mancha; but to avoid the disgrace of flying before a detachment, he occupied the Escurial

mountain, and placed his army across the roads
leading from the passes of the Guadarama to Madrid. While in this position Wellington's advanced
guard, composed of D'Urban's Portuguese a troop
of horse artillery and a battalion of infantry, passed
the Guadarama, and the 10th the whole army was
over the mountains. Then the king, retaining
only eight thousand men in position, sent the rest of
his troops to protect the march of his court, which
quitted Madrid the same day, with two or three
thousand carriages of different kinds and nearly
twenty thousand persons of all ages and sexes.

The 11th D'Urban drove back Trielhard's cavalry
posts, and entered Majadahonda, whilst some German infantry, Bock's heavy cavalry, and a troop of
horse artillery, occupied Las Rozas about a mile
in his rear. In the evening, Trielhard, reinforced
by Schiazzetti's Italian dragoons and the lancers of
Berg, returned, whereupon D'Urban called up the
horse artillery and would have charged the enemy's
leading squadrons, but the Portuguese cavalry fled.
The artillery officer thus abandoned, made a vigorous effort to save his guns, yet three of them being
overturned on the rough ground were taken, and the
victorious cavalry passed through Majadahonda in
pursuit. The German dragoons, although surprised
in their quarters, mounted and stopped the leading
French squadrons until Schiazzetti's Italians came
up, when the fight was like to end badly ; but Ponsonby's cavalry and the seventh division arrived, and
Trielhard immediately abandoned Majadahonda,
leaving the captured guns behind him, yet carrying
away prisoners, the Portuguese general Visconde de
Barbacena, the colonel of the German cavalry, and
others of less rank. The whole loss of the allies

was above two hundred, and when the infantry
passed through Rozas, a few hours after the combat,
the German dead were lying thickly in the streets,
many of them in their shirts and trousers, and thus
stretched across the sills of the doors, they furnished
proof at once of the suddenness of the action and of
their own bravery. Had the king been prepared to
follow up this blow with his whole force the allies
must have suffered severely, for Wellington, trusting to the advanced guard, had not kept his divisions very close together.

After this combat the king retired to Valdemoro
where he met his convoy from Madrid, and when
the troops of the three different nations forming his
army thus came together, a horrible confusion
arose; the convoy was plundered, and the miserable
people who followed the court, were made a prey
by the licentious soldiers. Marshal Jourdan, a man
at all times distinguished for the noblest sentiments,
immediately threw himself into the midst of the
disorderly troops, and aided by the other generals,
with great personal risk arrested the mischief, and
succeeded in making the multitude file over the
bridge of Aranjues. The procession was however
lugubrious and shocking, for the military line of
march was broken by crowds of weeping women
and children and by despairing men, and courtiers
of the highest rank were to be seen in full dress,
desperately struggling with savage soldiers for the
possession of even the animals on which they were
endeavouring to save their families. The cavalry
of the allies could have driven the whole before
them into the Tagus, yet Lord Wellington did not
molest them. Either from ignorance of their situation, or what is more probable compassionating

their misery, and knowing that the troops by abandoning the convoy could easily escape over the river, he would not strike where the blow could only fall on helpless people without affecting the military operations. Perhaps also he thought it wise to leave Joseph the burthen of his court.

In the evening of the 13th the whole multitude was over the Tagus, the garrisons of Aranjues and Toledo joined the army, order was restored, and the king received letters from Soult and Suchet. The first named marshal opposed the evacuation of Andalusia; the second gave notice, that the Sicilian expedition had landed at Alicant, and that a considerable army was forming there. Then irritated by Soult and alarmed for the safety of Suchet, the king relinquished his march towards the Morena and commenced his retreat to Valencia. The 15th the advanced guard moved with the sick and wounded, who were heaped on country cars, and the main body of the convoy followed under charge of the infantry, while the cavalry, spreading to the right and left, endeavoured to collect provisions. But the people, remembering the wanton devastation committed a few months before by Montbrun's troops, on their return from Alicant, fled with their property; and as it was the hottest time of the year, and the deserted country was sandy and without shade, this march, of one hundred and fifty miles to Almanza, was one of continual suffering. The Partida chief Chaleco hovered constantly on the flanks and rear, killing without mercy all persons, civil or military, who straggled or sunk from exhaustion; and while this disastrous journey was in progress, another misfortune befel the French on the side of Requeña. For the hussars and infantry belonging to

Suchet's army, having left Madrid to succour Cuenca
before the king returned from Segovia, carried off
the garrison of that place in despite of the Empecinado, and made for Valencia; but Villa Campa
crossing their march on the 25th of August, at the
passage of a river, near Utiel, took all their baggage, their guns, and three hundred men. And
after being driven away from Cuenca the Empecinado invested Guadalaxara where the enemy had
left a garrison of seven hundred men.

Wellington seeing that the king had crossed the
Tagus in retreat entered Madrid, a very memorable
event were it only from the affecting circumstances
attending it. He, a foreigner and marching at the
head of a foreign army, was met and welcomed to
the capital of Spain by the whole remaining population. The multitude who before that hour had
never seen him, came forth to hail his approach,
not with feigned enthusiasm, not with acclamations
extorted by the fear of a conqueror's power, nor yet
excited by the natural proneness of human nature
to laud the successful, for there was no tumultuous
exultation; famine was amongst them, and long-
endured misery had subdued their spirits, but
with tears, and every other sign of deep emotion,
they crowded around his horse, hung upon his stirrups, touched his clothes, or throwing themselves
upon the earth, blessed him aloud as the friend of
Spain. His triumph was as pure, and glorious, as
it was uncommon, and he felt it to be so.

Madrid was however still disturbed by the presence of the enemy. The Retiro contained enormous stores, twenty thousand stand of arms, more
than one hundred and eighty pieces of artillery, and
the eagles of two French regiments, and it had a gar-

rison of two thousand fighting men, besides invalids and followers, but its inherent weakness was soon made manifest. The works consisted of an interior fort called La China, with an exterior entrenchment; but the fort was too small, the entrenchment too large, and the latter could be easily deprived of water. In the lodgings of a French officer also was found an order, directing the commandant to confine his real defence to the fort, and accordingly, in the night of the 13th, being menaced, he abandoned the entrenchment, and the next day accepted honourable terms, because La China was so contracted and filled with combustible buildings, that his fine troops would with only a little firing have been smothered in the ruins; yet they were so dissatisfied that many broke their arms and their commander was like to have fallen a victim to their wrath. They were immediately sent to Portugal, and French writers with too much truth assert, that the escort basely robbed and murdered many of the prisoners. This disgraceful action was perpetrated, either at Avila or on the frontier of Portugal, wherefore the British troops, who furnished no escorts after the first day's march from Madrid, are guiltless.

Coincident with the fall of the Retiro was that of Guadalaxara, which surrendered to the Empecinado. This mode of wasting an army, and its resources, was designated by Napoleon as the most glaring and extraordinary of all the errors committed by the king and by Marmont. And surely it was so. For including the garrisons of Toro, Tordesillas, Zamora and Astorga, which were now blockaded, six thousand men had been delivered, as it were bound, to the allies, and with them, stores and equipments sufficient for a new

army. These forts had been designed by the
emperor to resist the partidas, but his lieutenants
exposed them to the British army, and thus the
positive loss of men from the battle of Salamanca
was doubled.

Napoleon had notice of Marmont's defeat as early
as the 2d of September, a week before the great
battle of Borodino ; the news was carried by colonel
Fabvier, who made the journey from Valladodid in
one course, and having fought on the 22d of July
at the Arapiles, was wounded on the heights of
Moskowa the 7th of September ! However, the
duke of Ragusa, suffering alike in body and in
mind, had excused himself with so little strength,
or clearness, that the emperor contemptuously re-
marking, that the despatch contained more com-
plicate stuffing than a clock, desired his war minister
to demand, why Marmont had delivered battle
without the orders of the king ? why he had not
made his operations subservient to the general
plan of the campaign ? why he broke from defensive
into offensive operations before the army of the
centre joined him ? why he would not even wait two
days for Chauvel's cavalry, which he knew were
close at hand ? " From personal vanity," said the
emperor, with seeming sternness, " the duke of
Ragusa has sacrificed the interests of his country,
and the good of my service, he is guilty of the
crime of insubordination, and is the author of all
this misfortune."

But Napoleon's wrath so just, and apparently so
dangerous, could not, even in its first violence,
overpower his early friendship. With a kindness,
the recollection of which must now pierce Marmont's
inmost soul, twice, in the same letter, he desired

that these questions might not even be put to his
unhappy lieutenant until his wounds were cured
and his health re-established.   Nor was this generous feeling shaken by the arrival of the king's
agent, colonel Désprez, who reached Moscow the
18th of October, just after Murat had lost a battle
at the outposts and when all hopes of peace with
Russia were at an end.   Joseph's dispatches bitter
against all the generals, were especially so against
Marmont and Soult; the former for having lost the
battle, the latter because of his resistance to the
royal plan.   The recal of the duke of Dalmatia
was demanded imperatively, because he had written
a letter to the emperor, extremely offensive to the
king; and it was also hinted, that Soult designed to
make himself king of Andalusia.   Idle stories of that
marshal's ambition seem always to have been resorted
to, when his skilful plans were beyond the military
judgement of ordinary generals ; but Marmont was
deeply sunk in culpable misfortune, and the king's
complaints against him were not unjust.   Napoleon had however then seen Wellington's dispatch,
which was more favourable to the duke of Ragusa,
than Joseph's report ; for the latter was founded on
a belief, that the unfortunate general, knowing the
army of the centre was close at hand, would not
wait for it ; whereas the partidas had intercepted
so many of Joseph's letters, it is doubtful if any
reached Marmont previous to the battle.   It was in
vain therefore, that Desprez pressed the king's
discontent on the emperor ; that great man, with
unerring sagacity, had already disentangled the
truth, and Desprez was thus roughly interrogated as
to the conduct of his master.

Why was not the army of the centre in the field

a month sooner to succour Marmont? Why was
the emperor's example, when, in a like case, he
marched from Madrid against Sir John Moore,
forgotten? Why, after the battle, was not the
Duero passed, and the beaten troops rallied on the
army of the centre? Why were the passes of the
Guadarama so early abandoned? Why was the
Tagus crossed so soon? Finally, why were the
stores and gun-carriages in the Retiro not burnt,
the eagles and the garrison carried off?

To these questions the king's agent could only
reply by excuses which must have made the energetic
emperor smile ; but when, following his instructions,
Desprez harped upon Soult's demeanour, his designs
in Andalusia, and still more upon the letter so personally offensive to the king, and which shall be
noticed hereafter, Napoleon replied sharply, that he
could not enter into such pitiful disputes while he
was at the head of five hundred thousand men
and occupied with such immense operations. With
respect to Soult's letter, he said he knew his brother's real feelings, but those who judged Joseph by
his language could only think with Soult, whose
suspicions were natural and partaken by the other
generals ; wherefore he would not, by recalling
him, deprive the armies in Spain of the only military
head they possessed. And then in ridicule of
Soult's supposed treachery, he observed, that the
king's fears on that head must have subsided, as the
English newspapers said the duke of Dalmatia was
evacuating Andalusia, and he would of course unite
with Suchet and with the army of the centre to
retake the offensive.

The emperor, however, admitted all the evils
arising from these disputes between the generals and

the king, but said that at such a distance he could not
give precise orders for their conduct. He had foreseen the mischief he observed, and regretted more
than ever that Joseph had disregarded his counsel
not to return to Spain in 1811, and thus saying he
closed the conversation, but this expression about
Joseph not returning to Spain is very remarkable. Napoleon spoke of it as of a well known
fact, yet Joseph's letters shew that he not only
desired but repeatedly offered to resign the crown
of Spain and live a private man in France ! Did
the emperor mean that he wished his brother to
remain a crowned guest at Paris ? or had some
subtle intriguers misrepresented the brothers to each
other ? The noblest buildings are often defiled in
secret by vile and creeping things.

OBSERVATIONS.

1°. *Menace your enemy's flanks, protect your
own, and be ready to concentrate on the important
points :*

These maxims contain the whole spirit of Napoleon's instructions to his generals, after Badajos
was succoured in 1811. At that time he ordered the
army of Portugal to occupy the valley of the Tagus
and the passes of the Gredos mountains, in which
position it covered Madrid, and from thence it
could readily march to aid either the army of the
south, or the army of the north. Dorsenne, who
commanded the latter, could bring twenty-six thousand men to Ciudad Rodrigo, and Soult could
bring a like number to Badajos, but Wellington

could not move against one or the other without
having Marmont upon his flank; he could not
move against Marmont, without having the others
on both flanks, and he could not turn his opponent's
flanks save from the ocean. If notwithstanding
this combination he took Ciudad Rodrigo and
Badajos, it was by surprise, and because the
French did not concentrate on the important
points, which proved indeed his superiority to the
executive general opposed to him but in no manner affected the principle of Napoleon's plan.

Again, when the preparations for the Russian
war had weakened the army of the north, the
emperor, giving Marmont two additional divisions,
ordered him to occupy Castile, not as a defensive
position, but as a central offensive one from whence
he could keep the Gallicians in check, and by
prompt menacing movements, prevent Wellington
from commencing serious operations elsewhere.
This plan also had reference to the maxim respecting flanks. For Marmont was forbidden to
invade Portugal while Wellington was on the
frontier of Beira, that is when he could not assail
him in flank; and he was directed to guard the
Asturias carefully as a protection to the great line
of communication with France; in May also he
was rebuked for having withdrawn Bonet from
Oviedo, and for delaying to reoccupy the Asturias
when the incursion against Beira terminated. But
neither then nor afterwards did the duke of Ragusa
comprehend the spirit of the Emperor's views, and
that extraordinary man, whose piercing sagacity
seized every chance of war, was so disquieted by
his lieutenant's want of perception, that all the

pomp, and all the vast political and military combinations of Dresden, could not put it from his
thoughts.

" Twice," said he, " has the duke of Ragusa
placed an interval of thirty leagues between his
army and the enemy, contrary to all the rules of
war ; the English general goes where he will, the
French general loses the initial movements and is
of no weight in the affairs of Spain.   Biscay and
the north are exposed by the evacuation of the
Asturias; Santona and St. Sebastian are endangered, and the guerillas communicate freely with
the coast.   If the duke of Ragusa has not kept
some bridges on the Agueda, he cannot know what
Wellington is about, and he will retire before light
cavalry instead of operating so as to make the
English general concentrate his whole army.   The
false direction already given to affairs by marshal
Marmont, makes it necessary that Caffarelli should
keep a strong corps always in hand ; that the commander of the reserve, at Bayonne, should look to
the safety of St. Sebastian, holding three thousand
men always ready to march ; finally that the provisional battalions, and troops from the depôts of
the interior, should immediately reinforce the reserve at Bayonne, be encamped on the Pyrennees,
and exercised and formed for service.   *If Marmont's oversights continue, these troops will prevent
the disasters from becoming extreme.*"

Napoleon was supernaturally gifted in warlike
matters.   It has been recorded of Cæsar's generalship, that he foretold the cohorts mixed with his
cavalry would be the cause of victory at Pharsalia.
But this letter was written by the French emperor
on the 28th of May before the allies were even

collected on the Agueda, and when a hundred
thousand French troops were between the English
general and Bayonne, and yet its prescience was
vindicated at Burgos in October !

2°. To fulfil the conditions of the emperor's
design, Marmont should have adopted Soult's recommendation, that is, leaving one or two divisions
on the Tormes he should have encamped near
Baños, and pushed troops towards the upper
Agueda to watch the movements of the allies.
Caffarelli's divisions could then have joined those
on the Tormes, and thus Napoleon's plan for 1811
would have been exactly renewed ; Madrid would
have been covered, a junction with the king would
have been secured, Wellington could scarcely have
moved beyond the Agueda, and the disaster of
Salamanca would have been avoided.

The duke of Ragusa, apparently because he
would not have the king in his camp, run counter
both to the emperor and to Soult.   1°. He kept no
troops on the Agueda, which might be excused
on the ground that the feeding of them there was
beyond his means ; but then he did not concentrate
behind the Tormes to sustain his forts, neither did
he abandon his forts, when he abandoned Salamanca, and thus eight hundred men were sacrificed
merely to secure the power of concentrating behind the Duero. 2°. He adopted a line of operations perpendicular to the allies' front, instead of
lying on their flank ; he abandoned sixty miles of
country between the Tormes and the Agueda, and
he suffered Wellington to take the initial movements of the campaign. 3°. He withdrew Bonet's
division from the Asturias, whereby he lost Caffarelli's support and realized the emperor's fears

for the northern provinces. It is true that he regained the initial power, by passing the Duero on
the 18th, and had he deferred the passage until the
king was over the Guadarama, Wellington must
have gone back upon Portugal with some shew of
dishonour if not great loss. But if Castaños, instead of remaining with fifteen thousand Gallicians,
before Astorga, a weak place with a garrison of
only twelve hundred men, had blockaded it with
three or four thousand, and detached Santocildes
with eleven or twelve thousand down the Esla to
co-operate with Silveira and D'Urban, sixteen thousand men would have been acting upon Marmont's
right flank in June; and as Bonet did not join until
the 8th of July the line of the Duero would
scarcely have availed the French general.

3°. The secret of Wellington's success is to be
found in the extent of country occupied by the
French armies, and the impediments to their military communication. Portugal was an impregnable central position, from whence the English
general could rush out unexpectedly against any
point. This strong post was however of his own
making, he had chosen it, had fortified it, had
defended it, he knew its full value and possessed
quickness and judgement to avail himself of all
its advantages ; the battle of Salamanca was accidental in itself, but the tree was planted to bear
such fruit, and Wellington's profound combinations
must be estimated from the general result. He
had only sixty thousand disposable troops, and
above a hundred thousand French were especially
appointed to watch and controul him, yet he passed
the frontier, defeated forty-five thousand in a
pitched battle, and drove twenty thousand others

from Madrid in the greatest confusion, without
risking a single strategic point, of importance to
his own operations. His campaign up to the conquest of Madrid was therefore strictly in accord
with the rules of art, although his means and resources have been shewn to be precarious, shifting,
and uncertain. Indeed the want of money alone
would have prevented him from following up his
victory if he had not persuaded the Spanish authorities, in the Salamanca country, to yield him the
revenues of the government in kind under a promise of repayment at Cadiz. No general was ever
more entitled to the honours of victory.

4°. The success of Wellington's daring advance
would seem to indicate a fault in the French plan
of invasion. The army of the south, numerous, of
approved valour and perfectly well commanded, was
yet of so little weight in this campaign as to prove
that Andalusia was a point pushed beyond the true
line of operations. The conquest of that province
in 1811 was an enterprize of the king's, on which
he prided himself, yet it seems never to have been
much liked by Napoleon, although he did not absolutely condemn it. The question was indeed a
very grave one. While the English general held
Portugal, and while Cadiz was unsubdued, Andalusia was a burthen, rather than a gain. It would
have answered better, either to have established
communications with France by the southern line
of invasion, which would have brought the enterprize within the rules of a methodical war, or to
have held the province partially by detachments,
keeping the bulk of the army of the south in Estremadura, and thus have strengthened the northern
line of invasion. For in Estremadura, Soult would

have covered the capital, and have been more strictly
connected with the army of the centre; and his
powerful cooperation with Massena in 1810 would
probably have obliged the English general to quit
Portugal. The same result could doubtless have
been obtained by reinforcing the army of the south,
with thirty or forty thousand men, but it is questionable if Soult could have fed such a number;
and in favour of the invasion of Andalusia it may
be observed, that Seville was the great arsenal of
Spain, that a formidable power might have been
established there by the English without abandoning Portugal, that Cadiz would have compensated
for the loss of Lisbon, and finally that the English
ministers were not at that time determined to defend Portugal.

5°. When the emperor declared that Soult possessed the only military head in the Peninsula he referred to a proposition made by that marshal which
shall be noticed in the next chapter; but having
regard merely to the disputes between the duke of
Dalmatia, Marmont, and the king, Suchet's talents
not being in question, the justice of the remark
may be demonstrated. Napoleon always enforced
with precept and example, the vital military principle of concentration on the important points; but
the king and the marshals, though harping continually upon this maxim, desired to follow it out, each
in his own sphere. Now to concentrate on a wrong
point, is to hurt yourself with your own sword,
and as each French general desired to be strong,
the army at large was scattered instead of being
concentrated.

The failure of the campaign was, by the king,
attributed to Soult's disobedience, inasmuch as the

passage of the Tagus by Drouet would have enabled the army of the centre to act, before Palombini's division arrived. But it has been shewn that
Hill could have brought Wellington an equal, or
superior reinforcement, in less time, whereby the
latter could either have made head until the French
dispersed for want of provisions, or, by a rapid
counter-movement, he could have fallen upon Andalusia. And if the king had menaced Ciudad Rodrigo in return it would have been no diversion, for
he had no battering train, still less could he have
revenged himself by marching on Lisbon, because
Wellington would have overpowered Soult and
established a new base at Cadiz, before such an
operation could become dangerous to the capital of
Portugal. Oporto might indeed have been taken,
yet Joseph would have hesitated to exchange Madrid for that city. But the ten thousand men
required of Soult by the king, on the 19th of June,
could have been at Madrid before August, and thus
the passes of the Guadarama could have been defended until the army of Portugal was reorganized!
Aye! but Hill could then have entered the valley of
the Tagus, or, being reinforced, could have invaded
Andalusia while Wellington kept the king's army in
check. It would appear therefore that Joseph's
plan of operations, if all its combinations had been
exactly executed, might have prevented Wellington's progress on some points, but to effect this the
French must have been concentrated in large
masses from distant places without striking any
decisive blow, which was the very pith and marrow
of the English general's policy. Hence it follows
that Soult made the true and Joseph the false application of the principle of concentration.

6°. If the king had judged his position truly he would have early merged the monarch in the general, exchanged the palace for the tent; he would have held only the Retiro and a few fortified posts in the vicinity of Madrid, he would have organized a good pontoon train and established his magazines in Segovia, Avila, Toledo, and Talavera; finally he would have kept his army constantly united in the field, and exercised his soldiers, either by opening good roads through the mountains, or in chasing the partidas, while Wellington remained quiet. Thus acting, he would have been always ready to march north or south, to succour any menaced point. By enforcing good order and discipline in his own army, he would also have given a useful example, and he could by vigilance and activity have ensured the preponderance of force in the field on whichever side he marched. He would thus have acquired the esteem of the French generals, and obtained their willing obedience, and the Spaniards would more readily have submitted to a warlike monarch. A weak man may safely wear an inherited crown, it is of gold and the people support it; but it requires the strength of a warrior to bear the weight of an usurped diadem, it is of iron.

7°. If Marmont and the king were at fault in the general plan of operations, they were not less so in the particular tactics of the campaign.

On the 18th of July the army of Portugal passed the Douro in advance. On the 30th it repassed that river in retreat, having, in twelve days, marched two hundred miles, fought three combats, and a general battle. One field-marshal, seven generals, twelve thousand five hundred men and officers had Appendix, Nos. 19, 20.

been killed, wounded, or taken; and two eagles, besides those taken in the Retiro, several standards, twelve guns, and eight carriages, exclusive of the artillery and stores captured at Valladolid, fell into the victors' hands. In the same period, the allies marched one hundred and sixty miles, and had one field-marshal, four generals, and somewhat less than six thousand officers and soldiers killed or wounded.

This comparison furnishes the proof of Wellington's sagacity, when he determined not to fight except at great advantage. The French army, although surprised in the midst of an evolution and instantly swept from the field, killed and wounded six thousand of the allies; the eleventh and sixty-first regiments of the sixth division had not together more than one hundred and sixty men and officers left standing at the end of the battle; twice six thousand then would have fallen in a more equal contest, the blow would have been less decisive, and as Chauvel's cavalry and the king's army were both at hand, a retreat into Portugal would probably have followed a less perfect victory. Wherefore this battle ought not, and would not have been fought, but for Marmont's false movement on the 22d. Yet it is certain that if Wellington had retired without fighting, the murmurs of his army, already louder than was seemly, would have been heard in England, and if an accidental shot had terminated his career all would have terminated. The cortez, ripe for a change, would have accepted the intrusive king, and the American war, just declared against England, would have rendered the complicated affairs of Portugal so extremely embarrassed that no new man could have continued the contest. Then the cries of disappointed politicians would have been raised. Wellington, it would have been said, Wellington, desponding, and distrusting his brave troops, dared not venture a battle on even terms, hence these misfortunes! His name would have been made, as Sir John Moore's was, a butt for the malice and falsehood of faction, and his military genius would have been measured by the ignorance of his detractors.

8°. In the battle Marmont had about forty-two thousand sabres and bayonets; Wellington who had received some detachments on the 19th had above forty-six thousand, but the excess was principally Spanish. The French had seventy-four guns, the Appendix,
Nos.19,20. allies, including a Spanish battery, had only sixty pieces. Thus, Marmont, over-matched in cavalry and infantry, was superior in artillery, and the fight would have been most bloody, if the generals had been equal, for courage and strength were in even balance until Wellington's genius struck the beam. Scarcely can a fault be detected in his conduct. It might indeed be asked why the cavalry reserves were not, after Le Marchant's charge, brought up closer to sustain the fourth, fifth, and sixth divisions and to keep off Boyer's dragoons, but it would seem ill to cavil at an action which was described at the time by a French officer, as the " *beating of forty thousand men in forty minutes.*"

9°. The battle of Salamanca remarkable in many points of view, was not least so in this that it was the first decided victory gained by the allies in the Peninsula. In former actions the French had been repulsed, here they were driven headlong as it were before a mighty wind, without help or stay, and the results were proportionate. Joseph's secret nego-ciations with the Cortez were crushed, his partizans in every part of the Peninsula were abashed, and the sinking spirit of the Catalans was revived ; the clamours of the opposition in England were checked, the provisional government of France was dismayed, the secret plots against the French in Germany were resuscitated, and the shock, reaching even to Moscow, heaved and shook the colossal structure of Napoleon's power to its very base.

Nevertheless Salamanca was as most great battles are, an accident ; an accident seized upon with astonishing vigour and quickness, but still an accident.   Even its results were accidental, for the French could never have repassed the Tormes as an army, if Carlos D'España had not withdrawn the garrison from Alba, and hidden the fact from Wellington ; and this circumstance alone would probably have led to the ruin of the whole campaign, but for another of those chances, which, recurring so frequently in war, render bad generals timid, and make great generals trust their fortune under the most adverse circumstances.   This is easily shewn. Joseph was at Blasco Sancho on the 24th, and notwithstanding his numerous cavalry, the army of Portugal passed in retreat across his front at the distance of only a few miles, without his knowledge ; he thus missed one opportunity of effecting his junction with Clauzel.   On the 25th this junction could still have been made at Arevalo, and Wellington, as if to mock the king's generalship, halted that day behind the Zapardiel ; yet Joseph retreated towards the Guadarama, wrathful that Clauzel made no effort to join him, and forgetful that as a beaten and pursued army must march, it was for him to join Clauzel.   But the true cause of these errors was the different inclinations of the generals.   The king wished to draw Clauzel to Madríd, Clauzel desired to have the king behind the Duero, and if he had succeeded the probable result may be thus traced.

Clauzel during the first confusion wrote that only twenty thousand men could be reorganised, but in this number he did not include the stragglers and marauders who always take advantage of a defeat to seek their own interest ; a reference to the French loss proves that there were nearly thirty thousand fighting men left, and in fact Clauzel did in a fortnight reorganise twenty thousand infantry, two thousand cavalry and fifty guns, besides gaining a knowledge of five thousand stragglers and marauders. In fine no soldiers rally quicker after a defeat, than the French, and hence as Joseph brought to Blasco Sancho thirty guns and fourteen thousand men of which above two thousand were horsemen, forty thousand infantry, and more than six thousand cavalry with a powerful artillery, might then have been rallied behind the Duero, exclusive of Caffarelli's divisions. Nor would Madrid have been meanwhile exposed to an insurrection, nor to the operation of a weak detachment from Wellington's army ; for the two thousand men, sent by Suchet, had arrived in that capital on the 30th, and there were in the several fortified points of the vicinity, six or seven thousand other troops who could have been united at the Retiro, to protect that depôt and the families attached to the intrusive court.

Thus Wellington without committing any fault, would have found a more powerful army than Marmont's, again on the Duero, and capable of renewing the former operations with the advantage of former errors as warning beacons. But his own army would not have been so powerful as before, for the reinforcements sent from England did not even suffice to replace the current consumption of men; and neither the fresh soldiers nor the old Walcheren regiments were able to sustain the toil of the recent operations. Three thousand troops had joined since the battle, yet the general decrease, including the killed and wounded, was above eight thousand men, and the number of sick was rapidly augmenting from the extreme heat. It may therefore be said that if Marmont was stricken deeply by Wellington the king poisoned the wound. The English general had fore-calculated all these superior resources of the enemy, and it was only Marmont's flagrant fault, on the 22d, that could have wrung the battle from him; yet he fought it as if his genius disdained such trial of its strength. I saw him late in the evening of that great day, when the advancing flashes of cannon and musketry, stretching as far as the eye could command, shewed in the darkness how well the field was won; he was alone, the flush of victory was on his brow, and his eyes were eager and watchful, but his voice was calm, and even gentle. More than the rival of Marlborough, since he had defeated greater warriors than Marlborough ever encountered, with a prescient pride he seemed only to accept this glory, as an earnest of greater things.

BOOK XIX.

CHAPTER I.

As Wellington's operations had now deeply affected the French affairs in the distant provinces, it is necessary again to revert to the general progress of the war, lest the true bearings of his military policy should be overlooked. The battle of Salamanca, by clearing all the centre of Spain, had reduced the invasion to its original lines of operation. For Palombini's division having joined the army of the centre, the army of the Ebro was broken up ; Caffarelli had concentrated the scattered troops of the army of the north; and when Clauzel had led back the vanquished army of Portugal to Burgos, the whole French host was divided in two distinct parts, each having a separate line of communication with France, and a circuitous, uncertain, attenuated line of correspondence with each other by Zaragoza instead of a sure and short one by Madrid. But Wellington was also forced to divide his army in two parts, and though, by the advantage of his central position, he retained the initial power, both of movement and concentration, his lines of communication were become long, and weak because the enemy was powerful at either flank. Wherefore on his own simple strength in the centre of Spain he could not rely, and the diversions he had projected against the enemy's rear and flanks became more important than ever. To these we must now turn.

EASTERN OPERATIONS.

See Book
XVII.
Chap. II.
It will be recollected that the narrative of Catalonian affairs ceased at the moment when Decaen, after fortifying the coast line and opening new roads beyond the reach of shot from the English ships, was gathering the harvest of the interior. Lacy, inefficient in the field and universally hated, was thus confined to the mountain chain which separates the coast territory from the plains of Lerida, and from the Cerdaña. The insurrectionary

Captain
Adding-
ton's
correspon-
dence.
MSS.
spirit of the Catalonians was indeed only upheld by Wellington's successes, and by the hope of English succour from Sicily ; for Lacy, devoted to the republican party in Spain, had now been made captain general as well as commander-in-chief, and sought to keep down the people, who were generally of the priestly and royal faction. He publicly spoke of exciting a general insurrection, yet, in his intercourse with the English naval officers, avowed his wish to repress the patriotism of the Somatenes ; he was not ashamed to boast of his assassination plots, and received with honour, a man who had murdered the

History of
the conspi-
racies
against the
French
army in
Catalonia,
published
at
Barcelona,
1813.
aid-de-camp of Maurice Mathieu ; he sowed dissentions amongst his generals, intrigued against all of them in turn, and when Eroles and Manso, who were the people's favourites, raised any soldiers, he transferred the latter as soon as they were organized to Sarzfield's division, at the same time calumniating that general to depress his influence. He quarrelled incessantly with captain Codrington, and had no desire to see an English force in Catalonia lest a general insurrection should take place, for he feared

that the multitude once gathered and armed would
drive him from the province and declare for the opponents of the cortez. And in this view the constitution itself, although emanating from the cortez,
was long withheld from the Catalans, lest the newly
declared popular rights should interfere with the
arbitrary power of the chief.

Such was the state of the province when intelligence that the Anglo-Sicilian expedition had arrived
at Mahon, excited the hopes of the Spaniards and
the fears of the French. The coast then became the
great object of interest to both, and the Catalans
again opened a communication with the English
fleet by Villa Nueva de Sitjes, and endeavoured
to collect the grain of the Campo de Taragona.
Decaen, coming to meet Suchet who had arrived at
Reus with two thousand men, drove the Catalans to
the hills again; yet the Lerida district was thus
opened to the enterprises of Lacy, because it was at
this period that Reille had detached general Paris
from Zaragoza to the aid of Palombini; and that
Severoli's division was broken up to reinforce the
garrisons of Lerida, Taragona, Barcelona, and
Zaragoza. But the army of the Ebro being dissolved, Lacy resolved to march upon Lerida, where
he had engaged certain Spaniards in the French
service to explode the powder magazine when he
should approach; and this odious scheme, which
necessarily involved the destruction of hundreds of
his own countrymen, was vainly opposed by Eroles
and Sarzfield.

On the 12th of July, Eroles' division, that general
being absent, was incorporated with Sarzfield's and
other troops at Guisona, and the whole journeying
day and night reached Tremp on the 13th. Lacy

CHAP.
I.

1812.
July.

See Book
XVII.
Chap. II.

having thus turned Lerida, would have resumed the
march at mid-day, intending to attack the next
morning at dawn, but the men were without food,
and exhausted by fatigue, and fifteen hundred had
fallen behind. A council of war being then held,
Sarzfield, who thought the plot wild, would have
returned, observing that all communication with the
sea was abandoned, and the harvests of the Camps
de Taragona and Valls being left to be gathered by
the enemy, the loss of the corn would seriously
affect the whole principality. Displeased at the
remonstrance, Lacy immediately sent him back
to the plain of Urgel with some infantry and the
cavalry, to keep the garrison of Balaguer in check;
but in the night of the 16th when Sarzfield had
reached the bridge of Alentorna on the Segre, fresh
orders caused him to return to Limiana on the
Noguera. Meanwhile Lacy himself had advanced
by Agen towards Lerida, the explosion of the
magazine took place, many houses were thrown
down, two hundred inhabitants and one hundred
and fifty soldiers were destroyed ; two bastions fell,
and the place was laid open.

Henriod the governor, although ignorant of the
vicinity of the Spaniards, immediately manned the
breaches, the garrison of Balaguer, hearing the
explosion marched to his succour, and when the
Catalan troops appeared, the citizens enraged by
the destruction of their habitations aided the
French; Lacy then fled back to Tremp, bearing
the burthen of a crime which he had not feared
to commit, but wanted courage to turn to his
country's advantage. To lessen the odium thus
incurred, he insidiously attributed the failure to
Sarzfield's disobedience; and as that general, to

punish the people of Barbastro for siding with the French and killing twenty of his men, had raised a heavy contribution of money and corn in the district, he became so hateful, that some time after, when he endeavoured to raise soldiers in those parts, the people threw boiling water at him from the windows as he passed.

CHAP.
I.

1812.
July.

Captain
Codring-
ton's
Papers,
MSS.

Before this event Suchet had returned to Valencia, and Dacaen and Maurice Mathieu marched against colonel Green, who was entrenched in the hermitage of St. Dimas, one of the highest of the peaked rocks overhanging the convent of Montserrat. Manso immediately raised the Somatenes to aid Green, and as the latter had provisions the inaccessible strength of his post seemed to defy capture; yet he surrendered in twenty-four hours, and at a moment when the enemy, despairing of success, were going to relinquish the attack. He excused himself as being forced by his own people, but he signed the capitulation. Decaen then set fire to the convent of Montserrat and the flames seen for miles around was the signal that the warfare on that holy mountain was finished. After this the French general marched to Lerida to gather corn and Lacy again spread his troops in the mountains.

Idem.

Laffaille's
Campaigns
in Catalo-
nia.

During his absence Eroles had secretly been preparing a general insurrection to break out when the British army should arrive, and it was supposed that his object was to effect a change in the government of the province; for though Lacy himself again spoke of embodying the Somatenes if arms were given to him by Sir Edward Pellew, there was really no scarcity of arms, the demand was a deceit to prevent the muskets from being given to the people, and there was no levy. Hence

Codring-
ton's Pa-
pers, MSS.

the discontent increased and a general desire for
the arrival of the British troops became preva-
lent; the miserable people turned anxiously towards any quarter for aid, and this expression of
conscious helplessness was given in evidence by
the Spanish chiefs, and received as proof of enthusiasm by the English naval commanders, who
were more sanguine of success than experience
would warrant. All eyes were however directed
towards the ocean, the French in fear, the Catalans
in hope; and the British armament did appear off
Palamos, but after three days, spread its sails
again and steered for Alicant, leaving the principality stupified with grief and disappointment.

This unexpected event was the natural result of
previous errors on all sides, errors which invariably
attend warlike proceedings when not directed by
a superior genius, and even then not always to be
avoided. It has been shewn how ministerial vacillation marred lord William Bentinck's first intention of landing in person with ten or twelve thousand men on the Catalonian coast; and how after
much delay general Maitland had sailed to Palma
with a division of six thousand men, Calabrians,
Sicilians and others, troops of no likelihood save
that some three thousand British and Germans were
amongst them. This force was afterwards joined
by the transports from Portugal having engineers
and artillery officers on board, and that honoured
battering train which had shattered the gory walls of
Badajos. Wellington had great hopes of this expedition; he had himself sketched the general plan
of operations; and his own campaign had been conceived in the expectation, that lord William Bentinck, a general of high rank and reputation, with
ten thousand good troops, aided with at least as

many Spanish soldiers, disciplined under the two British officers Whittingham and Roche, would have early fallen on Catalonia to the destruction of Suchet's plans. And when this his first hope was quashed, he still expected that a force would be disembarked of strength, sufficient, in conjunction with the Catalan army, to take Taragona.

Roche's corps was most advanced in discipline, but the Spanish government delayed to place it under general Maitland, and hence it first sailed from the islands to Murcia, then returned without orders, again repaired to Murcia, and at the moment of general Maitland's arrival off Palamos, was, under the command of Joseph O'Donel, involved in a terrible catastrophe already alluded to and hereafter to be particularly narrated. Whittingham's levy remained, but when inspected by the quarter-mas-ter general Donkin it was found in a raw state, scarcely mustering four thousand effective men, amongst which were many French deserters from the island of Cabrera. The sumptuous clothing and equipments of Whittingham's and Roche's men, their pay regularly supplied from the British subsidy, and very much exceeding that of the other Spanish corps, excited envy and dislike; there was no public inspection, no check upon the expenditure, nor upon the delivery of the stores, and Roche's proceedings on this last head, whether justly or unjustly I know not, were very generally and severely censured. Whittingham acknowledged that he could not trust his people near the enemy without the aid of British troops, and though the captain-general Coupigny desired their departure, his opinion was against a descent in Catalonia. Maitland hesitated, but Sir Edward Pellew urged this descent so very strongly, that he finally assented

Gen. Donkin's papers, MSS.

BOOK
XIX.
———
1812.
August.
and reached Palamos with nine thousand men of all nations on the 31st of July, yet in some confusion as to the transport service, which the staff officers attributed to the injudicious meddling of the naval chiefs.

Maitland's first care was to open a communication with the Spanish commanders. Eroles came on board at once and vehemently and unceasingly urged an immediate disembarkation, declaring that the fate of Catalonia and his own existence depended upon it; the other generals shewed less eagerness, and their accounts differed greatly with respect to the relative means of the Catalans and the French. Lacy estimated the enemy's disposable troops at fifteen thousand, and his own at seven thousand infantry and three hundred cavalry; and even that number he said he could with difficulty feed or provide with ammunition. Sarzfield judged the French to be, exclusive of Suchet's moveable column, eighteen thousand infantry and five hundred cavalry; he thought it rash to invest Taragona with a less force, and that a free and constant communication with the fleet was absolutely essential in any operation. Eroles rated the enemy at thirteen thousand infantry and five hundred cavalry, including Suchet's column; but the reports of the deserters gave twenty-two thousand infantry, exclusive of Suchet's column and of the garrisons and Miguelettes in the enemy's service.

Notes by
general
Maitland,
MSS.
General
Donkin's
papers,
MSS.

No insurrection of the Somatenes had yet taken place, nor was there any appearance that such an event would happen, as the French were descried conducting convoys along the shore with small escorts, and concentrating their troops for battle without molestation. The engineers demanded from six to ten days to reduce Taragona after investment, and Decaen and Maurice Mathieu were then near Montserrat with seven or eight thousand good troops, which number could be doubled in a few days; the Catalans could not so soon unite and join Maitland's force, and there was a general, although apparently, an unjust notion abroad, that Lacy was a Frenchman at heart. It was feared also, that the Toulon fleet might come out and burn the transports at their anchorage during the siege, and thus Wellington's battering train and even the safety of the army would be involved in an enterprize promising little success. A full council of war was unanimous not to land, and the reluctance of the people to rise, attributed by captain Codrington to the machinations of traitors, was visible; Maitland also was farther swayed by the generous and just consideration, that as the Somatenes had not voluntarily taken arms, it would be cruel to excite them to such a step, when a few days might oblige him to abandon them to the vengeance of the enemy. Wherefore as Palamos appeared too strong for a sudden assault, the armament sailed towards Valencia with intent to attack that place, after a project, furnished by the quarter-master general Donkin and in unison with lord Wellington's plan of operations; but Maitland, during the voyage, changed his mind and proceeded at once to Alicant.

The Catalans were not more displeased than the British naval commanders at seeing the principality thus shaken off; yet the judgment of the latter seems to have been swayed partly from having given stronger hopes of assistance to the former than the circumstances would rigorously warrant; partly from that confidence, which inspired by con-

BOOK
XIX.
———
1812.
August

Captain
Codring-
ton's pa-
pers, MSS.
tinual success, is strength on their own element,
but rashness on shore. Captain Codrington, from
the great interest he took in the struggle, was
peculiarly discontented; yet his own description of
the state of Catalonia at the time, shows that his
hopes rested more on some vague notions of the
Somatenes' enthusiasm, than upon any facts which
a general ought to calculate upon. Lord Wellington
indeed said, that he could see no reason why the
plan he had recommended, should not have been
successful; an observation made, however, when he
was somewhat excited by the prospect of having
Suchet on his own hands, and probably under some
erroneous information. He had been deceived about
the strength of the forts at Salamanca, although
close to them; and as he had only just established
a sure channel of intelligence in Catalonia, it was
probable that he was also deceived with respect to
Taragona, which if not strong in regular works was
well provided and commanded by a very bold active
governor, and offered great resources in the facility
of making interior retrenchments.

The force of the Catalans lord Wellington knew
principally from sir Edward Pellew, who had derived
his information chiefly from Eroles, who very much
exaggerated it, and lessened the enemy's power in
proportion. And general Maitland could scarcely be
called a commander-in-chief, for lord William Bentinck forbade him to risk the loss of his division lest
Sicily itself should thereby be endangered; and to
avoid mischief from the winter season, he was instructed to quit the Spanish coast in the second week
of September. Lord William and lord Wellington
were therefore not agreed in the object to be attained.
The first considered the diversion on the Spanish

coast as secondary to the wants of Sicily, whereas
Wellington looked only to the great interests at
stake in the Peninsula, and thought Sicily in no
danger until the French should reinforce their army
in Calabria. He desired vigorous combined efforts
of the military and naval forces, to give a new aspect
to the war in Catalonia, and his plan was that
Taragona should be attacked ; if it fell the warfare
he said would be once more established on a good
base in Catalonia; if it was succoured by the concentration of the French troops, Valencia would
necessarily be weak, and the armament could then
proceed to attack that place, and if unsuccessful
return to assail Taragona again.

This was an excellent plan no doubt, but Napoleon never lost sight of that great principle of war,
so concisely expressed by Sertorius when he told
Pompey that a good general should look behind
him rather than before. The emperor acting on the
proverb that fortune favours the brave, often urged
his lieutenants to dare desperately with a few men
in the front, but he invariably covered their communications with heavy masses, and there is no
instance of his plan of invasion being shaken by a
flank or rear attack, except where his instructions
were neglected. His armies made what are called
points, in war, such as Massena's invasion of Portugal, Moncey's attack on Valencia, Dupont's on
Andalusia ; but the general plan of operation was
invariably supported by heavy masses protecting
the communications. Had his instructions, sent
from Dresden, been strictly obeyed, the walls of
Lerida and Taragona would have been destroyed,
and only the citadels of each occupied with small
garrisons easily provisioned for a long time. The

field army would thus have been increased by at least three thousand men, the moveable columns spared many harassing marches, and Catalonia would have offered little temptation for a descent.

But notwithstanding this error of Suchet, Maitland's troops were too few, and too ill-composed to venture the investment of Taragona. The imperial muster-rolls give more than eighty thousand men, including Reille's divisions at Zaragosa, for the armies of Aragon and Catalonia, and twenty-seven thousand of the first and thirty-seven thousand of the second, were actually under arms with the eagles ; wherefore to say that Decaen could have brought at once ten thousand men to the succour of Taragona, and, by weakening his garrisons, as many more in a very short time, is not to over-rate his power ; and this without counting Paris' brigade, three thousand strong, which belonged to Reille's division and was disposable. Suchet had just before come to Reus with two thousand select men of all arms, and as O'Donel's army had since been defeated near Alicant, he could have returned with a still greater force to oppose Maitland.

Now the English fleet was descried by the French off Palamos on the evening of the 31st of July, although it did not anchor before the 1st of August ; Decaen and Maurice Mathieu with some eight thousand disposable men were then between Montserrat and Barcelona, that is to say, only two marches from Taragona ; Lamarque with from four to five thousand, was between Palamos and Mataro, five marches from Taragona ; Quesnel with a like number was in the Cerdaña, being about seven marches off ; Suchet and Paris could have arrived in less than eight days, and from the garrisons, and minor posts, smaller succours might have been drawn; Tortoza alone could have furnished two thousand. But Lacy's division was at Vich, Sarzfield's at Villa Franca, Eroles' divided between Montserrat and Urgel, Milan's in the Grao D'Olot, and they required five days even to assemble; when united, they would not have exceeded seven thousand men, and with their disputing, captious generals, would have been unfit to act vigorously; nor could they have easily joined the allies without fighting a battle in which their defeat would have been certain.

Sarzfield judged that ten days at least were necessary to reduce Taragona, and positively affirmed that the army must be entirely fed from the fleet, as the country could scarcely supply the Catalonian troops alone. Thus Maitland would have had to land his men, his battering train and stores, and to form his investment, in the face of Decaen's power, or, following the rules of war, have defeated that general first. But Decaen's troops numerically equal, without reckoning the garrison of Taragona two thousand strong, were in composition vastly superior to the allies, seeing that only three thousand British and German troops in Maitland's army, were to be at all depended upon in battle; neither does it appear that the platforms, sand-bags, fascines and other materials, necessary for a siege, were at this period prepared and on board the vessels.

It is true Maitland would, if he had been able to resist Decaen at first, which seems doubtful, have effected a great diversion, and Wellington's object would have been gained if a re-embarkation had been secure; but the naval officers, having reference to the nature of the coast, declared that a safe re-embarkation could not be depended upon.   The soundness of this opinion has indeed been disputed by many seamen, well acquainted with the coast, who maintain, that even in winter the Catalonian shore is remarkably safe and tranquil; and that Cape Salou, a place in other respects admirably adapted for a camp, affords a certain retreat, and facility of re-embarking on one or other of its sides in all weather.   However, to Maitland the coast of Catalonia was represented as unsafe, and this view of the question is also supported by very able seamen likewise acquainted with that sea.

OPERATIONS IN MURCIA.

The Anglo-Sicilian armament arrived at Alicant at a critical moment; the Spanish cause was there going to ruin.   Joseph O'Donel, brother to the regent, had with great difficulty organized a new Murcian army after Blake's surrender at Valencia, and this army, based upon Alicant and Carthagena, was independent of a division under general Frere, which always hung about Baza, and Lorca, on the frontier of Grenada, and communicated through the Alpuxaras with the sea-coast.   Both Suchet and Soult were paralyzed in some degree by the neighbourhood of these armies, which holding a central position were supported by fortresses, supplied by sea from Gibraltar to Cadiz, and had their existence guaranteed by Wellington's march into Spain, by his victory of Salamanca, and by his general combinations.   For the two French commanders were forced to watch his movements, and to support at the same time, the one a blockade of the Isla de Leon, the other the fortresses in Catalonia; hence they were in no condition to follow up the prolonged opera-

tions necessary to destroy these Murcian armies,
which were moreover supported by the arrival of
general Ross with British troops at Carthagena.

O'Donel had been joined by Roche in July, and
Suchet, after detaching Maupoint's brigade towards
Madrid, departed himself with two thousand men
for Catalonia, leaving general Harispe with not more
than four thousand men beyond the Xucar. General
Ross immediately advised O'Donel to attack him,
and to distract his attention a large fleet, with
troops on board, which had originally sailed from
Cadiz to succour Ballesteros at Malaga, now
appeared off the Valencian coast. At the same
time Bassecour and Villa Campa, being free to act
in consequence of Palombini's and Maupoint's departure for Madrid, came down from their haunts
in the mountains of Albaracyn upon the right flank See Plan 6.
and rear of the French positions. Villa Campa
penetrated to Liria, and Bassecour to Cofrentes on
the Xucar ; but ere this attack could take place,
Suchet, with his usual celerity, returned from Reus.
At first he detached men against Villa Campa, but
when he saw the fleet, fearing it was the Sicilian
armament, he recalled them again, and sent for
Paris' brigade from Zaragoza, to act by Teruel
against Bassecour and Villa Campa. Then he concentrated his own forces at Valencia, but a storm
drove the fleet off the coast, and meanwhile
O'Donel's operations brought on the

FIRST BATTLE OF CASTALLA.

Harispe's posts were established at Biar, Castalla,
and Onil on the right ; at Ibi and Alcoy on the
left. This line was not more than one march from
Alicant. Colonel Mesclop, with a regiment of in-

fantry and some cuirassiers held Ibi, and was supported by Harispe himself with a reserve at Alcoy. General Delort, with another regiment of infantry, was at Castalla, having some cuirassiers at Onil on his left, and a regiment of dragoons with three companies of foot at Biar on his right. In this exposed situation the French awaited O'Donel, who directed his principal force, consisting of six thousand infantry, seven hundred cavalry, and eight guns, against Delort; meanwhile Roche with three

See Plan 7. thousand men was to move through the mountains of Xixona, so as to fall upon Ibi simultaneously with the attack at Castalla. O'Donel hoped thus to cut the French line, and during these operations, Bassecour, with two thousand men, was to come down from Cofrentes to Villena, on the right flank of Delort.

Suchet's
official
correspon-
dence,
MSS.

Suchet's
Memoirs.

Roche's
correspon-
dence,
MSS.

General
Delort's
official re-

Roche, who marched in the night of the 19th, remained during the 20th in the mountains, but the next night he threaded a difficult pass, eight miles long, reached Ibi at day-break on the 21st, and sent notice of his arrival to O'Donel; and when that general appeared in front of Delort, the latter abandoned Castalla, which was situated in the same valley as Ibi, and about five miles distant from it. But he only retired skirmishing to a strong ridge behind that town, which also extended behind Ibi; this secured his communication with Mesclop, of whom he demanded succour, and at the same time he called in his own cavalry and infantry from Onil and Biar. Mesclop, leaving some infantry, two guns, and his cuirassiers, to defend Ibi and a small fort on the hill behind it, marched at once towards Delort, and thus Roche, finding only a few men before him, got possession of the town after a sharp skirmish, yet he could not take the fort.

At first O'Donel who had advanced beyond Castalla, only skirmished with and cannonaded the French in his front, for he had detached the Spanish cavalry to operate by the plains of Villena, to turn the enemy's right and communicate with Bassecour. While expecting the effects of this movement he was astonished to see the French dragoons come trotting through the pass of Biar, on his left flank; they were followed by some companies of infantry, and only separated from him by a stream over which was a narrow bridge without parapets, and at the same moment the cuirassiers appeared on the other side coming from Onil. The Spanish cavalry had made no effort to interrupt this march from Biar, nor to follow the French through the de- See Appendix, No. 15. file, nor any effort whatever. In this difficulty O'Donel turned two guns against the bridge and supported them with a battalion of infantry, but the French dragoons observing this battalion to be unsteady, braved the fire of the guns, and riding furiously over the bridge seized the battery, and then dashed against and broke the infantry. Delort's line advanced at the same moment, the cuirassiers charged into the town of Castalla, and the whole Spanish army fled outright. Several hundred sought refuge in an old castle and there surrendered, and of the others three thousand were killed, wounded, or taken, and yet the victors had scarcely fifteen hundred men engaged, and did not lose two hundred. O'Donel attributed his defeat to the disobedience and inactivity of St. Estevan, who commanded his cavalry, but the great fault was the placing that cavalry beyond the defile of Biar instead of keeping it in hand for the battle.

This part of the action being over, Mesclop, who

had not taken any share in it, was reinforced and returned to succour Ibi, to which place also Harispe was now approaching from Alcoy; but Roche favoured by the strength of the passes escaped, and reached Alicant with little hurt, while the remains of O'Donel's divisions, pursued by the cavalry on the road of Jumilla, fled to the city of Murcia. Bassecour who had advanced to Almanza was then driven back to his mountain-haunts, where Villa Campa rejoined him. It was at this moment that Maitland's armament disembarked and the remnants of the Spanish force rallied. The king, then flying from Madrid, immediately changed the direction of his march from the Morena to Valencia, and one more proof was given that it was England and not Spain which resisted the French; for Alicant would have fallen, if not as an immediate consequence of this defeat, yet surely when the king's army had joined Suchet.

That general, who had heard of the battle of Salamanca, the evacuation of Madrid and the approach of Joseph, and now saw a fresh army springing up in his front, hastened to concentrate his disposable force in the positions of San Felippe de Xativa and Moxente which he entrenched, as well as the road to Almanza with a view to secure his junction with the king. At the same time he established a new bridge and bridge-head at Alberique in addition to that at Alcira on the Xucar; and having called up Paris from Teruel and Maupoint from Cuenca resolved to abide a battle, which the slowness and vacillation of his adversaries gave him full time to prepare for.

Maitland arrived the 7th, and though his force was not all landed before the 11th, the French were still scattered on various points, and a vigorous commander would have found the means to drive them over the Xucar, and perhaps from Valencia itself. However the British general had scarcely set his foot on shore when the usual Spanish vexations overwhelmed him. Three principal roads led towards the enemy; one on the left, passed through Yecla and Fuente La Higuera, and by it the remnant of O'Donel's army was coming up from Murcia; another passed through Elda, Sax, Villena, and Fuente de la Higuera, and the third through Xixona, Alcoy, and Albayda. Now O'Donel, whose existence as a general was redeemed by the appearance of Maitland, instantly demanded from the latter a pledge, that he would draw nothing either by purchase or requisition, save wine and straw, from any of these lines, nor from the country between them. The English general assented and instantly sunk under the difficulties thus created. For his intention was to have attacked Harispe at Alcoy and Ibi on the 13th or 14th, but he was only able to get one march from Alicant as late as the 16th, he could not attack before the 18th, and it was on that day, that Suchet concentrated his army at Xativa. The delay had been a necessary consequence of the agreement with O'Donel.

Maitland was without any habitude of command, his commissariat was utterly inefficient, and his field-artillery had been so shamefully ill-prepared in Sicily that it was nearly useless. He had hired mules at a great expense for the transport of his guns, and of provisions, from Alicant, but the owners of the mules soon declared they could not fulfil their contract unless they were fed by the British, and this O'Donel's restrictions as to the roads prevented. Many of the muleteers also, after receiving their money, deserted with both mules and provisions; and on the first day's march a convoy, with six days' supply, was attacked by an armed banditti called a guerilla, and the convoy was plundered or dispersed and lost.

Maitland suffering severely from illness, was disgusted at these things, and fearing for the safety of his troops, would have retired at once, and perhaps have re-embarked, if Suchet had not gone back to Xativa; then however, he advanced to Elda, while Roche entered Alcoy; yet both apparently without an object, for there was no intention of fighting, and the next day Roche retired to Xixona and Maitland retreated to Alicant. To cover this retreat general Donkin pushed forward, with a detachment of Spanish and English cavalry, through Sax, Ibi, and Alcoy, and giving out that an advanced guard of five thousand British was close behind him, coasted all the French line, captured a convoy at Olleria, and then returned through Alcoy. Suchet kept close himself, in the camp of Xativa, but sent Harispe to meet the king who was now near Almanza, and on the 25th the junction of the two armies was effected; at the same time Maupoint, escaping Villa Campa's assault, arrived from Cuenca with the remnant of his brigade.

When the king's troops arrived, Suchet pushed his outposts again to Villena and Alcoy, but apparently occupied in providing for Joseph's army and court he neglected to press the allies, which he might have done to their serious detriment. Meanwhile O'Donel who had drawn off Frere's division from Lorca came up to Yecla with five or six thou-

sand men, and Maitland reinforced with some CHAP.
I.
detachments from Sicily, commenced fortifying a
camp outside Alicant; but his health was quite 1812.
August.
broken, and he earnestly desired to resign, being
filled with anxiety at the near approach of Soult.
That marshal had abandoned Andalusia, and his
manner of doing so shall be set forth in the next
chapter; for it was a great event, leading to great
results, and worthy of deep consideration by those
who desire to know upon what the fate of kingdoms
may depend.

CHAPTER II.

OPERATIONS IN ANDALUSIA.

BOOK XIX.

1812.
August.

SUCHET found resources in Valencia to support the king's court and army, without augmenting the pressure on the inhabitants, and a counter-stroke could have been made against the allies, if the French commanders had been of one mind and had looked well to the state of affairs; but Joseph exasperated by the previous opposition of the generals, and troubled by the distresses of the numerous families attached to his court, was only intent upon recovering Madrid as soon as he could collect troops enough to give Wellington battle. He had demanded from the French minister of war, money, stores, and a reinforcement of forty thousand men, and he had imperatively commanded Soult to abandon Andalusia ; that clear-sighted commander,

Appendix No. 3.

could not however understand why the king, who had given him no accurate details of Marmont's misfortunes, or of his own operations, should yet order him to abandon at once, all the results, and all the interests, springing from three years' possession of the south of Spain. He thought it a great question not to be treated lightly, and as his vast capacity enabled him to embrace the whole field of

operations, he concluded that rumour had exaggerated the catastrophe at Salamanca and that the
abandoning of Andalusia would be the ruin of the
French cause.

"To march on Madrid," he said, "would probably
produce another pitched battle, which should be
carefully avoided, seeing that the whole frame-
work of the French invasion was disjointed, and
no resource would remain after a defeat. On the
other hand, Andalusia, which had hitherto been
such a burthen to the invasion, now offered means
to remedy the present disasters, and to sacrifice that
province with all its resources, for the sake of
regaining the capital of Spain, appeared a folly.
It was purchasing a town at the price of a kingdom. Madrid was nothing in the emperor's policy,
though it might be something for a king of Spain;
yet Philip the Vth had thrice lost it and preserved his
throne. Why then should Joseph set such a value
upon that city? The battle of the Arapiles was
merely a grand duel which might be fought again
with a different result; but to abandon Andalusia
with all its stores and establishments; to raise the
blockade of Cadiz; to sacrifice the guns, the
equipments, the hospitals and the magazines, and
thus render null the labours of three years, would be
to make the battle of the Arapiles a prodigious histo-
rical event, the effect of which would be felt all over
Europe and even in the new world. And how was
this flight from Andalusia to be safely effected? The
army of the south had been able to hold in check
sixty thousand enemies disposed on a circuit round
it, but the moment it commenced its retreat towards
Toledo those sixty thousand men would unite to
follow, and Wellington himself would be found on

the Tagus in its front. On that line then the army
of the south could not march, and a retreat through
Murcia would be long and difficult. But why retreat at all? Where," exclaimed this able warrior,
" where is the harm though the allies should possess
the centre of Spain?"

"Your majesty," he continued, " should collect the
army of the centre, the army of Aragon, and if possible, the army of Portugal, and you should march
upon Andalusia, even though to do so should involve
the abandonment of Valencia. If the army of Portugal comes with you, one hundred and twenty thousand men will be close to Portugal ; if it cannot or
will not come, let it remain, because while Burgos
defends itself, that army can keep on the right of the
Ebro and the emperor will take measures for its
succour. Let Wellington then occupy Spain from
Burgos to the Morena, it shall be my care to provide
magazines, stores, and places of arms in Andalusia ;
and the moment eighty thousand French are assembled in that province the theatre of war is changed !
The English general must fall back to save Lisbon,
the army of Portugal may follow him to the Tagus,
the line of communication with France will be
established by the eastern coast, the final result of
the campaign turns in our favour, and a decisive
battle may be delivered without fear at the gates
of Lisbon. March then with the army of the
centre upon the Despenas Peros, unite all our forces
in Andalusia, and all will be well ! Abandon that
province and you lose Spain ! you will retire behind
the Ebro and famine will drive you thence before
the emperor can, from the distant Russia, provide
a remedy ; his affairs even in that country will suffer by the blow, and America dismayed by our misfortunes will perhaps make peace with England."

Neither the king's genius, nor his passions, would permit him to understand the grandeur and vigour of this conception. To change even simple lines of operation suddenly, is at all times a nice affair, but thus to change the whole theatre of operations and regain the initial movements after a defeat, belongs only to master spirits in war. Now the emperor had recommended a concentration of force, and Joseph would not understand this save as applied to the recovery of Madrid; he was uneasy for the frontiers of France; as if Wellington could possibly have invaded that country while a great army menaced Lisbon; in fine he could see nothing but his lost capital on one side, and a disobedient lieutenant on the other, and peremptorily repeated his orders. Then Soult, knowing that his plan could only be effected by union and rapidity, and dreading the responsibility of further delay, took immediate steps to abandon Andalusia; but mortified by this blighting of his fruitful genius, and stung with anger at such a termination to all his political and military labours, his feelings overmastered his judgment. Instead of tracing the king's rigid counteraction of his scheme to the narrowness of the monarch's military genius, he judged it part of a design to secure his own fortune at the expense of his brother, an action quite foreign to Joseph's honest and passionate nature. Wherefore making known this opinion to six generals, who were sworn to secrecy, unless interrogated by the Emperor, he wrote to the French minister of war Appendix No. 4. expressing his doubts of the king's loyalty towards the emperor, and founding them on the following facts.

1°. That the extent of Marmont's defeat had been made known to him only by the reports of the

enemy, and the king, after remaining for twenty-
three days, without sending any detailed information of the operations in the north of Spain,
although the armies were actively engaged, had
peremptorily ordered him to abandon Andalusia,
saying it was the only resource remaining for the
French. To this opinion Soult said he could not
subscribe, yet being unable absolutely to disobey
the monarch, he was going to make a movement
which must finally lead to the loss of all the
French conquests in Spain, seeing that it would
then be impossible to remain permanently on the
Tagus, or even in the Castiles.

2°. This operation ruinous in itself was insisted
upon at a time, when the newspapers of Cadiz
affirmed, that Joseph's ambassador at the court of
Petersburgh, had joined the Prussian army in the
field ; that Joseph himself had made secret over-
tures to the government in the Isla de Leon ; that
Bernadotte, his brother-in-law, had made a treaty
with England and had demanded of the Cortez a
guard of Spaniards, a fact confirmed by information
obtained through an officer sent with a flag of truce
to the English admiral ; finally that Moreau and
Blucher were at Stockholm, and the aid-du-camp
of the former was in London.

Reflecting upon all these circumstances he feared
that the object of the king's false movements, might
be to force the French army over the Ebro, in the
view of making an arrangement for Spain, separate
from France ; fears, said the duke of Dalmatia,
which may be chimerical, but it is better in such a
crisis to be too fearful than too confident. This
letter was sent by sea, and the vessel having touched
at Valencia at the moment of Joseph's arrival there,
the despatch was opened, and it was then, in the

first burst of his anger, that the king despatched
Desprez on that mission to Moscow, the result of
which has been already related.

Soults' proceedings though most offensive to the
king and founded in error, because Joseph's letters,
containing the information required, were intercepted, not withheld, were prompted by zeal for his
master's service and cannot be justly condemned, yet
Joseph's indignation was natural and becoming.
But the admiration of reflecting men must ever
be excited by the greatness of mind, and the calm
sagacity, with which Napoleon treated this thorny
affair. Neither the complaints of his brother, nor
the hints of his minister of war (for the duke of
Feltre, a man of mean capacity and of an intriguing
disposition, countenanced Joseph's expressed sus- Appendix,
No. 5.
picions that the duke of Dalmatia designed to make
himself king of Andalusia) could disturb the temper
or judgment of the Emperor; and it was then,
struck with the vigour of the plan for concentrating
the army in Andalusia, he called Soult the only
military head in Spain. Nor was Wellington inat-
tentive of that general's movements, he knew his
talents, and could foresee and appreciate the importance of the project he had proposed. Anxiously
he watched his reluctant motions, and while apparently enjoying his own triumph amidst the
feasts and rejoicings of Madrid, his eye was fixed
on Seville; the balls and bull-fights of the capital
cloaked both the skill and the apprehensions of the
consummate general.

Before the allies had crossed the Guadarama,
Hill had been directed to hold his army in hand,
close to Drouet, and ready to move into the valley
of the Tagus, if that general should hasten to the

succour of the king. But when Joseph's retreat upon Valencia was known, Hill received orders to fight Drouet, and even to follow him into Andalusia; at the same time general Cooke was directed to prepare an attack, even though it should be an open assault on the French lines before Cadiz, while Ballesteros operated on the flank from Gibraltar. By these means Wellington hoped to keep Soult from sending any succour to the king, and even to force him out of Andalusia without the necessity of marching there himself; yet if these measures failed, he was resolved to take twenty thousand men from Madrid and uniting with Hill drive the French from that province.

Previous to the sending of these instructions, Laval and Villatte had pursued Ballesteros to Malaga, which place, after a skirmish at Coin, he entered, and was in such danger of capture, that the maritime expedition already noticed was detached from Cadiz, by sea, to carry him off. However the news of the battle of Salamanca having arrested the French movements, the Spanish general regained San Roque, and the fleet went on to Valencia. Meanwhile Soult, hoping the king would transfer the seat of war to Andalusia had caused Drouet to shew a bold front against Hill, extending from the Serena to Monas-terio, and to send scouting parties towards Merida; and large magazines were formed at Cordoba, a central point, equally suited for an advance by Estremadura, a march to La Mancha, or a retreat by Grenada. Wherefore Hill, who had not then received his orders to advance, remained on the defensive; nor would Wellington stir from Madrid, although his presence was urgently called for on the Duero, until he was satisfied that the duke of Dalmatia

meant to abandon Andalusia. The king, as we
have seen, finally forced this measure upon the
marshal; but the execution required very extensive
arrangements, for the quarters were distant, the
convoys immense, the enemies numerous, the line
of march wild, and the journey long. And it was
most important to present the imposing appearance
of a great and regular military movement and not
the disgraceful scene of a confused flight.

The distant minor posts, in the Condado de Niebla
and other places, were first called in, and then the
lines before the Isla were abandoned; for Soult,
in obedience to the king's first order, designed to
move upon La Mancha, and it was only by accident,
and indirectly, that he heard of Joseph's retreat
to Valencia. At the same time he discovered that
Drouet, who had received direct orders from the
king, was going to Toledo, and it was not without
difficulty, and only through the medium of his brother, who commanded Drouet's cavalry, that he could
prevent that destructive isolated movement. Murcia
then became the line of retreat but every thing was
hurried, because the works before the Isla were
already broken up in the view of retreating towards
La Mancha, and the troops were in march for Seville
although the safe assembling of the army at Grenada
required another arrangement.

On the 25th of August a thousand guns, stores in
proportion, and all the immense works of Chiclana,
St. Maria, and the Trocadero, were destroyed.
Thus the long blockade of the Isla de Leon was
broken up at the moment when the bombardment of
Cadiz had become very serious, when the opposition
to English influence was taking a dangerous direction, when the French intrigues were nearly ripe,

the cortez becoming alienated from the cause of
Ferdinand and the church; finally when the executive government was weaker than ever, because the
count of Abispal, the only active person in the
regency, had resigned, disgusted that his brother
had been superseded by Elio and censured in the
cortez for the defeat at Castalla. This siege or
rather defence of Cadiz, for it was never, strictly
speaking, besieged, was a curious episode in the
war. Whether the Spaniards would or would not
have effectually defended it without the aid of
British troops is a matter of speculation; but it
is certain that notwithstanding Graham's glorious
action at Barrosa, Cadiz was always a heavy burthen
upon Lord Wellington; the forces, there employed,
would have done better service under his immediate
command, and many severe financial difficulties to
say nothing of political crosses would have been
spared.

In the night of the 26th Soult quitting Seville,
commenced his march by Ossuna and Antequera,
towards Grenada; but now Wellington's orders had
set all the allied troops of Andalusia and Estremadura in motion. Hill advanced against Drouet;
Ballesteros moved by the Ronda mountains to hang
on the retiring enemy's flanks; the expedition sent
by sea to succour him, returned from Valencia;
colonel Skerrit and Cruz Murgeon disembarked
with four thousand English and Spanish troops, at
Huelva, and marching upon St. Lucar Mayor, drove
the enemy from thence, on the 24th. The 27th
they fell upon the French rear-guard at Seville,
and the suburb of Triana, the bridge, and the streets
beyond, were soon carried, by the English guards
and Downie's legion. Two hundred prisoners,

several guns and many stores were taken, but
Downie himself was wounded and made prisoner,
and treated very harshly, because the populace rising
in aid of the allies had mutilated the French soldiers
who fell into their hands. Scarcely was Seville taken,
when seven thousand French infantry came up from
Chiclana, but thinking all Hill's troops were before
them, instead of attacking Skerrit hastily followed
their own army, leaving the allies masters of the city.
But this attack though successful, was isolated and
contrary to lord Wellington's desire. A direct and
vigorous assault upon the lines of Chiclana by the
whole of the Anglo-Spanish garrison was his plan,
and such an assault, when the French were abandoning their works there, would have been a far
heavier blow to Soult.

That commander was now too strong to be meddled with. He issued eight days' bread to his army,
marched very leisurely, picked up on his route the
garrisons and troops who came into him at Antequera,
from the Ronda and from the coast; and at Grenada
he halted eleven days to give Drouet time to join him,
for the latter quitting Estremadura the 25th by the
Cordova passes, was marching by Jaen to Huescar.
Ballesteros had harassed the march, but the French
general had, with an insignificant loss, united seventy-two guns and forty-five thousand soldiers
under arms, of which six thousand were cavalry.
He was however still in the midst of enemies.
On his left flank was Hill; on his right flank
was Ballesteros; Wellington himself might come
down by the Despenas Perros; the Murcians were
in his front, Skerrit and Cruz Murgeon behind him,
and he was clogged with enormous convoys; his

sick and maimed men alone amounted to nearly
nine thousand; his Spanish soldiers were deserting
daily, and it was necessary to provide for several
hundreds of Spanish families who were attached
to the French interests. To march upon the city
of Murcia was the direct, and the best route for
Valencia; but the yellow fever raged there and at
Carthagena; moreover, Don S. Bracco, the English consul at Murcia, a resolute man, declared
his resolution to inundate the country if the
French advanced. Wherefore again issuing eight
days' bread Soult marched by the mountain ways
leading from Huescar to Cehejin, and Calasparra,
and then moving by Hellin, gained Almanza on
the great road to Madrid, his flank being covered
by a detachment from Suchet's army which skirmished with Maitland's advanced posts at San
Vicente close to Alicant. At Hellin he met the
advanced guard of the army of Aragon, and on
the 3rd of October the military junction of all the
French forces was effected.

The task was thus completed, and in a manner
worthy of so great a commander. For it must be
recollected that besides the drawing together of the
different divisions, the march itself was three hundred miles, great part through mountain roads, and
the population was every where hostile. General
Hill had menaced him with twenty-five thousand
men, including Morillo and Penne Villemur's forces;
Ballesteros, reinforced from Cadiz, and by the deserters, had nearly twenty thousand; there were
fourteen thousand soldiers still in the Isla; Skerrit
and Cruz Murgeon had four thousand, and the
Partidas were in all parts numerous: yet from the

midst of these multitudes the duke of Dalmatia carried off his army his convoys and his sick without any disaster. In this manner Andalusia, which had once been saved by the indirect influence of a single march, made by Moore from Salamanca, was, such is the complexity of war, after three years' subjection, recovered by the indirect effect of a single battle delivered by Wellington close to the same city.

During these transactions Maitland's proceedings had been anxiously watched by Wellington; for though the recovery of Andalusia was, both politically and militarily, a great gain, the result, he saw, must necessarily be hurtful to the ultimate success of his campaign by bringing together such powerful forces. He still thought that regular operations would not so effectually occupy Suchet, as a littoral warfare, yet he was contented that Maitland should try his own plan, and he advised that general to march by the coast, and have constant communication with the fleet, referring to his own campaign against Junot in 1808 as an example to be followed. But, the coast roads were difficult, the access for the fleet uncertain; and though the same obstacles, and the latter perhaps in a greater degree, had occurred in Portugal, the different constitution of the armies, and still more of the generals, was an insuperable bar to a like proceeding in Valencia.

General Maitland only desired to quit his command, and the more so that the time appointed by lord William Bentinck for the return of the troops to Sicily was approaching. The moment was critical, but Wellington without hesitation forbade their departure, and even asked the ministers to place them under his own command. Meanwhile with the utmost gentleness and delicacy, he showed to Maitland, who was a man of high honour, courage, and feeling, although inexperienced in command, and now heavily oppressed with illness, that his situation was by no means dangerous;— that the entrenched camp of Alicant might be safely defended,—that he was comparatively better off than Wellington himself had been when in the lines of Torres Vedras, and that it was even desirable that the enemy should attack him on such strong ground, because the Spaniards when joined with English soldiers in a secure position would certainly fight. He also desired that Carthagena should be well looked to by general Ross lest Soult should turn aside to surprise it. Then taking advantage of Elio's fear of Soult he drew him with the army that had been O'Donel's towards Madrid and so got some controul over his operations.

If the English general had been well furnished with money at this time, and if the yellow fever had not raged in Murcia, it is probable he would have followed Joseph rapidly, and rallying all the scattered Spanish forces, and the Sicilian armament on his own army, have endeavoured to crush the king and Suchet before Soult could arrive; or he might have formed a junction with Hill at Despenas Perros and so have fallen on Soult himself, during his march, although such an operation would have endangered his line of communication on the Duero. But these obstacles induced him to avoid operations in the south, which would have involved him in new and immense combinations, until he had

secured his northern line of operations by the capture of Burgos, meaning then with his whole army
united to attack the enemy in the south.

However he could not stir from Madrid until he
was certain that Soult would relinquish Andalusia,
and this was not made clear before Cordoba was
abandoned. Then Hill was ordered to advance on
Zalamea de la Serena, where he commanded equally,
the passes leading to Cordoba in front, those leading
to La Mancha on the left, and those leading by
Truxillo to the Tagus in the rear; so that he could
at pleasure either join Wellington, follow Drouet
towards Grenada, or interpose between Soult and
Madrid, if he should turn towards the Despenas
Perros : meanwhile Skerrit's troops were marching
to join him, and the rest of the Anglo-Portuguese
garrison of Cadiz sailed to Lisbon, with intent to
join Wellington by the regular line of operations.

During these transactions the affairs in Old
Castile had become greatly deranged, for where
Wellington was not, the French warfare generally
assumed a severe and menacing aspect. Castaños
had, in person, conducted the siege of Astorga, after
the battle of Salamanca, yet with so little vigour,
that it appeared rather a blockade than a siege.
The forts at Toro and Zamora had also been
invested, the first by the Partidas, the second by Silveira's militia, who with great spirit had passed their
own frontier, although well aware that they could
not be legally compelled to do so. Thus all the
French garrisons abandoned by Clauzel's retreat
were endangered, and though the slow progress of
the Spaniards before Astorga was infinitely disgraceful to their military prowess, final success
seemed certain.

General H. Clinton was at Cuellar, Santo Cildes occupied Valladolid, Anson's cavalry was in the valley of the Esqueva, and the front looked fair enough. But in the rear the line of communication, as far as the frontier of Portugal, was in great disorder; the discipline of the army was deteriorating rapidly, and excesses were committed on all the routes. A detachment of Portuguese, not more than a thousand strong, either instigated by want or by their hatred of the Spaniards, had perpetrated such enormities on their march from Pinhel to Salamanca, that as an example, five were executed and many others severely punished by stripes, yet even this did not check the growing evil, the origin of which may be partly traced to the license at the storming of Ciudad Rodrigo and Badajos, but principally to the sufferings of the soldiers.

All the hospitals in the rear were crowded, and Salamanca itself, in which there were six thousand sick and wounded, besides French prisoners, was the very abode of misery. The soldiers endured much during the first two or three days after the battle, and the inferior officers' sufferings were still more heavy and protracted. They had no money, and many sold their horses and other property to sustain life; some actually died of want, and though Wellington, hearing of this, gave orders that they should be supplied from the purveyor's stores in the same manner as the soldiers, the relief came late. It is a common, yet erroneous notion, that the English system of hospitals in the Peninsula was admirable, and that the French hospitals were neglected. Strenuous and unceasing exertions were made by lord Wellington and the chiefs of the medical staff to form good hospital establishments, but the want of money, and still

more the want of previous institutions, foiled their
utmost efforts.   Now there was no point of warfare
which more engaged Napoleon's attention than the
care of his sick and wounded ; and he being monarch
as well as general, furnished his hospitals with all
things requisite, even with luxuries.   Under his
fostering care also, baron Larrey justly celebrated,
were it for this alone, organized the establishment
called the hospital " *Ambulance;*" that is to say,
waggons of a peculiar construction, well horsed,
served by men trained and incorporated as soldiers,
and subject to a strict discipline. Rewarded for their
courage and devotion like other soldiers they were
always at hand, and whether in action or on a march,
ready to pick up, to salve, and to carry off wounded
men ; and the astonishing rapidity with which the
fallen French soldiers disappeared from a field of
battle attested the excellence of the institution.

But in the British army, the carrying off the
wounded, depended, partly upon the casual assistance of a weak waggon train, very badly disciplined,
furnishing only three waggons to a division, and not
originally appropriated to that service ; partly upon
the spare commissariat animals, but principally upon
the resources of the country, whether of bullock
carts, mules, or donkeys, and hence the most doleful
scenes after a battle, or when an hospital was to be
evacuated.   The increasing numbers of the sick
and wounded as the war enlarged, also pressed on
the limited number of regular medical officers,
and Wellington complained, that when he demanded more, the military medical board in London
neglected his demands, and thwarted his arrangements.   Shoals of hospital mates and students
were indeed sent out, and they arrived for the

most part ignorant alike of war, and their own profession; while a heterogeneous mass of purveyors
and their subordinates, acting without any military
organization or effectual superintendence, continually bade defiance to the exertions of those medical
officers, and they were many, whose experience,
zeal, and talents would, with a good institution to
work upon, have rendered this branch of the service
most distinguished. Nay, many even of the well-
educated surgeons sent out were for some time of
little use, for superior professional skill is of little
value in comparison of experience in military
arrangement; where one soldier dies from the want
of a delicate operation, hundreds perish from the
absence of military arrangement. War tries the
strength of the military frame-work; it is in peace
that the frame-work itself must be formed, otherwise barbarians would be the leading soldiers of
the world; a perfect army can only be made by
civil institutions, and those, rightly considered,
would tend to confine the horrors of war to the field
of battle, which would be the next best thing to the
perfection of civilization that would prevent war
altogether.

Such was the state of affairs on the allies' line of
communication, when, on the 14th of August, Clauzel suddenly came down the Pisuerga. Anson's
cavalry immediately recrossed the Duero at Tudela,
Santo Cildes, following Wellington's instructions,
fell back to Torrelobaton, and on the 18th the
French assembled at Valladolid to the number of
twenty thousand infantry, two thousand cavalry,
and fifty guns well provided with ammunition. Five
thousand stragglers, who in the confusion of defeat
had fled to Burgos and Vittoria, were also collected

Clauzel's
correspon-
dence.
MSS.

and in march to join. Clauzel's design was to be at hand when Joseph, reinforced from the south, should drive Wellington from Madrid, for he thought the latter must then retire by Avila, and the Valle de Ambles, and he purposed to gain the mountains of Avila himself, and harass the English general's flank. Meanwhile Foy proposed with two divisions of infantry and sixteen hundred cavalry, to succour the garrisons of Toro, Zamora, and Astorga, and Clauzel consented, though he appears to have been somewhat fearful of this dangerous experiment, and did not believe Astorga was so near its fall.

CHAP. II.

1812. August.

Foy's correspondence, MSS.

Foy wished to march on the 15th by Placentia, yet he was not dispatched until the evening of the 17th, and then by the line of Toro, the garrison of which place he carried off in passing. The 19th he sabred some of the Spanish rear-guard at Castro Gonzalo, on the Esla; the 20th, at three o'clock in the evening, he reached La Baneza, but was mortified to learn, that Castaños, by an artful negociation had, the day before, persuaded the garrison of Astorga, twelve hundred good troops, to surrender, although there was no breach, and the siege was actually being raised at the time. The Gallicians being safe in their mountains, the French general turned to the left, and marched upon Carvajales, hoping to enclose Silveira's militia, between the Duero and the Esla, and sweep them off in his course; then relieving Zamora, he purposed to penetrate to Salamanca, and seize the trophies of the Arapiles. And this would infallibly have happened, but for the judicious activity of sir Howard Douglas, who, divining Foy's object, sent Silveira with timeful notice into Portugal; yet so critical was the movement that

Foy's correspondence, MSS.

Sir H. Douglas's papers, MSS.

Foy's cavalry skirmished with the Portuguese rear-
guard near Constantin at day-break on the 24th.
The 25th the French entered Zamora, but Wellington was now in movement upon Arevalo, and
Clauzel recalled Foy at the moment when his infantry were actually in march upon Salamanca to
seize the trophies, and his cavalry was moving by
Ledesma, to break up the line of communication
with Ciudad Rodrigo.

That Foy was thus able to disturb the line of
communication was certainly Clinton's error. Wellington left eighteen thousand men, exclusive of
the troops besieging Astorga, to protect his flank and
rear, and he had a right to think it enough, because
he momentarily expected Astorga to fall, and the
French army, a beaten one, was then in full retreat.
It is true none of the French garrisons yielded before Clauzel returned, but Clinton alone had eight
thousand good troops, and might with the aid of
Santo Cildes and the partidas, have baffled the
French; he might even have menaced Valladolid,
after Foy's departure, which would have certainly
brought that general back. And if he dared not
venture so much, he should, following his instructions, have regulated his movements along the left
of the Duero, so as to be always in a condition to
protect Salamanca; that is, he should have gone to
Olmedo when Clauzel first occupied Valladolid,
but he retired to Arevalo, which enabled Foy to
advance.

The mere escape of the garrisons, from Toro and
Zamora, was by the English general thought no
misfortune. It would have cost him a long march
and two sieges in the hottest season to have reduced
them, which, in the actual state of affairs, was more

than they were worth; yet, to use his own words, *" it was not very encouraging to find, that the best Spanish army was unable to stand before the remains of Marmont's beaten troops; that in more than two months, it had been unable even to breach Astorga, and that all important operations must still be performed by the British troops."* The Spaniards, now in the fifth year of the war, were still in the state described by sir John Moore, *" without an army, without a government, without a general!"*

While these events were passing in Castile Popham's armament remained on the Biscay coast, and the partidas thus encouraged became so active, that with exception of Santona and Gueteria, all the littoral posts were abandoned by Caffarelli; Porlier, Renovalles, and Mendizabel, the nominal commanders of all the bands, immediately took possession of Castro, Santander, and even of Bilbao, and though general Rouget came from Vittoria to recover the last, he was after some sharp fighting obliged to retire again to Durango. Meanwhile Reille, deluded by a rumour that Wellington was marching through the centre of Spain upon Zaragoza, abandoned several important outposts, Aragon, hitherto so tranquil, became unquiet, and all the northern provinces were ripe for insurrection.

CHAPTER III.

WHILE the various military combinations, described in the foregoing chapter, were thickening, Wellington, as we have seen, remained in Madrid, apparently inactive, but really watching the fitting moment to push his operations, and consolidate his success in the north, preparatory to the execution of his designs in the south. The result was involved in a mixed question, of time, and of combinations dependant upon his central position, and upon the activity of the partidas in cutting off all correspondence between the French armies. His mode of paralyzing Suchet's and Caffarelli's armies, by the Sicilian armament in the east and Popham's armament in the north, has been already described, but his internal combinations, to oppose the united forces of Soult and the king, were still more important and extensive.

When it was certain that Soult had actually abandoned Andalusia, Hill was directed upon Toledo, by the bridge of Almaraz, and colonel Sturgeon's genius had rendered that stupendous ruin, although more lofty than Alcantara, passable for artillery. Elio also was induced to bring the army of Murcia to the same quarter, and Ballesteros was desired to take post on the mountain of Alcaraz, and look to the fortress of Chinchilla, which, situated at the confines of Murcia and La Mancha, and perched on a rugged isolated hill in a vast plain, was peculiarly strong both from construction and site, and it was the knot of all the great lines of communication. The partizan corps of Bassecour, Villa Campa, and the Empecinado, were desired to enter La Mancha, and thus, as Hill could bring up above twenty thousand men, and as the third, fourth, and light divisions, two brigades of cavalry, and Carlos D'España's troops, were to remain near Madrid, whilst the rest of the army marched into Old Castile, above sixty thousand men, thirty thousand being excellent troops and well commanded, would have been assembled, with the fortified post of Chinchilla in front, before Soult could unite with the king.

The British troops at Carthagena were directed, when Soult should have passed that city, to leave only small garrisons in the forts there, and join the army at Alicant, which with the reinforcements from Sicily, would then be sixteen thousand strong, seven thousand being British troops. While this force was at Alicant Wellington judged that the French could not bring more than fifty thousand against Madrid without risking the loss of Valencia itself. Not that he expected the heterogeneous mass he had collected could resist on a fair field the veteran and powerfully constituted army which would finally be opposed to them; but he calculated that ere the French generals could act seriously, the rivers would be full, and Hill could then hold his ground, sufficiently long to enable the army to come back from Burgos. Indeed he had little doubt of reducing that place, and being again on the Tagus in time to take the initial movements himself.

Meanwhile the allies had several lines of operation.

Ballasteros from the mountains of Alcaraz, could
harass the flanks of the advancing French, and
when they passed, could unite with Maitland to
overpower Suchet.

Hill could retire if pressed, by Madrid, or by
Toledo, and could either gain the passes of the
Guadarama or the valley of the Tagus.

Elio, Villa Campa, Bassecour, and the Empecinado could act by Cuenca and Requeña against
Suchet, or against Madrid if the French followed
Hill obstinately; or they could join Ballesteros.
And besides all these forces, there were ten or twelve
thousand new Spanish levies in the Isla waiting for
clothing and arms which under the recent treaty
were to come from England.

To lord Wellington, the English ministers had
nominally confided the distribution of these succours, but following their usual vicious manner of
doing business, they also gave Mr. Stuart a controul over it, without Wellington's knowledge, and
hence the stores, expected by the latter at Lisbon
or Cadiz, were by Stuart unwittingly directed to
Coruña, with which place the English general had
no secure communication; moreover there were
very few Spanish levies there, and no confidential
person to superintend the delivery of them. Other
political crosses, which shall be noticed in due
time, he also met with, but it will suffice here to
say that the want of money was an evil now become intolerable. The army was many months in
arrears; those officers who went to the rear sick
suffered the most cruel privations, and those who
remained in Madrid, tempted by the pleasures of

the capital, obtained some dollars at an exorbitant premium from a money-broker, and it was grievously suspected that his means resulted from the nefarious proceedings of an under commissary; but the soldiers, equally tempted, having no such resource, plundered the stores of the Retiro. In fine, discipline became relaxed throughout the army, and the troops kept in the field were gloomy, envying those who remained at Madrid.

That city exhibited a sad mixture of luxury and desolation. When it was first entered a violent, cruel, and unjust persecution of those who were called " *Afrancesados*," was commenced, and continued, until the English general interfered, and as an example made no distinction in his invitations to the palace feasts. Truly it was not necessary to increase the sufferings of the miserable people, for though the markets were full of provisions, there was no money wherewith to buy; and though the houses were full of rich furniture, there were neither purchasers nor lenders; even noble families secretly sought charity that they might live. At night the groans, and stifled cries of famishing people were heard, and every morning emaciated dead bodies, cast into the streets, shewed why those cries had ceased. The calm resignation with which these terrible sufferings were borne was a distinctive mark of the national character; not many begged, none complained, there was no violence, no reproaches, very few thefts; the allies lost a few animals, nothing more, and these were generally thought to be taken by robbers from the country. But with this patient endurance of calamity the " *Madrileños*" discovered a deep and unaffected gratitude for kindness received at the hands of the

British officers who contributed, not much for they
had it not, but, enough of money to form soup charities by which hundreds were succoured.   It was
the third division, and I believe the forty-fifth regiment which set the example, and surely this is not
the least of the many honourable distinctions those
brave men have earned.

Wellington desirous of obtaining shelter from the
extreme heat for his troops, had early sent four
divisions and the cavalry, to the Escurial and St.
Ildefonso, from whence they could join Hill by the
valley of the Tagus, or Clinton by Arevalo ; but
when he knew that the king's retreat upon Valencia
was decided, that Soult had abandoned Cordoba,
and that Clinton was falling back before Clauzel,
he ordered the first, fifth, and seventh divisions,
Pack's and Bradford's Portuguese brigades, Ponsonby's light horsemen, and the heavy German
cavalry, to move rapidly upon Arevalo, and on the
1st of September quitted Madrid himself to take
the command.   Yet his army had been so diminished by sickness that only twenty-one thousand
men, including three thousand cavalry, were assembled in that town, and he had great difficulty
to feed the Portuguese soldiers, who were also very
ill equipped.

The regency instead of transmitting money and
stores to supply their troops, endeavoured to throw
off the burthen entirely by an ingenious device ;
for having always had a running account with the
Spanish government, they now made a treaty, by
which the Spaniards were to feed the Portuguese
troops, and check off the expense on the national
account which was then in favour of the Portuguese ; that is, the soldiers were to starve under the

sanction of this treaty, because the Spaniards could
not feed their own men, and would not, if they
could, have fed the Portuguese.   Neither could
the latter take provisions from the country, because
Wellington demanded the resources of the valleys
of the Duero and Pisuerga for the English soldiers,
as a set-off against the money advanced by Sir
Henry Wellesley to the Spanish regency at Cadiz.
Wherefore to force the Portuguese regency from
this shameful expedient he stopped the payments
of their subsidy from the chest of aids.   Then the
old discontents and disputes revived and acquired
new force; the regency became more intractable
than ever, and the whole military system of Portugal was like to fall to pieces.

On the 4th the allies quitted Arevalo, the 6th
they passed the Duero by the ford above Puente de
Duero, the 7th they entered Valladolid, and meanwhile the Gallicians, who had returned to the Esla,
when Foy retreated, were ordered to join the
Anglo-Portuguese army.   Clauzel abandoned Valladolid in the night of the 6th, and though closely
followed by Ponsonby's cavalry, crossed the Pisuerga
and destroyed the bridge of Berecal on that river.
The 8th the allies halted, for rest, and to await
the arrival of Castaños ; but seldom during this
war did a Spanish general deviate into activity;
and Wellington observed that in his whole intercourse with that people, from the beginning of the
revolution to that moment, he had not met with an
able Spaniard, while amongst the Portuguese he
had found several.   The Gallicians came not, and
the French retreated slowly up the beautiful
Pisuerga and Arlanzan valleys, which, in denial
of the stories about French devastation, were care-

fully cultivated and filled to repletion with corn, wine, and oil.

Nor were they deficient in military strength. Off the high road, on both sides, ditches and rivulets impeded the troops, while cross ridges continually furnished strong parallel positions flanked by the lofty hills on either side. In these valleys Clauzel baffled his great adversary in the most surprising manner. Each day he offered battle, but on ground which Wellington was unwilling to assail in front, partly because he momentarily expected the Gallicians up, but chiefly because of the declining state of his own army from sickness, which, combined with the hope of ulterior operations in the south, made him unwilling to lose men. By flank movements he dislodged the enemy, yet each day darkness fell ere they were completed, and the morning's sun always saw Clauzel again in position. At Cigales and Dueñas, in the Pisuerga valley; at Magoz, Torquemada, Cordobilla, Revilla, Vallejera, and Pampliega in the valley of the Arlanzan, the French general thus offered battle, and finally covered Burgos on the 16th, by taking the strong position of Cellada del Camino.

But eleven thousand Spanish infantry, three hundred cavalry, and eight guns, had now joined the allies, and Wellington would have attacked frankly on the 17th, had not Clauzel, alike wary and skilful, observed the increased numbers and retired in the night to Frandovinez; his rear-guard was however next day pushed sharply back to the heights of Burgos, and in the following night he passed through that town leaving behind him large stores of grain. Caffarelli who had come down to place the castle of Burgos in a state of defence, now joined him, and

the two generals retreated upon Briviesca, where
they were immediately reinforced by that reserve
which, with such an extraordinary foresight, the
emperor had directed to be assembled and exercised on the Pyrennees, in anticipation of Marmont's
disaster. The allies entered Burgos amidst great
confusion, for the garrison of the castle had set fire
to some houses impeding the defence of the fortress,
the conflagration spread widely, and the Partidas
who were already gathered like wolves round a carcass, entered the town for mischief. Mr. Sydenham,
an eye-witness, and not unused to scenes of war, thus
describes their proceedings, " What with the flames
and the plundering of the Guerillas, who are as
bad as Tartars and Cossacks of the Kischack or
Zagatay hordes, I was afraid Burgos would be
entirely destroyed, but order was at length restored
by the manful exertions of Don Miguel Alava."

The series of beautiful movements executed by
Clauzel, merit every praise, but it may be ques-
tioned if the English general's marches were in the
true direction, or made in good time; for though
Clinton's retreat upon Arevalo influenced, it did not
absolutely dictate the line of operations. Wellington had expected Clauzel's advance to Valladolid; it
was therefore no surprise, and on the 26th of August,
Foy was still at Zamora. At that period the English
general might have had his army, Clinton's troops
excepted, at Segovia; and as the distance from
thence to Valladolid, is rather less than from Valladolid to Zamora, a rapid march upon the former,
Clinton advancing at the same time, might have
separated Clauzel from Foy. Again, Wellington
might have marched upon Burgos by Aranda de

Duero and Lerma, that road being as short as by Valladolid; he might also have brought forward the third, or the light division, by the Somosierra, from Madrid, and directed Clinton and the Spaniards to close upon the French rear. He would thus have turned the valleys of the Pisuerga and the Arlanzan, and could from Aranda, or Lerma, have fallen upon Clauzel while in march. That general having Clinton and the Gallicians on his rear, and Wellington, reinforced by the divisions from Madrid, on his front or flank, would then have had to fight a decisive battle under every disadvantage. In fine the object was to crush Clauzel, and this should have been effected though Madrid had been entirely abandoned to secure success. It is however probable that want of money and means of transport decided the line of operations, for the route by the Somosierra was savage and barren, and the feeding of the troops even by Valladolid was from hand to mouth, or painfully supported by convoys from Portugal.

SIEGE OF THE CASTLE OF BURGOS.

Caffarelli had placed eighteen hundred infantry, besides artillery-men, in this place, and general Dubreton the governor, was of such courage and skill that he surpassed even the hopes of his sanguine and warlike countryman. The castle and its works enclosed a rugged hill, between which and the river, the city of Burgos was situated. An old wall with a new parapet and flanks constructed by the French offered the first line of defence; the second line, which was within the other, was earthen, of the nature of a field retrenchment and

Colonel
Jones's
Sieges,
2nd edit.

well palisaded; the third line was similarly constructed and contained the two most elevated
points of the hill, on one of which was an entrenched building called the White Church, and on
the other the ancient keep of the castle; this last
was the highest point, and was not only entrenched
but surmounted with a heavy casemated work called
the Napoleon battery. Thus there were five separate enclosures.

The Napoleon battery commanded every thing
around it, save to the north, where at the distance
of three hundred yards there was a second height
scarcely less elevated than that of the fortress.
It was called the Hill of San Michael, and was
defended by a large horn-work with a hard sloping
scarp twenty-five, and a counterscarp ten feet
high. This outwork was unfinished and only closed See Plan 4.
by strong palisades, but it was under the fire of
the Napoleon battery, was well flanked by the
castle defences, and covered in front by slight
entrenchments for the out picquets. The French
had already mounted nine heavy guns, eleven field-
pieces, and six mortars or howitzers in the fortress,
and as the reserve artillery and stores of the army
of Portugal were also deposited there, they could
increase their armament.

FIRST ASSAULT.

The batteries so completely commanded all
the bridges and fords over the Arlanzan that two
days elapsed ere the allies could cross; but
on the 19th the passage of the river being
effected above the town, by the first division,
major Somers Cocks, supported by Pack's Portu-

guese, drove in the French outposts on the hill
of San Michael. In the night, the same troops,
reinforced with the forty-second regiment, stormed
the horn-work. The conflict was murderous. For
though the ladders were fairly placed by the bear-
ers of them, the storming column, which, covered
by a firing party, marched against the front, was
beaten with great loss, and the attack would have
failed if the gallant leader of the seventy-ninth
had not meanwhile forced an entrance by the
gorge. The garrison was thus actually cut off,
but Cocks, though followed by the second battalion of the forty-second regiment, was not closely
supported, and the French being still five hundred
strong, broke through his men and escaped. This
assault gave room for censure, the troops complained of each other, and the loss was above four
hundred, while that of the enemy was less than
one hundred and fifty.

Wellington was now enabled to examine the
defences of the castle. He found them feeble and
incomplete, and yet his means were so scant that
he had slender hopes of success, and relied more
upon the enemy's weakness than upon his own
power. It was however said that water was scarce
with the garrison and that their provision magazines
could be burned, wherefore encouraged by this information he adopted the following plan of attack.

Twelve thousand men composing the first and
sixth divisions and the two Portuguese brigades,
were to undertake the works; the rest of the
troops, about twenty thousand, exclusive of the
Partidas, were to form the covering army.

The trenches were to be opened from the suburb

CHAP.
III.

1812.
September

Jones's
Sieges.

of San Pedro, and a parallel formed in the direction of the hill of San Michael.

A battery for five guns was to be established close to the right of the captured horn-work.

A sap was to be pushed from the parallel as near the first wall as possible, without being seen into from the upper works, and from thence the engineer was to proceed by gallery and mine.

When the first mine should be completed, the battery on the hill of San Michael was to open against the second line of defence, and the assault was to be given on the first line. If a lodgement was formed, the approaches were to be continued against the second line, and the battery on San Michael was to be turned against the third line, in front of the White Church, because the defences there were exceedingly weak. Meanwhile a trench for musketry was to be dug along the brow of San Michael, and a concealed battery was to be prepared within the horn-work itself, with a view to the final attack of the Napoleon battery.

The head-quarters were fixed at Villa Toro, colonel Burgoyne conducted the operations of the engineers, colonel Robe and colonel Dickson those of the artillery, which consisted of three eighteen-pounders, and the five iron twenty-four-pound howitzers used at the siege of the Salamanca forts; and it was with regard to these slender means, rather than the defects of the fortress, that the line of attack was chosen.

When the horn-work fell a lodgement had been immediately commenced in the interior, and it was continued vigorously, although under a destructive

fire from the Napoleon battery, because the besiegers feared the enemy would at day-light endeavour to retake the work by the gorge; good
cover was, however, obtained in the night, and the
first battery was also begun.

The 21st the garrison mounted several fresh
field-guns, and at night kept up a heavy fire of
grape, and shells, on the workmen who were dig-
ging the musketry trench in front of the first
battery.

The 22d the fire of the besieged was redoubled,
but the besiegers worked with little loss, and their
musketeers galled the enemy. In the night the
first battery was armed with two eighteen-pounders
and three howitzers, and the secret battery within
the horn-work was commenced; but lord Wellington, deviating from his first plan, now resolved
to try an escalade against the first line of defence.
He selected a point half-way between the suburb
of San Pedro and the horn-work, and at midnight
four hundred men provided with ladders were
secretly posted, in a hollow road, fifty yards from
the wall, which was from twenty-three to twenty-
five feet high but had no flanks; this was the
main column, and a Portuguese battalion was also
assembled in the town of Burgos to make a combined flank attack on that side.

SECOND ASSAULT.

The storm was commenced by the Portuguese,
but they were repelled by the fire of the common
guard alone, and the principal escalading party
which was composed of detachments from different
regiments under major Lawrie 79th regiment,

though acting with more courage, had as little
success. The ladders were indeed placed, and the
troops entered the ditch, yet all together, and con-
fusedly; Lawrie was killed and the bravest soldiers who first mounted the ladders were bayonetted;
combustible missiles were then thrown down in
great abundance, and after a quarter of an hour's
resistance, the men gave way, leaving half their
number behind. The wounded were brought off
the next day under a truce. It is said that on the
body of one of the officers killed the French found
a complete plan of the siege, and it is certain that
this disastrous attempt, which delayed the regular
progress of the siege for two days, increased the
enemy's courage, and produced a bad effect upon
the allied troops, some of whom were already dispirited by the attack on the horn-work.

The original plan being now resumed, the hollow way from whence the escaladers had advanced,
and which at only fifty yards' distance run along
the front of defence, was converted into a parallel,
and connected with the suburb of San Pedro.
The trenches were made deep and narrow to secure
them from the plunging shot of the castle, and
musketeers were also planted to keep down the
enemy's fire; but heavy rains incommoded the
troops, and though the allied marksmen got the
mastery over those of the French immediately in
their front, the latter, having a raised and pallisaded work on their own right which in some
measure flanked the approaches, killed so many of See Plan 4.
the besiegers that the latter were finally withdrawn.

In the night a flying sap was commenced, from
the right of the parallel, and was pushed within

twenty yards of the enemy's first line of defence; but the directing engineer was killed, and with him many men, for the French plied their musketry sharply, and rolled large shells down the steep side of the hill. The head of the sap was indeed so commanded as it approached the wall, that a six-feet trench, added to the height of the gabion above, scarcely protected the workmen, wherefore the gallery of the mine was opened, and worked as rapidly as the inexperience of the miners, who were merely volunteers from the line, would permit.

The concealed battery within the horn-work of San Michael being now completed, two eighteen-pounders were removed from the first battery to arm it, and they were replaced by two iron howitzers, which opened upon the advanced palisade below, to drive the French marksmen from that point; but after firing one hundred and forty rounds without success this project was relinquished, and ammunition was so scarce that the soldiers were paid to collect the enemy's bullets.

This day also a zigzag was commenced in front of the first battery and down the face of San Michael, to obtain footing for a musketry trench to overlook the enemy's defences below ; and though the workmen were exposed to the whole fire of the castle, at the distance of two hundred yards, and were knocked down fast, the work went steadily on.

On the 26th the gallery of the mine was advanced eighteen feet, and the soil was found favourable, but the men in passing the sap, were hit fast by the French marksmen, and an assistant engineer was killed. In the night the parallel was prolonged on the right within twenty yards of the enemy's ramparts, with a view to a second gallery

and mine, and musketeers were planted there to
oppose the enemy's marksmen and to protect the
sap; at the same time the zigzag on the hill of
San Michael was continued, and the musket trench
there was completed under cover of gabions, and
with little loss, although the whole fire of the
castle was concentrated on the spot.

The 27th the French were seen strengthening
their second line, and they had already cut a step,
along the edge of the counterscarp, for a covered
way, and had palisaded the communication. Meanwhile the besiegers finished the musketry trench on
the right of their parallel, and opened the gallery
for the second mine; but the first mine went on
slowly, the men in the sap were galled and disturbed, by stones, grenades, and small shells,
which the French threw into the trenches by hand;
and the artillery fire also knocked over the gabions
of the musketry trench, on San Michael, so fast,
that the troops were withdrawn during the day.

In the night a trench of communication forming
a second parallel behind the first was begun and
nearly completed from the hill of San Michael
towards the suburb of San Pedro, and the musketry
trench on the hill was deepened.

The 28th an attempt was made to perfect this
new parallel of communication, but the French
fire was heavy, and the shells, which passed over,
came rolling down the hill again into the trench, so
the work was deferred until night and was then
perfected. The back roll of the shells continued
indeed to gall the troops, but the whole of this
trench, that in front of the horn-work above, and
that on the right of the parallel below, were filled
with men whose fire was incessant. Moreover

the first mine was now completed and loaded
with more than a thousand weight of powder, the
gallery was strongly tamped for fifteen feet with
bags of clay, and all being ready for the explosion
Wellington ordered the

THIRD ASSAULT.

At midnight the hollow road, fifty yards from
the mine, was lined with troops to fire on the defences, and three hundred men, composing the
storming party, were assembled there, attended by
others who carried tools and materials to secure the
lodgement when the breach should be carried. The
mine was then exploded, the wall fell, and an
officer with twenty men rushed forward to the
assault. The effect of the explosion was not so
great as it ought to have been, yet it brought the
wall down, the enemy was stupified, and the for-
lorn hope, consisting of a sergeant and four daring
soldiers, gained the summit of the breach, and
there stood until the French, recovering, drove them
down pierced with bayonet wounds. Meanwhile the
officer and the twenty men, who were to have been
followed by a party of fifty, and these by the remainder of the stormers, missed the breach in the
dark, and finding the wall unbroken, returned, and
reported that there was no breach. The main body
immediately regained the trenches, and before the
sergeant and his men returned with streaming
wounds to tell their tale, the enemy was reinforced;
and such was the scarcity of ammunition that no
artillery practice could be directed against the
breach, during the night; hence the French were
enabled to raise a parapet behind it and to place

obstacles on the ascent which deterred the besiegers
from renewing the assault at daylight.

This failure arose from the darkness of the night, and the want of a conducting engineer, for out of four regular officers, of that branch, engaged in the siege, one had been killed, one badly wounded, and one was sick, wherefore the remaining one was necessarily reserved for the conducting of the works. The aspect of affairs was gloomy. Twelve days had elapsed since the siege commenced, one assault had succeeded, two had failed, twelve hundred men had been killed, or wounded, little progress had been made, and the troops generally shewed symptoms of despondency, especially the Portuguese, who seemed to be losing their ancient spirit. Discipline was relaxed, the soldiers wasted ammunition, and the work in the trenches was avoided or neglected both by officers and men; insubordination was gaining ground, and reproachful orders were issued, the guards only being noticed as presenting an honourable exception.

In this state it was essential to make some change in the operations, and as the French marksmen, in the advanced palisadoed work below, were now become so expert that every thing which could be seen from thence was hit, the howitzer battery on San Michael was reinforced with a French eight-pounder, by the aid of which this mischievous post was at last demolished. At the same time the gallery of the second mine was pushed forward, and a new breaching battery for three guns was constructed behind it, so close to the enemy's defences that the latter screened the work from the artillery fire of their upper fortress; but the parapet of the battery was only made musket-proof because the besieged had no guns on the lower line of this front.

In the night the three eighteen-pounders were brought from the hill of San Michael without being discovered, and at daylight, though a very galling fire of muskets thinned the workmen, they persevered until nine o'clock when the battery was finished and armed. But at that moment the watchful Dubreton brought a howitzer down from the upper works, and with a low charge threw shells into the battery; then making a hole through a flank wall, he thrust out a light gun which sent its bullets whizzing through the thin parapet at every round, and at the same time his marksmen plied their shot so sharply that the allies were driven from their pieces without firing a shot. More French cannon were now brought from the upper works, the defences of the battery were quite demolished, two of the gun-carriages were disabled, a trunnion was knocked off one of the eighteen-pounders, and the muzzle of another was split. And it was in vain that the besiegers' marksmen, aided by some officers who considered themselves good shots, endeavoured to quell the enemy's fire, the French being on a height were too well covered and remained masters of the fight.

In the night a second and more solid battery was formed at a point a little to the left of the ruined one, but at daylight the French observed it; and their fire plunging from above made the parapet fly off so rapidly, that the English general relinquished his intention and returned to his galleries and mines, and to his breaching battery on the hill of San Michael. The two guns still serviceable were therefore removed towards the

upper battery to beat down a retrenchment formed
by the French behind the old breach. It was intended to have placed them on this new position in
the night of the 3d, but the weather was very wet
and stormy, and the workmen, those of the guards
only excepted, abandoned the trenches; hence at
daylight the guns were still short of their destination and nothing more could be done until the
following night.

On the 4th, at nine o'clock in the morning, the
two eighteen-pounders, and three iron howitzers,
again opened from San Michael's, and at four o'clock
in the evening, the old breach being cleared of
all incumbrances, and the second mine being
strongly tamped for explosion, a double assault was
ordered. The second battalion of the twenty-fourth
British regiment, commanded by captain Hedder-
wick was selected for this operation, and was formed
in the hollow way, having one advanced party,
under Mr. Holmes, pushed forward as close to the
new mine as it was safe to be, and a second party
under Mr. Frazer in like manner pushed towards
the old breach.

FOURTH ASSAULT.

At five o'clock the mine was exploded with a
terrific effect, sending many of the French up into
the air and breaking down one hundred feet of the
wall, the next instant Holmes and his brave men
went rushing through the smoke and crumbling
ruins, and Frazer, as quick and brave as his
brother officer, was already fighting with the
defenders on the summit of the old breach. The
supports followed closely,, and in a few minutes
both points were carried with a loss to the as-

sailants of thirty-seven killed and two hundred wounded, seven of the latter being officers and amongst them the conducting engineer. During the night lodgements were formed, in advance of the old, and on the ruins of the new breach, yet very imperfectly, and under a heavy destructive fire from the upper defences. But this happy attack revived the spirits of the army, vessels with powder were coming coastwise from Coruña, a convoy was expected by land from Ciudad Rodrigo, and as a supply of ammunition sent by sir Home Popham had already reached the camp, from Santander, the howitzers continued to knock away the palisades in the ditch, and the battery on San Michael's was directed to open a third breach at a point where the first French line of defence was joined to the second line.

This promising state of affairs was of short duration.

On the 5th, at five o'clock in the evening, while the working parties were extending the lodgements, three hundred French came swiftly down the hill, and sweeping away the labourers and guards from the trenches, killed or wounded a hundred and fifty men, got possession of the old breach, destroyed the works, and carried off all the tools. However in the night the allies repaired the damage and pushed saps from each flank to meet in the centre near the second French line, and to serve as a parallel to check future sallies. Meanwhile the howitzers on the San Michael continued their fire, yet ineffectually, against the palisades; the breaching battery in the horn-work also opened, but it was badly constructed, and the guns being unable to see the wall sufficiently low, soon ceased to speak, the embrasures were therefore masked. On the other hand

the besieged were unable, from the steepness of the
castle-hill, to depress their guns sufficiently to bear
on the lodgement at the breaches in the first line,
but their musquetry was destructive, and they rolled
down large shells to retard the approaches towards
the second line.

On the 7th the besiegers had got so close to
the wall below that the howitzers above could no
longer play without danger to the workmen, wherefore two French field-pieces, taken in the horn-work,
were substituted and did good service. The breaching battery on San Michael's being altered, also renewed its fire, and at five o'clock had beaten down
fifty feet from the parapet of the second line; but the
enemy's return was heavy, and another eighteen-
pounder lost a trunnion. However in the night block-
carriages with supports for the broken trunnions
were provided, and the disabled guns were enabled
to recommence their fire yet with low charges. But
a constant rain had now filled the trenches, the
communications were injured, the workmen were
negligent, the approaches to the second line went
on slowly, and again Dubreton came thundering
down from the upper ground, driving the guards
and workmen from the new parallel at the lodgements, levelling all the works, carrying off all the
tools, and killing or wounding two hundred men.
Colonel Cocks, promoted for his gallant conduct at
the storming of San Michael, restored the fight, and
repulsed the French, but he fell dead on the ground
he had recovered. He was a young man of a mo-
dest demeanour, brave, thoughtful, and enterprising,
and he lived and died a good soldier.

After this severe check the approaches to the

second line were abandoned, and the trenches were
extended so as to embrace the whole of the fronts
attacked; the battery on San Michael had meantime
formed a practicable breach twenty-five feet wide,
and the parallel, at the old breach of the first line,
was prolonged by zigzags on the left towards this new
breach, while a trench was opened to enable marksmen to fire upon the latter at thirty yards distance.
Nevertheless another assault could not be risked
because the great expenditure of powder had again
exhausted the magazines, and without a new supply, the troops might have found themselves without ammunition in front of the French army which
was now gathering head near Briviesca. Heated
shot were however thrown at the White Church with
a view to burn the magazines ; and the miners were
directed to drive a gallery, on the other side of the
castle, against the church of San Roman, a building
pushed out a little beyond the French external line
of defence on the side of the city.

On the 10th, when the besiegers' ammunition was
nearly all gone, a fresh supply arrived from Santander, but no effect had been produced upon the White
Church, and Dubreton had strengthened his works to
meet the assault; he had also isolated the new breach
See Plan,
No. 4.
on one flank by a strong stockade extending at right
angles from the second to the third line of defence.
The fire from the Napoleon battery had obliged the
besiegers again to withdraw their battering guns
within the horn-work, and the attempt to burn the
White Church was relinquished, but the gallery
against San Roman was continued. In this state
things remained for several days with little change,
save that the French, maugre the musketry from

the nearest zigzag trench, had scarped eight feet at the top of the new breach and formed a small trench at the back.

On the 15th the battery in the horn-work was again armed, and the guns pointed to breach the wall of the Napoleon battery; they were however overmatched and silenced in three-quarters of an hour, and the embrasures were once more altered, that the guns might bear on the breach in the second line. Some slight works and counter-works were also made on different points, but the besiegers were principally occupied repairing the mischief done by the rain, and in pushing the gallery under San Roman, where the French were now distinctly heard talking in the church, wherefore the mine there was formed and loaded with nine hundred pounds of powder.

On the 17th the battery of the horn-work being renewed, the fire of the eighteen-pounders cleared away the enemy's temporary defences at the breach, the howitzers damaged the rampart on each side, and a small mine was sprung on the extreme right of the lower parallel, with a view to take possession of a cavalier or mound which the French had raised there, and from which they had killed many men in the trenches; it was successful, and a lodgement was effected, but the enemy soon returned in force and obliged the besiegers to abandon it again. However on the 18th the new breach was rendered practicable, and Wellington ordered it to be stormed. The explosion of the mine under San Roman was to be the signal; that church was also to be assaulted; and at the same time a third detachment was to escalade the works in front of the ancient breach and thus connect the attacks.

FIFTH ASSAULT.

At half-past four o'clock the springing of the mine at San Roman broke down a terrace in front of that building, yet with little injury to the church itself; the latter was, however, resolutely attacked by colonel Browne, at the head of some Spanish and Portuguese troops, and though the enemy sprung a countermine which brought the building down, the assailants lodged themselves in the ruins. Meanwhile two hundred of the foot-guards, with strong supports, poured through the old breach in the first line, and escaladed the second line, beyond which in the open ground between the second and third lines, they were encountered by the French, and a sharp musketry fight commenced. At the same time a like number of the German legion, under major Wurmb, similarly supported, stormed the new breach, on the left of the guards, so vigourously, that it was carried in a moment, and some men, mounting the hill above, actually gained the third line. Unhappily at neither of these assaults did the supports follow closely, and the Germans being cramped on their left by the enemy's stockade, extended by their right towards the guards, and at that critical moment Dubreton, who held his reserves well in hand, came dashing like a torrent from the upper ground, and in an instant cleared the breaches. Wurmb and many other brave men fell, and then the French, gathering round the guards, who were still unsupported, forced them beyond the outer line. More than two hundred men and officers were killed or wounded in this combat, and the next night the enemy recovered San Roman by a sally.

The siege was thus virtually terminated, for

though the French were beaten out of St. Roman
again, and a gallery was opened from that church
against the second line ; and though two twenty-
four pounders, sent from Santander, by sir Home
Popham, had passed Reynosa on their way to
Burgos, these were mere demonstrations.   It is
now time to narrate the different contemporary
events which obliged the English general, with a
victorious army, to abandon the siege of a third-
rate fortress, strong in nothing but the skill and
bravery of the governor and his gallant soldiers.

CHAPTER IV.

BOOK
XIX.

1812.
October.

WHEN king Joseph retreated to Valencia he earnestly demanded a reinforcement of forty thousand men, from France, and, more earnestly, money. Three millions of francs he obtained from Suchet, yet his distress was greater even than that of the allies, and Wellington at one time supposed that this alone would drive the French from the Peninsula. The Anglo-Portuguese soldiers had not received pay for six months, but the French armies of the south, of the centre, and of Portugal, were a whole year behindhand; and the salaries of the ministers, and civil servants of the court, were two years in arrears. Suchet's army, the only one which depended entirely on the country, was by that marshal's excellent management regularly paid, and the effect on its discipline was conformable; his troops refrained from plunder themselves, and repressed some excesses of Joseph's and Soult's soldiers so vigorously, as to come to blows in defence of the inhabitants. And thus it will ever be, since paid soldiers only may be kept under discipline. Soldiers without money must become robbers. Napoleon knew the king's necessity to be extreme, but the war with Russia had so absorbed the resources of France, that little money, and only twenty thousand men, principally conscripts, could be sent to Spain.

The army of Portugal, at the moment when the

siege of the castle commenced, had been quartered
between Vittoria and Burgos; that is to say, at Pancorbo and along the Ebro as far as Logroña, an advanced guard only remaining at Briviesca; on this
line they were recruited and reorganized, and Massena was appointed with full powers to command in
the northern provinces. A fine opportunity to revenge
his own retreat from Torres Vedras, was thus furnished to the old warrior; but whether he doubted
the issue of affairs, or was really tamed by age, he
pleaded illness, and sent general Souham to the
army of Portugal. Then arose contentions, for
Marmont had designated Clauzel as the fittest to
lead, Massena insisted that Souham was the abler
general, and the king desired to appoint Drouet.
Clauzel's abilities were certainly not inferior to
those of any French general, and to more perfect Letter from
acquaintance with the theatre of war, he added a the duke of
Feltre to
better knowledge of the enemy he had to contend King Joseph, 4th
with; he was also more known to his own soldiers, Oct. 1812,
MSS.
and had gained their confidence by his recent operations, no mean considerations in such a matter.
However, Souham was appointed.

Caffarelli anxious to succour the castle of Burgos,
which belonged to his command, had united at Vittoria a thousand cavalry, sixteen guns, and eight thousand infantry, of which three thousand were of the
young guard. The army of Portugal, reinforced from
France with twelve thousand men, had thirty-five
thousand present under arms, reorganized in six
divisions, and by Clauzel's care, its former excellent discipline had been restored. Thus forty-four
thousand good troops were, in the beginning of Official report of gen-
October, ready to succour the castle of Burgos; eral Souham, MSS.
but the generals, although anxious to effect that

BOOK
XIX.
————
1812.
October.
object, awaited, first the arrival of Souham, and then news from the king, with whose operations it was essential to combine their own.   They had no direct tidings from him because the lines of correspondence were so circuitous, and so beset by the Partidas, that the most speedy as well as certain mode of communication, was through the minister of war at Paris; and that functionary found the information, best suited to his purpose, in the English newspapers.   For the latter, while deceiving the British public by accounts of battles which were never fought, victories which were never gained, enthusiasm and vigour which never existed, did, with most accurate assiduity, enlighten the enemy upon the numbers, situation, movements, and reinforcements of the allies.

Duke of
Feltre's
correspon-
dence,
MSS.

Souham arrived the 3rd of October with the last of the reinforcements from France, but he imagined that lord Wellington had sixty thousand troops around Burgos, exclusive of the Partidas, and that three divisions were marching from Madrid to his aid; whereas none were coming from that capital, and little more than thirty thousand were present under arms round Burgos, eleven thousand being Gallicians scarcely so good as the Partidas.   Wellington's real strength was in his Anglo-Portuguese, then not twenty thousand, for besides those killed or wounded at the siege, the sick had gone to the rear faster than the recovered men came up.   Some unattached regiments and escorts were, indeed, about Segovia, and other points north of the Guadarama, and a reinforcement of five thousand men had been sent from England in September; but the former belonged to Hill's army, and of the latter, the lifeguards and blues had gone to Lisbon.   Hence a

Souham's
official cor-
respon-
dence,
MSS.

regiment of foot guards, and some detachments for CHAP.
IV.
the line, in all about three thousand, were the only
available force in the rear. 1812.
October.

During the first part of the siege, the English
general seeing the French scattered along the Ebro,
and only reinforced by conscripts, did not fear any
interruption, and the less so, that sir Home Popham
was again menacing the coast line. Even now,
when the French were beginning to concentrate their
troops, he cared little for them, and was resolved
to give battle; for he thought that Popham and the
guerillas would keep Caffarelli employed, and he
felt himself a match for the army of Porugal. Nor
were the Partidas inactive on any point, and their
successes though small in themselves, were exceedingly harassing to the enemy.

Mina having obtained two or three thousand stand of English arms had re-entered Aragon
and domineered on the left bank of the Ebro,
while Duran, with four thousand men, operated
uncontrolled on the right bank. The Empecinado,
Villacampa, and Bassecour descended from Cuenca,
the first against Requeña, the others against Albacete. The Frayle interrupted the communications between Valencia and Tortoza. Saornil,
Cuesta, Firmin, and others, were in La Mancha
and Estremadura, Juan Palarea, called the Medico,
was near Segovia, and though Marquinez had been
murdered by one of his own men, his partida and
that of Julian Sanchez acted as regular troops with
Wellington's army. Meanwhile sir Home Popham,
in conjunction with Mendizabel, Porlier, and Renovales, who had gathered all the minor partidas
under their banners, assailed Gueteria; but unsuc-
cessfully; for on the 30th of September, the

Spanish chiefs were driven away, and Popham lost some guns which had been landed. About the same time the Empecinado being defeated at Requeña, retired to Cuenca, yet he failed not from thence to infest the French quarters.

Duran, when Soria was abandoned, fell upon Calatayud, but was defeated by Severoli, who withdrew the garrison. Then the Spanish chief attacked the castle of Almunia, which was only one march from Zaragoza, and when Severoli succoured this place also, and dismantled the castle, Duran attacked Borja between Tudela and Zaragoza, and took it before Severoli could come up. Thus Zaragoza was gradually deprived of its out-posts, on the right of the Ebro ; on the left, Mina hovered close to the gates, and his lieutenant, Chaplangara, meeting, near Ayerbe, with three hundred Italians, killed forty, and would have destroyed the whole but for the timely succour of some mounted gens-d'armes. At last Reille being undeceived as to Wellington's march, restored the smaller posts which he had abandoned, and Suchet ordered the castle of Almunia to be refitted, but during these events, Bassecour and Villa Campa united to infest Joseph's quarters about Albacete.

Soult's march from Andalusia and his junction with the king, has been described ; but while he was yet at Grenada, Hill, leaving three Portuguese regiments of infantry and one of cavalry at Almendralejo and Truxillo, to protect his line of supply, had marched to cross the Tagus at Almaraz, and Arzobispo. He entered Toledo the 28th of September, and the same day Elio took a small French garrison left in Consuegra. Hill soon after occupied a line from Toledo to Aranjuez, where he

was joined by the fourth division, Victor Alten's
cavalry, and the detachments quartered about Ilde-
fonsos and Segovia. On the 8th, hearing of Soult's
arrival at Hellin, he pushed his cavalry to Belmonte
on the San Clemente road, and here in La Mancha
as in Old Castile the stories of French devastation
were belied by the abundance of provisions.

Bassecour, Villa Campa, and the Empecinado
now united on the road leading from Cuenca to
Valencia, while the Medico and other chiefs gathered in the Toledo mountains. In this manner
the allies extended from Toledo on the right, by
Belmonte, Cuenca, and Calatayud to near Jacca on
the left, and were in military communication with
the coast; for Caffarelli's disposable force was now
concentrated to relieve Burgos, and Mina had free
intercourse with Mendizabal and Renovales, and
with Popham's fleet. But the French line of correspondence between the armies in the eastern and Appendix, No. 8, B.
northern provinces, was so interrupted that the
English newspapers became their surest, quickest,
and most accurate channels of intelligence.

Souham, who over-rated the force of his adversary, and feared a defeat as being himself the only
barrier left between Wellington and France, was
at first so far from meditating an advance, that he
expected and dreaded an attack from the allies;
and as the want of provisions would not let him
concentrate his army permanently near Monasterio,
his dispositions were made to fight on the Ebro. Duke of
The minister of war had even desired him to Feltre's official
detach a division against the partidas. But when correspon-dence,
by the English newspapers, and other information MSS.
sent from Paris, he learned that Soult was in march
from Grenada,—that the king intended to move

BOOK
XIX.

1812.
October.

General
Souham's
official
correspon-
dence,
MSS.

upon Madrid,—that no English troops had left that capital to join Wellington,—that the army of the latter was not very numerous, and that the castle of Burgos was sorely pressed, he called up Caffarelli's troops from Vittoria, concentrated his own at Briviesca and resolved to raise the siege.

On the 13th a skirmish took place on the stream beyond Monasterio, where captain Perse of the sixteenth dragoons was twice forced from the bridge and twice recovered it in the most gallant manner, maintaining his post until colonel F. Ponsonby, who commanded the reserves, arrived. Ponsonby and Perse were both wounded, and this demonstration was followed by various others until the evening of the 18th, when the whole French army was united, and the advanced guard captured a picquet of the Brunswickers which contrary to orders had remained in St. Olalla. This sudden movement apparently prevented Wellington from occupying the position of Monasterio, his out-posts fell back on the 19th to Quintanapala and Olmos, and on the ridges behind those places he drew up his army in order of battle. The right was at Ibeas on the Arlanzan; the centre at Riobena and Majarradas on the main road behind Olmos ; the left was thrown back near Soto Palaccio, and rested on a small river.

The 20th, Maucune, with two divisions of infantry and one of cavalry, drove the allies from Quintanapala, but Olmos was successfully defended by the Chasseurs Brittaniques, and Maucune, having no supports, was immediately outflanked on the right and forced back to Monasterio, by two divisions under sir Edward Paget. There were now in position, including Pack's Portuguese, which blockaded the castle, about thirty-three thousand men under arms, namely, twenty-one thousand Anglo-Portuguese infantry and cavalry, eleven thousand Gallicians, and the horsemen of Marquinez and Julian Sanchez. Thus, there were four thousand troopers, but only two thousand six hundred of these were British and German, and the Spanish horsemen regular or irregular, could scarcely be counted in the line of battle. The number of guns and howitzers was only forty-two, including twelve Spanish pieces, extremely ill equipped and scant of ammunition.

Lord Wellington had long felt the want of artillery and had sent a memoir upon the subject, to the British government, in the beginning of the year, yet his ordnance establishment had not been augmented, hence his difficulties during the siege; and in the field, instead of ninety British and Portuguese cannon, which was the just complement for his army, he had now only fifty serviceable pieces, of which twenty-four were with general Hill; and all were British, for the Portuguese artillery had from the abuses and the poverty of their government entirely melted away. Now the French had, as I have before stated, forty-four thousand men, of which nearly five thousand were cavalry, and they had more than sixty guns, a matter of no small importance; for besides the actual power of artillery in an action, soldiers are excited when the noise is greatest on their side. Wellington stood, therefore, at disadvantage in numbers, composition, and real strength. In his rear was the castle, and the river Arlanzan, the fords and bridges of which were commanded by the guns of the fortress; his generals of division, Paget excepted, were not of

Official
state of the
army given
to Massena
MSS.

any marked ability, his troops were somewhat desponding, and deteriorated in discipline. His situation was therefore dangerous, and critical ; a
victory could scarcely be expected, and a defeat
would have been destructive ; he should not have
provoked a battle, nor would he have done so had
he known that Caffarelli's troops were united to
Souham's.

On the other hand, Souham should by all means
have forced on an action, because his ground was
strong, his retreat open, his army powerful and
compact, his soldiers full of confidence, his lieutenants Clauzel, Maucune, and Foy, men of distinguished talents, able to second, and able to succeed
him in the chief command. The chances of victory and the profit to be derived were great, the
chances of defeat, and the dangers to be incurred
comparatively small. And it was thus indeed that
he judged the matter himself, for Maucune's advance was intended to be the prelude to a great
battle, and the English general, as we have seen,
was willing to stand the trial. But generals are not
absolute masters of events, and as the extraneous
influence which restrained both sides, on this
occasion, came from afar, it was fitting to show how,
in war, movements, distant, and apparently unconnected with those immediately under a general's
eye, will break his measures, and make him appear
undecided or foolish when in truth he is both wise
and firm.

While Wellington was still engaged with the
siege, the cortez made him commander of all the
Spanish armies. He had before refused this responsible situation, but the circumstances were now
changed, for the Spaniards, having lost nearly all

Appendix,
No. 8. A.

their cavalry and guns in the course of the war,
could not safely act, except in connexion with the
Anglo-Portuguese forces, and it was absolutely
necessary that one head should direct. The English
general therefore demanded leave of his own government to accept the offer, although he observed,
that the Spanish troops were not at all improved in
their discipline, their equipments, or their military
spirit; but he thought that conjoined with the
British they might behave well, and so escape
any more of those terrible disasters which had here-
tofore overwhelmed the country and nearly brought
the war to a conclusion. He was willing to save
the dignity of the Spanish government, by leaving
it a certain body of men wherewith to operate after
its own plans; but that he might exercise his own
power efficiently, and to the profit of the troops
under himself, he desired that the English government would vigorously insist upon the strict application of the subsidy to the payment of the Spanish
soldiers acting with the British army, otherwise
the care of the Spanish troops, he said, would only
cramp his own operations.

In his reply to the Cortez, his acceptance of the
offer was rendered dependent upon the assent of
his own government; and he was careful to guard
himself from a danger, not unlikely to arise, namely,
that the Cortez, when he should finally accept the
offer, would in virtue of that acceptance assume
the right of directing the whole operations of the
war. The intermediate want of power to move the
Spanish armies, he judged of little consequence,
because hitherto his suggestions having been cheer-
fully attended to by the Spanish chiefs, he had no

reason to expect any change in that particular, but there he was grievously mistaken.

Previous to this offer the Spanish government had, at his desire, directed Ballesteros to cross the Morena, and place himself at Alcaraz and in support of the Chinchilla fort, where joined by Cruz Murgeon, by Elio, and by the Partidas, he would have had a corps of thirty thousand men, would have been supported by Hill's army, and, having the mountains behind him for a retreat, could have safely menaced the enemy's flank, and delayed the march against Madrid or at least have obliged the king to leave a strong corps of observation to watch him. But Ballesteros, swelling with arrogant folly, never moved from Grenada, and when he found that Wellington was created generalissimo, he published a manifesto appealing to the Spanish pride against the degradation of serving under a foreigner; he thus sacrificed to his own spleen the welfare of his country, and with a result he little expected; for while he judged himself a man to sway the destinies of Spain, he suddenly found himself a criminal and nothing more. The Cortez caused him to be arrested in the midst of his soldiers, who, indifferent to his fate, suffered him to be sent a prisoner to Ceuta. The count of Abisbal was then declared captain general of Andalusia, and the duke del Parque was appointed to command Ballesteros' army, which general Verues immediately led by Jaen towards La Mancha, but Soult was then on the Tormes.

That marshal united with the king on the 3d of October. His troops required rest, his numerous sick were to be sent to the Valencian hospitals, and

his first interview with Joseph was of a warm
nature, for each had his griefs and passions to declare. Finally the monarch yielded to the superior mental power of his opponent and resolved to
profit from his great military capacity, yet reluctantly and more from prudence than liking; for the
duke of Feltre, minister of war at Paris, although
secretly an enemy of Soult, and either believing, or
pretending to believe in the foolish charges of disorderly ambition made against that commander, opposed any decided exercise of the king's authority
until the emperor's will was known : yet this would
not have restrained the king if the marshals Jourdan
and Suchet had not each declined accepting the
duke of Dalmatia's command when Joseph offered
it to them.

Soult's first operation was to reduce Chinchilla,
a well-constructed fort, which, being in the midst
of his quarters, commanded the great roads so as to
oblige his army to move under its fire or avoid it
by circuitous routes. A vigorous defence was
expected, but on the 6th it fell, after a few hours'
attack ; for a thunder-storm suddenly arising in a
clear sky had discharged itself upon the fort, and
killed the governor and many other persons, whereupon the garrison, influenced, it is said, by a superstitious fear, surrendered. This was the first bitter
fruit of Ballesteros' disobedience, for neither could
Soult have taken Chinchilla, nor scattered his troops,
as he did, at Albacete, Almanza, Yecla, and Hellin,
if thirty thousand Spaniards had been posted between Alcaraz and Chinchilla, and supported by
thirty thousand Anglo-Portuguese at Toledo under
Hill. These extended quarters were however essential for the feeding of the French general's num-

bers, and now, covered by the fort of Chinchilla, his troops were well lodged, his great convoys of sick and maimed men, his Spanish families, and other impediments, safely and leisurely sent to Valencia, while his cavalry scouring the country of La Mancha in advance, obliged Bassecour and Villa Campa to fall back upon Cuenca.

The detail of the operations which followed, belongs to another place. It will suffice to say here, that the king, being at the head of more than seventy thousand men, was enabled without risking Valencia to advance towards the Tagus, having previously sent Souham a specific order to combine his movements in cooperation but strictly to avoid fighting. General Hill also finding himself threatened by such powerful forces, and reduced by Ballesteros' defection to a simple defence of the Tagus, at a moment when that river was becoming fordable in all places, gave notice of his situation to lord Wellington. Joseph's letter was dispatched on the 1st, and six others followed in succession day by day, yet the last carried by colonel Lucotte, an officer of the royal staff, first reached Souham; the advantages derived from the allies' central position, and from the Partidas, were here made manifest; for Hill's letter, though only dispatched the 17th, reached Wellington at the same moment that Joseph's reached Souham. The latter general was thus forced to relinquish his design of fighting on the 20th; nevertheless having but four days' provisions left, he designed when those should be consumed, to attack notwithstanding the king's prohibition, if Wellington should still confront him. But the English general considering that his own army, already in a very critical situation, would be quite isolated if the king should, as was

Appendix,
No. 8. A.

most probable, force the allies from the Tagus, now resolved, though with a bitter pang, to raise the siege and retreat so far as would enable him to secure his junction with Hill.

While the armies were in presence some fighting had place at Burgos, Dubreton had again obtained possession of the ruins of the church of San Roman and was driven away next morning; and now in pursuance of Wellington's determination to retreat, mines of destruction were formed in the horn-work by the besiegers, and the guns and stores were removed from the batteries to the parc at Villa Toro. But the greatest part of the draught animals had been sent to Reynosa, to meet the powder and artillery coming from Santander, and hence, the eighteen-pounders could not be carried off, nor, from some error, were the mines of destruction exploded. The rest of the stores and the howitzers were put in march by the road of Villaton and Frandovinez for Celada del Camino. Thus the siege was raised, after five assaults, several sallies and thirty-three days of investment, during which the besiegers lost more than two thousand men and the besieged six hundred in killed or wounded; the latter had also suffered severely, from continual labour, want of water, and bad weather, for the fortress was too small to afford shelter for the garrison and the greater part bivouacked between the lines of defence.

RETREAT FROM BURGOS.

This operation was commenced on the night of the 21st by a measure of great nicety and boldness, for the road, divaricating at Gamonal, led by See Plan 5. Villatoro to the bridge of Villaton on the one hand,

and the bridge of Burgos on the other, and Wellington chose the latter, which was the shortest, though it passed the Arlanzan river close under the guns of the castle. The army quitted the position after dark without being observed, and having the artillery-wheels muffled with straw, defiled over the bridge of Burgos with such silence and celerity, that Dubreton, watchful and suspicious as he was, knew nothing of their march until the Partidas, failing in nerve, commenced galloping; then he poured a destructive fire down, but soon lost the range. By this delicate operation the infantry gained Cellada del Camino and Hormillas that night, but the light cavalry halted at Estepar and the bridge of Villa Baniel. Souham, who did not discover the retreat until late in the evening of the 22d, was therefore fain to follow, and by a forced march, to overtake the allies, whereas, if Wellington to avoid the fire of the castle had gone by Villaton, and Frandovinez, the French might have forestalled him at Cellada del Camino.

The 23d the infantry renewing their march crossed the Pisuerga, at Cordovillas, and Torquemada, a little above and below its junction with the Arlanzan; but while the main body made this long march, the French having passed Burgos in the night of the 22d, vigorously attacked the allies' rear-guard. This was composed of the cavalry and some horse-artillery, commanded by Norman Ramsay and Major Downman; of two battalions of Germans under Colin Halket; and of the Partidas of Marquinez and Sanchez, the latter being on the left of the Arlanzan and the whole under the command of Sir Stapleton Cotton. The piquets of light cavalry were vigorously driven from the bridge of Baniel as early as seven o'clock in the morning; but they rallied upon their reserves and gained the Hormaza stream which was disputed for some time, and a charge made by captain Perse of the sixteenth dragoons, was of distinguished bravery. However the French cavalry finally forced the passage and the British retiring behind Cellada Camino took post in a large plain. On their left was a range of hills the summit of which was occupied by the Partida of Marquinez, and on their right was the Arlanzan, beyond which Julian Sanchez was posted. Across the middle of the plain run a marshy rivulet cutting the main road, and only passable by a little bridge near a house called the Venta de Pozo, and half way between this stream and Cellada there was a broad ditch with a second bridge in front of a small village. Cotton immediately retired over the marshy stream, leaving Anson's horsemen and Halket's infantry as a rear-guard beyond the ditch; and Anson to cover his own passage of that obstacle left the eleventh dragoons and the guns at Cellada Camino, which was situated on a gentle eminence.

COMBAT OF VENTA DE POZO.

When the French approached Cellada, major Money of the eleventh, who was in advance, galloping out from the left of the village at the head of two squadrons, overturned their leading horsemen, and the artillery plied them briskly with shot, but the main body advancing at a trot along the road soon outflanked the British, and obliged Money's squadrons to rejoin the rest of the regiment while the guns went on beyond the bridge of Venta de Pozo. Meanwhile the French general Curto with a brigade of hussars ascended the hills on the left, and being followed by Boyer's dragoons, put Marquinez' Partida to flight; but a deep ravine run along the foot of these hills, next the plain, it could only be passed at certain places, and towards the first of these the Partidas galloped, closely chased by the hussars, at the moment when the leading French squadrons on the plain were forming in front of Cellada to attack the eleventh regiment. The latter charged and drove the first line upon the second, but then both lines coming forward together, the British were pushed precipitately to the ditch, and got over by the bridge with some difficulty, though with little loss, being covered by the fire of Halket's infantry which was in the little village behind the bridge.

The left flank of this new line was already turned by the hussars on the hills, wherefore Anson fell back covered by the sixteenth dragoons, and in good order, with design to cross the second bridge at Venta de Pozo; during this movement Marquinez' Partida came pouring down from the hills in full flight, closely pursued by the French hussars, who mixed with the fugitives, and the whole mass fell upon the flank of the sixteenth dragoons; and at the same moment, these last were also charged by the enemy's dragoons, who had followed them over the ditch. The commander of the Partida was wounded, colonel Pelly with another officer, and thirty men of the sixteenth, fell into the enemy's hands, and all were driven in confusion upon the reserves. But while the French were reforming their scattered squadrons after this charge, Anson got his people over the bridge of Venta de Pozo and drew up beyond the rivulet and to the left

of the road, on which Halket's battalions and the
guns had already taken post, and the heavy German cavalry, an imposing mass, stood in line on
the right, and farther in the rear than the artillery.

Hitherto the action had been sustained by the
cavalry of the army of Portugal, but now Caffarelli's horsemen consisting of the lancers of Berg,
the fifteenth dragoons and some squadrons of "*gens
d'armes*," all fresh men, came down in line to the
rivulet, and finding it impassable, with a quick
and daring decision wheeled to their right, and
despite of the heavy pounding of the artillery,
trotted over the bridge, and again formed line, in
opposition to the German dragoons, having the
stream in their rear. The position was dangerous
but they were full of mettle, and though the Germans, who had let too many come over, charged
with a rough shock and broke the right, the French
left had the advantage and the others rallied ; then
a close and furious sword contest had place, but
the "*gens d'armes*" fought so fiercely, that the
Germans, maugre their size and courage, lost
ground and finally gave way in disorder. The
French followed on the spur with shrill and eager
cries, and Anson's brigade which was thus outflanked and threatened on both sides, fell back also,
but not happily, for Boyer's dragoons having continued their march by the hills to the village of Bal-
baces there crossed the ravine and came thundering
in on the left. Then the British ranks were broken,
the regiments got intermixed, and all went to the
rear in confusion; finally however the Germans,
having extricated themselves from their pursuers
turned and formed a fresh line on the left of the
road, and the others rallied upon them.

The "*gens d'armes*" and lancers, who had suffered severely from the artillery, as well as in the sword-fight, now halted, but Boyer's dragoons forming ten squadrons, again came to the charge, and with the more confidence that the allies' ranks appeared still confused and wavering. When within a hundred yards, the German officers rode gallantly out to fight, and their men followed a short way, but the enemy was too powerful, disorder and tumult again ensued, the swiftness of the English horses alone prevented a terrible catastrophe, and though some favourable ground enabled the line to reform once more, it was only to be again broken. However Wellington, who was present, had placed Halket's infantry and the guns in a position to cover the cavalry, and they remained tranquil until the enemy, in full pursuit after the last charge, came galloping down and lent their left flank to the infantry; then the power of this arm was made manifest; a tempest of bullets emptied the French saddles by scores, and their hitherto victorious horsemen after three fruitless attempts to charge, each weaker than the other, reined up and drew off to the hills, the British cavalry covered by the infantry made good their retreat to Quintana la Puente near the Pisuerga, and the bivouacs of the enemy were established at Villadrigo. The loss in this combat was very considerable on both sides, the French suffered most, but they took a colonel and seventy other prisoners, and they had before the fight, also captured a small commissariat store near Burgos.

While the rear-guard was thus engaged, drunkenness and insubordination, the usual concomitants of an English retreat, were exhibited at Torquema-

da, where the well-stored wine-vaults became the
prey of the soldiery: it is said, that twelve thousand men were to be seen at one time in a state of
helpless inebriety. This commencement was bad,
and the English general, who had now retreated
some fifty miles, seeing the enemy so hot and menacing in pursuit, judged it fitting to check his course;
for though the arrangements were surprisingly well
combined, the means of transport were so scanty and
the weather so bad, that the convoys of sick and
wounded were still on the wrong side of the Duero.
Wherefore, having with a short march crossed the
Carion river on the 24th at its confluence with the
Pisuerga, he turned and halted behind it.

Here he was joined by a regiment of the guards,
and by detachments coming from Coruña, and
his position extending from Villa Muriel to Dueñas below the meeting of the waters, was strong.
The troops occupied a range of hills, lofty, yet descending with an easy sweep to the Carion; that
river covered the front, and the Pisuerga did the same
by the right wing. A detachment had been left to destroy the bridge of Baños on the Pisuerga; colonel
Campbell with a battalion of the royals was sent to aid
the Spaniards in destroying the bridges at Palencia;
and in Wellington's immediate front some houses
and convents beyond the rivers, furnished good
posts to cover the destruction of the bridges of
Muriel and San Isidro on the Carion, and that of
Dueñas on the Pisuerga.

Souham excited by his success on the 23d followed from Villadrigo early on the 24th, and having
cannonaded the rear-guard at Torquemada passed
the Pisuerga. He immediately directed Foy's division upon Palencia, and ordered Maucune with the

advanced guard to pursue the allies to the bridges
of Baños, Isidro, and Muriel; but he halted himself
at Magoz, and, if fame does not lie, because the number of French drunkards at Torquemada were even
more numerous than those of the British army.

COMBAT ON THE CARION.

Before the enemy appeared, the summits of the
hills were crowned by the allies, all the bridges
were mined and that of San Isidro was strongly
protected by a convent which was filled with troops.
The left of the position was equally strong, yet
general Oswald, who had just arrived from England
and taken the command of the fifth division on the
instant, overlooked the advantages to be derived
from the dry bed of a canal with high banks,
which, on his side, run parallel with the Carion,
and he had not occupied the village of Muriel in
sufficient strength. In this state of affairs Foy
reached Palencia, where, according to some French
writers, a treacherous attempt was made under cover
of a parley, to kill him ; he however drove the allies
with some loss from the town and in such haste
that all the bridges were abandoned in a perfect
condition, and the French cavalry crossing the river
and spreading abroad gathered up both baggage
and prisoners.

This untoward event obliged Wellington to throw
back his left, composed of the fifth division and the
Spaniards, at Muriel, thus offering two fronts, the
one facing Palencia, the other the Carion. Oswald's
error then became manifest ; for Maucune having dispersed the eighth caçadores who were defending a ford
between Muriel and San Isidro, fell with a strong

body of infantry and guns upon the allies at Muriel,
and this at the moment when the mine having been
exploded, the party covering the bridge were passing the broken arch by means of ladders. The
play of the mine which was effectual, checked
the advance of the French for an instant, but
suddenly a horseman darting out at full speed
from the column, rode down under a flight of
bullets, to the bridge, calling out that he was a
deserter; he reached the edge of the chasm made
by the explosion, and then violently checking his
foaming horse, held up his hands, exclaiming
that he was a lost man, and with hurried accents
asked if there was no ford near. The good-na-
tured soldiers pointed to one a little way off and
the gallant fellow having looked earnestly for a few
moments as if to fix the exact point, wheeled his
horse round, kissed his hand in derision, and bend-
ing over his saddle-bow dashed back to his own
comrades, amidst showers of shot, and shouts of
laughter from both sides. The next moment
Maucune's column covered by a concentrated fire
of guns passed the river at the ford thus discovered, made some prisoners in the village, and
lined the dry bed of the canal.

Lord Wellington who came up at this instant immediately turned some guns upon the enemy and desired
that the village and canal might be retaken; Oswald
thought that they could not be held, yet Wellington,
whose retreat was endangered by the presence of the
enemy on that side of the river was peremptory; he
ordered one brigade under general Barnes to attack
the main body, while another brigade under general
Pringle, cleared the canal, and he strengthened the
left with the Spanish troops and Brunswickers. A

very sharp fire of artillery and musquetry ensued,
and the allies suffered some loss, especially by cannon-shot which from the other side of the river
plumped into the reserves. The Spaniards, unequal
to any regular movement, got into confusion, and
were falling back, when their fiery countryman
Miguel Alava, running to their head, with exhortation and example, for though wounded he would
not retire, urged them forward to the fight; finally
the enemy was driven over the river, the village was reoccupied in force, and the canal was
lined by the allied troops. During these events at
Villa Muriel, other troops attempted without success to seize the bridge of San Isidro, and the mine
was exploded; but they were more fortunate at
the bridge of Baños on the Pisuerga, for the mine
there failed, and the French cavalry galloping
over, made both the working and covering party
prisoners.

The strength of the position was now sapped,
for Souham could assemble his army on the allies'
left, by Palencia, and force them to an action with
their back upon the Pisuerga, or he could pass that
river on his own left, and forestall them on the
Duero at Tudela. If Wellington pushed his army
over the Pisuerga by the bridge of Duenas, Souham,
having the initial movement, might be first on the
ground, and could attack the heads of the allied columns while Foy's division came down on the rear. If
Wellington, by a rapid movement along the right
bank of the Pisuerga, endeavoured to cross at
Cabezon, which was the next bridge in his rear, and
so gain the Duero, Souham by moving along the
left bank, might fall upon him while in march to
the Duero, and hampered between that river the

Pisuerga and the Esquevilla. An action under
such circumstances would have been formidable,
and the English general once cut off from the Duero
must have retired through Valladolid and Simancas
to Tordesillas, or Toro, giving up his communications with Hill. In this critical state of affairs
Wellington made no delay. He kept good watch
upon the left of the Pisuerga, and knowing that the
ground there was rugged, and the roads narrow and
bad, while on the right bank they were good and
wide, sent his baggage in the night to Valladolid,
and withdrawing the troops before day-break on
the 26th, made a clean march of sixteen miles to
Cabezon, where he passed to the left of the Pisuerga
and barricaded and mined the bridge. Then
sending a detachment to hold the bridge of Tudela
on the Duero behind him, he caused the seventh
division, under lord Dalhousie, to secure the bridges
of Valladolid, Simancas, and Tordesillas. His retreat
behind the Duero, which river was now in full
water, being thus assured, he again halted, partly
because the ground was favourable, partly to give
the commissary general Kennedy time for some indispensible arrangements.

This functionary, who had gone to England sick
in the latter end of 1811, and had returned to the
army only the day before the siege of Burgos was
raised, in passing from Lisbon by Badajoz to Madrid, and thence to Burgos, discovered that the inexperience of the gentleman who conducted the department during his absence had been productive of some
serious errors. The magazines established between
Lisbon and Badajos, and from thence by Almaraz to
the valley of the Tagus, for the supply of the army
in Madrid, had not been removed again when the

retreat commenced, and Soult would have found
them full, if his march had been made rapidly on
that side; on the other hand the magazines on the
line of operations, between Lisbon and Salamanca,
were nearly empty.   Kennedy had therefore the
double task on hand to remove the magazines from
the south side of the Tagus, and to bring up stores
upon the line of the present retreat; and his dispositions were not yet completed when Wellington
desired him to take measures for the removal of the
sick and wounded, and every other incumbrance,
from Salamanca, promising to hold his actual position
on the Pisuerga until the operation was effected. Now
there was sufficient means of transport for the
occasion, but the negligence of many medical and
escorting officers, conducting the convoys of sick to
the rear, and the consequent bad conduct of the
soldiers, for where the officers are careless the
soldiers will be licentious, produced the worst effects.
Such outrages were perpetrated on the inhabitants
along the whole line of march that terror was every
where predominant, and the ill-used drivers and muleteers deserted, some with, some without their cattle,
by hundreds.   Hence Kennedy's operation in some
measure failed, the greatest distress was incurred,
and the commissariat lost nearly the whole of the
animals and carriages employed; the villages were
abandoned, and the under-commissaries were be-
wildered, or paralyzed, by the terrible disorder thus
spread along the line of communication.

Souham having repaired the bridges on the
Carion, resumed the pursuit on the 26th, by the
right of the Pisuerga, being deterred probably from
moving to the left bank, by the rugged nature of the
ground, and by the king's orders not to risk a serious

action. In the morning of the 27th his whole army
was collected in front of Cabezon, but he contented
himself with a cannonade and a display of his
force; the former cost the allies colonel Robe of the
artillery, a practised officer and a worthy man; the
latter enabled the English general, for the first
time, to discover the numbers he had to contend
with, and they convinced him that he could hold
neither the Pisuerga nor the Duero permanently.
However his object being to gain time, he held his
position, and when the French, leaving a division in
front of Cabezon, extended their right, by Cigales
and Valladolid, to Simancas, he caused the bridges at
the two latter places to be destroyed in succession.

Congratulating himself that he had not fought
in front of Burgos with so powerful an army,
Wellington now resolved to retire behind the Duero
and finally, if pressed, behind the Tormes. But
as the troops on the Tagus would then be exposed to a flank attack, similar to that which the
siege of Burgos had been raised to avoid on his
own part; and as this would be more certain if any
ill fortune befell the troops on the Duero, he ordered Hill to relinquish the defence of the Tagus
at once and retreat, giving him a discretion as to
the line, but desiring him, if possible, to come by
the Guadarama passes; for he designed, if all went
well, to unite on the Adaja river in a central position, intending to keep Souham in check with a
part of his army, and with the remainder to fall
upon Soult.

On the 28th Souham, still extending his right,
with a view to dislodge the allies by turning their
left, endeavoured to force the bridges at Valladolid See plan 5.
and Simancas on the Pisuerga, and that of Torde-

sillas on the Duero. The first was easily defended
by the main body of the seventh division, but
Halket, an able officer, finding the French strong
and eager at the second, destroyed it, and detached
the regiment of Brunswick Oels to ruin that of
Tordesillas. It was done in time, and a tower behind the ruins was occupied by a detachment, while
the remainder of the Brunswickers took post in a
pine-wood at some distance. The French arrived
and seemed for some time at a loss, but very soon
sixty French officers and non-commissioned officers,
headed by captain Guingret, a daring man, formed
a small raft to hold their arms and clothes, and
then plunged into the water, holding their swords
with their teeth, and swimming and pushing their
raft before them. Under protection of a cannonade, they thus crossed this great river, though
it was in full and strong water, and the weather
very cold, and having reached the other side, naked
as they were, stormed the tower. The Brunswick
regiment then abandoned its position, and these
gallant soldiers remained masters of the bridge.

Wellington having heard of the attack at Simancas,
and having seen the whole French army in march
to its right along the hill beyond the Pisuerga on
the evening of the 28th, destroyed the bridges at
Valladolid and Cabeçon, and crossed the Duero at
Tudela and Puente de Duero on the 29th, but
scarcely had he effected this operation when intelligence of Guingret's splendid action at Tordesillas
reached him. With the instant decision of a great
captain he marched by his left, and having reached
the heights between Rueda and Tordesillas on the
30th, fronted the enemy and forbad further progress
on that point; the bridge was indeed already

repaired by the French, but Souham's main body

had not yet arrived, and Wellington's menacing position was too significant to be misunderstood. The bridges of Toro and Zamora were now destroyed by detachments, and though the French, spreading along the river bank, commenced repairing the former, the junction with Hill's army was insured; and the English general, judging that the bridge of Toro could not be restored for several days, even hoped to maintain the line of the Duero permanently, because he expected that Hill, of whose operations it is now time to speak, would be on the Adaja by the 3d of November.

CHAPTER V.

FRENCH PASSAGE OF THE TAGUS—RETREAT
FROM MADRID.

BOOK
XIX.
———
1812.
October.
See plan 6.
King Joseph's first intention was to unite a great
part of Suchet's forces as well as Soult's with his
own, and Soult, probably influenced by a false report that Ballesteros had actually reached La
Mancha, urged this measure. Suchet resisted, observing that Valencia must be defended against the
increasing power of the Anglo-Sicilian and Spanish
armies at Alicant, and the more so that, until the
French army could cross the Tagus and open a new
line of communication with Zaragoza, Valencia
would be the only base for the king's operations.
Joseph then resolved to incorporate a portion of the
army of the south with the army of the centre,
giving the command to Drouet, who was to move
by the road of Cuenca and Tarancon towards the
Tagus; but this arrangement, which seems to have
been dictated by a desire to advance Drouet's authority, was displeasing to Soult. He urged that
his army, so powerfully constituted, physically and
morally, as to be the best in the Peninsula, owed
its excellence to its peculiar organization and it
would be dangerous to break that up. Nor was
there any good reason for this change; for if
Joseph only wished to have a strong body of

troops on the Cuenca road, the army of the centre
could be reinforced with one or two divisions, and
the whole could unite again on the Tagus without
injury to the army of the south. It would however
be better, he said, to incorporate the army of the
centre with the army of the south and march altogether by the road of San Clemente, leaving only a
few troops on the Cuenca road, who might be reinforced by Suchet. But if the king's plan arose
from a desire to march in person with a large body
he could do so with greater dignity by joining the
army of the south, which was to act on the main
line of operations. Joseph's reply was a peremptory order to obey or retire to France, and Drouet
marched to Cuenca.

Soult's army furnished thirty-five thousand infantry,
six thousand excellent cavalry under arms with se- Imperial
venty-two guns, making with the artillerymen a total muster-
rolls,MSS.
of forty-six thousand veteran combatants. The army
of the centre including the king's guards furnished
about twelve thousand, of which two thousand were
good cavalry with twelve guns. Thus fifty-eight Joseph's
correspon-
thousand fighting men, eight thousand being cavalry, dence,
MSS.
with eighty-four pieces of artillery, were put in motion to drive Hill from the Tagus. Joseph's project
was to pass that river, and operate against Wellington's rear, if he should continue the siege of Burgos ; but if he concentrated on the Tagus, Souham
was in like manner to operate on his rear by Aranda official papers from
de Duero, and the Somosierra, sending detachments the Bureau
de la Guerre
towards Guadalaxara to be met by other detach- MSS.
ments, coming from the king through Sacedon.
Finally if Wellington, as indeed happened, should
abandon both Burgos and Madrid, the united
French forces were to drive him into Portugal.

The conveying of Soult's convoys of sick men to
Valencia and other difficulties, retarded the commencement of operations to the king's great discontent, and meanwhile he became very uneasy for his
supplies, because the people of La Mancha, still
remembering Montbrun's devastations, were flying
with their beasts and grain, and from frequent repetition, were become exceedingly expert in evading the researches of the foragers. Such however
is the advantage of discipline and order, that while
La Mancha was thus desolated from fear, confidence
and tranquillity reigned in Valencia.

However on the 18th of October Joseph marched
from Requeña upon Cuenca, where he found Drouet
with a division of Soult's infantry and some cavalry.
He then proceeded to Tarancon, which was the
only artillery road, on that side, leading to the
Tagus, and during this time Soult marched by San
Clemente upon Ocaña and Aranjuez. General Hill
immediately sent that notice to Lord Wellington
which caused the retreat from Burgos, but he was
in no fear of the enemy, for he had withdrawn all
his outposts and united his whole force behind the
Tagus. His right was at Toledo, his left at Fuente
Dueñas, and there were Spanish and Portuguese
troops in the valley of the Tagus extending as far as
Talavera. The Tagus was however fordable, from its
junction with the Jarama near Aranjuez, upwards;
and moreover, this part of the line, weak from its
extent, could not easily be supported, and the troops
guarding it, would have been too distant from the
point of action if the French should operate against
Toledo. Hill therefore drew his left behind the Ta-
juna which is a branch of the Jarama, and running
nearly parallel to the Tagus. His right occupied

very strong ground from Añover to Toledo, he destroyed the bridges at Aranjuez, and securing that
below the confluence of the Jarama and Henares,
called the Puente Larga, threw one of boats over
the former river a little above Bayona. The light
division and Elio's troops forming the extreme left
were directed to march upon Arganda, and the head-
quarters were fixed at Cienpozuelos.

The bulk of the troops were thus held in hand,
ready to move to any menaced point, and as Skerrit's brigade had just arrived from Cadiz, there was,
including the Spanish regulars, forty thousand men
in line, and a multitude of partidas were hovering
about. The lateral communications were easy and
the scouts passing over the bridge of Toledo covered
all the country beyond the Tagus. In this state of
affairs the bridges at each end of the line furnished
the means of sallying upon the flanks of any force
attacking the front; the French must have made
several marches to force the right, and on the left
the Jarama with its marshy banks, and its many
confluents, offered several positions, to interpose between the enemy and Madrid.

Drouet passed the Tagus the 29th at the abandoned fords of Fuente Dueñas and Villa Maurique,
and the king, with his guards, repaired to Zarza de la
Cruz. Meanwhile Soult whose divisions were coming
fast up to Ocaña, restored the bridge of Aranjuez,
and passed the Tagus also with his advanced guard.
On the 30th he attacked General Cole who commanded at the Puente Larga with several regiments
and some guns, but though the mines failed and
the French attempted to carry the bridge with the
bayonet they were vigorously repulsed by the forty-
seventh under Colonel Skerrit. After a heavy can-

nonade and a sharp musketry which cost the allies
sixty men, Soult relinquished the attempt and
awaited the arrival of his main body. Had the Puente
Larga been forced, the fourth division which was at
Soult's
official cor-
respond-
ence with
the king,
MSS.
Añover would have been cut off from Madrid, but
the weather being thick and rainy, Soult could not
discover what supporting force was on the high
land of Valdemoro behind the bridge and was
afraid to push forward too fast.

The king discontented with this cautious mode of
proceeding now designed to operate by Toledo, but
during the night the Puente Larga was abandoned,
and Soult, being still in doubt of Hill's real object,
advised Joseph to unite the army of the centre at
Arganda and Chinchon, throwing bridges for retreat
at Villa Maurique and Fuente Dueñas as a precaution in case a battle should take place. Hill's
movement was however a decided retreat, which
would have commenced twenty-four hours sooner
but for the failure of the mines and the combat at
the Puente Larga. Wellington's orders had reached
him at the moment when Soult first appeared on the
Tagus, and the affair was so sudden, that the light
division, which had just come from Alcala to Arganda to close the left of the position, was obliged,
without halting, to return again in the night, the
total journey being nearly forty miles.

Wellington, foreseeing that it might be difficult
for Hill to obey his instructions, had given him a
discretionary power to retire either by the valley
of the Tagus, or by the Guadarama; and a position
taken up in the former, on the flank of the enemy,
would have prevented the king from passing the
Guadarama, and at the same time have covered
Lisbon; whereas a retreat by the Guadarama ex-

posed Lisbon. Hill, thinking the valley of the
Tagus, in that advanced season, would not support
the French army, and knowing Wellington to be
pressed by superior forces in the north, chose the
Guadarama. Wherefore, burning his pontoons, and
causing La China and the stores remaining there to
be destroyed in the night of the 30th, he retreated
by different roads, and united his army on the 31st
of October near Majadahonda. Meanwhile the
magazines along the line of communication to
Badajos were, as I have already noticed, in danger
if the enemy had detached troops to seize them,
neither were the removal and destruction of the
stores in Madrid effected without disorders of a
singular nature.

The municipality had demanded all the provision
remaining there as if they wanted them for the enemy,
and when this was refused, they excited a mob to
attack the magazines ; some firing even took place,
and the assistance of the fourth division was required to restore order ; a portion of wheat was finally
given to the poorest of the people, and Madrid was
abandoned. It was affecting to see the earnest
and true friendship of the population. Men and
women, and children, crowded around the troops
bewailing their departure. They moved with them
in one vast mass, for more than two miles, and left
their houses empty at the very instant when the
French cavalry scouts were at the gates on the other
side. This emotion was distinct from political feeling, because there was a very strong French party
in Madrid ; and amongst the causes of wailing the
return of the plundering and cruel partidas, un-
checked by the presence of the British, was very
loudly proclaimed. The " Madrileños" have been

stigmatized as a savage and faithless people, the
British army found them patient, gentle, generous,
and loyal; nor is this fact to be disputed, because
of the riot which occurred in the destruction of the
magazines, for the provisions had been obtained by
requisition from the country around Madrid, under
an agreement with the Spanish government to pay
at the end of the war; and it was natural for the
people, excited as they were by the authorities, to
endeavour to get their own flour back, rather than
have it destroyed when they were starving.

With the Anglo-Portuguese troops marched
Penne Villemur, Morillo, and Carlos D'España, and
it was Wellington's wish that Elio, Bassecour, and
Villa Campa should now throw themselves into the
valley of the Tagus, and crossing the bridge of Arzobispo, join Ballesteros's army, now under Virues.
A great body of men, including the Portuguese
regiments left by Hill in Estremadura, would thus
have been placed on the flank of any French army
marching upon Lisbon, and if the enemy neglected
this line, the Spaniards could operate against Madrid
or against Suchet at pleasure.   Elio, however, being
cut off from Hill by the French advance, remained
at the bridge of Auñion, near Sacedon, and was
there joined by Villa Campa and the Empecinado.

Soult now brought up his army as quickly as
possible to Valdemoro, and his information, as to
Hill's real force, was becoming more distinct; but
there was also a rumour that Wellington was close
at hand with three British divisions, and the French
general's movements were consequently cautious, lest
he should find himself suddenly engaged in battle
before his whole force was collected, for his rear
was still at Ocaña, and the army of the centre had

not yet passed the Tajuña. This disposition of his
troops was probably intentional to prevent the king
from fighting, for Soult did not think this a fitting
time for a great battle unless upon great advantage.
In the disjointed state of their affairs, a defeat
would have been more injurious to the French than
a victory would have been beneficial; the former
would have lost Spain, the latter would not have
gained Portugal.

On the 1st of November, the bulk of Soult's
army being assembled at Getafé, he sent scouting
parties in all directions to feel for the allies, and
to ascertain the direction of their march; the next
·day the army of the centre and that of the south
were reunited not far from Madrid, but Hill was
then in full retreat for the Guadarama covered by
a powerful rear-guard under general Cole.

The 3d Soult pursued the allies, and the king
entering Madrid, placed a garrison in the Retiro
for the protection of his court and of the Spanish
families attached to his cause; this was a sensible
relief, for hitherto in one great convoy they had impeded the movements of the army of the centre.
On the 4th Joseph rejoined Soult at the Guadarama
with his guards, which always moved as a separate
body ; but he had left Palombini beyond the Tagus
near Tarancon to scour the roads on the side of
Cuenca, and some dragoons being sent towards
Huete were surprised by the partidas, and lost
forty men, whereupon Palombini rejoined the army.

General Hill was moving upon Arevalo, slowly
followed by the French, when fresh orders from
Wellington, founded on new combinations, changed
the direction of his march. Souham had repaired
the bridge of Toro on the 4th, several days sooner

than the English general had expected, and thus when he was keenly watching for the arrival of Hill on the Adaja, that he might suddenly join him and attack Soult, his designs were again baffled; for he dared not make such a movement lest Souham, possessing both Toro and Tordesillas, should fall upon his rear; neither could he bring up Hill to the Duero and attack Souham, because he had no means to pass that river, and meanwhile Soult moving by Fontiveros would reach the Tormes. Seeing then that his combinations had failed, and his central position no longer available, either for offence or defence, he directed Hill to gain Alba de Tormes at once by the road of Fontiveros, and on the 6th he fell back himself, from his position in front of Tordesillas, by Naval del Rey and Pituega to the heights of San Christoval.

See Plans
3 and 5.

Joseph, thinking to prevent Hill's junction with Wellington, had gained Arevalo by the Segovia road on the 5th and 6th; the 8th Souham's scouts were met with at Medina del Campo, and for the first time, since he had quitted Valencia, the king obtained news of the army of Portugal. One hundred thousand combatants, of which above twelve thousand were cavalry, with a hundred and thirty pieces of artillery, were thus assembled on those plains over which, three months before, Marmont had marched with so much confidence to his own destruction. Soult then expelled from Andalusia by Marmont's defeat, was now, after having made half the circuit of the Peninsula, come to drive into Portugal, that very army whose victory had driven him from the south; and thus, as Wellington had foreseen and foretold, the acquisition of Andalusia,

politically important and useful to the cause, proved
injurious to himself at the moment, insomuch as the
French had concentrated a mighty power, from
which it required both skill and fortune to escape.
Meanwhile the Spanish armies let loose by this
union of all the French troops, kept aloof, or coming
to aid, were found a burthen, rather than a help.

On the 7th Hill's main body passed the Tormes,
at Alba, and the bridge there was mined ; the
light division and Long's cavalry remained on the
right bank during the night but the next day the
former also crossed the river. Wellington himself
was in the position of San Christoval, and it is
curious, that the king, even at this late period, Joseph's
was doubtful if Ballesteros's troops had or had not correspon-
dence,
joined the allied army at Avila. Wellington also MSS.
was still uncertain of the real numbers of the enemy,
but he was desirous to maintain the line of the
Tormes permanently, and to give his troops repose.
He had made a retreat of two hundred miles ; Hill
had made one of the same distance besides his
march from Estremadura ; Skerrit's people had
come from Cadiz, and the whole army required
rest, for the soldiers, especially those who besieged
Burgos, had been in the field, with scarcely an
interval of repose, since January ; they were barefooted, and their equipments were spoiled, the
cavalry were becoming weak, their horses were out
of condition, and the discipline of all was failing.

The excesses committed on the retreat from
Burgos have already been touched upon, and during
the first day's march from the Tagus to Madrid,
some of general Hill's men had not behaved better.
Five hundred of the rear-guard under Cole, chiefly
of one regiment, finding the inhabitants had fled

according to their custom whichever side was approaching, broke open the houses, plundered and
got drunk.   A multitude were left in the cellars of
Valdemoro, and two hundred and fifty fell into the
hands of the enemy.   The rest of the retreat being
unmolested, was made with more regularity, but
the excesses still committed by some of the soldiers
were glaring and furnished proof that the moral
conduct of a general cannot be fairly judged by
following in the wake of a retreating army.   On
this occasion there was no want of provisions, no
hardships to exasperate the men, and yet I the
author of this history, counted on the first day's
march from Madrid, seventeen bodies of murdered
peasants ; by whom killed, or for what, whether by
English, or Germans, by Spaniards, or Portuguese,
whether in dispute, in robbery, or in wanton vil-
lany, I know not, but their bodies were in the
ditches, and a shallow observer might thence have
drawn the most foul and false conclusions against
the English general and nation.

Another notable thing was the discontent of the
veteran troops with the arrangements of the staff
officers.   For the assembling of the sick men, at the
place and time prescribed to form the convoys,
was punctually attended to by the regimental officers ; not so by the others, nor by the commissaries
who had charge to provide the means of transport ;
hence delay and great suffering to the sick and the
wearing out of the healthy men's strength by waiting with their packs on for the negligent.   And
when the light division was left on the right bank
of the Tormes to cover the passage at Alba, a prudent order that all baggage or other impediments,
should pass rapidly over the narrow bridge at that

place without halting at all on the enemy's side, was, by those charged with the execution, so rigorously interpreted, as to deprive the light division of their ration bullocks and flour mules, at the very moment of distribution; and the tired soldiers, thus absurdly denied their food, had the farther mortification to see a string of commissariat carts deliberately passing their post many hours afterwards. All regimental officers know that the anger and discontent thus created is one of the surest means of ruining the discipline of an army, and it is in these particulars that the value of a good and experienced staff is found.

Lord Wellington's position extended from Christoval to Aldea Lengua on the right bank of the Tormes, and on the left of that river, to the bridge of Alba, where the castle which was on the right bank was garrisoned by Howard's brigade of the second division. Hamilton's Portuguese were on the left bank as a reserve for Howard; the remainder of the second division watched the fords of Huerta and Enciña, and behind them in second line the third and fourth divisions occupied the heights of Calvariza de Ariba. The light division and the Spanish infantry entered Salamanca, the cavalry were disposed beyond the Tormes, covering all the front, and thus posted, the English general desired to bring affairs to the decision of a battle. For the heights of Christoval were strong and compact, the position of the Arapiles on the other side of the Tormes was glorious as well as strong, and the bridge of Salamanca, and the fords furnished the power of concentrating on either side of that river by a shorter line than the enemy could move upon.

But while Wellington prepared for a battle, he also looked to a retreat. His sick were sent to the rear, small convoys of provisions were ordered up from Ciudad Rodrigo to certain halting places between that place and Salamanca; the overplus of ammunition in the latter town was destroyed daily by small explosions, and large stores of clothing, of arms and accoutrements, were delivered to the Spanish troops, who were thus completely furnished; one hour after the English general had the mortification to see them selling their equipments even under his own windows. Indeed Salamanca presented an extraordinary scene, and the Spaniards, civil and military, began to evince hatred of the British. Daily did they attempt or perpetrate murder, and one act of peculiar atrocity merits notice. A horse, led by an English soldier, being frightened, backed against a Spanish officer commanding at a gate, he caused the soldier to be dragged into his guard-house and there bayonetted him in cold blood, and no redress could be had for this or other crimes, save by counter-violence, which was not long withheld. A Spanish officer while wantonly stabbing at a rifleman was shot dead by the latter; and a British volunteer slew a Spanish officer at the head of his own regiment in a sword fight, the troops of both nations looking on, but here there was nothing dishonourable on either side.

The civil authorities, not less savage, were more insolent than the military, treating every English person with an intolerable arrogance. Even the prince of Orange was like to have lost his life; for upon remonstrating about quarters with the sitting junta, they ordered one of their guards to

kill him; and he would have been killed had
not Mr. Steele of the forty-third, a bold athletic
person, felled the man before he could stab; yet
both the prince and his defender were obliged to
fly instantly to avoid the soldier's comrades. The
exasperation caused by these things was leading to
serious mischief when the enemy's movements gave
another direction to the soldiers' passions.

On the 9th Long's cavalry had been driven in
upon Alba, and on the 10th Soult opened a concentrated fire of eighteen guns against that place. The
castle, which crowned a bare and rocky knoll, had
been hastily entrenched, and furnished scarcely any
shelter from this tempest; for two hours the garrison could only reply with musketry, but finally
it was aided by the fire of four pieces from the left
bank of the river, and the post was defended until
dark, with such vigour that the enemy dared not
venture on an assault. During the night general
Hamilton reinforced the garrison, repaired the damaged walls, and formed barricades, but the next
morning after a short cannonade, and some musketry firing the enemy withdrew. This combat cost
the allies above a hundred men.

On the 11th the king coming up from Medina del
Campo reorganized his army. That is, he united the
army of the centre with the army of the south, placing
the whole under Soult, and he removed Souham from
the command of the army of Portugal to make way
for Drouet. Caffarelli had before this returned to
Burgos, with his divisions and guns, and as Souham,
besides his losses and stragglers, had placed garrisons in Toro, Tordesillas, Zamora, and Valladolid;
and as the king also, had left a garrison in the
Retiro, scarcely ninety thousand combatants of all

arms were assembled on the Tormes; but twelve thousand were cavalry, nearly all were veteran troops, and they had at least one hundred and twenty pieces of artillery. Such a mighty power could not remain idle, for the country was exhausted of provisions, the soldiers were already wanting bread, and the king, eager enough for battle, for he was of a brave spirit and had something of his brother's greatness of soul, sought counsel how to deliver it with most advantage.

Jourdan with a martial fire unquenched by age, was for bringing affairs to a crisis by the boldest and shortest mode. He had observed that Welling-
Appendix,
No. 9. ton's position was composed of three parts, namely, the right at Alba; the centre at Calvariza Ariba; the left, separated from the centre by the Tormes, at San Christoval; the whole distance being about fifteen miles. Now the Tormes was still fordable in many places above Salamanca, and hence he proposed to assemble the French army in the night, pass the river at day-break, by the fords between Villa Gonzalo and Huerta, and so make a concentrated attack upon Calvariza de Ariba, which would force Wellington to a decisive battle.

French
Official
correspon-
dence,
MSS. Soult opposed this project, he objected to attacking Wellington in a position which he was so well acquainted with, which he might have fortified, and where the army must fight its way, even from the fords, to gain room for an order of battle. He proposed instead, to move by the left to certain fords, three in number, between Exéme and Galisancho, some seven or eight miles above Alba de Tormes. They were easy in themselves, he said, and well suited from the conformation of the banks, for forcing a passage if it should be disputed; and by

making a slight circuit the troops in march could
not be seen by the enemy. Passing there, the
French army would gain two marches upon the
allies, would be placed upon their flank and rear,
and could fight on ground chosen by its own generals, instead of delivering battle on ground chosen
by the enemy ; or it could force on an action in a
new position whence the allies could with difficulty
retire in the event of disaster. Wellington must
then fight to disadvantage, or retire hastily, sacrificing part of his army to save the rest ; and the
effect, whether militarily or politically, would be the
same as if he was beaten by a front attack. Jourdan
replied, that this was prudent, and might be successful if Wellington accepted battle, but that
general could not thereby be forced to fight,
which was the great object ; he would have time to
retreat before the French could reach the line of
his communications with Ciudad Rodrigo, and it
was even supposed by some generals that he would
retreat to Almeida at once by San Felices and Barba
de Puerco.

Neither Soult nor Jourdan knew the position of
the Arapiles in detail, and the former, though he Letter to
the king,
urged his own plan, offered to yield if the king was MS.
so inclined. Jourdan's proposition was supported
by all the generals of the army of Portugal, except
Clausel who leaned to Soult's opinion ; but as that
marshal commanded two-thirds of the army, while
Jourdan had no ostensible command, the question
was finally decided agreeably to his counsel. Nor
is it easy to determine which was right, for though
Jourdan's reasons were very strong, and the result
did not bear out Soult's views, we shall find the
failure was only in the execution. Nevertheless it

would seem so great an army and so confident, for
the French soldiers eagerly demanded a battle,
should have grappled in the shortest way; a just
and rapid development of Jourdan's plan would probably have cut off Hamilton's Portuguese and the brigade in the castle of Alba, from Calvariza Ariba.

On the other hand, Wellington, who was so well
acquainted with his ground, desired a battle on either
side of the Tormes; his hope was indeed to prevent
the passage of that river until the rains rendered
it unfordable, and thus force the French to retire
from want of provisions, or engage him on the position of Christoval; yet he also courted a fight on
the Arapiles, those rocky monuments of his former
victory. He had sixty-eight thousand combatants
under arms, fifty-two thousand of which, including
Letter to
lord Liver-
pool, MS. four thousand British cavalry, were Anglo-Portuguese, and he had nearly seventy guns. This force
he had so disposed, that besides Hamilton's Portuguese, three divisions guarded the fords, which
were moreover defended by entrenchments, and the
whole army might have been united in good time
upon the strong ridges of Calvariza Ariba, and on
the two Arapiles, where the superiority of fifteen
thousand men would scarcely have availed the
French. A defeat would only have sent the allies
to Portugal, whereas a victory would have taken
them once more to Madrid. To draw in Hamilton's
Portuguese, and the troops from Alba, in time,
would have been the vital point; but as the French,
if they did not surprise the allies, must have fought
their way up from the river, this danger might
have proved less than could have been supposed
at first view. In fine the general was Wellington
and he knew his ground.

FRENCH PASSAGE OF THE TORMES.   RETREAT
TO CIUDAD RODRIGO.

Soult's plan being adopted, the troops in the
distant quarters were brought up; the army of
Portugal was directed to make frequent demonstrations against Christoval, Aldea Lengua, and the
fords between Huerta and Alba; the road over the
hills to the Galisancho fords was repaired, and two
trestle-bridges were constructed for the passage of
the artillery. The design was to push over the
united armies of the centre and the south, by these
fords; and if this operation should oblige the allies
to withdraw from Alba de Tormes, the army of
Portugal was to pass by the bridge at that place
and by the fords, and assail Wellington's rear; but
if the allies maintained Alba, Drouet was to follow
Soult at Galisancho.

At daybreak on the 14th the bridges were thrown,
the cavalry and infantry passed by the fords, the
allies' outposts were driven back, and Soult took a
position at Mozarbes, having the road from Alba to
Tamames, under his left flank. Meanwhile Wellington remained too confidently in Salamanca,
and when the first report informed him that the
enemy were over the Tormes, made the caustic
observation, that he would not recommend it to
some of them. Soon, however, the concurrent
testimony of many reports convinced him of his
mistake, he galloped to the Arapiles, and having
ascertained the direction of Soult's march drew off
the second division, the cavalry, and some guns
to attack the head of the French column. The
fourth division and Hamilton's Portuguese remained
at Alba, to protect this movement; the third

division secured the Arapiles rocks until the troops
from San Christoval should arrive; and Wellington
was still so confident to drive the French back over
the Tormes, that the bulk of the troops did not
quit San Christoval that day. Nevertheless when
he reached Mozarbes, he found the French, already
assembled there, too strong to be seriously meddled
with. However under cover of a cannonade, which
kept off their cavalry, he examined their position,
which extended from Mozarbes to the heights of
Nuestra Señora de Utiero, and it was so good that
the evil was without remedy; wherefore drawing off
the troops from Alba, and destroying the bridge,
he left three hundred Spaniards in the castle,
with orders, if the army retired the next day, to
abandon the place and save themselves as they
best could.

During the night and the following morning the
allied army was united in the position of the Arapiles, and Wellington still hoped the French would
give battle there; yet he placed the first division
at Aldea Tejada, on the Junguen stream, to secure
that passage in case Soult should finally oblige him
to choose between Salamanca and Ciudad Rodrigo.
Meantime the army of Portugal finding the bridge
of Alba broken, and the castle occupied, crossed
the Tormes at Galisancho, and moved up to the
ridge of Señora de Utiera; Soult, who had commenced fortifying Mozarbes, extended his left at the
same time to the height of Señora de la Buena, near
the Ciudad Rodrigo road, yet slowly because the
ground was heavy, deep, and the many sources of
the Junguen and the Valmusa streams were fast
filling from the rain and impeded his march.
This evolution was nearly the same as that prac-

tised by the duke of Ragusa at the battle of Salamanca; but it was made on a wider circle, by a
second range of heights enclosing as it were those
by which the duke of Ragusa moved on that day,
and consequently, beyond the reach of such a
sudden attack and catastrophe. The result in each
case was remarkable. Marmont closing with a short
quick turn, a falcon striking at an eagle, received a
buffet that broke his pinions, and spoiled his flight.
Soult, a wary kite, sailing slowly and with a wide
wheel to seize a helpless prey, lost it altogether.

About two o'clock lord Wellington, feeling himself too weak to attack, and seeing the French
cavalry pointing to the Ciudad Rodrigo road,
judged the king's design was to establish a fortified head of cantonments at Mozarbes, and then
operate against the allies' communication with
Ciudad Rodrigo; wherefore suddenly casting his
army into three columns, he crossed the Junguen,
and then covering his left flank with his cavalry
and guns, defiled, in order of battle, before the
enemy at little more than cannon-shot. With a
wonderful boldness and facility, and good fortune
also, for there was a thick fog and a heavy rain
which rendered the bye-ways and fields, by which
the enemy moved, nearly impassable, while the
allies had the use of the high roads, he carried his
whole army in one mass quite round the French left:
thus he gained the Valmusa river, where he halted
for the night, in the rear of those who had been
threatening him in front, only a few hours before.
This exploit was certainly surprising, but it was
not creditable to the generalship on either side; for
first it may be asked why the English commander,
having somewhat carelessly suffered Soult to pass

the Tormes and turn his position, waited so long on the Arapiles as to render this dangerous movement necessary, a movement which a combination of bad roads, bad weather, and want of vigour on the other side, rendered possible and no more.

It has been said, that the only drawback to the duke of Dalmatia's genius, is his want of promptness to strike at the decisive moment. It is certainly a great thing to fight a great battle; and against such a general as Wellington, and such troops as the British, a man may well be excused, if he thinks twice, ere he puts his life and fame, and the lives and fame of thousands of his countrymen, the weal or woe of nations, upon the hazard of an event, which may be decided by the existence of a ditch five feet wide, or the single blunder of a single fool, or the confusion of a coward, or by any other circumstance however trivial. To make such a throw for such a stake is no light matter. It is no mean consideration, that the praise or the hatred of nations, universal glory or universal, perhaps eternal contempt, waits on an action, the object of which may be more safely gained by other means, for in war there is infinite variety. But in this case it is impossible not to perceive, that the French general vacillated after the passage of the river, purposely perhaps to avoid an action, since, as I have before shown, he thought it unwise, in the disjointed state of the French affairs and without any fixed base or reserves in case of defeat, to fight a decisive battle. Nor do I blame this prudence, for though it be certain that he who would be great in war must be daring, to set all upon one throw belongs only to an irresponsible chief, not to a lieutenant whose

task is but a portion of the general plan; neither
is it wise, in monarch or general, to fight when
all may be lost by defeat, unless all may be won
by victory. However, the king, more unfettered
than Soult, desired a battle, and with an army so
good and numerous, the latter's prudence seems
misplaced; he should have grappled with his
enemy, and, once engaged at any point, Wellington could not have continued his retreat, especially
with the Spaniards, who were incapable of dexterous movements.

On the 16th the allies retired by the three roads
which lead across the Matilla stream, through Tamames, San Munos, and Martin del Rio, to Ciudad
Rodrigo; the light division and the cavalry closed
the rear, and the country was a forest, penetrable in
all directions. The army bivouacked in the evening
behind the Matilla stream; but though this march
was not more than twelve miles, the stragglers were
numerous, for the soldiers meeting with vast herds
of swine, quitted their colours by hundreds to shoot
them, and such a rolling musketry echoed through
the forest, that Wellington at first thought the
enemy was upon him. It was in vain that the staff
officers rode about to stop this disgraceful practice,
which had indeed commenced the evening before;
it was in vain that Wellington himself caused two
offenders to be hanged, the hungry soldiers still
broke from the columns, the property of whole districts was swept away in a few hours, and the
army was in some degree placed at the mercy of
the enemy. The latter however were contented to
glean the stragglers, of whom they captured two
thousand, and did not press the rear until evening near Matilla where their lancers fell on, but

were soon checked by the light companies of the twenty-eighth, and afterwards charged by the fourteenth dragoons.

The 17th presented a different yet a not less curious scene. During the night the cavalry immediately in front of the light division, had, for some unknown reason, filed off by the flanks to the rear without giving any intimation to the infantry, who, trusting to the horsemen, had thrown out their picquets at a very short distance in front. At daybreak, while the soldiers were rolling their blankets and putting on their accoutrements, some strange horsemen were seen in the rear of the bivouac and were at first taken for Spaniards, but very soon their cautious movements and vivacity of gestures, shewed them to be French; the troops stood to arms, and in good time, for five hundred yards in front, the wood opened on to a large plain on which, in place of the British cavalry, eight thousand French horsemen were discovered advancing in one solid mass, yet carelessly and without suspecting the vicinity of the British. The division was immediately formed in columns, a squadron of the fourteenth dragoons and one of the German hussars came hastily up from the rear, Julian Sanchez' cavalry appeared in small parties on the right flank, and every precaution was taken to secure the retreat. This checked the enemy, but as the infantry fell back, the French though fearing to approach their heavy masses in the wood, sent many squadrons to the right and left, some of which rode on the flanks near enough to bandy wit, in the Spanish tongue, with the British soldiers, who marched without firing. Very soon however the signs of mischief became visible, the road was

strewed with baggage, and the bât-men came running in for protection, some wounded, some without arms, and all breathless as just escaped from a
surprise. The thickness of the forest had enabled
the French horsemen to pass along unperceived on
the flanks of the line of march, and, as opportunity
offered, they galloped from side to side, sweeping
away the baggage and sabring the conductors and
guards; they had even menaced one of the columns
but were checked by the fire of the artillery. In one
of these charges general Paget was carried off, as it
were from the midst of his own men, and it might
have been Wellington's fortune, for he also was
continually riding between the columns and without
an escort. However the main body of the army
soon passed the Huebra river and took post behind
it, the right at Tamames, the left near Boadilla,
the centre at San Munoz, Buena Barba, and
Gallego de Huebra.

When the light division arrived at the edge of
the table-land, which overhangs the fords at the
last-named place, the French cavalry suddenly
thickened, and the sharp whistle of musket-bullets
with the splintering of branches on the left showed
that their infantry were also up. Soult in the
hope of forestalling the allies at Tamames, had
pushed his columns towards that place, by a road
leading from Salamanca through Vecinos, but finding Hill's troops in his front turned short to his right
in hopes to cut off the rear-guard, which led to the

COMBAT OF THE HUEBRA.

The English and German cavalry, warned by the
musketry, crossed the fords in time, and the light

division should have followed without delay ; because the forest ended on the edge of the table-land, and the descent from thence to the river, about eight hundred yards, was open and smooth, and the fords of the Huebra were deep.   Instead of taking the troops down quickly, an order, more respectful to the enemy's cavalry than to his infantry, was given to form squares. The officers looked at each other in amazement but at that moment Wellington fortunately appeared, and under his directions the battalions instantly glided off to the fords, leaving four companies of the forty-third and one of the riflemen to cover the passage.   These companies, spreading as skirmishers, were immediately assailed in front and on both flanks, and with such a fire that it was evident a large force was before them ; moreover a driving rain and mist prevented them from seeing their adversaries, and being pressed closer each moment, they gathered by degrees at the edge of the wood, where they maintained their ground for a quarter of an hour, then seeing the division was beyond the river, they swiftly cleared the open slope of the hill, and passed the fords under a very sharp musketry. Only twenty-seven soldiers fell, for the tempest, beating in the Frenchmen's faces, baffled their aim, and Ross's guns, playing from the low ground with grape, checked the pursuit, but the deep bellowing of thirty pieces of heavy French artillery showed how critically timed was the passage.

The banks of the Huebra were steep and broken, but the enemy spread his infantry to the right and left along the edge of the forest, making demonstrations on every side, and there were several fords to be guarded ; the fifty-second and the Portuguese

defended those below, Ross's guns supported by the
riflemen and the forty-third defended those above,
and behind the right of the light division, on higher
ground was the seventh division. The second division, Hamilton's Portuguese, and a brigade of cavalry, were in front of Tamames, and thus the bulk of the army was massed on the right, hugging the Pena de Francia, and covering the roads leading to Ciudad, as well as those leading to the passes of the Gata hills.

In this situation one brisk attempt made to force the fords guarded by the fifty-second, was vigorously repulsed by that regiment, but the skirmishing, and the cannonade, which never slackened, continued until dark; and heavily the French artillery played upon the light and seventh divisions. The former, forced to keep near the fords, and in column, lest a sudden rush of cavalry should carry off the guns on the flat ground, were plunged into at every round, yet suffered little loss, because the clayey soil, saturated with rain, swallowed the shot and smothered the shells; but it was a matter of astonishment to see the seventh division kept on open and harder ground by its commander, and in one huge mass tempting the havoc of this fire for hours, when a hundred yards in its rear the rise of the hill, and the thick forest, would have entirely covered it without in any manner weakening the position.

On the 18th the army was to have drawn off before daylight, and the English general was anxious about the result, because the position of the Huebra, though good for defence, was difficult to remove from at this season; the roads were hollow and narrow, and led up a steep bank to a table-land, which was open, flat, marshy, and scored with water gullies ; and from the overflowing of one of the streams the principal road was impassable a mile in rear of the position ; hence to bring the columns off in time, without jostling, and if possible without being attacked, required a nice management. All the baggage and stores had marched in the night, with orders not to halt until they reached the high lands near Ciudad Rodrigo, but if the preceding days had produced some strange occurrences, the 18th was not less fertile in them.

In a former part of this work it has been observed, that even the confirmed reputation of lord Wellington could not protect him from the vanity and presumption of subordinate officers. The allusion fixes here. Knowing that the most direct road was impassable, he had directed the divisions by another road, longer, and apparently more difficult ; this seemed such an extraordinary proceeding to some general officers, that, after consulting together, they deemed their commander unfit to conduct the army, and led their troops by what appeared to them the fittest line of retreat ! Meanwhile Wellington, who had, before day-light, placed himself at an important point on his own road, waited impatiently for the arrival of the leading division until dawn, and then suspecting something of what had happened, galloped to the other road and found the would-be commanders, stopped by that flood which his arrangements had been made to avoid. The insubordination, and the danger to the whole army, were alike glaring, yet the practical rebuke was so severe and well timed, the humiliation so complete, and so deeply felt, that, with one proud sarcastic observation, indicating contempt more than

anger, he led back the troops and drew off all his
forces safely. However some confusion and great
danger still attended the operation, for even on
this road one water-gully was so deep that the
light division, which covered the rear, could only
pass it man by man over a felled tree, and it was
fortunate that Soult unable to feed his troops a
day longer, stopped on the Huebra with his main
body and only sent some cavalry to Tamames.
Thus the allies retired unmolested, but whether
from necessity, or from negligence in the subordinates, the means of transport were too scanty for
the removal of the wounded men, most of whom
were hurt by cannon-shot; many were left behind,
and as the enemy never passed the Huebra at this
point, those miserable creatures perished by a horrible and lingering death.

The marshy plains, over which the army was
now marching, exhausted the strength of the
wearied soldiers, thousands straggled, the depre-
dations on the herds of swine were repeated, and
the temper of the army, generally, prognosticated
the greatest misfortunes if the retreat should be
continued. This was however the last day of trial,
for towards evening the weather cleared up, the
hills near Ciudad Rodrigo afforded dry bivouacs
and fuel, the distribution of good rations restored
the strength and spirits of the men, and the next
day Ciudad Rodrigo and the neighbouring villages
were occupied in tranquillity. The cavalry was
then sent out to the forest, and being aided by
Julian Sanchez' Partidas, brought in from a thousand to fifteen hundred stragglers who must otherwise have perished. During these events Joseph
occupied Salamanca, but colonel Miranda, the Spanish officer left at Alba de Tormes, held that place

until the 27th and then carried off his garrison in
the night.

Thus ended the retreat from Burgos. The
French gathered a good spoil of baggage; what
the loss of the allies, in men, was, cannot be
exactly determined, because no Spanish returns
were ever seen. An approximation may however be
easily made. According to the muster-rolls, the
Anglo-Portuguese under Wellington, had about
one thousand men killed, wounded, and missing
between the 21st and 29th of October, which was
the period of their crossing the Duero, but this
only refers to loss in action; Hill's loss between
the Tagus and the Tormes was, including stragglers, about four hundred, and the defence of the
castle of Alba de Tormes cost one hundred. Now
if the Spanish regulars, and Partidas, marching
with the two armies, be reckoned to have lost a
thousand, which considering their want of discipline is not exaggerated, the whole loss, previous
to the French passage of the Tormes, will amount
perhaps to three thousand men. But the loss
between the Tormes and the Agueda was certainly
greater, for nearly three hundred were killed and
wounded at the Huebra, many stragglers died in
the woods, and we have marshal Jourdan's testimony, that the prisoners, Spanish Portuguese and
English, brought into Salamanca up to the 20th
November, were three thousand five hundred and
twenty. The whole loss of the double retreat cannot therefore be set down at less than nine thousand
including the cost of men in the siege of Burgos.

I have been the more precise on this point, because some French writers have spoken of ten
thousand being taken between the Tormes and the
Agueda, and general Souham estimated the previ-

See Ap-
pendix,
No. 9.

ous loss, including the siege of Burgos, at seven
thousand. But the king in his despatches called
the whole loss twelve thousand, including therein
the garrison of Chinchilla, and he observed that if
the generals of cavalry, Soult and Tilley, had followed the allies vigorously from Salamanca, the
loss would have been much greater. Certainly the
army was so little pressed that none would have
supposed the French horsemen were numerous.
On the other hand English authors have most un-
accountably reduced the British loss to as many
hundreds.

Although the French halted on the Huebra, the
English general kept his troops together behind
the Agueda, because Soult retired with the troops
under his immediate command to Los Santos on the
Upper Tormes, thus pointing towards the pass of
Baños, and it was rumoured he designed to march
that way, with a view to invade Portugal by the
valley of the Tagus. Wellington disbelieved this
rumour, but he could not disregard it, because
nearly all his channels of intelligence had been
suddenly dried up by a tyrannical and foolish
decree of the Cortez, which obliged every man to
justify himself for having remained in a district
occupied by the enemy, and hence to avoid persecution, those who used to transmit information, fled
from their homes. Hill's division was therefore
moved to the right as far as Robledo, to cover the
pass of Perales, the rest of the troops were ready to
follow, and Penne Villemur, leading the fifth Spanish army over the Gata mountains occupied Coria.

Joseph, after hesitating whether he should leave
the army of the south, or the army of Portugal in
Castile, finally ordered the head-quarters of the

latter to be fixed at Valladolid, and of the former at Toledo ; the one to maintain the country between the Tormes and the Esla, the other to occupy La Mancha with its left, the valley of the Tagus, as far as the Tietar, with its centre, and Avila with its right. The army of the centre went to Segovia, where the king joined it with his guards, and when these movements, which took place in December, were known, Wellington placed his army also in winter quarters.

The fifth Spanish army crossing the Tagus at Alcantara entered Estremadura.

Hill's division occupied Coria, and Placentia, and held the town of Bejar by a detachment.

Two divisions were quartered on a second line behind Hill about Castello Branco, and in the Upper Beira.

The light division remained on the Agueda, and the rest of the infantry were distributed along the Duero from Lamego downwards.

The Portuguese cavalry were placed in Moncorvo, and the British cavalry, with the exception of Victor Alten's brigade which was attached to the light division, occupied the valley of the Mondego.

Carlos D'España's troops garrisoned Ciudad Rodrigo, and the Gallicians marched through the Tras os Montes to their own country.

In these quarters the Anglo-Portuguese were easily fed, because the improved navigation of the Tagus, the Douro, and the Mondego, furnished water carriage close to all their cantonments ; moreover the army could be quickly collected on either frontier, for the front line of communication from Estremadura passed by the bridge of Alcantara to Coria, and from thence through the pass of Perales to the Agueda. The second line run by Penama- cor and Guinaldo, and both were direct; but the post of Bejar, although necessary to secure Hill's quarters from a surprise, was itself exposed.

The French also had double and direct communications across the Gredos mountains. On their first line they restored a Roman road leading from Horcajada, on the Upper Tormes, by the Puerto de Pico to Monbeltran, and from thence to Talavera. To ease their second line they finished a road, begun the year before by Marmont, leading from Avila, by the convent of Guisando and Escalona to Toledo. But these communications though direct, were in winter so difficult, that general Laval crossing the mountains from Avila was forced to harness forty horses to a carriage ; moreover Wellington having the interior and shorter lines, was in a more menacing position for offence, and a more easy position for defence ; wherefore, though he had ordered all boats to be destroyed at Almaraz, Arzobispo, and other points where the great roads came down to the Tagus, the French, as anxious to prevent him from passing that river, as he was to prevent them, sent parties to destroy what had been overlooked. Each feared that the other would move, and yet neither wished to continue the campagin, Wellington, because his troops wanted rest, more than one-third being in the hospitals ! the French because they could not feed their men and had to refix their general base of operations, broken up and deranged as it was by the Guerillas.

The English general was however most at his ease. He knew that the best French officers thought it useless to continue the contest in Spain, unless the British army was first mastered, Soult's

intercepted letters showed him how that general desired to fix the war in Portugal, and there was now a
most powerful force on the frontier of that kingdom.
But on the other hand Badajos, Ciudad Rodrigo,
and Almeida blocked the principal entrances, and
though the two former were very ill provided
by the Spaniards, they were in little danger because
the last compaign had deprived the French of all
their ordnance, arsenals, and magazines, in Andalusia, Almaraz, Madrid, Salamanca, and Valladolid;
and it was nearly impossible for them to make any
impression upon Portugal, until new establishments
were formed. Wherefore Wellington did not fear
to spread his troops in good and tranquil quarters,
to receive reinforcements, restore their equipments,
and recover their health and strength.

This advantage was not reciprocal. The secondary warfare which the French sustained, and which
it is now time again to notice, would have been
sufficient to establish the military reputation of
any nation before Napoleon's exploits had raised.the
standard of military glory. For when disembarrassed
of their most formidable enemy, they were still
obliged to chase the Partidas, to form sieges, to recover and restore the posts they had lost by concentrating their armies, to send moveable columns
by long winter marches over a vast extent of country for food, fighting for what they got, and living
hard because the magazines filled from the fertile
districts were of necessity reserved for the field
operations against Wellington. Certainly it was a
great and terrible war they had in hand, and good
and formidable soldiers they were to sustain it so
long and so manfully amidst the many errors of their
generals.

CHAPTER VI.

CONTINUATION OF THE PARTIZAN WARFARE.

In the north, while Souham was gathering in front CHAP.
of Wellington, some of Mendizabel's bands block-   VI.
                                                  1812.
aded Santona by land, and Popham, after his failure
at Gueteria blockaded it by sea. It was not very
well provisioned, but Napoleon, always watchful,
had sent an especial governor, general Lameth, and
a chosen engineer, general D'Abadie, from Paris
to complete the works. By their activity a hundred and twenty pieces of cannon were soon mounted,
and they had including the crew of a corvette a garrison of eighteen hundred men. Lameth who was
obliged to fight his way into the place in September,
also formed an armed flotilla, with which, when the
English squadron was driven off the port by gales
of wind, he made frequent captures. Meanwhile
Mendizabel surprised the garrison of Briviesca,
Longa captured a large convoy with its escort, near
Burgos, and all the bands had visibly increased in
numbers and boldness.

When Caffarelli returned from the Duero, Reille
took the command of the army of Portugal, Drouet
assumed that of the army of the centre, and Souham being thus cast off returned to France. The
army of Portugal was then widely spread over
the country. Avila was occupied, Sarrut took
possession of Leon, the bands of Marquinez and

Salazar were beaten, and Foy marching to seize
Astorga, surprised and captured ninety men employed to dismantle that fortress ; but above twenty
breaches had already been opened and the place
ceased to be of any importance.   Meanwhile Caffarelli troubled by the care of a number of convoys, one
of which under general Frimont, although strongly
escorted, and having two pieces of cannon, fell into
Longa's hands the 30th of November, was unable
to commence active operations until the 29th of
December.   Then his detachments chased the bands
from Bilbao, while he marched himself to succour
and provision Santona and Gueteria, and to re-
establish his other posts along the coasts ; but while
he was near Santona the Spaniards attacked St.
Domingo in Navarre, and invested Logroña.

Sir Home Popham had suddenly quitted the Bay
of Biscay with his squadron, leaving a few vessels to
continue the littoral warfare, which enabled Caffarelli to succour Santona ; important events followed
but the account of them must be deferred as belonging to the transactions of 1813.   Meanwhile tracing the mere chain of Guerilla operations from
Biscay to the other parts, we find Abbé, who
commanded in Pampeluna, Severoli who guarded
the right of the Ebro, and Paris who had returned
from Valencia to Zaragoza, continually and at times
successfully attacked in the latter end of 1812 ; for
after Chaplangarra's exploit near Jacca, Mina intercepted all communication with France, and on the
22d of November surprised and drove back to Zaragoza with loss a very large convoy.   Then he besieged the castle of Huesca, and when a considerable
force, coming from Zaragoza, forced him to desist,
he reappeared at Barbastro.   Finally in a severe

action fought on the heights of Señora del Poya,
towards the end of December, his troops were dispersed by Colonel Colbert, yet the French lost
seventy men, and in a few weeks Mina took the
field again, with forces more numerous than he had
ever before commanded.

About this time Villa Campa, who had entrenched
himself near Segorbé to harass Suchet's rear, was
driven from thence by general Panetier, but being
afterwards joined by Gayan, they invested the castle
of Daroca with three thousand men. Severoli marching from Zaragoza succoured the place, yet Villa
Campa reassembled his whole force near Cariñeña
behind Severoli who was forced to fight his way home
to Zaragoza. The Spaniards reappeared at Almunia,
and on the 22nd of December, another battle was
fought, when Villa Campa being defeated with considerable slaughter retired to New Castile, and there
soon repaired his losses. Meanwhile, in the centre
of Spain, Elio, Bassecour, and Empecinado, having
waited until the great French armies passed in pursuit of Hill came down upon Madrid. Wellington,
when at Salamanca, expected that this movement
would call off some troops from the Tormes, but the
only effect was to cause the garrison left by Joseph to
follow the great army, which it rejoined, between the
Duero and the Tormes, with a great encumbrance
of civil servants and families. The Partidas then
entered the city and committed great excesses, treating the people as enemies.

Soult and Joseph had been earnest with Suchet to
send a strong division by Cuenca as a protection for
Madrid, and that marshal did move in person with
a considerable body of troops as far as Requeña on
the 28th of November, but being in fear for his line

towards Alicant soon returned to Valencia in a state of indecision, leaving only one brigade at Requeña. He had been reinforced by three thousand fresh men from Catalonia, yet he would not undertake any operation until he knew something of the king's progress, and at Requeña he had gained no intelligence even of the passage of the Tagus. The Spaniards being thus uncontrolled gathered in all directions.

The duke del Parque advanced with Ballesteros' army to Villa Nueva de los Infantes, on the La Mancha side of the Sierra Morena, his cavalry entered the plains and some new levies from Grenada, came to Alcaraz on his right. Elio and Bassecour, leaving Madrid to the Partidas, marched to Albacete, without hindrance from Suchet, and re-opened the communication with Alicant ; hence exclusive of the Sicilian army, nearly thirty thousand regular Spanish troops were said to be assembled on the borders of Murcia, and six thousand new levies came to Cordoba as a reserve. However on the 3d of December, Joseph at the head of his guards and the army of the centre, drove all the Partidas from the capital, and re-occupied Guadalaxara and the neighbouring posts ; Soult entered Toledo and his cavalry advanced towards Del Parque, who immediately recrossed the Morena, and then the French horsemen swept La Mancha to gather contributions and to fill the magazines at Toledo.

By these operations, Del Parque, now joined by the Grenadan troops from Alcaraz, was separated from Elio, and Suchet was relieved from a danger which he had dreaded too much, and by his own inaction contributed to increase. It is true he had

all the sick men belonging to the king's and to Soult's
army on his hands, but he had also many effective
men of those armies; and though the yellow fever had
shewn itself in some of his hospitals, and though he
was also very uneasy for the security of his base in
Aragon, where the Partida warfare was reviving,
yet, with a disposable force of fifteen thousand infantry, and a fine division of cavalry, he should not
have permitted Elio to pass his flank in the manner
he did. He was afraid of the Sicilian army which
had indeed a great influence on all the preceding
operations, for it is certain that Suchet would otherwise have detached troops to Madrid by the Cuenca
road, and then Soult would probably have sought
a battle between the Tagus and the Guadarama
mountains; but this influence arose entirely from
the position of the Alicant army, not from its operations, which were feeble and vacillating.

Maitland had resigned in the beginning of
October, and his successor Mackenzie immediately
pushed out some troops to the front, and there was
a slight descent upon Xabea by the navy, but the
general remained without plan or object, the only
signs of vitality being a fruitless demonstration
against the castle of Denia, where general Donkin
disembarked on the 4th of October with a detachment of the eighty-first regiment. The walls had
been represented as weak, but they were found to
be high and strong, and the garrison had been unexpectedly doubled that morning, hence no attack
took place, and in the evening a second reinforcement arrived, whereupon the British re-embarked.
However the water was so full of pointed rocks that
it was only by great exertions lieutenant Penruddocke
of the Fame could pull in the boats, and the soldiers

wading and fighting, got on board with little loss
indeed but in confusion.

Soon after this, general William Clinton came
from Sicily to take the command, and Wellington
who was then before Burgos, thinking Suchet would
weaken his army to help the king, recommended an
attempt upon the city of Valencia either by a coast
attack or by a land operation, warning Clinton
however to avoid an action in a cavalry country.
This was not very difficult, because the land
was generally rocky and mountainous, but Clinton
would not stir without first having possession of the
citadel of Alicant, and thus all things fell into disorder and weakness. For the jealous Spanish governor would not suffer the British to hold even a gate
of the town, nay, he sent Elio a large convoy of
clothing and other stores with an escort of only
twenty men, that he might retain two of that general's battalions to resist the attempt which he believed or pretended to believe Clinton would make
on the citadel. Meanwhile that general, leaving
Whittingham and Roche at Alcoy and Xixona,
drew in his other troops from the posts previously
occupied in front by Mackenzie; he feared Suchet's
cavalry, but the marshal, estimating the allied

armies at more than fifty thousand men, would
undertake no serious enterprize while ignorant
of the king's progress against lord Wellington.
He however diligently strengthened his camp at
St. Felipe de Xativa, threw another bridge over the
Xucar, entrenched the passes in his front, covered
Denia with a detachment, obliged Whittingham to
abandon Alcoy, dismantled the extensive walls of
Valencia, and fortified a citadel there.

It was in this state of affairs that Elio came down

to Albacete, and priding himself upon the dexterity CHAP. VI.
with which he had avoided the French armies, proposed to Clinton a combined attack upon Suchet. 1812.
Elio greatly exaggerated his own numbers, and
giving out that Del Parque's force was under his command, pretended that he could bring forty thousand men into the field, four thousand being cavalry.
But the two Spanish armies if united would scarcely
have produced twenty thousand really effective in- General Donkin's
fantry; moreover Del Parque, a sickly unwieldy correspon-dence,
person, was extremely incapable, his soldiers were MS.
discontented and mutinous, and he had no intention
of moving beyond Alcaraz.

With such allies it was undoubtedly difficult for
the English general to co-operate, yet it would seem,
something considerable might have been effected
while Suchet was at Requeña, even before Elio
arrived, and more surely after that general had
reached Albacete. Clinton had then twelve thousand men, of which five thousand were British:
there was a fleet to aid his operations, and the
Spanish infantry under Elio were certainly ten
thousand. Nothing was done, and it was because
nothing was attempted, that Napoleon, who watched
this quarter closely, assured Suchet, that however Official
difficult his position was from the extent of country correspon-dence of
he had to keep in tranquillity, the enemy in his the duke of Feltre,
front was not really formidable. Events justified MS.
this observation. The French works were soon
completed and the British army fell into such dis-
repute, that the Spaniards with sarcastic malice
affirmed it was to be put under Elio to make it useful.

Meanwhile Roche's and Whittingham's division General Donkin's
continued to excite the utmost jealousy in the other correspon-dence, MSS.

BOOK
XIX.

1812.

Appendix,
No. 17.

Spanish troops, who asked, very reasonably, what they did to merit such advantages? England paid and clothed them and the Spaniards were bound to feed them; they did not do so, and Canga Arguelles, the intendant of the province, asserted that he had twice provided magazines for them in Alicant, which were twice plundered by the governor; and yet it is certain that the other Spanish troops were far worse off than these divisions. But on every side intrigues, discontent, vacillation, and weakness were visible, and again it was shewn that if England was the stay of the Peninsula, it was Wellington alone who supported the war.

On the 22d of November the obstinacy of the governor being at last overcome he gave up the citadel of Alicant to the British, yet no offensive operations followed, though Suchet on the 26th drove Roche's troops out of Alcoy with loss, and defeated the Spanish cavalry at Yecla. However on the 2d of December, general Campbell arriving from Sicily, with four thousand men, principally British, assumed the command, making the fourth general-in-chief in the same number of months. His presence, the strong reinforcement he brought, and the intelligence that lord William Bentinck was to follow with another reinforcement, again raised the public expectation, and Elio immediately proposed that the British should occupy the enemy on the Lower Xucar, while the Spaniards crossing that river attacked Requeña. However general Campbell after making some feeble demonstrations declared he would await lord William Bentinck's arrival. Then the Spanish general, who had hitherto abstained from any disputes with the British, became extremely discontented, and dispersed his army for

subsistence. On the other hand the English general complained that Elio had abandoned him.

Suchet expecting Campbell to advance had
withdrawn his outposts to concentrate at Xativa,
but when he found him as inactive as his predecessors and saw the Spanish troops scattered, he surprised one Spanish post at Onteniente, another in Ibi,
and reoccupied all his former offensive positions in
front of Alicant. Soult's detachments were now
also felt in La Mancha, wherefore Elio retired into
Murcia, and Del Parque, as we have seen, went
over the Morena. Thus the storm which had menaced the French disappeared entirely, for Camp-
bell, following his instructions, refused rations to Appendix. No. 17,18.
Whittingham's corps and desired it to separate for
the sake of subsistence; and as the rest of the
Spanish troops were actually starving, no danger
was to be apprehended from them : nay, Habert
marched up to Alicant, killed and wounded some
men almost under the walls, and the Anglo-Italian
soldiers deserted to him by whole companies when
opportunity offered.

Suchet did as he pleased towards his front but he
was unquiet for his rear, for besides the operations
of Villa Campa, Gayan, Duran and Mina in Aragon,
the Frayle and other partida chiefs continually
vexed his communications with Tortoza. Fifty men
had been surprised and destroyed near Segorbe the
22d of November, by Villa Campa; and general
Panetier, who was sent against that chief, though
he took and destroyed his entrenched camp was
unable to bring him to action or to prevent him
from going to Aragon, and attacking Daroca as I
have before shown. Meanwhile the Frayle sur-

BOOK
XIX.
—————
1812.
prised and destroyed an ordnance convoy, took
several guns and four hundred horses, and killed in
cold blood after the action above a hundred artillery-men and officers. A moveable column being immediately despatched against him, destroyed his depôts and many of his men, but the Frayle himself escaped and soon reappeared upon the communications.
The loss of this convoy was the first disgrace of
the kind which had befallen the army of Aragon,
Suchet,
official cor-
respond-
ence with
the king,
MSS.
and to use Suchet's expression a battle would have
cost him less.

Nor were the Spaniards quite inactive in Catalonia, although the departure of general Maitland
had so dispirited them that the regular warfare
Captain
Codring-
ton's pa-
pers, MS.
was upon the point of ceasing altogether. The
active army was indeed stated to be twenty thousand strong, and the tercios of reserve forty-five thousand ; yet a column of nine hundred French controuled the sea-line and cut off all supplies landed
for the interior. Lacy who remained about Vich
with seven thousand men affirmed that he could not
feed his army on the coast, but captain Codrington
says that nineteen feluccas laden with flour had in
two nights only, landed their cargoes between Mattaro and Barcelona for the supply of the latter city,
and that these and many other ventures of the same
kind might have been captured without difficulty ;
that Claros and Milans continued corruptly to con-
nive at the passage of French convoys ; that the rich
merchants of Mattaro and Arens invited the enemy
to protect their contraband convoys going to France,
and yet accused him publicly of interrupting their
lawful trade when in fact he was only disturbing a
treasonable commerce, carried on so openly that he
was forced to declare a blockade of the whole coast.

A plot to deliver up the Medas islands was also
discovered, and when Lacy was pressed to call out the Somatenes, a favorite project with the English naval officers, he objected that he could scarcely feed and provide ammunition for the regular troops. He also observed that the general efforts of that nature hitherto made, and under more favourable circumstances, had produced only a waste of life, of treasure, of provisions, of ammunition and of arms, and now the French possessed all the strong places.

At this time so bitter were the party dissensions that Sir Edward Pellew anticipated the ruin of the principality from that cause alone. Lacy, Sarzfield, Eroles and captain Codrington, continued their old disputes, and Sarzfield who was then in Aragon had also quarrelled with Mina ; Lacy made a formal requisition to have Codrington recalled, the junta of Catalonia made a like demand to the regency respecting Lacy, and meanwhile such was the misery of the soldiers that the officers of one regiment actually begged at the doors of private houses to obtain old clothing for their men, and even this poor succour was denied. A few feeble isolated efforts by some of the partizan generals, were the only signs of war when Wellington's victory at Salamanca again raised the spirit of the province. Then also for the first time the new constitution adopted by the cortez was proclaimed in Catalonia, the junta of that province was suppressed, Eroles the people's favorite obtained greater powers, and was even flattered with the hope of becoming captain general, for the regency had agreed at last to recal Lacy. In fine the aspect of affairs changed and many thousand English muskets and other weapons were by Sir Edward Pellew, given to the partizans as well as to the regular troops which enabled them to receive cartridges from the ships instead of the loose powder formerly demanded on account of the difference in the bore of the Spanish muskets. The effect of these happy coincidences was soon displayed. Eroles who had raised a new division of three thousand men, contrived in concert with Codrington, a combined movement in September against Taragona. Marching in the night of the 27th from Reus to the mouth of the Francoli he was met by the boats of the squadron and having repulsed a sally from the fortress, drove some Catalans in the French service, from the ruins of the Olivo, while the boats swept the mole, taking five vessels. After this affair Eroles encamped on the hill separating Lerida, Taragona, and Tortoza, meaning to intercept the communication between those places and to keep up an intercourse with the fleet, now the more necessary because Lacy had lost this advantage eastward of Barcelona. While thus posted he heard that a French detachment had come from Lerida to Arbeca, wherefore making a forced march over the mountains he surprised and destroyed the greatest part on the 2d of October, and then returned to his former quarters.

Meanwhile Lacy embarked scaling ladders and battering guns on board the English ships, and made a pompous movement against Mattaro with his whole force, yet at the moment of execution changed his plan and attempted to surprise Hostalrich, but he let this design be known, and as the enemy prepared to succour the place, he returned to Vich without doing any thing. During these operations Manso defeated two hundred French near Molino del Rey, gained some advantages over one Pelligri, a French miguelette partizan, and captured some French boats at Mattaro after Lacy's departure. However Sarzfield's mission to raise an army in Aragon had failed, and Decaen desiring to check the reviving spirit of the Catalans, made a combined movement against Vich in the latter end of October. Lacy immediately drew Eroles, Manso, and Milans towards that point, and thus the fertile country about Reus was again resigned to the French, the intercourse with the fleet totally lost, and the garrison of Taragona, which had been greatly straitened by the previous operations of Eroles, was relieved. Yet the defence of Vich was not secured, for on the 3d of November one division of the French forced the main body of the Spaniards, under Lacy and Milans, at the passes of Puig Gracioso and Congosto, and though the other divisions were less successful against Eroles and Manso, at St. Filieu de Codenas, Decaen reached Vich the 4th. The Catalans, who had lost altogether above five hundred men, then separated; Lacy went to the hills near Momblanch, Milans and Rovira towards Olot, and Manso to Montserrat.

Eroles returned to Reus, and was like to have surprised the Col de Balaguer, for he sent a detachment under colonel Villamil, dressed in Italian uniforms which had been taken by Rovira in Figueras, and his men were actually admitted within the palisade of the fort before the garrison perceived the deceit. A lieutenant with sixteen men placed outside were taken, and this loss was magnified so much to Eroles that he ordered Villamil to make a more regular attack. To aid him Codrington brought up the Blake, and landed some marines, yet no impression was made on the garrison, and the allies retired on the

17th at the approach of two thousand men sent from Tortoza. Eroles and Manso then vainly united near Manresa to oppose Decaen, who, coming down from Vich, forced his way to Reus, seized a vast quantity of corn, supplied Taragona, and then marched to Barcelona.

These operations indisputably proved that there was no real power of resistance in the Catalan army, but as an absurd notion prevailed that Soult, Suchet, and Joseph were coming with their armies in one body, to France, through Catalonia, Lacy endeavoured to cover his inactivity by pretending a design to raise a large force in Aragon, with which to watch this retreat, and to act as a flanking corps to lord Wellington, who was believed to be then approaching Zaragoza. Such rumours served to amuse the Catalans for a short time, but the sense of their real weakness soon returned. In December Bertoletti, the governor of Taragona, marched upon Reus, and defeated some hundred men who had reassembled there ; and at the same time a French convoy for Barcelona, escorted by three thousand men, passed safely in the face of six thousand Catalan soldiers, who were desirous to attack but were prevented by Lacy.

The anger of the people and of the troops also, on this occasion was loudly expressed, Lacy was openly accused of treachery, and was soon after recalled. However, Eroles who had come to Cape Salou to obtain succour from the squadron for his suffering soldiers, acknowledged that the resources of Catalonia were worn out, the spirit of the people broken by Lacy's misconduct, and the army, reduced to less than seven thousand men, naked and famishing. Affairs were so bad, that expecting to be made

captain-general he was reluctant to accept that CHAP.
office, and the regular warfare was in fact extin- VI.
guished, for Sarzfield was now acting as a partizan 1812.
on the Ebro. Nevertheless the French were greatly
dismayed at the disasters in Russia; their force was
weakened by the drafts made to fill up the ranks of
Napoleon's new army; and the war of the partidas
continued, especially along the banks of the Ebro,
where Sarzfield, at the head of Eroles' ancient
division, which he had carried with him out of
Catalonia, acted in concert with Mina, Duran,
Villa Campa, the Frayle, Pendencia, and other
chiefs, who were busy upon Suchet's communication between Tortoza and Valencia.

Aragon being now unquiet, and Navarre and
Biscay in a state of insurrection, the French forces
in the interior of Spain were absolutely invested.
Their front was opposed by regular armies, their
flanks annoyed by the British squadrons, and their
rear, from the Bay of Biscay to the Mediterranean,
plagued and stung by this chain of partidas and
insurrections. And England was the cause of all
this. England was the real deliverer of the Peninsula. It was her succours thrown into Biscay that
had excited the new insurrection in the northern
provinces, and enabled Mina and the other chiefs
to enter Aragon, while Wellington drew the great
masses of the French towards Portugal. It was
that insurrection, so forced on, which, notwithstanding the cessation of the regular warfare in Catalonia, gave life and activity to the partidas of the
south. It was the army from Sicily which, though
badly commanded, by occupying the attention of
Suchet in front, obliged him to keep his forces
together instead of hunting down the bands on his

communications. In fine, it was the troops of
England who had shocked the enemy's front of
battle, the fleets of England which had menaced
his flanks with disembarkations, the money and
stores of England which had supported the partidas. Every part of the Peninsula was pervaded
by her influence, or her warriors, and a trembling
sense of insecurity was communicated to the French
wherever their armies were not united in masses.

Such then were the various military events of the
year 1812, and the English general taking a view of
the whole, judged that however anxious the French
might be to invade Portugal, they would be content
during the winter to gather provisions and wait for
reinforcements from France wherewith to strike a
decisive blow at his army. But those reinforcements never came. Napoleon, unconquered of man,
had been vanquished by the elements. The fires
and the snows of Moscow combined, had shattered
his strength, and in confessed madness, nations and
rulers rejoiced, that an enterprize, at once the
grandest, the most provident, the most beneficial,
ever attempted by a warrior-statesman, had been
foiled : they rejoiced that Napoleon had failed to
re-establish unhappy Poland as a barrier against the
most formidable and brutal, the most swinish tyranny, that has ever menaced and disgraced European civilization.

CHAPTER VII.

GENERAL OBSERVATIONS.

Lord Wellington exasperated by the conduct of the army and by the many crossings he had experienced during the campaign, had no sooner taken his winter-quarters, than he gave vent to his indignation in a circular letter, addressed to the superior officers, which, being ill-received by the army at the time, has been frequently referred to since with angry denunciations of its injustice. In substance it declared, " that discipline had deteriorated during the campaign *in a greater degree than he had ever witnessed or ever read of in any army*, and this without any disaster, any unusual privation or hardship save that of inclement weather; that the officers had, from the first, lost all command over their men, and hence excesses, outrages of all kinds, and inexcusable losses had occurred ; that no army had ever made shorter marches in retreat, or had longer rests; no army had ever been so little pressed by a pursuing enemy, and that the true cause of this unhappy state of affairs was to be found in the habitual neglect of duty by the regimental officers."

These severe reproaches were generally deserved, and only partially unjust; yet the statements, on which they were founded, were in some particulars unintentionally inaccurate, especially as regarded the retreat from Salamanca. The marches, though short as to distance, after quitting the Tormes, were

long as to time, and it is the time an English soldier
bears his burthen, for like the ancient Roman he
carries the load of an ass, that crushes his strength.
Some regiments had come from Cadiz without
halting, and as long garrison duty had weakened
their bodies, both their constitutions and their inexperience were too heavily taxed.   The line of march
from Salamanca was through a flooded, and flat,
clayey country, not much easier to the allies than
the marshes of the Arnus were to Hannibal's army;
and mounted officers, as that great general well knew
when he placed the Carthaginian cavalry to keep
up the Gallic rear, never judge correctly of a foot-
soldier's exertions; they measure his strength by
their horses' powers.   On this occasion the troops,
stepping ankle-deep in clay, mid-leg in water, lost
their shoes, and with strained sinews heavily made
their way, and withal they had but two rations in
five days.

Wellington thought otherwise, for he knew not
that the commissariat stores, which he had ordered
up, did not arrive regularly because of the extreme
fatigue of the animals who carried them; and those
that did arrive were not ⎰available for the troops,
because, as the rear of an army, and especially a
retreating army, is at once the birth-place and the
recipient of false reports, the subordinate commissaries and conductors of the temporary dépôts,
alarmed with rumours that the enemy's cavalry had
forestalled the allies on the march, carried off
or destroyed the field-stores: hence the soldiers
were actually feeding on acorns when their commander supposed them to be in the receipt of good
rations.   The destruction of the swine may be
therefore, in some measure, palliated; but there is
neither palliation nor excuse to be offered for the

excesses and outrages committed on the inhabitants,

nor for many officers' habitual inattention to their duty, of which the general justly complained. Certainly the most intolerable disorders had marked the retreat, and great part of the sufferings of the army arose from these and previous disorders, for it is too common with soldiers, first to break up the arrangements of their general by want of discipline, and then to complain of the misery which those arrangements were designed to obviate. Nevertheless Wellington's circular was not strictly just, because it excepted none from blame, though in conversation he admitted the reproach did not apply to the light division nor to the guards.

With respect to the former the proof of its discipline was easy though Wellington had not said so much in its favour; for how could those troops be upbraided, who held together so closely with their colours, that, exclusive of those killed in action, they did not leave thirty men behind. Never did the extraordinary vigour and excellence of their discipline merit praise more than in this retreat. But it seems to be a drawback to the greatness of lord Wellington's character, that while capable of repressing insubordination, either by firmness or dexterity as the case may require, capable also of magnanimously disregarding, or dangerously resenting injuries, his praises and his censures are bestowed indiscriminately, or so directed as to acquire partizans and personal friends rather than the attachment of the multitude. He did not make the hard-working military crowd feel that their honest unobtrusive exertions were appreciated. In this he differs not from many other great generals and statesmen, but he thereby fails to influence masses, and his genius falls short of that sublime flight by which Hannibal in ancient, and Napoleon in modern times, commanded the admiration of the world. Nevertheless it is only by a comparison with such great men that he can be measured, nor will any slight examination of his exploits suffice to convey a true notion of his intellectual power and resources. Let this campaign be taken as an example.

It must be evident that it in no manner bears out the character of an easy and triumphant march, which English writers have given to it. Nothing happened according to the original plan. The general's operations were one continual struggle to overcome obstacles, occasioned by the enemy's numbers, the insubordination of his own troops, the slowness, incapacity, and unfaithful conduct of the Spanish commanders, the want of money, and the active folly of the different governments he served. For first his design was to menace the French in Spain so as to bring their forces upon him from other parts, and then to retire into Portugal, again to issue forth when want should cause them to disperse. He was not without hopes indeed to strike a decisive blow, yet he was content, if the occasion came not, to wear out the French by continual marching, and he trusted that the frequent opportunities thus given to the Spaniards would finally urge them to a general effort. But he found his enemy, from the first, too powerful for him, even without drawing succour from distant parts, and he would have fallen back at once, were it not for Marmont's rashness. Nor would the victory of the Arapiles itself have produced any proportionate effect but for the errors of the king, and his rejection of Soult's advice. Those errors caused the evacuation of Andalusia, yet it was only to concentrate an overwhelming force with which the French finally drove the victors back to Portugal.

Again, Wellington designed to finish his campaign in the southern provinces, and circumstances obliged him to remain in the northern provinces. He would have taken Burgos and he could not ; he would have rested longer on the Carrion, and his flanks were turned by the bridges of Palencia and Baños; he would have rested behind the Douro, to profit of his central position, but the bridge at Tordesillas was ravished from him, and the sudden reparation of that at Toro, obliged him to retire. He would have united with Hill on the Adaja, and he could only unite with him behind the Tormes; and on this last river also he desired either to take his winter quarters, or to have delivered a great battle with a view to regain Madrid, and he could do neither. Finally he endeavoured to make an orderly and an easy retreat to Ciudad Rodrigo, and his army was like to have dissolved altogether. And yet in all these varying circumstances, his sagacity as to the general course of the war, his promptness in taking advantage of particular opportunities, was conspicuous. These are the distinguishing characteristics of real genius.

Passing over as already sufficiently illustrated that master-stroke, the battle of Salamanca, the reader would do well to mark, how this great commander did, after that event, separate the king's army from Marmont's, forcing the one to retreat upon Burgos, and driving the other from Madrid; how he thus broke up the French combinations, so that many weeks were of necessity required to reunite a power capable of disturbing him in the field ; how he posted Clinton's division and the Gallicians, to repress any light excursion by the beaten army of Portugal; how, foreseeing Soult's plan to establish a new base of operations in Andalusia, he was prepared, by a sudden descent from Madrid, to drive Soult himself from that province; how promptly, when the siege of Burgos failed, and his combinations were ruined by the fault of others, how promptly I say, he commenced his retreat, sacrificing all his high-wrought expectation of triumph in a campaign which he burned to finish, and otherwise would have finished, even with more splendour than it had commenced.

If Burgos, a mean fortress of the lowest order, had fallen early, the world would have seen a noble stroke. For the Gallicians, aided by a weak division of Wellington's army, and by the British reinforcements making up from Coruña, would, covered by Burgos, have sufficed to keep the army of Portugal in check, while Popham's armament would have fomented a general insurrection of the northern provinces. Meanwhile Wellington, gathering forty-five thousand Anglo-Portuguese, and fifteen thousand Spaniards, on the Tagus, would have marched towards Murcia; Ballesteros' army, and the sixteen thousand men composing the Alicant army, would there have joined him, and with a hundred thousand soldiers he would have delivered such a battle to the united French armies, if indeed they could have united, as would have shaken all Europe with its martial clangor. To exchange this glorious vision, for the cold desolate reality of a dangerous winter retreat was, for Wellington, but a momentary mental struggle, and it was simultaneous with that daring conception, the

passage of the bridge of Burgos under the fire of
the castle.

Let him be traced now in retreat. Pursued by a
superior army and seeing his cavalry defeated, he
turned as a savage lion at the Carrion, nor would
he have removed so quickly from that lair, if the
bridges at Palencia and Baños had been destroyed
according to his order. Neither is his cool self-
possession to be overlooked ; for when both his
flanks were thus exposed, instead of falling back
in a hurried manner to the Duero, he judged exactly the value of the rugged ground on the left
bank of the Pisuerga, in opposition to the double
advantage obtained by the enemy at Palencia and
Baños; nor did the difficulty which Souham and
Caffarelli, independent commanders and neither of
them accustomed to move large armies, would find
in suddenly changing their line of operations escape him. His march to Cabeçon and his position
on the left of the Pisuerga was not a retreat, it
was the shift of a practised captain.

When forced to withdraw Hill from the Tagus,
he, on the instant, formed a new combination to
fight that great battle on the Adaja which he had
intended to deliver near the Guadalaviar ; and
though the splendid exploit of captain Guingret, at
Tordesillas, baffled this intent, he, in return, baffled
Souham by that ready stroke of generalship, the
posting of his whole army in front of Rueda,
thus forbidding a passage by the restored bridge.
Finally, if he could not maintain the line of the
Duero, nor that of the Tormes, it was because rivers can never be permanently defended against superior forces, and yet he did not quit the last without a splendid tactical illustration. I mean that

surprising movement from the Arapiles to the Valmusa, a movement made not in confusion and half
flight, but in close order of battle, his columns
ready for action, his artillery and cavalry skirmishing, passing the Junguen without disorder, filing
along the front of and winding into the rear of
a most powerful French army, the largest ever collected in one mass in the Peninsula, an army
having twice as many guns as the allies, and twelve
thousand able horsemen to boot. And all these
great and skilful actions were executed by lord
Wellington with an army composed of different
nations; soldiers, fierce indeed, and valiant, terrible
in battle, but characterised by himself, as more
deficient in good discipline than any army of which
he had ever read !

Men engaged only in civil affairs and especially
book-men are apt to undervalue military genius,
talking as if simple bravery were the highest qua-
lification of a general; and they have another
mode of appeasing an inward sense of inferiority,
namely, to attribute the successes of a great captain, to the prudence of some discreet adviser, who
in secret rules the general, amends his errors, and
leaves him all the glory. Thus Napoleon had
Berthier, Wellington has sir George Murray ! but
in this, the most skilful, if not the most glorious of
Wellington's campaigns, sir George Murray was
not present, and the staff of the army was governed
by three young lieutenant-colonels, namely, lord
Fitzroy Somerset,Waters, and Delancey ; for though
sir Willoughby Gordon joined the army as quarter-
master-general after the battle of Salamanca, he
was inexperienced, and some bodily suffering impeded his personal exertions.

Such then were the principal points of skill displayed by Wellington; yet so vast and intricate an
art is war, that the apophthegm of Turenne will
always be found applicable: "*he who has made no
mistakes in war, has seldom made war.*" Some
military writers, amongst them the celebrated
Jomini, blame the English general, that with a
conquering army, and an insurgent nation at his
beck, he should in three months after his victory
have attempted nothing more than the unsuccessful
siege of Burgos. This censure is not entirely
unfounded; the king certainly escaped very easily
from Madrid; yet there are many points to be
argued ere the question can be decided. The want
of money, a want progressively increasing, had
become almost intolerable. Wellington's army was
partly fed from Ciudad Rodrigo, partly from the
valley of the Pisuerga, Hill's troops were fed from
Lisbon; the Portuguese in their own country, and
the Spaniards every where, lived as the French did,
by requisition; but the British professed to avoid
that mode of subsistence, and they made it a
national boast to all Europe that they did so; the
movements of the army were therefore always subservient to this principle, and must be judged accordingly, because want of money was with them
want of motion.

Now four modes of operation were open to
Wellington.

1°. *After the victory of Salamanca to follow the
king to Valencia, unite with the Alicant army, and,
having thus separated Soult from Joseph and Suchet,
to act according to events.*

To have thus moved at once, without money, into
Valencia, or Murcia, new countries where he had

no assured connexions, and which were scarcely able
to feed the French armies, would have exposed him
to great difficulties; and he must have made extensive arrangements with the fleet ere he could have
acted vigorously, if, as was probable, the French
concentrated all their forces behind the Guadalaviar.
Meanwhile the distance between the main allied army
and those troops necessarily left in the north, being
considered, the latter must have been strengthened
at the expense of those in the south, unless the army
of Portugal joined the king, and then Wellington
would have been quite overmatched in Valencia;
that is, if Soult also joined·the king, and if not he
would have placed the English general between
two fires.   If a force was not left in the north the
army of Portugal would have had open field, either
to march to the king's assistance by Zaragoza, or
to have relieved Astorga, seized Salamanca, recovered the prisoners and the trophies of the Arapiles,
and destroyed all the great lines of magazines and
dépôts even to the Tagus.   Moreover, the yellow
fever raged in Murcia, and this would have compelled the English general to depend upon the
contracted base of operations offered by Alicant,
because the advance of Clauzel would have rendered
it impossible to keep it on the Tagus.   Time, therefore, was required to arrange the means of operating
in this manner, and meanwhile the army was not
unwisely turned another way.

2⁰.   *To march directly against Soult in Andalusia.*

This project Wellington was prepared to execute,
when the king's orders rendered it unnecessary,
but if Joseph had adopted Soult's plan a grand
field for the display of military art would have been

opened. The king going by the Despenas Peros,

and having the advantage of time in the march,
could have joined Soult, with the army of the centre, before the English general could have joined
Hill. The sixty thousand combatants thus united
could have kept the field until Suchet had also
joined ; but they could scarcely have maintained
the blockade of Cadiz also, and hence the error
of Wellington seems to have been, that he did
not make an effort to overtake the king, either
upon or beyond the Tagus ; for the army of the
centre would certainly have joined Soult by the
Despenas Peros, if Maitland had not that moment
landed at Alicant.

3°. *To follow the army of Portugal after the victory of Salamanca.*

The reasons for moving upon Madrid instead of
adopting this line of operations having been already
shewn in former observations, need not be here
repeated, yet it may be added that the destruction
of the great arsenal and dépôt of the Retiro was no
small object with reference to the safety of Portugal.

4°. *The plan which was actually followed.*

The English general's stay in the capital was
unavoidable, seeing that to observe the development
of the French operations in the south was of such
importance. It only remains therefore to trace
him after he quitted Madrid. Now the choice of
his line of march by Valladolid certainly appears
common-place, and deficient in vigour, but it was
probably decided by the want of money, and of means
of transport ; to which may be added the desire to
bring the Gallicians forward, which he could only
attain by putting himself in actual military communication with them, and covering their advance.

Yet this will not excuse the feeble pursuit of Clauzel's retreating army up the valley of the Pisuerga. The Spaniards would not the less have come up if that general had been defeated, nor would the want of their assistance have been much felt in the action. Considerable loss would, no doubt, have been suffered by the Anglo-Portuguese, and they could ill bear it, but the result of a victory would have amply repaid the damage received; for the time gained by Clauzel was employed by Caffarelli to strengthen the castle of Burgos, which contained the greatest French dépôt in this part of Spain. A victory therefore would have entirely disarranged the enemy's means of defence in the north, and would have sent the twice-broken and defeated army of Portugal, behind the Ebro; then neither the conscript reinforcements, nor the junction of Caffarelli's troops, would have enabled Clauzel, with all his activity and talent, to re-appear in the field before Burgos would have fallen. But that fortress would most probably have fallen at once, in which case the English general might have returned to the Tagus, and perhaps in time to have met Soult as he issued forth from the mountains in his march from Andalusia.

It may be objected, that as Burgos did not yield, it would not have yielded under any circumstances without a vigorous defence. This is not so certain, the effect of a defeat would have been very different from the effect of such a splendid operation as Clauzel's retreat; and it appears also, that the prolonged defence of the castle may be traced to some errors of detail in the attack, as well as to want of sufficient artillery means. In respect of the great features of the campaign, it may be assumed that

Wellington's judgement on the spot, and with a full knowledge both of his own and his adversaries' situations, is of more weight than that of critics, however able and acute, who knew nothing of his difficulties. But in the details there was something of error exceedingly strange. It is said, I believe truly, that Sir Howard Douglas being consulted, objected to the proceeding by gallery and mine against an outward, a middle, and an inward line of defence, as likely to involve a succession of tedious and difficult enterprizes, which even if successful, would still leave the White Church, and the upper castle or keep, to be carried ;—that this castle, besides other artillery armament, was surmounted by a powerful battery of heavy guns, bearing directly upon the face of the horn-work of San Michael, the only point from which it could be breached, and until it was breached, the governor, a gallant man, would certainly not surrender. It could not however be breached without a larger battering train than the allies possessed, and would not, as he supposed, be effected by mines; wherefore proposing to take the guns from two frigates, then lying at Santander, he proffered to bring them up in time.

In this reasoning lord Wellington partly acquiesced, but his hopes of success were principally founded on the scarcity of water in the castle, and upon the facility of burning the provision magazines; nor was he without hope that his fortune would carry him through, even with the scanty means he possessed. Towards the end of the siege, however, he did resort, though too late, to the plan of getting guns up from Santander. But while Sir Howard Douglas thus counselled him on the spot, Sir Edward Pakenham, then in Madrid, assured the author of this history, at the time, that he also, foreseeing the artillery means were too scanty, had proposed to send by the Somosierra twelve fine Russian battering guns, then in the Retiro; and he pledged himself to procure, by an appeal to the officers in the capital, animals sufficient to transport them and their ammunition to Burgos in a few days. The offer was not accepted.

Something also may be objected to the field operations, as connected with the siege; for it is the rule, although not an absolute one, that the enemy's active army should first be beaten, or driven beyond some strong line, such as a river, or chain of mountains, before a siege is commenced. Now if Wellington had masked the castle after the horn-work was carried on the 19th, and had then followed Clauzel, the French generals, opposed to him, admit, that they would have gone over the Ebro, perhaps even to Pampeluna and St. Sebastian. In that case all the minor dépôts must have been broken up, and the reorganization of the army of Portugal retarded at least a month; before that time, the guns from Santander would have arrived and the castle of Burgos would have fallen. In Souham's secret despatches, it is said, of course on the authority of spies, that Castaños urged an advance beyond Burgos instead of a siege; of this I know nothing, but it is not unlikely, because to advance continually, and to surround an enemy, constituted, with Spanish generals, the whole art of war. Howbeit on this occasion, the advice, if given, was not unreasonable; and it needed scarcely even to delay the siege while the covering army advanced, because one division of infantry might have come up from Madrid, still leaving two of the finest in the army, and a brigade of cavalry, at that capital, which was sufficient, seeing that Hill was coming up to Toledo, that Ballesteros' disobedience was then unknown, and that the king was in no condition to advance before Soult arrived.

The last point to which it is fitting to advert, was the stopping too long on the Tormes in hopes of fighting in the position of the Arapiles. It was a stirring thought indeed for a great mind, and the error was brilliantly redeemed, but the remedy does not efface the original fault; and this subject leads to a consideration, of some speculative interest, namely, why Wellington, desirous as he was to keep the line of the Tormes, and knowing with what difficulty the French fed their large army, did not order every thing in his rear to take refuge in Ciudad Rodrigo and Almeida, and entrench himself on St. Christoval and in Salamanca. Thus posted with a bridge-head on the left bank that he might operate on either side of the Tormes, he might have waited until famine obliged the enemy to separate, which would have been in a very few days; but perhaps the answer would be that the Spaniards had left Ciudad Rodrigo in a defenceless state.

Turning now to the French side we shall find that they also committed errors.

Souham's pursuit after the cavalry combat at Vente de Pozo was feeble. Wellington, speaking of his own army, said, "no troops were ever less pressed by an enemy." The king's orders were however positive not to fight, and as the English general continually offered Souham battle in strong positions, the man had no power to do mischief. Soult's pursuit of Hill, which was also

remarkably cautious, arose from other motives.
He was not desirous of a battle, and until the
Guadarama was passed, Hill had the larger force,
for then only was the whole French army united.
The duke of Dalmatia wished to have marched in
one great mass through La Mancha, leaving only a
small corps, or a detachment of Suchet's army, on
the Cuenca road; but the king united the whole of
the army of the centre, his own guards and seven
thousand men of the army of the south, on the
Cuenca line, and there were no good cross communications except by Taracon.   Soult therefore advanced towards the Tagus with only thirty-five thousand men, and from commissariat difficulties and
other obstacles, he was obliged to move by divisions,
which followed each other at considerable distances;
when his advanced guard was at Valdemoro, his rear-
guard not having reached Ocaña was two marches
distant.   The danger of this movement is evident.
Hill might have turned and driven him over the
Tagus; or if his orders had permitted him to act
offensively at first, he might, after leaving a small
corps on the Upper Tagus, to watch the king, have
passed that river at Toledo, and without abandoning
his line of operations by the valley of the Tagus,
have attacked Soult while on the march towards
Ocaña.   The latter in despite of his numerous cavalry
must then have fallen back to concentrate his forces,
and this would have deranged the whole campaign.

The duke of Dalmatia, who thought Ballesteros
was with Hill, naturally feared to press his adversary
under such a vicious disposition of the French
army, neither could that disposition be changed
during the operation, because of the want of good
cross roads, and because Souham had been taught

that the king would meet him on the side of Guadalaxara. In fine Soult had learned to respect his
adversaries, and with the prudence of a man whose
mental grasp embraced the whole machinery of the
war, he avoided a doubtful battle where a defeat
would, from the unsettled state of the French
affairs, have lost the whole Peninsula. Wellington
had Portugal to fall back upon, but the French
armies must have gone behind the Ebro.

These seem to be the leading points of interest
in this campaign, but it will not be uninteresting
to mark the close affinities between Wellington's retreat and that of Sir John Moore. This last-named
general marched from Portugal into the north of
Spain, with the political view of saving Andalusia,
by drawing on himself the French power, having
before-hand declared that he expected to be overwhelmed. In like manner Wellington moved into
the same country, to deliver Andalusia, and thus
drew on himself the whole power of the enemy;
like Moore declaring also before-hand, that the political object being gained, his own military position would be endangered. Both succeeded, and
both were, as they had foretold, overwhelmed by
superior forces. Moore was to have been aided by
Romana's Spanish army, but he found it a burthen;
so also Wellington was impeded, not assisted, by the
Gallicians, and both generals were without money.

Moore having approached Soult, and menaced
Burgos, was forced to retreat, because Napoleon
moved from Madrid on his right flank and towards
his rear. Wellington having actually besieged Burgos was obliged to raise the siege and retire, lest the
king, coming through Madrid, should pass his right
flank and get into his rear. Moore was only followed

by Soult to the Esla, Wellington was only followed by Souham to the Duero. The one general looked to the mountains of Gallicia for positions which he could maintain, but the apathy of the Spanish people, in the south, permitted Napoleon to bring up such an overwhelming force that this plan could not be sustained; the other general had the same notion with respect to the Duero, and the defection of Ballesteros enabled the king to bring up such a power that further retreat became necessary.

Moore's soldiers at the commencement of the operation evinced want of discipline, they committed great excesses at Valderas, and disgraced themselves by their inebriety at Bembibre and Villa Franca. In like manner Wellington's soldiers broke the bonds of discipline, disgraced themselves by drunkenness at Torquemada and on the retreat from the Puente Larga to Madrid; and they committed excesses every where. Moore stopped behind the Esla river to check the enemy, to restore order, and to enable his commissariat to remove the stores; Wellington stopped behind the Carrion for exactly the same purposes. The one general was immediately turned on his left, because the bridge of Mancilla was abandoned unbroken to Franceschi; the other general was also turned on his left, because the bridge of Palencia was abandoned unbroken to Foy.

Moore's retreat was little short of three hundred miles; Wellington's was nearly as long, and both were in the winter season. The first halted at Benevente, at Villa Franca, and at Lugo; the last halted at Duenas, at Cabeçon, Tordesillas, and Salamanca. The principal loss sustained by the one, was in the last marches between Lugo and

Coruña; so also the principal loss sustained by the other, was in the last marches between the Tormes and the Agueda. Some of Moore's generals murmured against his proceedings, some of Wellington's generals, as we have seen, went further; the first were checked by a reprimand, the second were humbled by a sarcasm. Finally both generals reproached their armies with want of discipline, both attributed it to the negligence of the officers generally, and in both cases the justice of the reproaches was proved by the exceptions. The reserve and the foot-guards in Moore's campaign, the light division and the foot-guards in Wellington's, gave signal proof, that it was negligence of discipline, not hardships, though the latter were severe in both armies, that caused the losses. Not that I would be understood to say that those regiments only preserved order; it is certain that many others were eminently well conducted, but those were the troops named as exceptions at the time.

Such were the resemblances of these two retreats. The differences were, that Moore had only twenty-three thousand men in the first part of his retreat, and only nineteen thousand in the latter part, whereas Wellington had thirty-three thousand in the first part of his retreat, and sixty-eight thousand men in the latter part. Moore's army were all of one nation and young soldiers, Wellington's were of different nations but they were veterans. The first marched through mountains, where the weather was infinitely more inclement than in the plains, over which the second moved, and until he reached the Esla, Moore's flank was quite exposed, whereas Wellington's flank was covered by Hill's army until he gained the Tormes.   Wellington with veteran troops was opposed to Souham, to Soult, to the king, and to Jourdan, men not according in their views, and their whole army, when united, did not exceed the allies by more than twenty thousand men. Moore with young soldiers was at first opposed to four times, and latterly to three times his own numbers, for it is remarkable, that the French army assembled at Astorga was above eighty thousand, including ten thousand cavalry, which is nearly the same as the number assembled against Wellington on the Tormes; but Moore had little more than twenty thousand men to oppose to this overwhelming mass, and Wellington had nearly seventy thousand.   The Partidas abounded at the time of Wellington's retreat, they were unknown at the time of Moore's retreat, and this general was confronted by Napoleon, who, despotic in command, was also unrivalled in skill, in genius, and in vigour. Wellington's army was not pressed by the enemy, and he made short marches, yet he lost more stragglers than Moore, who was vigorously pressed, made long marches, and could only secure an embarkation by delivering a battle, in which he died most honourably. His character was immediately vilified. Wellington was relieved from his pursuers by the operation of famine, and had therefore no occasion to deliver a battle, but he also was vilified at the time, with equal injustice; and if he had then died it would have been with equal malice. His subsequent successes, his great name and power, have imposed silence upon his detractors, or converted censure into praise, for it is the nature of mankind, especially of the ignorant, to cling to fortune.

Moore attributed his difficulties to the apathy of

the Spaniards; his friends charged them on the
incapacity of the English government. Wellington
attributed his ultimate failure to the defection of
Ballesteros; his brother, in the House of Lords,
charged it on the previous contracted policy of
Perceval's government, which had crippled the
general's means; and certainly Wellington's reasoning, relative to Ballesteros, was not quite sound.
That general, he said, might either have forced
Soult to take the circuitous route of Valencia,
Requeña, and Cuenca, or leave a strong corps in
observation, and then Hill might have detached
men to the north. He even calculated upon Ballesteros being able to stop both Soult and Souham,
altogether; for as the latter's operations were prescribed by the king, and dependent upon his proceedings, Wellington judged that he would have
remained tranquil if Joseph had not advanced.
This was the error. Souham's despatches
clearly shew, that the king's instructions checked, Appendix,
No. 8, A.
instead of forwarding his movements; and that
it was his intention to have delivered battle
at the end of four days, without regard to the
king's orders; and such was his force, that Wellington admitted his own inability to keep the field.
Ballesteros' defection therefore cannot be pleaded
in bar of all further investigation; but whatever
failures there were, and however imposing the
height to which the English general's reputation
has since attained, this campaign, including the
sieges of Ciudad Rodrigo, Badajos, the forts of
Salamanca, and of Burgos, the assault of Almaraz,
and the battle of Salamanca, will probably be considered his finest illustration of the art of war.

Waterloo may be called a more glorious exploit because of the great man who was there vanquished; Assye may be deemed a more wonderful action, one indeed to be compared with the victory which Lucullus gained over Tygranes, but Salamanca will always be referred to as the most skilful of Wellington's battles.

BOOK XX.

CHAPTER I.

WHILE the armies were striving, the political CHAP.
affairs had become exceedingly complicated and ———
unsteady. Their workings were little known or
observed by the public, but the evils of bad government in England, Spain, and Portugal, the incon-
gruous alliance of bigoted aristocracy with awakened
democracy, and the inevitable growth of national
jealousies as external danger seemed to recede,
were becoming so powerful, that if relief had not
been obtained from extraneous events, even the
vigour of Wellington must have sunk under the
pressure. The secret causes of disturbance shall
now be laid bare, and it will then be seen that the
catastrophe of Napoleon's Russian campaign was
absolutely necessary to the final success of the
British arms in the Peninsula. I speak not of the
physical power which, if his host had not withered
on the snowy wastes of Muscovy, the emperor could
have poured into Spain, but of those moral obstacles, which, springing up on every side, corrupted
the very life-blood of the war.

If Russia owed her safety in some degree to the
contest in the Peninsula, it is undoubted that the
fate of the Peninsula was in return, decided on

the plains of Russia; for had the French veterans
who there perished, returned victorious, the war
could have been maintained for years in Spain,
with all its waste of treasures and of blood, to
the absolute ruin of England, even though her
army might have been victorious in every battle.
Yet who shall say with certainty what termination
any war will ever have? Who shall prophecy of
an art always varying, and of such intricacy that
its secrets seem beyond the reach of human intellect? What vast preparations, what astonishing
combinations were involved in the plan, what vigour
and ability displayed in the execution of Napoleon's
march to Moscow! And yet when the winter
came, only four days sooner than he expected,
the giant's scheme seemed a thing for children to
laugh at!

Nevertheless the political grandeur of that expedition will not be hereafter judged from the wild
triumph of his enemies, nor its military merits from
the declamation which has hitherto passed as the
history of the wondrous, though unfortunate enter-
prise. It will not be the puerilities of Labaume,
of Segur, and their imitators, nor even that splendid
military and political essay of general Jomini, called
the " *Life of Napoleon*," which posterity will accept as the measure of a general, who carried four
hundred thousand men across the Niemen, and a
hundred and sixty thousand men to Moscow. And
with such a military providence, with such a vigilance, so disposing his reserves, so guarding his
flanks, so guiding his masses, that while constantly
victorious in front, no post was lost in his rear, no
convoy failed, no courier was stopped, not even a
letter was missing: the communication with his

capital was as regular and certain as if that immense march had been but a summer excursion of pleasure! However it failed, and its failure was the safety of the Peninsula.

In England the retreat from Burgos was viewed with the alarm and anger which always accompanies the disappointment of high-raised public expectation; the people had been taught to believe the French weak and dispirited, they saw them so strong and daring, that even victory could not enable the allies to make a permanent stand beyond the frontiers of Portugal. Hence arose murmurs, and a growing distrust as to the ultimate result, which would not have failed to overturn the war faction, if the retreat of the French from Moscow, the defection of Prussia, and the strange unlooked-for spectacle of Napoleon vanquished, had not come in happy time as a counterpoise.

When the parliament met, lord Wellesley undertook, and did very clearly show, that if the successes in the early part of the year had not been, by his brother, pushed to the extent expected, and had been followed by important reverses, the causes were clearly to be traced to the imbecile administration of Mr. Perceval and his coadjutors, whose policy he truly characterized as having in it "*nothing regular but confusion.*" With a very accurate knowledge of facts he discussed the military question, and maintained that twelve thousand infantry and three thousand cavalry, added to the army in the beginning of the year, would have rendered the campaign decisive, because the Russian contest, the incapacity of Joseph, and the dissentions of the French generals in Spain, had produced the most favourable crisis for striking a

vital blow at the enemy's power. The cabinet were
aware of this, and in good time, but though there
were abundance of soldiers idling at home, when
the welfare of the state required their presence in
the Peninsula, nay, although the ministers had actually sent within five thousand as many men as
were necessary, they had, with the imbecility which
marked all their proceedings, so contrived, that
few or none should reach the theatre of war until
the time for success had passed away. Then touching upon the financial question, with a rude hand
he tore to pieces the minister's pitiful pretexts, that
the want of specie had necessarily put bounds to
their efforts, and that the general himself did not
complain. " No!" exclaimed lord Wellesley, " he
does not complain because it is the sacred duty of
a soldier not to complain. But he does not say
that with greater means he could not do greater
things, and his country will not be satisfied if these
means are withheld by men, who having assumed
the direction of affairs in such a crisis, have
only incapacity to plead in extenuation of their
failures."

This stern accuser was himself fresh from the
ministry, versed in state matters, and of unques-
tionable talents ; he was well acquainted with the
actual resources and difficulties of the moment; he
was sincere in his opinions because he had abandoned office rather than be a party to such a
miserable mismanagement of England's power; he
was in fine no mean authority against his former
colleagues, even though the facts did not so clearly
bear him out in his views.

That England possessed the troops and that they

were wanted by Wellington is undeniable. Even in
September there were still between fifty and sixty
thousand soldiers present under arms at home, and
that any additional force could have been fed in
Portugal is equally beyond doubt, because the reserve magazines contained provisions for one hundred
thousand men for nine months. The only question
then was the possibility of procuring enough of specie
to purchase those supplies which could not be had
on credit. Lord Wellington had indeed made the
campaign almost without specie, and a small additional force would certainly not have overwhelmed
his resources; but setting this argument aside, what
efforts, what ability, what order, what arrangements were made by the government to overcome
the difficulties of the time? Was there less extravagance in the public offices, the public works,
public salaries, public contracts? The very snuff-
boxes and services of plate given to diplomatists,
the gorgeous furniture of palaces, nay the gaudy
trappings wasted on Whittingham's, Roche's, and
Downie's divisions, would almost have furnished the
wants of the additional troops demanded by lord
Wellesley. Where were all the millions lavished
in subsidies to the Spaniards, where the millions
which South America had transmitted to Cadiz,
where those sums spent by the soldiers during the
war? Real money had indeed nearly disappeared
from England, and a base paper had usurped its
place; but gold had not disappeared from the
world, and an able ministry would have found it.
These men only knew how to squander.

The subsidy granted to Portugal was paid by
the commercial speculation of lord Wellington

BOOK
XX.
————
1812.
Stuart's
Correspon-
dence
MSS.

and Mr. Stuart, speculations which also fed the
army, saved the whole population of Portugal from
famine, and prevented the war from stopping in
1811 ; and yet so little were the ministers capable
even of understanding, much less of making such
arrangements, that they now rebuked their general
for having adopted them and after their own imbecile manner insisted upon a new mode of providing supplies. Every movement they made
proved their incapacity. They had permitted lord
William Bentinck to engage in the scheme of invading Italy when additional troops were wanted
in Portugal; and they suffered him to bid, in the
money-market, against lord Wellington, and thus
sweep away two millions of dollars at an exorbitant premium, for a chimera, when the war in the
Peninsula was upon the point of stopping altogether in default of that very money which Wellington could have otherwise procured — nay, had
actually been promised at a reasonable cost. Nor
was this the full measure of their folly.

Lord Wellesley affirmed, and they were unable to
deny the fact, that dollars might have been obtained
from South America to any amount, if the government would have consented to pay the market-price
for them ; they would not do it, and yet afterwards
sought to purchase the same dollars at a higher
rate in the European markets. He told them, and
they could not deny it, that they had empowered
five different agents, to purchase dollars for five different services, without any controlling head ; that
these independent agents were bidding against each
other in every money-market, and the restrictions
as to the price were exactly in the inverse propor-

tion to the importance of the service : the agent
for the troops in Malta was permitted to offer the
highest price, lord Wellington was restricted to
the lowest. And besides this folly lord Wellesley
shewed that they had, under their licensing system,
permitted French vessels to bring French goods,
silks and gloves, to England, and to carry bullion
away in return. Napoleon thus paid his army in
Spain with the very coin which should have subsisted the English troops.

Incapable however as the ministers were of
making the simplest arrangements ; neglecting, as
they did, the most obvious means of supplying the
wants of the army; incapable even, as we have
seen, of sending out a few bales of clothing and
arms for the Spaniards without producing the utmost confusion, they were heedless of the counsels
of their general, prompt to listen to every intriguing
adviser, and ready to plunge into the most absurd
and complicated measures, to relieve that distress
which their own want of ability had produced.
When the war with the United States broke out, a
war provoked by themselves, they suffered the
Admiralty, contrary to the wishes of Mr. Stuart, to
reduce the naval force at Lisbon, and to neglect
Wellington's express recommendation as to the sta-
tioning of ships for the protection of the merchant-
men bringing flour and stores to Portugal. Thus
the American privateers, being unmolested, run down
the coast of Africa, intercepted the provision trade
from the Brazils, which was one of the principal resources of the army, and then, emboldened by impunity, infested the coast of Portugal, captured
fourteen ships loaded with flour off the Douro, and

a large vessel in the very mouth of the Tagus. These things happened also when the ministers were censuring and interfering with the general's commercial transactions, and seeking to throw the feeding of his soldiers into the hands of British speculators; as if the supply of an army was like that of a common market! never considering that they thus made it the merchant's interest to starve the troops with a view to increase profits; never considering that it was by that very commerce, which they were putting an end to, that the general had paid the Portuguese subsidy for them, and had furnished his own military chest with specie, when their administrative capacity was quite unequal to the task.

Never was a government better served than the British government was by lord Wellington and Mr. Stuart. With abilities, vigilance, and industry seldom equalled, they had made themselves masters of all that related to the Portuguese policy, whether foreign or domestic, military, or civil, or judicial. They knew all the causes of mischief, they had faithfully represented them both to the Portuguese and British governments, and had moreover devised effectual remedies. But the former met them with the most vexatious opposition, and the latter, neglecting their advice, lent themselves to those foolish financial schemes which I have before touched upon as emanating from Mr. Villiers, Mr. Vansittart, and the count of Funchal. The first had been deficient as an ambassador and statesman, the second was universally derided as a financier, and the third, from his long residence in London, knew very little of the state of Portugal, had derived that little from

the information of his brother, the restless Principal
Souza, and in all his schemes had reference only to
his own intrigues in the Brazils. Their plans were
necessarily absurd. Funchal revived the old project
of an English loan, and in concert with his coadjutors
desired to establish a bank after the manner of the
English institution ; and they likewise advanced a
number of minor details and propositions, most of
which had been before suggested by Principal
Souza and rejected by lord Wellington, and all of
which went to evade, not to remedy the evils. Finally
they devised, and the English cabinet actually entertained the plan, of selling the crown and church property of Portugal. This spoliation of the Catholic
church was to be effected by commissioners, one of
whom was to be Mr. Sydenham, an Englishman and
a Protestant ; and as it was judged that the pope
would not readily yield his consent, they resolved
to apply to his nuncio, who being in their power
they expected to find more pliable.

Having thus provided for the financial difficulties
of Portugal, the ministers turned their attention to
the supply of the British army, and in the same
spirit concocted what they called a modified system
of requisitions after the manner of the French
armies ! Their speeches, their manifestoes, their
whole scheme of policy, which in the working had
nearly crushed the liberties of England and had
plunged the whole world into war ; that policy
whose aim and scope was, they said, to support
established religion, the rights of monarchs, and the
independence of nations, was now disregarded or
forgotten. Yes, these men, to remove difficulties
caused by their own incapacity and negligence,
were ready to adopt all that they had before con-

demned and reviled in the French; they were eager
to meddle, and in the most offensive manner, with
the catholic religion, by getting from the nuncio,
who was in their power, what they could not get
from the pope voluntarily; they were ready to interfere with the rights of the Portuguese crown by
selling its property, and finally they would have
adopted that system of requisitions which they had
so often denounced as rendering the very name of
France abhorrent to the world.

All these schemes were duly transmitted to lord
Wellington and to Mr. Stuart, and the former had,
in the field, to unravel the intricacies, to detect the
fallacies, and to combat the wild speculations of
men, who, in profound ignorance of facts, were
giving a loose to their imaginations on such complicated questions of state.   It was while preparing
to fight Marmont that he had to expose the futility
of relying upon a loan; it was on the heights of
San Christoval, on the field of battle itself, that he
demonstrated the absurdity of attempting to establish a Portuguese bank; it was in the trenches of
Burgos that he dissected Funchal's and Villiers's
schemes of finance, and exposed the folly of attempting the sale of church property; it was at the termination of the retreat that with a mixture of rebuke and reasoning he quelled the proposal to live
by forced requisitions; and on each occasion he
shewed himself as well acquainted with these subjects as he was with the mechanism of armies.

Reform abuses, raise your actual taxes with
vigour and impartiality, pay your present debt
before you contract a new one, was his constant
reply to the propositions for loans.   And when the
English ministers pressed the other plans, which,

besides the bank, included a recoinage of dollars
into cruzados, in other words the depreciation of
the silver standard, he with an unsparing hand laid
their folly bare. The military and political state of
Portugal he said was such that no man in his senses,
whether native or foreigner, would place his capital where he could not withdraw it at a moment's
notice. When Massena invaded that country unreasonable despondency had prevailed amongst the
ministers, and now they seemed to have a confidence as wild as their former fear; but he who
knew the real state of affairs; he who knew the
persons that were expected to advance money; he
who knew the relative forces of the contending
armies, the advantages and disadvantages attending
each; he who knew the absolute weakness of the
Portuguese frontier as a line of defence, could only
laugh at the notion that the capitalists would take
gold out of their own chests to lodge it in the chests
of the bank and eventually in those of the Portuguese treasury, a treasury deservedly without credit.
The French armies opposed to him in the field (he
was then on San Christoval) were, he said, just
double his own strength, and a serious accident to
Ballesteros, a rash general with a bad army, would
oblige the Anglo-Portuguese force to retire into
Portugal and the prospects of the campaign would
vanish; and this argument left out of the question
any accident which might happen to himself or
general Hill. Portugal would, he hoped, be saved
but its security was not such as these visionaries
would represent it.

But they had proposed also a British security,
in jewels, for the capital of their bank, and their
reasonings on this head were equally fallacious.

This security was to be supported by collecting the
duties on wines, exported from Portugal to England, and yet they had not even ascertained whether the existence of these duties was conformable
to the treaty with England. Then came the former
question. Would Great Britain guarantee the capital of the subscribers whether Portugal was lost or
saved? If the country should be lost, the new
possessors would understand the levying the duties upon wines as well as the old; would England
make her drinkers of port pay two duties, the one
for the benefit of the bank capitalists, the other for
the benefit of the French conquerors? If all these
difficulties could be got over, a bank would be the
most efficacious mode in which England could use
her credit for the benefit of Portugal; but all the
other plans proposed were mere spendthrift schemes
to defray the expenses of the war, and if the English government could descend to entertain them
they would fail, because the real obstacle, scarcity
of specie, would remain.

A nation desirous of establishing public credit
should begin, he said, by acquiring a revenue equal
to its fixed expenditure, and must manifest an inclination to be honest by performing its engage-
ments with respect to public debts. This maxim
he had constantly enforced to the Portuguese government, and if they had minded it, instead of
trusting to the fallacious hope of getting loans in
England, the deficiency of their revenue would have
been made up, without imposing new taxes, and
even with the repeal of many which were oppressive and unjust. The fair and honest collection of
taxes, which ought to exist, would have been sufficient. For after protracted and unsparing exertions,

and by refusing to accept their paper money on any
other condition in his commissariat transactions, he
had at last forced the Portuguese authorities to pay
the interest of that paper and of their exchequer
bills, called " *Apolocies grandes*," and the effect had
been to increase the resources of the government
though the government had even in the execution
evinced its corruption. Then showing in detail how
this benefit had been produced he traced the mischief created by men whom he called the *sharks* of
Lisbon and other great towns, meaning speculators, principally Englishmen, whose nefarious cupidity led them to cry down the credit of the
army-bills, and then purchase them, to the injury
of the public and of the poor people who furnished
the supplies.

A plan of recoining the Spanish dollars and so
gaining eight in the hundred of pure silver which
they contained above that of the Portuguese cruzado, he treated as a fraud, and a useless one.   In
Lisbon, where the cruzado was current, some gain
might perhaps be made ; but it was not even there
certain, and foreigners, Englishmen and Americans,
from whom the great supplies were purchased,
would immediately add to their prices in proportion
to the deterioration of the coin.   Moreover the
operations and expenditure of the army were not
confined to Lisbon, nor even to Portugal, and the
cruzado would not pass for its nominal value in
Spain ; thus instead of an advantage, the greatest inconvenience would result from a scheme at the best
unworthy of the British government.   In fine the
reform of abuses, the discontinuance of useless expenses, economy and energy were the only remedies.

Such was his reasoning but it had little effect on his persecutors ; for when his best men were falling by hundreds, his brightest visions of glory fading on the smoky walls of Burgos, he was again forced to examine and refute anew, voluminous plans of Portuguese finance, concocted by Funchal and Villiers, with notes by Vansittart. All the old schemes of the Principal Souza, which had been so often before analyzed and rejected as impracticable, were revived with the addition of a mixed Anglo-Portuguese commission for the sale of the crown and church lands. And these projects were accompanied with complaints that frauds had been practised on the custom-house, and violence used towards the inhabitants by the British commissaries, and it was insinuated such misconduct had been the real cause of the financial distresses of Portugal. The patient industry of genius was never more severely taxed.

Wellington began by repelling the charges of exactions and frauds, as applied to the army ; he showed that to reform the custom-house so as to prevent frauds, had been his unceasing recommendation to the Portuguese government; that he had as repeatedly, and in detail, shewed the government, how to remedy the evils they complained of, how to increase their customs, how to levy their taxes, how in fine to arrange their whole financial system in a manner that would have rendered their revenues equal to their expenses, and without that oppression and injustice which they were in the habit of practising ; for the extortions and violence complained of, were not perpetrated by the English but by the Portuguese commissariat, and yet the troops of that nation were starving. Having exposed Funchal's ignorance of financial facts in detail, and challenged him to the proof of the charges against the British army, he entered deeply into the consideration of the great question of the sale of the crown and church lands, which it had been proposed to substitute for that economy and reform of abuses which he so long, so often, and so vainly had pressed upon the regency. The proposal was not quite new. " I have already," he observed, " had before me a proposition for the sale or rather transfer, to the creditors of the ' *Junta de Viveres*' of crown lands; but these were the uncultivated lands in Alemtejo, and I pointed out to the government the great improbability that any body would take such lands in payment, and the injury that would be done to the public credit by making the scheme public if not likely to be successful. My opinion is that there is nobody in Portugal possessed of capital who entertains, or who ought to entertain, such an opinion of the state of affairs in the Peninsula, as to lay out his money in the purchase of crown lands. The loss of a battle, not in the Peninsula even, but elsewhere, would expose his estate to confiscation, or at all events to ruin by a fresh incursion of the enemy. Even if any man could believe that Portugal is secure against the invasion of the enemy, and his estate and person against the ' *violence, exactions, and frauds*' (these were Funchal's words respecting the allied army) of the enemy, he is not, during the existence of the war, according to the Conde de Funchal's notion, exempt from those evils from his own countrymen and their allies. Try this experiment, offer the estates of the crown for sale, and it will be seen whether I have formed a correct judgment on this subject." Then running with a rapid hand over many minor though intricate fallacies for raising the value of the Portuguese paper-money, he thus treated the great question of the church lands.

First, as in the case of crown lands, there would be no purchasers, and as nothing could render the measure palatable to the clergy, the influence of the church would be exerted against the allies, instead of being, as hitherto, strongly exerted in their favour. It would be useless if the experiment of the crown lands succeeded, and if that failed the sale of church lands could not succeed; but the attempt would alienate the good wishes of a very powerful party in Spain, as well as in Portugal. Moreover if it should succeed, and be honestly carried into execution, it would entail a burthen on the finances of five in the hundred, on the purchase-money, for the support of the ecclesiastical owners of the estates. The best mode of obtaining for the state eventually the benefit of the church property, would be to prevent the monasteries and nunneries from receiving novices, and thus, in the course of time, the pope might be brought to consent to the sale of the estates, or the nation might assume possession when the ecclesiastical corporations thus became extinct. He however thought that it was no disadvantage to Spain or Portugal, that large portions of land should be held by the church. The bishops and monks were the only proprietors who lived on their estates, and spent the revenues amongst the labourers by whom those revenues had been produced; and until the habits of the new landed proprietors changed, the transfer of the property in land from the clergy to the laymen would be a misfortune.

This memoir, sent from the trenches of Burgos,

quashed Funchal's projects; but that intriguer's
object was not so much to remove financial difficulties, as to get rid of his brother's opponents in
the regency by exciting powerful interests against
them; wherefore failing in this proposal, he ordered
Redondo, now marquis of Borba, the minister of
finance, to repair to the Brazils, intending to supply
his place with one of his own faction.   Wellington
and Stuart were at this time doggedly opposed by
Borba, but as the credit of the Portuguese treasury
was supported by his character for probity, they
forbade him to obey the order, and represented
the matter so forcibly to the prince regent, that
Funchal was severely reprimanded for his audacity.

It was amidst these vexations that Wellington
made his retreat, and in such destitution that he
declared all former distress for money had been
slight in comparison of his present misery.   So
low were the resources, that British naval stores
had been trucked for corn in Egypt; and the English
ministers, finding that Russia, intent upon pushing
her successes, was gathering specie from all quarters,
desired Mr. Stuart to prevent the English and
American captains of merchant vessels from carrying coin away from Lisbon; a remedial measure,
indicating their total ignorance of the nature of
commerce.   It was not attempted to be enforced.
Then also they transmitted their plan of supplying
the English army by requisitions on the country,
a plan the particulars of which may be best gathered
from the answers to it.

Mr. Stuart, firm in opposition, shortly observed
that it was by avoiding and reprobating such a
system, although pursued alike by the natives and
by the enemy, that the British character, and credit,

had been established so firmly as to be of the greatest use in the operations of the war. Wellington entered more deeply into the subject.

Nothing, he said, could be procured from the country in the mode proposed by the ministers' memoir, unless resort was also had to the French mode of enforcing their requisitions. The proceedings of the French armies were misunderstood. It was not true, as supposed in the memoir, that the French never paid for supplies. They levied contributions where money was to be had, and with this paid for provisions in other parts ; and when requisitions for money or clothing were made, they were taken on account of the regular contributions due to the government. They were indeed heavier than even an usurping government was entitled to demand, still it was a regular government account, and it was obvious the British army could not have recourse to a similar plan without depriving its allies of their own legitimate resources.

The requisitions were enforced by a system of terror. A magistrate was ordered to provide for the troops, and was told that the latter would, in case of failure, take the provisions and punish the village or district in a variety of ways. Now were it expedient to follow this mode of requisition there must be two armies, one to fight the enemy and one to enforce the requisitions, for the Spaniards would never submit to such proceedings without the use of force. The conscription gave the French armies a more moral description of soldiers, but even if this second army was provided, the British troops could not be trusted to inflict an exact measure of punishment on a disobedient village,

they would plunder it as well as the others readily
enough, but their principal object would be to get
at and drink as much liquor as they could, and then
to destroy as much valuable property as should fall
in their way; meanwhile the objects of their mission, the bringing of supplies to the army and the
infliction of an exact measure of punishment on the
magistrates or district would not be accomplished at
all. Moreover the holders of supplies in Spain being
unused to commercial habits, would regard payment for these requisitions by bills of any description,
to be rather worse than the mode of contribution
followed by the French, and would resist it as forcibly. And upon such a nice point did the war
hang, that if they accepted the bills, and were once
to discover the mode of procuring cash for them by
discounting high, it would be the most fatal blow
possible to the credit and resources of the British
army in the Peninsula. The war would then soon
cease.

The memoir asserted that Sir John Moore had
been well furnished with money, and that nevertheless the Spaniards would not give him provisions;
and this fact was urged as an argument for enforcing
requisitions. But the assertion that Moore was
furnished with money, which was itself the index to
the ministers' incapacity, Wellington told them was
not true. " Moore," he said, " had been even worse
furnished than himself ; that general had borrowed
a little, a very little money at Salamanca, but he had
no regular supply for the military chest until the
army had nearly reached Coruña; and the Spaniards
were not very wrong in their reluctance to meet his
wants, for the debts of his army were still unpaid in

BOOK
XX.
———
1812.

the latter end of 1812." In fine there was no mode by which supplies could be procured from the country without payment on the spot, or soon after the transaction, except by prevailing on the Spanish government to give the English army a part of the government contributions, and a part of the revenues of the royal domains, to be received from the people in kind at a reasonable rate. This had been already done by himself in the province of Salamanca with success, and the same system might be extended to other provinces in proportion as the legitimate government was re-established. But this only met a part of the evil, it would indeed give some supplies, cheaper than they could otherwise be procured, yet they must afterwards be paid for at Cadiz in specie, and thus less money would come into the militaay chest, which, as before noticed, was only supported by the mercantile speculations of the general.

Such were the discussions forced upon Wellington when all his faculties were demanded on the field of battle, and such was the hardiness of his intellect to sustain the additional labour. Such also were the men calling themselves statesmen who then wielded the vast resources of Great Britain. The expenditure of that country for the year 1812, was above one hundred millions, the ministers who controuled it, were yet so ignorant of the elementary principles of finance, as to throw upon their general, even amidst the clangor and tumult of battle, the task of exposing such fallacies. And to reduce these persons from the magnitude of statesmen to their natural smallness of intriguing debaters is called political prejudice! But though power may enable men to trample upon reason for a time with impunity, they cannot escape her ultimate vengeance, she reassumes her sway and history delivers them to the justice of posterity.

Perverse as the preceedings of the English ministers were, those of the Portuguese and Spanish governments were not less vexatious; and at this time the temper of the Spanish rulers was of infinite importance because of the misfortunes which had befallen the French emperor. The opportunity given to strike a decisive blow at his power in the Peninsula demanded an early and vigorous campaign in Spain, and the experience of 1812 had taught Wellington, that no aid could be derived from the Spaniards unless a change was made in their military system. Hence the moment he was assured that the French armies had taken winter-quarters, he resolved before all other matters, in person to urge upon the Cortez the necessity of giving him the real as well as the nominal command of their troops, seeing that without an immediate reformation the Spanish armies could not take the field in due season.

During the past campaign, and especially after the Conde de Abispal, indignant at the censure passed in the Cortez on his brother's conduct at Castalla, had resigned, the weakness of the Spanish government had become daily more deplorable; nothing was done to ameliorate the military system; an extreme jealousy raged between the Cortez and the regency; and when the former offered lord Wellington the command of their armies, Mr. Wellesley advised him to accept it, not so much in the hope of effecting any beneficial change, as to offer a point upon which the Spaniards who were still true to the English alliance and to the aristocratic cause might rally in case of reverse. The

disobedience of Ballesteros had been indeed promptly
punished ; but the vigour of the Cortez on that occasion, was more the result of offended pride than
any consideration of sound policy, and the retreat of
the allies into Portugal was the signal for a renewal
of those dangerous intrigues, which the battle of
Salamanca had arrested without crushing.

Lord Wellington reached Cadiz on the 18th of
December, he was received without enthusiasm, yet
with due honour, and his presence seemed agreeable
both to the Cortes and to the people ; the passions
which actuated the different parties in the state
subsided for the moment, and the ascendency of his
genius was so strongly felt, that he was heard with
patience, even when in private he strongly urged the
leading men to turn their attention entirely to the
war, to place in abeyance their factious disputes
and above all things not to put down the inquisition
lest they should drive the powerful church party
into the arms of the enemy. His exhortation upon
this last point, had indeed no effect save to encourage the Serviles to look more to England, yet it
did not prevent the Cortez yielding to him the
entire controul of fifty thousand men which were to
be paid from the English subsidy ; they promised also
that the commanders should not be removed, nor any
change made in the organization or destination of
such troops without his consent.

A fresh organization of the Spanish forces now
had place. They were divided into four armies
and two reserves.

The Catalans formed the first army.

Elio's troops including the divisions of Duran,
Bassecour, and Villa Campa, received the name of
the second army.

The forces in the Morena, formerly under Ballesteros, were constituted the third army, under Del
Parque.

The troops of Estremadura, Leon, Gallicia, and
the Asturias, including Morillo's, Penne Villemur's,
Downie's, and Carlos d'España's separate divisions,
were called the fourth army, and given to Castaños,
whose appointment to Catalonia was cancelled, and
his former dignity of captain-general in Estremadura and Gallicia restored. The Partidas of Longa,
Mina, Porlier, and the other chiefs in the northern
provinces were afterwards united to this army as
separate divisions.

The conde d'Abispal, made captain-general of
Andalusia, commanded the first reserve, and Lacy
recalled from Catalonia, where he was replaced by
Copons, was ordered to form a second reserve in the
neighbourhood of San Roque. Such were the new
dispositions, but when Wellington had completed
this important negociation with the Spanish government some inactivity was for the first time discovered
in his own proceedings. His stay was a little prolonged without apparent reason, and it was whis-
pered that if he resembled Cæsar, Cadiz could
produce a Cleopatra ; but whether true or not, he
soon returned to the army, first however visiting
Lisbon where he was greeted with extraordinary
honours, and the most unbounded enthusiasm, especially by the people.

His departure from Cadiz was the signal for all
the political dissentions to break out with more violence than before ; the dissentions of the liberals
and serviles became more rancorous, and the executive was always on the side of the latter, the
majority of the cortez on the side of the former ;

neither enjoyed the confidence of the people nor of
the allies, and the intrigues of Carlotta, which never
ceased, advanced towards their completion. A
strong inclination to make her sole regent was
manifested, and sir Henry Wellesley, tired of fruitless opposition remained neuter, with the approbation of his brother. One of the principal causes
of this feeling for Carlotta, was the violence she
had shewn against the insurgents of Buenos Ayres,
and another was the disgust given to the merchants
of Cadiz, by certain diplomatic measures which
lord Strangford had held with that revolted state.
The agents of the princess represented the policy of England towards the Spanish colonies as a
smuggling policy, and not without truth, for the
advice of lord Wellington upon that subject had
been unheeded. Lord Castlereagh had indeed of-
ferred a new mediation scheme, whereby the old
commission was to proceed under the Spanish restriction of not touching at Mexico, to which
country a new mission composed of Spaniards
was to proceed, accompanied by an English agent
without any ostensible character. This proposal
however ended as the others had done, and the
Spanish jealousy of England increased.

In the beginning of the year 1813, Carlotta's
cause ably and diligently served by Pedro Souza,
had gained a number of adherents even amongst the
liberals in the cortez. She was ready to sacrifice
even the rights of her posterity, and as she promised to maintain all ancient abuses, the clergy
and the serviles were in no manner averse to her
success. Meanwhile the decree to abolish the inquisition which was become the great test of political party, passed on the 7th of March, and the

regency were ordered to have it read in the churches. The clergy of Cadiz resisted the order, and intimated their refusal through the medium of a public letter, and the regency encouraged them by removing the governor of Cadiz, admiral Valdez, a known liberal and opponent of the inquisition, appointing in his stead general Alos, a warm advocate for that horrid institution. But in the vindication of official power the Spaniards are generally prompt and decided. On the 8th Augustin Arguelles moved, and it was instantly carried, that the sessions of the extraordinary cortez should be declared permanent, with a view to measures worthy of the nation, and to prevent the evils with which the state was menaced by the opposition of the regency and the clergy to the cortes. A decree was then proposed for suppressing the actual regency, and replacing it with a provisional government to be composed of the three eldest councillors of state. This being conformable to the constitution, was carried by a majority of eighty-six to fifty-eight, while another proposition, that two members of the cortez, publicly elected, should be added to the regency, was rejected as an innovation, by seventy-two against sixty-six. The councillors Pedro Agar, Gabriel Ciscar, and the cardinal Bourbon, archbishop of Toledo, were immediately installed as regents.

A committee which had been appointed to consider of the best means of improving a system of government felt by all parties to be imperfect, now recommended that the cardinal archbishop, who was of the blood royal, should be president of the regency, leaving Carlotta's claims unnoticed, and as Ciscar and Agar had been formerly removed from

the regency for incapacity, it was generally supposed that the intention was to make the archbishop in fact sole regent. Very soon however
Carlotta's influence was again felt, for a dispute
having arisen in the cortez between what were
called the Americans and the Liberals, about the
annual Acapulco-ship, the former to the number of
twenty joined the party of the princess, and it
was resolved that Ruiez Pedron, a distinguished
opponent of the inquisition, should propose her as
the head of the regency. They were almost sure
of a majority, when the scheme transpired, and
the people, who liked her not, became so furious
that her partizans were afraid to speak. Then the
opposite side, fearing her power, proposed on the
instant that the provisional regency should be made
permanent which was carried. Thus, chance rather
than choice ruling, an old prelate and two imbecile
councillors were entrusted with the government,
and the intrigues and rancour of the different
parties exploded more frequently as the pressure
from above became slight.

More than all others the clergy were, as might
be expected, violent and daring, yet the Cortez
was not to be frightened. Four canons of the
cathedrals were arrested in May, and orders were
issued to arrest the archbishop of St. Jago and
many bishops, because of a pastoral letter they had
published against the abolition of the inquisition;
for according to the habits of their craft of all
sects, they deemed religion trampled under foot
when the power of levying money and spilling
blood was denied to ministers professing the faith
of Christ. Nor amidst these broils did the English influence fail to suffer ; the democratic spirit

advanced hastily, the Cadiz press teemed with

writings, intended to excite the people against the
ultimate designs of the English cabinet, and every
effort was made to raise a hatred of the British
general and his troops. These efforts were not
founded entirely on falsehoods, and were far from
being unsuccessful, because the eager desire to
preserve the inquisition displayed by lord Wellington and his brother, although arising from military
considerations, was too much in accord with the
known tendency of the English cabinet's policy, not
to excite the suspicions of the whole liberal party.

The bishops of Logroño, Mondonedo, Astorga,
Lugo, and Salamanca, and the archbishop of St.
Jago were arrested, but several bishops escaped
into Portugal, and were there protected as martyrs
to the cause of legitimacy and despotism. The
bishop of Orense and the ex-regent Lardizabal had
before fled, the latter to Algarve, the former to the
Tras os Montes, from whence he kept up an active
intercourse with Gallicia, and the Cortez were far
from popular there ; indeed the flight of the bishops
created great irritation in every part of Spain, for
the liberal party of the Cortez was stronger in the
Isla than in other parts, and by a curious anomaly
the officers and soldiers all over Spain were generally their partizans while the people were generally the partisans of the clergy. Nevertheless the
seeds of freedom, though carelessly sown by the
French on one side, and by the Cortez on the other,
took deep root, and have since sprung up into
strong plants in due time to burgeon and bear
fruit.

When the bishops fled from Spain, Gravina, the
pope's Nuncio assumed such a tone of hostility,

that notwithstanding the good offices of sir Henry
Wellesley, which were for some time successful in
screening him from the vengeance of the Cortez,
the latter, encouraged by the English newspapers,
finally dismissed him and sequestered his benefices.
He also took refuge in Portugal, and like the rest
of the expelled clergy, sought by all means to
render the proceedings of the Cortez odious in
Spain. He formed a strict alliance with the Portuguese nuncio, Vicente Machiechi, and working
together with great activity, they interfered, not
with the concerns of Spain only, but with the
Catholics in the British army, and even extended
their intrigues to Ireland. Hence, as just and
honest government had never formed any part of
the English policy towards that country, alarm
pervaded the cabinet, and the nuncio, protected
when opposed to the Cortez, was now considered a
very troublesome and indiscreet person.

Such a state of feud could not last long without
producing a crisis, and one of a most formidable
and decisive nature was really at hand. Already
many persons in the Cortez held secret intercourse with Joseph, in the view of acknowledging
his dynasty, on condition that he would accede to the
general policy of the Cortez in civil government;
that monarch had as we have seen organized a
large native force, and the coasts of Spain and
Portugal swarmed with French privateers manned
with Spanish seamen. The victory at Salamanca
had withered these resources for the moment, but
Wellington's failure at Burgos and retreat into Portugal again revived them, and at the same time
gave a heavy shock to public confidence in the
power of England, a shock which nothing but the

misfortunes of Napoleon in Russia could have prevented from being fatal.

The Emperor indeed with that wonderful intellectual activity and energy which made him the
foremost man of the world, had raised a fresh army
and prepared once more to march into the heart of
Germany, yet to do this he was forced to withdraw
such numbers of old soldiers from Spain that the
French army could no longer hope permanently to
act on the offensive. This stayed the Peninsula
cause upon the very brink of a precipice, for in
that very curious, useful, and authentic work, called
" *Bourrienne and his errors*," it appears that early
in 1813, the ever factious Conde de Montijo, then
a general in Elio's army, had secretly made pro-
posals to pass over, with the forces under his command, to the king ; and soon afterwards the whole
army of Del Parque, having advanced into La
Mancha, made offers of the same nature.

They were actually in negociation with Joseph,
when the emperor's orders obliged the French
army to abandon Madrid, and take up the line of
the Duero. Then the Spaniards advertised of the
French weakness, feared to continue their negociations, Wellington soon afterwards advanced, and
as this feeling in favour of the intrusive monarch
was certainly not general, the resistance to the
invaders revived with the successes of the British
general. But if instead of diminishing his forces,
Napoleon, victorious in Russia, had strengthened
them, this defection would certainly have taken
place, and would probably have been followed by
others. The king at the head of a Spanish army
would then have reconquered Andalusia, Wellington would have been confined to the defence of

Portugal, and it is scarcely to be supposed that
England would have purchased the independence
of that country with her own permanent ruin.

This conspiracy is not related by me with entire
confidence, because no trace of the transaction is to
be found in the correspondence of the king taken
at Vittoria. Nevertheless there are abundant proofs
that the work called " *Bourrienne and his errors*,"
inasmuch as it relates to Joseph's transactions in
Spain, is accurately compiled from that monarch's
correspondence. Many of his papers taken at Vittoria were lost or abstracted at the time, and as in
a case involving so many persons' lives, he would
probably have destroyed the proofs of a conspiracy
which had failed, there seems little reason to doubt
that the general fact is correct. Napoleon also in
his memoirs, speaks of secret negociations with the
Cortez about this time, and his testimony is corro-
borated by the correspondence of the British embassy at Cadiz, and by the continued intrigues
against the British influence. The next chapter
will show that the policy of Spain was not the only
source of uneasiness to Lord Wellington.

CHAPTER II.

NOTHING could be more complicated than the political state of Portugal with reference to the situation of the English general. His object, as I have repeatedly shown, was to bring the whole resources of the country to bear on the war, but to effect this he had to run counter to the habits and customs, both of the people and of the government; to detect the intrigues of the subordinate authorities as well as those of the higher powers; to oppose the violence of factious men in the local government, and what was still more difficult, to stimulate the sluggish apathy and to combat the often honest obstinacy of those who were not factious. These things he was to effect without the power of recompensing or chastising, and even while forced to support those who merited rebuke, against the still more formidable intriguers of the court of Brazil; for the best men of Portugal actually formed the local government, and he was not foiled so much by the men as by the sluggish system which was national, and although dull for good purposes, vivacious enough for mischief. The dread of ultimate personal consequences attached, not to neglect of the war but to any vigorous exertions in support of it.

The proceedings of the court of Rio Janeiro were not less mischievous, for there the personal intrigues fostered by the peculiar disposition of the English envoy, by the weak yet dogged habits of the prince, and by the meddling nature and violent passions of the princess Carlotta, stifled all great national views. There also the power of the Souza's, a family deficient neither in activity nor in talent, was predominant, and the object of all was to stimulate the government in Portugal against the English general's military policy. To this he could, and had opposed, as we have seen, the power of the English government, with some effect at different times, but that resource was a dangerous one and only to be resorted to in extreme circumstances. Hence when to all these things is added a continual struggle with the knavery of merchants of all nations, his difficulties must be admitted, his indomitable vigour, his patience and his extraordinary mental resources admired, and the whole scene must be considered as one of the most curious and instructive lessons in the study of nations.

Wellington was not simply a general who with greater or less means, was to plan his military operations leaving to others the care of settling the political difficulties which might arise. He had, coincident with his military duties, to regenerate a whole people, to force them against the current of their prejudices and usages on a dangerous and painful course; he had to teach at once the populace and the government, to infuse spirit and order without the aid of rewards or punishments, to excite enthusiasm through the medium of corrupt oppressive institutions, and far from making any revolutionary appeal to suppress all tendency towards that resource of great minds on the like occasions. Thus only could he maintain an army at all, and as it was beyond the power of man to

continue such a struggle for any length of time
he was more than ever anxious to gather strength
for a decisive blow, which the enemy's situation
now rendered possible, that he might free himself from the critical and anomalous relation in
which he stood towards Portugal.

It may indeed be wondered that he so long
bore up against the encreasing pressure of these
distracting affairs, and certain it is that more than
once he was like to yield, and would have yielded
if fortune had not offered him certain happy military chances, and yet such as few but himself could
have profited from. In 1810, on the ridge of
Busaco, and in the lines, the military success was
rather over the Portuguese government than the
enemy. At Santarem in 1811 the glory of arms
scarcely compensated for the destitution of the
troops. At Fuentes Onoro and on the Caya, after
the second unsuccessful siege of Badajos, the Portuguese army had nearly dissolved; and the astonishing sieges of Ciudad Rodrigo and Badajos in
1812, were necessary to save the cause from dying
of inanition and despair. Even then the early
deliverance of Andalusia was frustrated, and time,
more valuable than gold or life, in war, was lost,
the enemy became the strongest in the field, and
in despite of the victory of Salamanca, the bad
effects of the English general's political situation
were felt in the repulse from Burgos, and in the
double retreat from that place and from Madrid.
Accumulated mischiefs were now to be encountered in Portugal.

It has been shown how obstinately the regency
opposed Wellington's plans of financial reform, how

they disputed and complained upon every circumstance, whether serious or trivial on which a complaint could be founded; for thinking Portugal no
longer in danger they were tired of their British
allies, and had no desire to aid nor indeed any wish
to see Spain delivered from her difficulties. They
designed therefore to harass the English general,
hoping either to drive him away altogether, or to
force him, and, through him, his government, to
grant them loans or new subsidies. But Wellington
knew that Portugal could, and he was resolved
it should find resources within itself, wherefore,
after the battle of Salamanca, when they demanded
a fresh subsidy he would not listen to them; and
when they adopted that scheme which I have
already exposed, of feeding, or rather starving their
troops, through the medium of a treaty with the
Spanish government, he checked the shameful and
absurd plan, by applying a part of the money in
the chest of aids intended for the civil service to
the relief of the Portuguese troops. Yet the regency did not entirely fail in their object inasmuch
as many persons dependent upon the subsidy were
thus deprived of their payments, and their complaints hurt the British credit, and reduced the
British influence with the people whose faithful
attachment to the alliance no intrigues had hitherto
been able to shake.

Into every branch of government, however minute, the regency now infused their own captious
and discontented spirit. They complained falsely
that general Campbell had insulted the nation by
turning some Portuguese residents publicly out of
Gibraltar in company with Jews and Moors; they
refused the wheat which was delivered to them by

lord Wellington in lieu of their subsidy, saying it
was not fit for food notwithstanding that the English troops were then living upon parcels of the
same grain, that their own troops were glad to get
it, and that no other was to be had. When a
wooden jetty was to be thrown in the Tagus for
the convenience of landing stores, they supported
one Caldas, a rich proprietor, in his refusal to permit
the trees, wanted for the purpose, to be felled,
alledging the rights of property, although he was to
be paid largely, and although they had themselves
then, and always, disregarded the rights of property,
especially when poor men were concerned, seizing
upon whatever was required either for the public
service, or for the support of their own irregularities,
without any payment at all and in shameful violation both of law and humanity.

The commercial treaty, and the proceedings of the
Oporto wine company, an oppressive corporation
unfair in all its dealings, irresponsible, established
in violation of that treaty, and supported without
regard either to the interests of the prince regent
or his British allies, furnished them with continual
subjects for disputes, and nothing was too absurd
or too gross for their interference. Under the management of Mr. Stuart who had vigorously enforced
Wellington's plans, their paper money had obtained
a reasonable and encreasing circulation, and their
custom-house resources had encreased, the expenses of their navy and of their arsenal had in some
degree been reduced ; and it was made evident that
an extensive and vigorous application of the same
principles would enable them to overcome all their
financial difficulties ; but there were too many personal interests, too much shameful profit made

under the abuses to permit such a reform. The naval establishment instead of being entirely transferred, as Wellington desired, to the Brazils, was continued in the Tagus, and with it the arsenal as its natural appendage. The infamous Junta de Viveres had been suppressed by the prince regent, yet the government under the false pretext of paying its debts still disbursed above ten thousand pounds a month in salaries to men whose offices had been formally abolished.

About this time also the opening of the Spanish ports in those provinces from whence the enemy had been driven, deprived Lisbon of a monopoly of trade enjoyed for the last three years, and the regency observing the consequent diminution of revenue, with inexpressible effrontery insisted that the grain, imported by Wellington, by which their army and their nation had been saved from famine, and by which their own subsidy had been provided, should enter the public warehouses under specific regulations and pay duty for so doing. So tenaciously did they hold to this point that Wellington was forced to menace a formal appeal to the English cabinet, for he knew that the subordinate officers of the government, knavish in the extreme, would have sold the secrets of the army magazines to the speculators ; and the latter, in whose hands the furnishing of the army would under the new plan of the English ministers be placed, being thus accurately instructed of its resources would have regulated their supplies with great nicety so as to have famished the soldiers, and paralyzed the operations at the greatest possible expense.

But the supply of the army under any system was now becoming extremely precarious, for besides the activity of the American privateers English ships of war used, at times, to capture the vessels secretly employed in bringing provision under licenses from Mr. Stuart and Mr. Forster. Nay the captain of a Scotch merchant vessel engaged in the same trade and having no letter of marque, had the piratical insolence to seize in the very mouth of the Tagus, and under the Portuguese batteries, an American vessel sailing under a license from Mr. Forster, and to carry her into Greenock, thus violating at once the license of the English minister, the independence of Portugal, and the general law of nations. Alarm immediately spread far and wide amongst the American traders, the indignation of the Portuguese government was strongly and justly excited, and the matter became extremely embarrassing, because no measure of punishment could be inflicted without exposing the secret of a system which had been the principal support of the army. However the Congress soon passed an act forbidding neutrals to ship flour in the American ports, and this blow, chiefly aimed at the Portuguese ships, following upon the non-importation act, and being combined with the illegal violence of the English vessels, nearly dried up this source of supply, and threw the army principally upon the Brazil trade, which by the negligence of the Admiralty was, as I have before noticed, exposed to the enterprize of the United States' privateers.

During Wellington's absence in Spain the military administration of Portugal was necessarily in the hands of the regency and all the ancient abuses were fast reviving. The army in the field received no succours, the field artillery had entirely disap-

peared, the cavalry was in the worst condition, the
infantry was reduced in numbers, the equipments
of those who remained were scarcely fit for service,
and the spirit of the men had waned from enthusiasm to despondency. There was no money in the
military chest, no recruits in the depôts, and the
transport service was neglected altogether. Beresford's severity had failed to check desertion, because
want, the parent of crimes, had proved too strong
for fear; the country swarmed with robbers, and
as no fault civil or military was punished by the
regency, every where knaves triumphed over the
welfare of the nation.

Meanwhile all persons whose indolence or ti-
midity led them to fly from the active defence of
their country to the Brazils, were there received
and cherished as martyrs to their personal affections
for the prince; they were lauded for their opposition to the regency, and were called victims to
the injustice of Beresford, and to the encroachments
of the English officers. This mischief was accompanied by another of greater moment, for the prince
continually permitted officers possessing family interest to retire from active service retaining their
pay and rank, thus offering a premium for bad
men to enter the army with the intent of quitting it
in this disgraceful manner. Multitudes did so, pro-
motion became rapid, the nobility whose influence
over the poor classes was very great, and might
have been beneficially employed in keeping up the
zeal of the men, disappeared rapidly from the regiments, and the foul stream of knaves and cowards
thus continually pouring through the military ranks
destroyed all cohesion and tainted every thing as it
passed.

Interests of the same nature, prevailing with the regency, polluted the civil administration. The rich and powerful inhabitants, especially those of the great cities, were suffered to evade the taxes and to disobey the regulations for drawing forth the re- sources of the country in the military service; and during Wellington's absence in Spain, the English under-commissaries, and that retinue of villains which invariably gather on the rear of armies, being in some measure freed from the immediate dread of his vigilance and vigour, violated all the regu- lations in the most daring manner. The poor husbandmen were cruelly oppressed, their farming animals were constantly carried off to supply food for the army, and agriculture was thus stricken at the root; the breed of horned cattle and of horses had rapidly and alarmingly decreased, and but- cher's meat was scarcely to be procured even for the troops who remained in Portugal.

These irregularities, joined to the gross miscon- duct of the military detachments and convoys of sick men, on all the lines of communication, not only produced great irritation in the country but offered the means for malevolent and factious per- sons to assail the character and intentions of the English general; every where writings and stories were circulated against the troops, the real out- rages were exaggerated, others were invented and the drift of all was to render Wellington, and the English, odious to the nation at large. Nor was this scheme confined to Portugal alone, agents were also busy to the same purpose in London, and when the enthusiasm, which Wellington's presence at Lisbon had created amongst the people, was known at Cadiz, the press there teemed with abuse. Divers agents of the democratic party in Spain came to Lisbon to aid the Portuguese malcontents, writings were circulated accusing Wellington of an intention to subjugate the Peninsula for his own ambitious views, and, as consistency is never regarded on such occasions, it was diligently insinuated that he encouraged the excesses of his troops out of personal hatred to the Portuguese people; the old baseness of sending virulent anonymous letters to the Englsh general was also revived. In fine the republican spirit was extending beyond the bounds of Spain, and the Portuguese regency, terrified at its approach, appealed to Mr. Stuart for the assistance of England to check its formidable progress. Neither were they wanting to themselves. They forbade the Portuguese newspapers to admit any observations on the political events in Spain, they checked the introduction of Spanish democratic publications, they ordered their diplomatists at Cadiz to encourage writings of an opposite tendency, and to support the election of deputies who were known for their love of despotism. This last measure was however baffled by the motion of Arguelles, already mentioned, which rendered the old Cortez permanent; and Mr. Stuart, judging the time unfavourable, advised the Portuguese government to reserve the exertion of its power against the democrats, until the military success which the state of the continent, and the weakness of the French troops in Spain, promised, should enable the victors to put down such doctrines with effect; advice which was not unmeaning as I shall have occasion hereafter to show.

All these malignant efforts Wellington viewed with indifference. " Every leading man," he said,

" was sure to be accused of criminal personal ambition, and, if he was conscious of the charge being
false, the accusation did no harm." Nevertheless
his position was thereby rendered more difficult, and
these intrigues were accompanied by other mischiefs
of long standing and springing from a different
source, but even of a more serious character, for
the spirit of captious discontent had reached the inferior magistracy, who endeavoured to excite the
people against the military generally. Complaints
came in from all quarters of outrages on the part of
the troops, some too true, but many of them false,
or frivolous ; and when the English general ordered
court-martials for the trial of the accused, the magistrates refused to attend as witnesses, because
Portuguese custom rendered such an attendance
degrading, and by Portuguese law a magistrate's
written testimony was efficient in courts-martial.
Wellington in vain assured them that English law
would not suffer him to punish men upon such testimony ; in vain he pointed out the mischief which
must infallibly overwhelm the country if the soldiers
discovered they might thus do evil with impunity. He offered to send in each case, lists of
Portuguese witnesses required that they might be
summoned by the native authorities, but nothing
could overcome the obstinacy of the magistrates ;
they answered that his method was insolent ; and
with a sullen malignity they continued to accumulate
charges against the troops, to refuse attendance in
the courts, and to call the soldiers, their own as
well as the British, " licensed spoliators of the
community."

For a time the generous nature of the poor peo-

ple, resisted all these combining causes of discontent ; neither real injuries nor the exaggerations, nor
the falsehoods of those who attempted to stir up
wrath, produced any visible effect upon the great
bulk of the population ; yet by degrees affection
for the British cooled, and Wellington expressed
his fears that a civil war would commence between
the Portuguese people on the one hand, and the
troops of both nations on the other. Wherefore
his activity was redoubled to draw, while he could
still controul affairs, all the military strength to a
head, and to make such an irruption into Spain as
would establish a new base of operations beyond
the power of such fatal dissensions.

These matters were sufficiently vexatious and
alarming, but what made him tremble, was, the
course, which the misconduct of the Portuguese
government, and the incapacity of the English
cabinet, had forced upon the native furnishers of
the supplies. Those persons, coming in the winter
to Lisbon to have their bills on the military chest
paid, could get no money, and in their distress had
sold the bills to speculators, the Portuguese holders, at a discount of fifteen, the Spanish holders
at a discount of forty in the hundred. The credit
of the chest immediately fell, prices rose in proportion, and as no military enterprize could carry
the army beyond the flight of this harpy, and no
revenues could satisfy its craving, the contest must
have ceased, if Mr. Stuart had not found a momentary and partial remedy, by publicly guaranteeing
the payment of the bills and granting interest until
they could be taken up. The expense was thus augmented, but the increase fell far short of the en-

hanced cost of the supplies which had already
resulted even from this restricted practice of the
bill-holders, and of two evils the least was chosen.
It may seem strange that such transactions should
belong to the history of the military operations in
the Peninsula, that it should be the general's instead of the minister's task, to encounter such
evils, and to find the remedy. Such however was
the nature of the war, and no adequate notion of
lord Wellington's vigorous capacity and Herculean
labours can be formed, without an intimate knowledge of the financial and political difficulties which
oppressed him, and of which this work has necessarily only given an outline.

The disorders of the Portuguese military system
had brought Beresford back to Lisbon while the
siege of Burgos was still in progress, and now,
under Wellington's direction, he strained every
nerve to restore the army to its former efficient state.
To recruit the regiments of the line he disbanded
all the militia men fit for service, replacing them
with fathers of families ; to restore the field artillery, he embodied all the garrison artillery-men,
calling out the ordenança gunners to man the fortresses and coast-batteries ; the worst cavalry regiments he reduced to render the best more efficient,
but several circumstances prevented this arm from
attaining any excellence in Portugal. Meanwhile
Lord Wellington and Mr. Stuart strenuously grappled
with the disorders of the civil administration and
their efforts produced an immediate and considerable increase of revenue. But though the regency
could not deny this beneficial effect, though they
could not deny the existence of the evils which
they were urged to remedy, though they admitted

that the reform of their custom-house system was
still incomplete, that their useless navy consumed
large sums which were wanted for the army, and
that the taxes especially the " *Decima*," were partially collected, and unproductive, because the rich
people in the great towns, who had benefited
largely by the war, escaped the imposts which the
poor people in the country, who had suffered most
from the war, paid; though they acknowledged that
while the soldiers' hire was in arrears, the transport
service neglected, and all persons, having just
claims upon the government, suffering severe privations, the tax-gatherers were allowed to keep a
month's tribute in their hands even in the districts
close to the enemy ; though all these things were
admitted, the regency would not alter their system,
and Borba, the minister of finance, combatted Wellington's plans in detail with such unusual obstinacy, that it became evident nothing could be obtained save by external pressure. Wherefore as the
season for military operations approached, Mr.
Stuart called upon lord Castlereagh to bring the
power of England to bear at once upon the court
of Rio Janeiro; and Wellington, driven to extremity,
sent the Portuguese prince-regent one of those
clear, powerful, and nervous statements, which left
those to whom they were addressed, no alternative
but submission, or an acknowledgement that sense
and justice were to be disregarded.

" I call your highness's attention," he said, " to
the state of your troops and of all your establishments ; the army of operations has been unpaid
since September, the garrisons since June, the
militia since February 1812. The transport service
has never been regularly paid, and has received

nothing since June. To these evils I have in vain
called the attention of the local government, and I
am now going to open a new campaign, with troops
to whom greater arrears of pay are due than when
the last campaign terminated, although the subsidy
from Great Britain, granted especially for the main-
tenance of those troops, has been regularly and
exactly furnished ; and although it has been proved
that the revenue for the last three months has
exceeded, by a third, any former quarter. The
honour of your highness's arms, the cause of your
allies, is thus seriously affected, and the uniform
refusal of the governors of the kingdom to attend to any one of the measures which I have
recommended, either for permanent or temporal
relief, has at last obliged me to go as a com-
plainant into your royal highness's presence, for
here I cannot prevail against the influence of the
chief of the treasury.

"I have recommended the entire reform of the customs system, but it has only been partially carried
into effect. I have advised a method of actually and
really collecting the taxes, and of making the rich
merchants, and capitalists, pay the tenth of their annual profits as an extraordinary contribution for the
war. I declare that no person knows better than I
do, the sacrifices and the sufferings of your people,
for there is no one for the last four years has lived
so much amongst those people; but it is a fact, sir,
that the great cities, and even some of the smallest
places, have gained by the war and the mercantile
class has enriched itself; there are divers persons
in Lisbon and Oporto who have amassed immense
sums. Now your government is, both from remote
and recent circumstances, unable to draw resources

from the capitalists by loans; it can only draw upon them by taxes. It is not denied that the regular tributes nor the extraordinary imposts on the mercantile profits are evaded; it is not denied that the measures I have proposed, vigorously carried into execution, would furnish the government with pecuniary resources, and it remains for that government to inform your highness, why they have neither enforced my plans, nor any others which the necessity of the times calls for. They fear to become unpopular, but such is the knowledge I have of the people's good sense and loyalty, such my zeal for the cause, that I have offered to become responsible for the happy issue, and to take upon myself all the odium of enforcing my own measures. I have offered in vain!

" Never was a sovereign in the world so ill served as your highness has been by the '*Junta de Viveres*,' and I zealously forwarded your interests when I obtained its abolition; and yet, under a false pretext of debt, the government still disburse fifty millions of reis monthly on account of that board. It has left a debt undoubtedly, and it is of importance to pay it, although not at this moment; but let the government state in detail how these fifty millions, granted monthly, have been applied; let them say if all the accounts have been called in and liquidated? who has enforced the operation? to what does the debt amount? has it been classified? how much is really still due to those who have received instalments? finally, have these millions been applied to the payment of salaries instead of debt? But were it convenient now to pay the debt, it cannot be denied that to pay the army which is to defend the country, to protect it from the sweeping destructive hand of the enemy, is of more pressing importance; the troops will be neither able nor willing to fight if they are not paid."

Then touching upon the abuse of permitting the tax-gatherers to hold a month's taxes in their hands, and upon the opposition he met with from the regency, he continued,

"I assure your royal highness that I give my advice to the governor of the kingdom actuated solely by an earnest zeal for your service without any personal interest. I can have none relative to Portugal, and none with regard to individuals, for I have no private relation with, and scarcely am acquainted with those who direct, or would wish to direct your affairs. Those reforms recommended by me, and which have at last been partially effected in the custom-house, in the arsenal, in the navy, in the payment of the interest of the national debt, in the formation of a military chest, have succeeded, and I may therefore say that the other measures I propose would have similar results. I am ready to allow that I may deceive myself on this point, but certainly they are suggested by a desire for the good of your service; hence in the most earnest and decided manner, I express my ardent wish, and it is common to all your faithful servants, that you will return to the kingdom, and take charge yourself of the government."

These vigorous measures to bring the regency to terms succeeded only partially. In May they promulgated a new system for the collection of taxes which relieved the financial pressure on the army for the moment, but which did not at all content Wellington, because it was made to square with old habits and prejudices, and thus left the roots of

all the evils alive and vigorous. Every moment
furnished new proofs of the hopelessness of rege-
nerating a nation through the medium of a corrupted government; and a variety of circumstances,
more or less serious, continued to embarrass the
march of public affairs.

In the Madeiras the authorities vexatiously prevented the English money agents from exporting
specie, and their conduct was approved of at Rio
Janeiro. At Bisao, in Africa, the troops had mu-
tinied for want of pay, and in the Cape de Verde
Islands disturbances arose from the over-exaction
of taxes; for when the people were weak, the
regency were vigorous; pliant only to the powerful. These commotions were trifling and soon
ended of themselves, yet expeditions were sent
against the offenders in both places, and the troops
thus employed immediately committed far worse
excesses, and did more mischief than that which
they were sent to suppress. At the same time
several French frigates finding the coast of Africa
unguarded, cruized successfully against the Brazil
trade, and aided the American privateers to contract
the already too straitened resources of the army.

Amidst all these difficulties however the extraordinary exertions of the British officers had restored
the numbers, discipline, and spirit of the Portuguese
army. Twenty-seven thousand excellent soldiers
were again under arms and ready to commence the
campaign, although the national discontent was
daily increasing; and indeed the very feeling of
security created by the appearance of such an army
rendered the citizens at large less willing to bear
the inconveniences of the war. Distant danger
never affects the multidude, and the billetting of

troops, who, from long habits of war, little regarded
the rights of the citizens in comparison with their
own necessities, being combined with requisitions,
and with a recruiting system becoming every year
more irksome, formed an aggregate of inconveniences intolerable to men who desired ease and no
longer dreaded to find an enemy on their hearth-
stones. The powerful classes were naturally more
affected than the poorer classes, because of their
indolent habits; but their impatience was aggravated because they had generally been debarred of
the highest situations, or supplanted, by the British
interference in the affairs of the country, and,
unlike those of Spain, the nobles of Portugal had
lost little or none of their hereditary influence.
Discontent was thus extended widely, and moreover
the old dread of French power was entirely gone;
unlimited confidence in the strength and resources
of England had succeeded ; and this confidence, to
use the words of Mr. Stuart, " being opposed to the
irregularities which have been practised by individuals, and to the difference of manners, and of
religion, placed the British in the singular position
of a class whose exertions were necessary for the
country, but who, for the above reasons, were in
every other respect as distinct from the natives as
persons with whom, from some criminal cause, it
was necessary to suspend communication."—Hence
he judged that the return of the prince-regent
would be a proper epoch for the British to retire
from all situations in Portugal not strictly military,
for if any thing should delay that event, the time
was approaching when the success of the army and
the tranquillity of the country would render it necessary to yield to the first manifestations of national

feeling. In fine, notwithstanding the great benefits
conferred upon the Portuguese by the British, the
latter were, and it will always be so on the like occasions, regarded by the upper classes as a captain
regards galley-slaves, their strength was required to
speed the vessel, but they were feared and hated.

The prince-regent did not return to Portugal
according to Wellington's advice, but Carlotta immediately prepared to come alone ; orders were
given to furnish her apartments in the different
palaces, and her valuable effects had actually
arrived. Ill health was the pretext for the voyage,
but the real object was to be near Spain to forward
her views upon the government there; for intent upon
mischief, indefatigable and of a violence approaching insanity, she had sold even her plate and jewels
to raise money wherewith to corrupt the leading
members of the cortez, and was resolved, if that
should not promise success, to distribute the money
amongst the Spanish partidas, and so create a
powerful military support for her schemes. Fortunately the prince dreading the intriguing advisers
of his wife would not suffer her to quit Rio Janeiro
until the wish of the British cabinet upon the
subject was known, and that was so decidedly adverse, that it was thought better to do without the
prince himself than to have him accompanied by
Carlotta ; so they both remained in the Brazils, and
this formidable cloud passed away, yet left no sun-
shine on the land.

It was at this period that the offer of a Russian
auxiliary force, before alluded to, being made to
Wellington by admiral Grieg, was accepted by him
to the amount of fifteen thousand men, and yet was
not fulfilled because the Russian ambassador in

London declared that the emperor knew nothing
of it! Alexander however proposed to mediate in
the dispute between Great Britain and America,
but the English ministers, while lauding him as a
paragon of magnanimity and justice, in regard to
the war against Napoleon, remembered the armed
neutrality and quadruple alliance, and wisely declined trusting England's maritime pretensions to
his faithless grasping policy. Neither would they
listen to Austria, who at this time, whether with
good faith or merely as a cloak I know not, desired
to mediate a general peace. However, amidst this
political confusion the progress of the military
preparations was visible ; and contemporary with
the Portuguese, the Spanish troops under Wellington's influence and providence acquired more con-
sistence than they had ever before possessed ; a
mighty power was in arms ; but the flood of war
with which the English general finally poured
into Spain, and the channels by which he directed
the overwhelming torrent, must be reserved for
another place. It is now time to treat of the
political situation of king Joseph, and to resume the
narrative of that secondary warfare which occupied
the French armies while Wellington was uninter-
ruptedly as far as the enemy were concerned, re-
organizing his power.

CHAPTER III.

In war it is not so much the positive strength, as
the relative situations of the hostile parties, which
gives the victory. Joseph's position, thus judged,
was one of great weakness, principally because he
was incapable of combining the materials at his
disposal, or of wielding them when combined by
others. France had been suddenly thrown by her
failure in Russia, into a new and embarrassing atti-
tude, more embarrassing even than it appeared to
her enemies, or than her robust warlike propor-
tions, nourished by twelve years of victory, indicated. Napoleon, the most indefatigable and active
of mankind, turned his enemy's ignorance on this
head to profit; for scarcely was it known that he
had reached Paris by that wise, that rapid journey,
from Smorghoni, which, baffling all his enemies'
hopes, left them only the power of foolish abuse;
scarcely I say, was his arrival at Paris known to the
world, than a new and enormous army, the con-
stituent parts of which he had with his usual foresight created while yet in the midst of victory, was
in march from all parts to unite in the heart of
Germany.

On this magical rapidity he rested his hopes to
support the tottering fabric of his empire; but well
aware of the critical state of his affairs, his design
was, while presenting a menacing front on every

side, so to conduct his operations that if he failed
in his first stroke, he might still contract his system
gradually and without any violent concussion. And
good reason for hope he had. His military power
was rather broken and divided than lessened, for it
is certain that the number of men employed in
1813 was infinitely greater than in 1812; in the
latter four hundred thousand, but in the former
more than seven hundred thousand men, and twelve
hundred field-pieces were engaged on different
points, exclusive of the armies in Spain. Then on
the Vistula, on the Oder, on the Elbe, he had
powerful fortresses, and numerous garrisons, or
rather armies, of strength and goodness to re-establish his ascendancy in Europe, if he could reunite
them in one system by placing a new host victo-
riously in the centre of Germany. And thus also
he could renew the adhesive qualities of those
allies, who still clung to him though evidently
feeling the attraction of his enemies' success.

But this was a gigantic contest, for his enemies,
by deceiving their subjects with false promises of
liberty, had brought whole nations against him.
More than eight hundred thousand men were in
arms in Germany alone; secret societies were in
full activity all over the continent; and in France a
conspiracy was commenced by men who desired
rather to see their country a prey to foreigners and
degraded with a Bourbon king, than have it independent and glorious under Napoleon. Wherefore that great monarch had now to make application, on an immense scale, of the maxim which
prescribes a skilful offensive as the best defence,
and he had to sustain two systems of operation not
always compatible; the one depending upon moral

force to hold the vast fabric of his former policy together, the other to meet the actual exigencies of the war. The first was infinitely more important than the last, and as Germany and France were the proper theatres for its display, the Spanish contest sunk at once from a principal into an accessary war. Yet this delicate conjuncture of affairs made it of vital importance, that Napoleon should have constant and rapid intelligence from Spain, because the ascendancy, which he yet maintained over the world by his astounding genius, might have been broken down in a moment if Wellington, overstepping the ordinary rules of military art, had suddenly abandoned the Peninsula, and thrown his army, or a part of it into France. For then would have been deranged all the emperor's calculations; then would the defection of all his allies have ensued; then would he have been obliged to concentrate both his new forces and his Spanish troops for the defence of his own country, abandoning all his fortresses and his still vast though scattered veteran armies in Germany and Poland, to the unrestrained efforts of his enemies beyond the Rhine. Nothing could have been more destructive to Napoleon's moral power, than to have an insult offered and commotions raised on his own threshold at the moment when he was assuming the front of a conqueror in Germany.

To obviate this danger or to meet it, alike required that the armies in the Peninsula should adopt a new and vigorous system, under which, relinquishing all real permanent offensive movements, they should yet appear to be daring and enterprising, even while they prepared to abandon their former conquests. But the emperor wanted old

officers and non-commissioned officers, and experienced soldiers, to give consistency to the young
levies with which he was preparing to take the
field, and he could only supply this want by drawing from the veterans of the Peninsula; wherefore
he resolved to recal the division of the young
guard, and with it many thousand men and officers
of the line most remarkable for courage and conduct. In lieu he sent the reserve at Bayonne into
Spain, replacing it with another, which was again
to be replaced in May by further levies; and besides this succour, twenty thousand conscripts were
appropriated for the Peninsula.

The armies thus weakened in numbers, and considerably so during the transit of the troops, were
also in quality greatly deteriorated, and at a very
critical time, for not only was Wellington being
powerfully reinforced, but the audacity, the spirit,
the organization, the discipline, and the numbers of
the Partidas, were greatly increased by English
supplies, liberally, and now usefully dealt out. And
the guerilla operations in the northern parts, being
combined with the British naval squadrons, had,
during the absence of the French armies, employed
to drive the allies back to Portugal, aroused anew
the spirit of insurrection in Navarre and Biscay; a
spirit exacerbated by some recent gross abuses of
military authority perpetrated by some of the French
local commanders.

The position of the invading armies was indeed
become more complicated than ever. They had
only been relieved from the crushing pressure of
lord Wellington's grand operations to struggle in
the meshes of the Guerilla and insurrectional warfare of the Spaniards. Nor was the importance of

these now to be measured by former efforts. The
Partida chiefs had become more experienced and
more docile to the suggestions of the British chief;
they had free communication with, and were constantly supplied with arms, ammunition, and money
from the squadrons on the coast; they possessed
several fortified posts and harbours, their bands
were swelling to the size of armies, and their military knowledge of the country and of the French
system of invasion was more matured; their own
dépôts were better hidden, and they could, and at
times did, bear the shock of battle on nearly equal
terms. Finally, new and large bands of another
and far more respectable and influential nature,
were formed or forming both in Navarre and Biscay,
where insurrectional juntas were organized, and
where men of the best families had enrolled numerous volunteers from the villages and towns.

Duke of
Feltre's
official
corres-
pondence,
MSS.

These volunteers were well and willingly supplied
by the country, and of course not obnoxious, like
the Partidas, from their rapine and violence. In
Biscay alone several battalions of this description,
each mustering a thousand men, were in the field,
and the communication with France was so completely interrupted, that the French minister of war
only heard that Joseph had received his dispatches
of the 4th of January, on the 18th of March, and
then through the medium of Suchet! The contributions could no longer be collected, the magazines
could not be filled, the fortresses were endangered,
the armies had no base of operations, the insurrection was spreading to Aragon, and the bands
of the interior were also increasing in numbers
and activity. The French armies, sorely pressed
for provisions, were widely disseminated, and every

where occupied, and each general was averse either
to concentrate his own forces or to aid his neigh-
bour. In fine the problem of the operations was
become extremely complicated, and Napoleon only
seems to have seized the true solution.

When informed by Caffarelli of the state of
affairs in the north, he thus wrote to the king,
" Hold Madrid only as a point of observation ; fix
your quarters not as monarch, but as general of the
French forces at Valladolid ; concentrate the armies
of the south, of the centre, and of Portugal around
you ; the allies will not and indeed cannot make
any serious offensive movement for several months ;
wherefore it is your business to profit from their
forced inactivity, to put down the insurrection in
the northern provinces, to free the communication
with France, and to re-establish a good base of
operations before the commencement of another
campaign, that the French army may be in condition to fight the allies if the latter advance towards France." Very important indeed did Napoleon deem this object, and so earnest was he to
have constant and rapid intelligence from his
armies in the Peninsula, that the couriers and
their escorts were directed to be dispatched twice
a week, travelling day and night at the rate of a
league an hour. He commanded also that the
army of the north should be reinforced even by
the whole army of Portugal, if it was necessary
to effect the immediate pacification of Biscay and
Navarre ; and while this pacification was in progress, Joseph was to hold the rest of his forces
in a position offensive towards Portugal, making
Wellington feel that his whole power was required
on the frontier, and that neither his main body nor

even any considerable detachment could safely embark to disturb France.   In short that he must
cover Lisbon strongly, and on the frontier, or expect to see the French army menacing that capital.
These instructions well understood, and vigourously executed, would certainly have put down
the insurrection in the rear of the king's position,
and the spring would have seen that monarch at
the head of ninety thousand men, having their retreat upon France clear of all impediments, and consequently free to fight the allies on the Tormes, the
Duero, the Pisuerga, and the Ebro ; and with several
supporting fortresses in a good state.

Joseph was quite unable to view the matter in this
common-sense point of view. He could not make his
kingly notions subservient to military science, nor his
military movements subservient to an enlarged policy.
Neither did he perceive that his beneficent notions
of government were misplaced amidst the din of
arms.   Napoleon's orders were imperative, but the
principle of them, Joseph could not previously
conceive himself nor execute the details after his
brother's conception.   He was not even acquainted
with the true state of the northern provinces, nor
would he at first credit it when told to him. Hence
while his thoughts were intent upon his Spanish
political projects, and the secret negociations with
Del Parque's army, the northern partidas and insurgents became masters of all his lines of communication in the north ; the Emperor's orders
dispatched early in January, and reiterated week
after week, only reached the king in the end of
February ; their execution did not take place until
the end of March, and then imperfectly. The time
thus lost was irreparable ; and yet as the emperor

King's
correspon-
dence,
MSS.

reproachfully observed, the bulletin which revealed
the extent of his disasters in Russia might alone
have taught the king what to do.

Joseph was nearly as immoveable in his resolutions as his brother, the firmness of the one being
however founded upon extraordinary sagacity, and
of the other upon the want of that quality. Regarding opposition to his views as the result of a
disloyal malevolence, he judged the refractory generals to be enemies to the emperor, as well as to
himself. Reille, Caffarelli, Suchet, alike incurred
his displeasure, and the duke of Feltre French
minister of war also, because of a letter in which,
evidently by the orders of the emperor, he rebuked
the king for having removed Souham from the
command of the army of Portugal.

Feltre's style, addressed to a monarch was very
offensive, and Joseph attributed it to the influence
of Soult, for his hatred of the latter was violent
and implacable even to absurdity. " The duke of King's
Dalmatia or himself," he wrote to the Emperor, correspondence,
" must quit Spain. At Valencia he had forgotten MSS.
his own injuries, he had suppressed his just indignation, and instead of sending marshal Soult to
France had given him the direction of the operations against the allies, but it was in the hope that
shame for the past combined with his avidity for
glory, would urge him to extraordinary exertions;
nothing of the kind had happened ; Soult was a
man not to be trusted. Restless, intriguing, ambitious, he would sacrifice every thing to his own
advancement, and possessed just that sort of talent
which would lead him to mount a scaffold when he
thought he was ascending the steps of a throne,

because he would want the courage to strike when the crisis arrived." He acquitted him, he said, with a coarse sarcasm, " of treachery at the passage of the Tormes, because there fear alone operated to prevent him from bringing the allies to a decisive action, but he was nevertheless treacherous to the emperor, and his proceedings in Spain were probably connected with the conspiracy of Malet at Paris."

Such was the language with which Joseph in his anger assailed one of the greatest commanders and most faithful servants of his brother ; and such the greetings which awaited Napoleon on his arrival at Paris after the disasters of Russia. In the most calm and prosperous state of affairs, coming from this source, the charges might well have excited the jealous wrath of the strongest mind; but in the actual crisis, when the emperor had just lost his great army, and found the smoking embers of a suppressed conspiracy at his very palace-gates, when his friends were failing, and his enemies accumulating, it seemed scarcely possible that these accusations should not have proved the ruin of Soult. Yet they did not even ruffle the temper of Napoleon. Magnanimous as he was sagacious, he smiled at the weakness of Joseph, and though he removed Soult from Spain, because the feud between him and the king would not permit them to serve beneficially together, it was only to make him the commander of the imperial guard ; and that no mark of his confidence might be wanting, he afterwards chose him, from amongst all his generals, to retrieve the affairs of the Peninsula when Joseph was driven from that country, an event the immediate causes of which were now being laid.

It has been already shown, that when Wellington took his winter-quarters, the French armies occupied a line stretching from the sea-coast at Valencia to the foot of the Gallician mountains. In these positions Suchet on the extreme left was opposed by the allies at Alicant. Soult, commanding the centre, had his head-quarters at Toledo, with one detachment at the foot of the Sierra Morena to watch the army of Del Parque, and two others in the valley of the Tagus. Of these last one was at Talavera and one on the Tietar. The first observed Morillo and Penne Villemur, who from Estremadura were constantly advancing towards the bridges on the Tagus, and menacing the rear of the French detachment which was on the Tietar in observation of general Hill then at Coria. Soult's advanced post in the valley of the Tagus communicated by the Gredos mountains with Avila, where Foy's division of the army of Portugal was posted partly for the sake of food, partly to watch Bejar and the Upper Tormes, because the allies, possessing the pass of Bejar, might have suddenly united north of the mountains, and breaking the French line have fallen on Madrid.

On the right of Foy, the remainder of the army of Portugal occupied Salamanca, Ledesma, and Alba on the Lower Tormes; Valladolid, Toro, and Tordesillas on the Duero; Benevente, Leon, and other points on the Esla, Astorga being, as I have before observed, dismantled by the Spaniards. Behind the right of this great line, the army of the north had retaken its old positions, and the army of the centre was fixed as before in and around Madrid, its operations being bounded on the right bank of the Tagus by the mountains which invest that capi-

tal, and on the left bank of the Tagus by the districts of Aranjuez, Tarancon, and Cuenca.

Joseph while disposing his troops in this manner,
issued a royal regulation marking the extent of
country which each army was to forage, requiring at the same time a certain and considerable
revenue to be collected by his Spanish civil authorities for the support of his court. The subsistence
of the French armies was thus made secondary to
the revenue of the crown, and he would have had
the soldiers in a time of war, of insurrectional
war, yield to the authority of the Spanish civilians; an absurdity heightened by the peculiarly
active, vigorous, and prompt military method of the
French, as contrasted with the dilatory improvident
promise-breaking and visionary system of the Spaniards. Hence scarcely was the royal regulation
issued when the generals broke through it in a
variety of ways, and the king was, as usual, involved in the most acrimonious disputes with all
the emperor's lieutenants. If he ordered one commander to detach troops to the assistance of another
commander, he was told that he should rather send
additional troops to the first. If he reprimanded
a general for raising contributions contrary to the
regulations, he was answered that the soldiers were
starving and must be fed. At all times also the
authority of the prefects and intendants was disregarded by all the generals; and this was in pursuance of Napoleon's order; for that monarch continually reminded his brother, that as the war was
carried on by the French armies their interests were
paramount; that the king of Spain could have no
authority over them, and must never use his military authority as lieutenant of the empire, in aid

King's
corres-
pondence.
MSS.

of his kingly views, for with those the French soldiers could have nothing to do; their welfare could
not be confided to Spanish ministers whose capacity
was by no means apparent and of whose fidelity the
emperor had no security.

Nothing could be clearer or wiser than these
instructions, but Joseph would not see this distinction between his military and his monarchical
duties, and continually defended his conduct by
reference to what he owed his subjects as king of
Spain. His sentiments, explained with great force
of feeling, and great beneficence of design, were
worthy of all praise if viewed abstractedly, but
totally inapplicable to the real state of affairs,
because the Spaniards were not his faithful and
attached subjects, they were his inveterate enemies;
and it was quite impossible to unite the vigour of a
war of conquest with the soft and benevolent government of a paternal monarch. Thus one constant
error vitiated all the king's political proceedings, an
error apparently arising from an inability to view his
situation as a whole instead of by parts, for his military operations were vitiated in the same manner.

As a man of state and of war he seems to have
been acute, courageous, and industrious, with respect to any single feature presented for his consideration, but always unable to look steadily on
the whole and consequently always working in the
dark. Men of his character being conscious of the
merit of labour and good intentions, are commonly
obstinate; and those qualities, which render them
so useful under the direction of an able chief, lead
only to mischief when they become chiefs themselves. For in matters of great moment, and in
war especially, it is not the actual importance but

the comparative importance of the operations which
should determine the choice of measures; and when
all are very important this choice demands judgment of the highest kind, judgment which no man
ever possessed more largely than Napoleon, and
which Joseph did not possess at all.

He was never able to comprehend the instructions of his brother, and never would accept the
advice of those commanders whose capacity approached in some degree to that of the emperor.
When he found that every general complained of
insufficient means, instead of combining their forces
so as to press with the principal mass against the
most important point, he disputed with each, and
turned to demand from the emperor additional succours for all; at the same time unwisely repeating
and urging his own schemes upon a man so infinitely his superior in intellect. The insurrection
in the northern provinces he treated not as a military but a political question, attributing it to the
anger of the people at seeing the ancient supreme
council of Navarre unceremoniously dismissed and
some of the members imprisoned by a French
general, a cause very inadequate to the effect.
Neither was his judgment truer with respect to the
fitness of time. He proposed, if a continuation
of the Russian war should prevent the emperor
from sending more men to Spain, to make Burgos
the royal residence, to transport there the archives,
and all that constituted a capital; then to have all
the provinces behind the Ebro, Catalonia excepted,
governed by himself through the medium of his
Spanish ministers and as a country at peace, while
those beyond the Ebro should be given up to the
generals as a country at war.

In this state his civil administration would he
said remedy the evils inflicted by the armies, would
conciliate the people by keeping all the Spanish
families and authorities in safety and comfort,
would draw all those who favoured his cause from
all parts of Spain, and would encourage the display
of that attachment to his person which he believed
so many Spaniards to entertain. And while he declared the violence and injustice of the French
armies to be the sole cause of the protracted resistance of the Spaniards, a declaration false in
fact, that violence being only one of many causes,
he was continually urging the propriety of beating
the English first and then pacifying the people by
just and benevolent measures. As if it were possible, off-hand, to beat Wellington and his veterans,
embedded as they were in the strong country of
Portugal, and having British fleets with troops and
succours of all kinds, hovering on the flanks of the
French, and feeding and sustaining the insurrection
of the Spaniards in their rear.

Napoleon was quite as willing and anxious as
Joseph could be to drive the English from the Peninsula, and to tranquillize the people by a regular
government; but with a more profound knowledge
of war, of politics and of human nature, he judged
that the first could only be done by a methodical
combination, in unison with that rule of art which
prescribes the establishment and security of the
base of operations, security which could not be
obtained if the benevolent but weak and visionary
schemes of the king, were to supersede military
vigour in the field. The emperor laughed in scorn
when his brother assured him that the Peninsulars
with all their fiery passions, their fanaticism and their

ignorance, would receive an equable government as a benefit from the hands of an intrusive monarch before they had lost all hope of resistance by arms.

Yet it is not to be concluded that Joseph was totally devoid of grounds for his opinions ; he was surrounded by difficulties and deeply affected by the misery which he witnessed, his Spanish minis- ters were earnest and importunate, and many of the French generals gave him but too much reason to complain of their violence. The length and muta- tions of the war had certainly created a large party willing enough to obtain tranquillity at the price of submission, while others were, as we have seen, not indisposed, if he would hold the crown on their terms, to accept his dynasty, as one essentially springing from democracy, in preference to the despotic, base, and superstitious family which the nation was called upon to uphold. It was not un- natural therefore for Joseph to desire to retain his capital while the negociations with Del Parque's army were still in existence, it was not strange that he should be displeased with Soult after reading that marshal's honest but offensive letter, and cer- tainly it was highly creditable to his character as a man and as a king that he would not silently suffer his subjects to be oppressed by the generals.

" I am in distress for money," he often exclaimed to Napoleon, " such distress as no king ever endured before, my plate is sold, and on state occasions the appearance of magnificence is supported by false metal. My ministers and household are actually starving, misery is on every face, and men, otherwise willing, are thus deterred from joining a king so little able to support them. My revenue is seized by the generals for the supply of their troops, and I

cannot as a king of Spain without dishonour par-
take of the resources thus torn by rapine from my
subjects whom I have sworn to protect; I cannot
in fine be at once king of Spain and general of the
French; let me resign both and live peaceably in
France. Your majesty does not know what scenes
are enacted, you will shudder to hear that men
formerly rich and devoted to our cause have been
driven out of Zaragoza and denied even a ration of
food. The marquis Cavallero, a councillor of state,
minister of justice, and known personally to your
majesty, has been thus used. He has been seen actually begging for a piece of bread!"

If this Caballero was the old minister to Charles
the IVth, no misery was too great a punishment
for his tyrannical rule under that monarch, yet it
was not from the hands of the French it should
have come; and Joseph's distress for money must
certainly have been great, since that brave and
honest man Jourdan, a marshal of France, major-
general of the armies, and a personal favourite of
the king's, complained that the non-payment of his Jourdan's
appointments had reduced him to absolute penury, Official
correspon-
and after borrowing until his credit was exhausted dence.
MSS.
he could with difficulty procure subsistence. It is
now time to describe the secondary operations of
the war, but as these were spread over two-thirds of
Spain, and were simultaneous, to avoid complexity
it will be necessary to class them under two great
heads, namely those which took place north and
those which took place south of the Tagus.

CHAPTER IV.

OPERATIONS SOUTH OF THE TAGUS.

BOOK
XX.

1813.

February.

IN December 1812 general Copons had been appointed captain-general of Catalonia instead of Eroles, but his arrival was delayed and the province was not relieved from Lacy's mischievous sway until February 1813, when Eroles, taking the temporary command, re-established the head-quarters at Vich. The French, being then unmolested, save by the English ships, passed an enormous convoy to France, but Eroles was not long idle. Through the medium of a double spy, he sent a forged letter to the governor of Taragona, desiring him to detach men to Villa Nueva de Sitjes, with carts to transport some stores; at the same time he gave out that he was himself going to the Cerdaña, which brought the French moveable column to that quarter, and then, Eroles, Manso, and Villamil, making forced marches from different points, reached Torre dem barra where they met the British squadron. The intention was to cut off the French detachment on its march to Villa Nueva and then to attack Taragona, but fortune rules in war; the governor received a letter from Maurice Mathieu of a different tenor from the forged letter, and with all haste regaining his fortress balked this well-contrived plan.

Sarzfield, at enmity with Eroles, was now combining his operations with Villa Campa, and they menaced Alcanitz in Aragon; but general Pannetier who had remained at Teruel to watch Villa

Campa, and to protect Suchet's communications,
immediately marched to Daroca, Severoli came
from Zaragoza to the same point, and the Spaniards,
alarmed by their junction, dispersed. Sarzfield returned to Catalonia, Bassecour and the Empecinado
remained near Cuenca, and Villa Campa as usual
hung upon the southern skirts of the Albaracyn
mountain, ready to pounce down on the Ebro or on
the Guadalquivir side as advantage might offer.
Meanwhile Suchet was by no means at ease. The
successes in Catalonia did not enable him to draw
reinforcements from thence, because Napoleon, true
to his principle of securing the base of operations,
forbad him to weaken the army there, and Montmarie's brigade was detached from Valencia to preserve the communication between Saguntum and Tortoza. But Aragon which was Suchet's place of arms
and principal magazine, being infested by Mina,
Duran, Villa Campa, the Empecinado, and Sarzfield,
was becoming daily more unquiet, wherefore Pannetier's brigade remained between Segorbé and
Daroca to aid Severoli. Thus although the two
armies of Aragon and Catalonia mustered more
than seventy thousand men, that of Aragon alone
having forty thousand, with fifty field-pieces, Suchet could not fight with more than sixteen thousand infantry, two thousand cavalry and perhaps
thirty guns beyond the Xucar. His right flank
was always liable to be turned by Requeña, his left
by the sea which was entirely at his adversary's
command, and his front was menaced by fifty thousand men, of which three thousand might be cavalry
with fifty pieces of artillery.

The component parts of the allied force were

the Anglo-Sicilians which, including Whittingham's and Roche's divisions, furnished eighteen
thousand soldiers. Elio's army furnishing twelve
thousand exclusive of the divisions of Bassecour,
Villa Campa, and the Empecinado, which, though
detached, belonged to him. Del Parque's army
reinforced by new levies from Andalusia, and on
paper twenty thousand. Numerically this was a
formidable power if it had been directed in mass
against Suchet; but on his right the duke of
Dalmatia, whose head-quarters were at Toledo,
sent forward detachments which occupied the army
of Del Parque; moreover the secret negociations
for the defection of the latter were now in full activity, and from the army of the centre a column
was sent towards Cuenca to draw Bassecour and the
Empecinado from Suchet's right flank; but those
chiefs had five thousand men, and in return continually harassed the army of the centre.

On the side of the Morena and Murcia, Soult's
operations were confined to skirmishes and foraging
parties. Early in January his brother, seeking' to
open a communication with Suchet by Albacete,
defeated some of Elio's cavalry with the loss of fifty
men, and pursued them until they rallied on their
main body, under Freyre; the latter offered battle
with nine hundred horsemen in front of the defile
leading to Albacete; but Soult, disliking his appearance turned off to the right, and passing through
Villa Nueva de los Infantes joined a French post
established in Valdepeña at the foot of the Morena,
where some skirmishes had also taken place with
Del Parque's cavalry. The elder Soult thus learned,
that Freyre, with two thousand five hundred horsemen, covered all the roads leading from La Mancha,

to Valencia and Murcia; that Elio's infantry was at Tobara and Hellin, Del Parque's head-quarters at Jaen; that the passes of the Morena were guarded, and magazines formed at Andujar, Linares, and Cordoba, while on the other side of La Mancha, the Empecinado had come to Hinojoso with fifteen hundred horsemen, and the column sent from the army of the centre was afraid to encounter him.

These dispositions, and the strength of the Spaniards, not only prevented the younger Soult from penetrating into Murcia, but delayed the march of a column, under general Daricau, destined to communicate with Suchet, and bring up the detachments baggage and stores, which the armies of the south and centre had left at Valencia. The scouting parties of both sides now met at different points, and on the 27th of January, a sharp cavalry fight happened at El Corral, in which the French commander was killed, and the Spaniards, though far the most numerous, defeated. Meanwhile Daricau, whose column had been reinforced, reached Utiel, opened the communication with Suchet by Requeña, cut off some small parties of the enemy, and then continuing his march received a great convoy, consisting of two thousand fighting men, six hundred travellers, and the stores and baggage belonging to Soult's and the king's armies. This convoy had marched for Madrid by the way of Zaragoza, but was recalled when Daricau arrived, and under his escort, aided by a detachment of Suchet's army placed at Yniesta, it reached Todelo in the latter end of February safely, though Villa Campa came down to the Cabriel River, to trouble the march.

During these different operations numerous absurd

and contradictory reports, principally originating
in the Spanish and English newspapers, obtained
credit in the French armies, such as, that sir Henry
Wellesley and Infantado had seized the government at Cadiz; that Clinton, by an intrigue, had
got possession of Alicant; that Ballesteros had
shewn Wellington secret orders from the cortez not
to acknowledge him as generalissimo, or even as a
grandee; that the cortez had removed the regency
because the latter permitted Wellington to appoint
intendants and other officers to the Spanish provinces; that Hill had devastated the frontier and
retired to Lisbon though forcibly opposed by Morillo; that a nephew of Ballesteros had raised the
standard of revolt; that Wellington was advancing,
and that troops had been embarked at Lisbon for a
maritime expedition, with other stories of a like
nature, which seem to have disturbed all the French
generals save Soult, whose information as to the
real state of affairs continued to be sure and accurate. He also at this time detected four or five
of Wellington's emissaries, amongst them, was a
Portuguese officer on his own staff; a man called
Piloti, who served and betrayed both sides; and an
amazon called Francisca de la Fuerte, who, though
only twenty-two years old, had already commanded
a partida of sixty men with some success, and was
now a spy. But in the latter end of February the
duke of Dalmatia was recalled, and the command of
his army fell to Gazan, whose movements belong
rather to the operations north of the Tagus.
Wherefore turning to Suchet, I shall proceed to
give an exact notion of his resources and of the
nature of the country where his operations were
conducted.

The city of Valencia, though nominally the seat of
his power, was not so. He had razed all the defences
constructed by the Spaniards, confining his hold to
the old walls and to a small fortified post within the
town sufficient to resist a sudden attack, and capable
of keeping the population in awe ; his real place
of arms was Saguntum, and between that and
Tortoza he had two fortresses, namely, Oropesa
and Peniscola; he had also another line of communication, but for infantry only, through Morella,
a fortified post, to Mequinenza. Besides these
lines there were roads both from Valencia and
Saguntum, leading through Segorbé to Teruel a
fortified post, and from thence to Zaragoza by Da- See Plan6.
roca another fortified post. These roads were eastward of the Guadalaviar, and westward of that river
Suchet had a line of retreat from Valencia to Madrid
by Requeña, which was also a fortified post. Now if
the whole of the French general's command be looked
to, his forces were very numerous, but that command
was wide, and in the field his army was, as I have
before shewn, not very numerous. Valencia was
in fact a point made on hostile ground which, now
that the French were generally on the defensive,
was only maintained with a view of imposing upon
the allies and drawing forth the resources of the
country as long as circumstances would permit.
The proper line for covering Valencia and the rich
country immediately around it was on the Xucar, or
rather beyond it, at San Felippe de Xativa and
Moxente, where a double range of mountains afforded strong defensive positions, barring the principal roads leading to Valencia. On this position
Suchet had formed his entrenched camp, much

talked of at the time, but slighter than fame represented it ; the real strength was in the natural formation of the ground.

Beyond his left flank the coast road was blocked
SeePlan7. by the castle of Denia, but his right could be turned
from Yecla and Almanza, through Cofrentes and
Requeña, and he was forced to keep strict watch
and strong detachments always towards the defile of
Almanza, lest Elio's army and Del Parque's should
march that way. This entrenched camp was Suchet's
permanent position of defence, but there were reasons why he should endeavour to keep his troops
generally more advanced ; the country in his front
was full of fertile plains, or rather coves, within the
hills, which run in nearly parallel ranges, and are
remarkably rocky and precipitous, enclosing the
plains like walls, and it was of great importance
who should command their resources. Hence as
the principal point in Suchet's front was the large
and flourishing town of Alcoy, he occupied it, and
from thence threw off smaller bodies to Biar, Castalla,
Ibi, and Onil, which were on the same strong ridge
as the position covering the cove of Alcoy. On his
right there was another plain in which Fuente La
Higuera, Villena, and Yecla were delineated at opposite points of a triangle, and as this plain and the
smaller valleys ministered to Suchet's wants because
of his superior cavalry, the subsistence of the French
troops was eased, while the cantonments and foraging
districts of the Sicilian army were contracted : the
outposts of the allied army were in fact confined
to a fourth and fifth parallel range of mountains
covering the towns of Elda, Tibi, Xixona, and Villa
Joyosa which was on the sea-coast.

Suchet thus assumed an insulting superiority over
an army more numerous than his own, but outward
appearances are deceitful in war; the French
general was really the strongest, because want,
ignorance, dissention, and even treachery, were in
his adversary's camps. Del Parque's army remained behind the Morena, Elio's was at Tobarra
and Hellin, and of the Anglo-Sicilian army, the
British only were available in the hour of danger,
and they were few. When general Campbell quarrelled with Elio the latter retired for a time towards
Murcia, but after Wellington's journey to Cadiz
he again came forward, and his cavalry entering La
Mancha skirmished with general Soult's and communicating with Bassecour and the Empecinado
delayed the progress of Daricau towards Valencia.
Meanwhile general Campbell remained quiet, in expectation that lord William Bentinck would come
with more troops to Alicant, but in February fresh
troubles broke out in Sicily, and in the latter end of
that month sir John Murray arriving, assumed the
command. Thus in a few months, five chiefs with
different views and prejudices successively came to
the command, and the army was still unorganized
and unequipped for vigorous service. The Sicilians,
Calabrese, and French belonging to it were eager
to desert, one Italian regiment had been broken for
misconduct by general Maitland, the British and
Germans were humiliated in spirit by the part they
were made to enact, and the Spaniards under Whit- Appendix,
No. 16, 17.
tingham and Roche were starving; for Wellington
knowing by experience how the Spanish government, though receiving a subsidy, would, if permitted, throw the feeding of their troops entirely

upon the British, forbade their being supplied from
the British stores, and the Spanish intendants neglected them.

Murray's first care was to improve the equipment
of his troops, and with the aid of Elio he soon put
them in a better condition. The two armies together furnished thirty thousand effective men, of
which about three thousand were cavalry, and they
had thirty-seven guns, yet very inadequately horsed,
and Whittingham's and Elio's cavalry were from
want of forage nearly unfit for duty. The transport
mules were hired at an enormous price, the expense
being at the rate of one hundred and thirty thousand
pounds annually, and yet the supply was bad, for
here as in all other parts of Spain, corruption and
misuse of authority prevailed. The rich sent their
fine animals to Alicant for sanctuary and bribed the
Alcaldes, the mules of the poor alone were pressed,
the army was ill provided, and yet the country was
harassed. In this state it was necessary to do something, and as the distress of Whittingham and
Roche's troops could not be removed, save by enlar-
ging their cantonments, Murray after some hesitation
resolved to drive the French from the mountains in
his front, and he designed, as the first step, to surprise
fifteen hundred men which they had placed in Alcoy. Now five roads led towards the French positions.
1°. On the left the great road from Alicant passing
through Monforte, Elda, Sax, Villena, and Fuente
de la Higuera, where it joins the great road from
Valencia to Madrid, which runs through Almanza.
This way turned both the ridges occupied by the
armies. 2°. A good road leading by Tibi to Castalla, from whence it sent off two branches, on the

left hand, one leading to Sax, the other through the
pass of Biar to Villena ; two other branches on the
right hand went, the one through Ibi to Alcoy, the
other through Onil to the same place. 3°. The road
from Alicant to Xixona, a bad road, leading over the
very steep rugged ridge of that name to Alcoy. At
Xixona also there was a narrow way on the right
hand, through the mountains to Alcoy, which was
followed by Roche when he attacked that place in
the first battle of Castalla. 4°. A carriage-road
running along the sea-coast as far as Villa Joyosa,
from whence a narrow mountain-way leads to the
village of Consentayna, situated in the cove of
Alcoy and behind that town.

On the 6th of March the allied troops moved in
four columns, one on the left by Elda, to watch the
great Madrid road ; one on the right composed of
Spanish troops under colonel Campbell, from Villa
Joyosa, to get to Consentayna behind Alcoy; a
third, under lord Frederick Bentinck, issuing by
Ibi, was to turn the French right ; the fourth
was to march from Xixona straight against Alcoy,
and to pursue the remainder of Habert's division,
which was behind that town. Lord Frederick
Bentinck attacked in due time, but as colonel
Campbell did not appear the surprise failed, and
when the French saw the main body winding down
the Sierra in front of Alcoy, they retired, pursued by
general Donkin with the second battalion of the
twenty-seventh regiment. The head of lord Frederick Bentinck's column was already engaged, but
the rear had not arrived, and the whole of Habert's
division was soon concentrated a mile beyond Alcoy,
and there offered battle; yet sir John Murray, instead
of pushing briskly forward, halted, and it was not

until several demands for support had reached him, that he detached the fifty-eighth to the assistance of the troops engaged, who had lost about forty men, chiefly of the twenty-seventh. Habert, fearing to be cut off by Consentayna, and seeing the fifty-eighth coming on, retreated, and the allies occupied Alcoy, which greatly relieved their quarters; but the want of vigour displayed by sir John Murray when he had gained Alcoy did not escape the notice of the troops.

After this affair the armies remained quiet until the 15th, when Whittingham forced the French posts with some loss from Albayda, and general Donkin, taking two battalions and some dragoons from Ibi, drove back their outposts from Rocayrente and Alsafara, villages situated beyond the range Plan 7. bounding the plain of Alcoy. He repassed the hills higher up with the dragoons and a company of the grenadiers of twenty-seventh, under captain Waldron, and returned by the main road to Alcoy, having in his course met a French battalion, through which the gallant Waldron broke with his grenadiers. Meanwhile sir John Murray, after much vacillation, at one time resolving to advance, at another to retreat, thinking it impossible first to force Suchet's entrenched camp, and then his second line behind the Xucar, a difficult river with muddy banks, believing also that the French general had his principal magazines at Valencia, conceived the idea of seizing the latter by a maritime expedition. He judged that the garrison which he estimated at eight hundred infantry, and one thousand cavalry, would be unable to resist, and that the town once taken the inhabitants would rise; Suchet could not then detach men enough to quell them without exposing himself to defeat on the

Xucar, and if he moved with all his force he could be closely followed by the allies and driven upon Requeña. In this view he made fresh dispositions.

On the 18th Roche's division reinforced by some troops from Elio's army and by a British grenadier battalion, was selected for the maritime attack, and the rest of the army was concentrated on the left at Castalla with the exception of Whittingham's troops which remained at Alcoy, for Suchet was said to be advancing, and Murray resolved to fight him. But to form a plan and to execute it vigorously, were with sir John Murray very different things. Although far from an incapable officer in the cabinet, he shewed none of the qualities of a commander in the field. His indecision was remarkable. On the morning of the 18th he resolved to fight in front of Castalla, and in the evening he assumed a weaker position behind that town, abandoning the command of a road, running from Ibi in rear of Alcoy, by which Whittingham might have been cut off. And when the strong remonstrances of his quarter-master general induced him to relinquish this ground, he adopted a third position, neither so strong as the first nor so defective as the last.

In this manner affairs wore on until the 26th, when Roche's division and the grenadier battalion marched to Alicant to embark, with orders, if they failed at Valencia, to seize and fortify Cullera at the mouth of the Xucar ; and if this also failed to besiege Denia. But now the foolish ministerial arrangements about the Sicilian army worked out their natural result. Lord Wellington, though he was permitted to retain the Anglo-Sicilian army in Spain beyond the period lord William Bentinck had assigned for its stay, had not the full command

given to him; he was clogged with reference
to the state of Sicily, until the middle of March,
and this new arrangement was still unknown to lord
William Bentinck and to sir John Murray. Thus
there were at this time, in fact, three commanding
officers; Wellington for the general operations,
Murray for the particular operations, and lord William Bentinck still empowered to increase or dimi-
nish the troops, and even upon emergency to
withdraw the whole. And now in consequence of
the continued dissentions in Sicily, the king of that
country having suddenly resumed the government,
lord William did recal two thousand of Murray's
best troops, and amongst them the grenadier battalion intended to attack Valencia. That enterprize instantly fell to the ground.

Upon this event sir John Murray, or some person
writing under his authority, makes the following
observations. " The most careful combination could
not have selected a moment when the danger of
such authority was more clearly demonstrated, more
severely felt. Had these orders been received a
very short time before, the allied army would not
have been committed in active operations; had they
reached sir John Murray a week later, there is
every reason to believe that the whole country from
Alicant to Valencia would have passed under the
authority of the allied army, and that marshal
Suchet cut off from his magazines in that province,
and in Aragon, would have been compelled to retire through a mountainous and barren country on
Madrid. But the order of lord William Bentinck
was peremptory, and the allied army which even
before was scarcely balanced, was now so inferior
to the enemy that it became an indispensible

necessity to adopt a system strongly defensive, and
all hope of a brilliant commencement of the campaign vanished."

Upon this curious passage it is necessary to remark, 1º. that Suchet's great magazines were not
at Valencia but at Saguntum; 2º. that from the
castle of Denia the fleet would have been descried,
and the strong garrison of Saguntum could have reinforced the troops in Valencia; Montmarie's brigade also would soon have come up from Oropesa.
These were doubtless contingencies not much to be
regarded in bar of such an enterprize, but Suchet
would by no means have been forced to retire by
Requeña upon Madrid, he would have retired to
Liria, the road to which steered more than five miles
clear of Valencia. He could have kept that city in
check while passing, in despite of sir John Murray,
and at Liria he would have been again in his natural position, that is to say, in full command of his
principal lines of communication. Moreover, however disagreeable to Suchet personally it might have
been to be forced back upon Madrid, that event
would have been extremely detrimental to the general cause, as tending to reinforce the king against
Wellington. But the singular part of the passage
quoted, is the assertion that the delay of a week in
lord William Bentinck's order would have ensured
such a noble stroke against the French army. Now
lord William Bentinck only required the troops to
proceed in the first instance to Mahon; what a
dull flagging spirit then was his, who dared not
delay obedience to such an order even for a week!

The recalled troops embarked for Sicily on the
5th of April, and Suchet alarmed at the offensive

position of the allies, which he attributed to the
general state of affairs, because the king's march to
Castile permitted all the Spanish armies of Andalusia to reinforce Elio, resolved to strike first, and
with the greater avidity because Elio had pushed
general Mijares with an advanced guard of three
or four thousand men to Yecla where they were
quite unsupported. This movement had been con-
certed in March, with Murray who was to occupy
Villena, and be prepared to fall upon the French
left, if the Spaniards were attacked at Yecla; and
in return the Spaniards were to fall on the French
right if Murray was attacked. Elio however neglected to strengthen his division at Yecla with
cavalry, which he had promised to do, nor did
Murray occupy Villena in force ; nevertheless Mijares remained at Yecla, Elio with the main body
occupied Hellin, and the cavalry were posted on
the side of Albacete, until the departure of the
troops for Sicily. Roche then joined the army at
Castalla, and Elio's main body occupied Elda and
Sax to cover the main road from Madrid to Alicant.

On the night of the 11th Suchet having by a
forced march assembled sixteen battalions of infantry, ten squadrons of cavalry, and twelve pieces
of artillery at Fuente la Higuera, marched straight
upon Caudete, while Harispe's division by a cross
road endeavoured to surprise the Spaniards at Yecla.
The latter retired fighting towards Jumilla by
the hills, but the French artillery and skirmishers
followed close, and at last the Spaniards being
pierced in the centre, one part broke and fled, and
the other part after some farther resistance surrendered. Two hundred were killed, and fifteen hun-

dred prisoners, including wounded, fell into the
hands of the victors, who lost about eighty men
and officers.

Suchet's movement on Fuente la Higuera was
known in the night of the 10th at Castalla, where
all the Anglo-Sicilian army was in position, because
Whittingham had come from Alcoy, leaving only a
detachment on that side. Hence while Harispe
was defeating Mijares at Yecla, Suchet in person
remained at Caudete with two divisions and the
heavy cavalry in order of battle, lest Murray
should advance by Biar and Villena. The latter
town, possessing an old wall and a castle, was occupied by the regiment of Velez-Malaga, a thousand
strong, and in the course of the day Murray also
came up with the allied cavalry and a brigade of
infantry. Here he was joined by Elio, without
troops, and when towards evening Harispe's fight
being over and the prisoners secured, Suchet advanced, Murray retired with the cavalry through
the pass of Biar leaving his infantry, under colonel
Adam, in front of that defile. He wished also to draw
the Spanish garrison from Villena but Elio would
not suffer it, and yet during the night, repenting of
his obstinacy, came to Castalla entreating Murray to
carry off that battalion. It was too late, Suchet had
broken the gates of the town the evening before, and
the castle with the best equipped and finest regiment
in the Spanish army had already surrendered.

Murray's final position was about three miles from
the pass of Biar. His left, composed of Whittingham's Spaniards, was entrenched on a rugged sierra
ending abruptly above Castalla, which, with its
old castle crowning an isolated sugar-loaf hill, See Plan 7.
closed the right of that wing and was occupied in
strength by Mackenzie's division.

A space between Whittingham's troops and the
town was left on the sierra for the advanced guard,
then in the pass of Biar ; Castalla itself, covered
by the castle, was prepared for defence, and the
principal approaches were commanded by strong
batteries, for Murray had concentrated nearly all
his guns at this point. The cavalry was partly
behind partly in front of the town on an extensive plain which was interspersed with olive
plantations.

The right wing, composed of Clinton's division
and Roche's Spaniards, was on comparatively low
ground, and extended to the rear at right angles
with the centre, but well covered by a "*barranco*" or
bed of a torrent, the precipitous sides of which
were, in some places, one hundred feet deep.

Suchet could approach this position, either
through the pass of Biar, or turning that defile,
by the way of Sax ; but the last road was supposed
to be occupied by Elio's army, and as troops
coming by it must make a flank march along the
front of the position, it was not a favourable line of
attack ; moreover the allies, being in possession of
the defiles of Biar, and of Alcoy, might have
gained the Xucar, either by Fuentes de la Higuera
or by Alcoy, seeing that Alicant, which was their
base, was safe, and the remnants of Elio's army
could easily have got away. Murray's army was
however scarcely active enough for such an operation, and Suchet advanced very cautiously, as it
behoved him to do, for the ground between Castalla and Biar was just such as a prompt opponent
would desire for a decisive blow.

The advanced guard, in the pass of Biar, about
two thousand five hundred men was composed of
two Italian regiments and a battalion of the twenty-

seventh British; two companies of German riflemen, a troop of foreign hussars and six guns, four
of which were mountain-pieces. The ground was
very strong and difficult but at two o'clock in the
afternoon the French, having concentrated in front
of the pass, their skirmishers swarmed up the steep
rocks on either flank, with a surprising vigour and
agility, and when they had gained the summit, the
supporting columns advanced. Then the allies who
had fought with resolution for about two hours
abandoned the pass with the loss of two guns and
about thirty prisoners, retreating however in good
order to the main position, for they were not followed beyond the mouth of the defile. The next day,
that is the 13th about one o'clock, the French cavalry, issuing cautiously from the pass, extended
to the left in the plain as far as Onil, and they
were followed by the infantry who immediately
occupied a low ridge about a mile in front of the
allies' left; the cavalry then gained ground to the
front, and closing towards the right of the allies
menaced the road to Ibi and Alcoy.

Murray had only occupied his ground the night
before, but he had studied it and entrenched it in
parts. His right wing was quite refused, and so
well covered by the barranco that nearly all the
troops could have been employed as a reserve to
the left wing, which was also very strongly posted
and presented a front about two miles in extent.
But notwithstanding the impregnable strength of
the ground the English general shrunk from the
contest, and while the head of the French column
was advancing from the defile of Biar, thrice he
gave his quarter-master general orders to put the
army in retreat, and the last time so peremptorily,

that obedience must have ensued if at that moment
the firing between the picquets and the French
light troops had not begun.

BATTLE OF CASTALLA.

Suchet's dispositions were made slowly and as if
he also had not made up his mind to fight, but a
crooked jut of the sierra, springing from about the
middle of the ridge, hid from him all the British
troops, and two-thirds of the whole army, hence
his first movement was to send a column towards
Castalla, to turn this jut of the sierra and discover
the conditions of the position. Meanwhile he
formed two strong columns immediately opposite
the left wing, and his cavalry, displaying a formidable line in the plain closed gradually towards the
barranco. The French general however soon discovered that the right of the allies was unattack-
able. Wherefore retaining his reserve on the low
ridge in front of the left wing, and still holding the
exploring column of infantry near Castalla, to protect his flank against any sally from that point, he
opened his artillery against the centre and right
wing of the allies, and forming several columns of
attack commenced the action against the allies' left
on both sides of the jut before spoken of.

The ascent in front of Whittingham's post, being
very rugged and steep, and the upper parts entrenched, the battle there resolved itself at once
into a fight of light troops, in which the Spaniards
maintained their ground with resolution ; but on
the other side of the jut, the French mounted the
heights, slowly indeed and with many skirmishers,
yet so firmly, that it was evident nothing but good
fighting would send them down again. Their light

troops spread over the whole face of the Sierra, and here and there attaining the summit were partially driven down again by the Anglo-Italian troops; but where the main body came upon the second battalion of the twenty-seventh there was a terrible crash. For the ground having an abrupt declination near the top enabled the French to form a line under cover, close to the British, who were lying down waiting for orders to charge; and while the former were unfolding their masses a grenadier officer, advancing alone, challenged the captain of the twenty-seventh grenadiers to single combat. Waldron an agile vigorous Irishman and of boiling courage instantly sprung forward, the hostile lines looked on without firing a shot, the swords of the champions glittered in the sun, the Frenchman's head was cleft in twain, and the next instant the twenty-seventh jumping up with a deafening shout, fired a deadly volley, at half pistol-shot distance, and then charged with such a shock that, maugre their bravery and numbers, the enemy's soldiers were overthrown and the side of the Sierra was covered with the killed and wounded. In Murray's despatch this exploit was erroneously attributed to colonel Adam, but it was ordered and conducted by colonel Reeves alone.

The French general seeing his principal column thus overthrown, and at every other point having the worst of the fight, made two secondary attacks to cover the rallying of the defeated columns, but these also failing, his army was separated in three parts, namely the beaten troops which were in great confusion, the reserve on the minor heights from whence the attacking columns had advanced, and the cavalry, which being far on the left in the

plain, was also separated from the point of action
by the bed of the torrent, a bridge over which was
commanded by the allies. A vigorous sally from
Castalla and a general advance would have obliged
the French reserves to fall back upon Biar in confusion before the cavalry could come to their assistance, and the victory might have been thus
completed; but Murray, who had remained during
the whole action behind Castalla, gave the French
full time to rally all their forces and retire in order
towards the pass of Biar. Then gradually passing
out by the right of the town, with a tedious pedan-
tic movement, he changed his front, forming two
lines across the valley, keeping his left at the foot of
the heights, and extending his right, covered by the
cavalry, towards the Sierra of Onil. Meanwhile
Mackenzie moving out by the left of Castalla with
three British, and one German battalion, and eight
guns followed the enemy more rapidly.

Suchet had by this time plunged into the pass
with his infantry cavalry and tumbrils in one mass,
leaving a rear-guard of three battalions with eight
guns to cover the passage; but these being pressed
by Mackenzie, and heavily cannonaded, were soon
forced to form lines and offer battle, answering gun
for gun. The French soldiers were heavily crushed
by the English shot, the clatter of musketry was
beginning, and one well-directed vigorous charge,
would have overturned and driven the French
in a confused mass upon the other troops then
wedged in the narrow defile; but Mackenzie's
movement had been made by the order of the
quarter-master-general Donkin, without Murray's
knowledge, and the latter instead of supporting it
strongly, sent repeated orders to withdraw the troops

already engaged, and in despite of all remonstrance caused them to fall back on the main body, when victory was in their grasp. Suchet thus relieved at a most critical moment immediately occupied a position across the defile with his flanks on the heights, and though Murray finally sent some light companies to attack his left the effort was feeble and produced no result ; he retained his position and in the night retired to Fuente de la Higuera.

On the 14th Murray marched to Alcoy where a small part of Whittingham's forces had remained in observation of a French detachment left to hold the pass of Albayda, and through this pass he proposed to intercept the retreat of Suchet, but his movements were slow, his arrangements bad, and the army became so disordered, that he halted the 15th at Alcoy. A feeble demonstration on the following days towards Albayda terminated his operations.

In this battle of Castalla, the allies had, including Roche's division, about seventeen thousand of all arms, and the French about fifteen thousand. Suchet says that the action was brought on, against his wish, by the impetuosity of his light troops, and that he lost only eight hundred men ; his statement is confirmed by Vacani the Italian historian. Sir John Murray affirms that it was a pitched battle and that the French lost above three thousand men. The reader may choose between these accounts. In favour of Suchet's version it may be remarked that neither the place, nor the time, nor the mode of attack, was such as might be expected from his talents and experience in war, if he had really intended a pitched battle ; and though the action was strongly contested on the principal point, it is scarcely possible that so many as three thousand men could have been killed and wounded. And yet eight hundred seems too few, because the loss of the victorious troops with all advantages of ground, was more than six hundred. One thing is however certain that if Suchet lost three thousand men, which would have been at least a fourth of his infantry, he must have been so disabled, so crippled, that what with the narrow defile of Biar in the rear, and the distance of his cavalry in the plain, to have escaped at all was extremely discreditable to Murray's generalship. An able commander having a superior force, and the allies were certainly the most numerous, would never have suffered the pass of Biar to be forced on the 12th, or if it were forced, he would have had his army well in hand behind it, ready to fall upon the head of the French column as it issued into the low ground.

Suchet violated several of the most important maxims of art. For without an adequate object, he fought a battle, having a defile in his rear, and on ground where his cavalry, in which he was superior, could not act. Neither the general state of the French affairs, nor the particular circumstances, invited a decisive offensive movement at the time, wherefore the French general should have been contented with his first successes against the Spaniards, and against Colonel Adam, unless some palpable advantage had been offered to him by Murray. But the latter's position was very strong indeed, and the French army was in imminent danger, cooped up between the pass of Biar and the allied troops; and this danger would have been increased if Elio had executed a movement which Murray

had proposed to him in the night of the 12th,
namely, to push troops into the mountains from
Sax, which would have strengthened Whittingham's
left and menaced the right flank of the enemy.
Elio disregarded this request, and during the
whole of the operations the two armies were unconnected, and acting without concert, although
only a few miles distant from each other. This
might have been avoided if they had previously
put the castle and town of Villena in a good
state of defence, and occupied the pass of Biar
in force behind it. The two armies would then
have been secure of a junction in advance, and the
plain of Villena would have been commanded. To
the courage of the troops belongs all the merit of
the success obtained, there was no generalship, and
hence though much blood was spilt no profit was
derived from victory.

CHAPTER V.

OPERATIONS NORTH OF THE TAGUS.

ON this side as in the south, one part of the French fronted lord Wellington's forces, while the rest warred with the Partidas, watched the English fleets on the coast, and endeavoured to maintain a free intercourse with France; but the extent of country was greater, the lines of communication longer, the war altogether more difficult, and the various operations more dissevered.

Four distinct bodies acted north of the Tagus.

1°. The army of Portugal, composed of six divisions under Reille, observing the allies from behind the Tormes; the Gallicians from behind the Esla.

2°. That part of the army of the south which, posted in the valley of the Tagus, observed Hill from behind the Tietar, and the Spaniards of Estremadura from behind the Tagus.

3°. The army of the north, under Caffarelli, whose business was to watch the English squadrons in the Bay of Biscay, to scour the great line of communication with France, and to protect the fortresses of Navarre and Biscay.

4°. The army of the centre, under count D'Erlon whose task was to fight the Partidas in the central pàrt of Spain, to cover Madrid and to connect the other armies by means of moveable columns radiating from that capital. Now if the reader will follow the operations of these armies in the order of their importance and will mark their bearing on the main action of the campaign, he will be led gradually to understand how it was, that in 1813, the French, although apparently in their full strength, were suddenly, irremediably and as it were by a whirlwind, swept from the Peninsula.

The army of the centre was composed of Darmagnac's and Barrois' French divisions, of Palombini's Italians, Casa Palacio's Spaniards, Trielhard's cavalry, and the king's French guards. It has been already shewn how, marching from the Tormes, it drove the Empecinado and Bassecour from the capital; but in passing the Guadarama one hundred and fifty men were frozen to death, a catastrophe produced by the rash use of ardent spirits. Palombini immediately occupied Alcala, and, having foraged the country towards Guadalaxara, brought in a large convoy of provisions to the capital. He would then have gone to Zaragoza to receive the recruits and stores which had arrived from Italy for his division, but Caffarelli was at this time so pressed that the Italian division finally marched to his succour, not by the direct road, such was the state of the northern provinces, but by the circuitous route of Valladolid and Burgos. The king's guards then replaced the Italians at Alcala, and excursions were commenced on every side against the Partidas, which being now recruited and taught by French deserters were become exceedingly wary and fought obstinately.

Vacani.

On the 8th of January, Espert, governor of Segovia, beat Saornil not far from Cuellar.

On the 3d of February, general Vichery, marching upon Medina Celi, routed a regiment of horse called the volunteers of Madrid, and took six hundred prisoners. The Empecinado with two thousand infantry and a thousand cavalry intercepted him on his return, but Vichery beat him with considerable slaughter, and made the retreat good with a loss of only seventy men. However the Guerilla chief being reinforced by Saornil and Abril, still kept the hills about Guadalaxara, and when D'Erlon sent fresh troops against him, he attacked a detachment under colonel Prieur, killed twenty men, took the baggage and recovered a heavy contribution.

During these operations the troops in the valley of the Tagus were continually harassed, especially by a chief called Cuesta who was sometimes in the Guadalupe mountains, sometimes on the Tietar, sometimes in the Vera de Placentia, and he was supported at times on the side of the Guadalupe by Morillo and Penne Villemur. The French were however most troubled by Hill's vicinity, for that general's successful enterprises had made a profound impression, and the slightest change of his quarters, or even the appearance of an English uniform beyond the line of cantonments caused a concentration of French troops as expecting one of his sudden blows.

Nor was the army of Portugal tranquil. The Gallicians menaced it from Puebla Senabria and the gorges of the Bierzo; Silveira from the Tras os Montes; the mountains separating Leon from the

Asturias were full of bands; Wellington was on the
Agueda; and Hill, moving from Coria by the pass
of Bejar might make a sudden incursion towards
Avila. Finally the communication with the army
of the north was to be kept up, and on every side
the Partidas were enterprising, especially the horsemen in the plains of Leon. Reille however did
not fail to war down these last.

Early in January Foy, returning from Astorga
to relieve general Leval, then at Avila, killed some
of Marquinez' cavalry in San Pedro, and more of
them at Mota la Toro; and on the 15th of that
month the French captain Mathis killed or took
four hundred of the same Partida at Valderas.
A convoy of Guerilla stores coming from the Asturias was intercepted by general Boyer's detachments, and one Florian, a celebrated Spanish Partizan in the French service, destroyed the band of
Garido, in the Avila district. The same Florian
on the 1st of February defeated the Medico and
another inferior chief, and soon after, passing the
Tormes, captured some Spanish dragoons who had
come out of Ciudad Rodrigo. On the 1st of
March he crushed the band of Tonto and at the same
time captain Mathis, acting on the side of the Carrion river, again surprised Marquinez' band at Mel-
gar Abaxo, and that Partida, reduced to two hundred men under two inferior chiefs called Tobar
and Marcos, ceased to be formidable.

Previous to this some Gallician troops having
advanced to Castro Gonzalo on the Esla, were attacked by Boyer who beat them through Benevente
with the loss of one hundred and fifty men, and
then driving the Spanish garrison from Puebla
Senabria, raised contributions with a rigour and

ferocity said to be habitual to him.   His detachments afterwards penetrating into the Asturias,
menaced Oviedo, and vexed the country in despite
of Porlier and Barceña who were in that province.
General Foy also having fixed his quarters at Avila,
feeling uneasy as to Hill's intentions, had endeavoured on the 20th of February to surprise Bejar
with the view of ascertaining if any large body was
collected behind it, but he was vigorously repulsed
by the fiftieth regiment and sixth caçadores under the
command of colonel Harrison.   However this attack
and the movements of Florian beyond the Tormes,
induced Lord Wellington to bring up another
division to the Agueda, which, by a reaction, caused
the French to believe the allies were ready to
advance.

During these events Caffarelli vainly urged
Reille to send him reinforcements, the insurrection
in the north gained strength, and the communications were entirely intercepted until Palombini,
driving away Mendizabal and Longa from Burgos,
enabled the great convoy and all Napoleon's despatches, which had been long accumulating there,
to reach Madrid in the latter end of February.
Joseph then reluctantly prepared to abandon his
capital and concentrate the armies in Castile, but
he neglected those essential ingredients of the
emperor's plan, rapidity and boldness.   By the
first Napoleon proposed to gain time for the suppression of the insurrection in the northern provinces.   By the second to impose upon Lord
Wellington and keep him on the defensive.   Joseph
did neither, he was slow and assumed the defensive
himself, and he and the other French generals expected to be attacked, for they had not fathomed

the English general's political difficulties; and
French writers since, misconceiving the character
of his warfare, have attributed to slowness in the
man what was really the long-reaching policy of a
great commander. The allied army was not so lithe
as the French army ; the latter carried on occasion
ten days' provisions on the soldiers' backs, or it
lived upon the country, and was in respect of its
organization and customs a superior military machine ; the former never carried more than three
days' provisions, never lived upon the country,
avoided the principle of making the war support
the war, payed or promised to pay for every thing,
and often carried in its marches even the corn for
its cavalry. The difference of this organization
resulting from the difference of policy between the
two nations, was a complete bar to any great and
sudden excursion on the part of the British general
and must always be considered in judging his
operations.

It is true that if Wellington had then passed
the Upper Tormes with a considerable force,
drawing Hill to him through Bejar, and moving
rapidly by Avila, he might have broken in upon
the defensive system of the king and beat his
armies in detail, and much the French feared such
a blow, which would have been quite in the manner
of Napoleon. But Wellington's views were directed by other than mere military principles.
Thus striking, he was not certain that his blow
would be decisive, his Portuguese forces would
have been ruined, his British soldiers seriously
injured by the attempt, and the resources of France
would have repaired the loss of the enemy, sooner
than he could have recovered the weakness which

must necessarily have followed such an unseasonable exertion.　His plan was to bring a great and
enduring power early into the field, for like Pho-
cion he desired to have an army fitted for a long
race and would not start on the short course.

Joseph though he conceived the probability and
dreaded the effect of such a sudden attack, could
by no means conceive the spirit of his brother's
plans.　It was in vain that Napoleon, while admitting the bad moral effect of abandoning the capital,
pointed out the difference between flying from it
and making a forward movement at the head of an
army; the king even maintained that Madrid was a
better military centre of operations than Valladolid,
because it had lines of communication by Segovia,
Aranda de Duero, and Zaragoza; nothing could
be more unmilitary, unless he was prepared to
march direct upon Lisbon if the allies marched
upon the Duero.　His extreme reluctance to quit
Madrid induced slowness, but the actual position
of his troops at the moment likewise presented
obstacles to the immediate execution of the emperor's orders; for as Daricau's division had not
returned from Valencia, the French outposts towards the Morena could not be withdrawn, nor
could the army of the centre march upon Valladolid
until the army of the south relieved it at Madrid.
Moreover Soult's counsels had troubled the king's
judgment; for that marshal agreeing that to abandon Madrid at that time was to abandon Spain,
offered a project for reconciling the possession of
the capital with the emperor's views.　This was to
place the army of Portugal, and the army of the
south, in position along the slopes of the Avila
mountains, and on the Upper Tormes menacing

Ciudad Rodrigo, while the king with the army of
the centre remained at Madrid in reserve. In this
situation he said they would be an over-match for
any force the allies could bring into the field, and
the latter could not move either by the valley of
the Tagus or upon the Duero without exposing
themselves to a flank attack.

The king objected that such a force could only
be fed in that country by the utter ruin of the
people, which he would not consent to; but he
was deceived by his ministers; the comfortable
state of the houses, the immense plains of standing
corn seen by the allies in their march from the
Esla to the Carrion proved that the people were
not much impoverished. Soult, well acquainted
with the resources of the country and a better and
more practised master of such operations, looked to
the military question rather than to the king's con-
ciliatory policy, and positively affirmed that the
armies could be subsisted; yet it does not appear
that he had taken into his consideration how the
insurrection in the northern provinces was to be
suppressed, which was the principal object of
Napoleon's plan. He no doubt expected that the
emperor would, from France send troops for that
purpose, but Napoleon knowing the true state of
his affairs foresaw that all the resources of France
would be required in another quarter.

Hatred and suspicion would have made Joseph
reject any plan suggested by Soult, and the more
so that the latter now declared the armies could
exist without assistance in money from France; yet
his mind was evidently unsettled by that marshal's
proposal, and by the coincidence of his ideas as
to holding Madrid, for even when the armies were

BOOK
XX.
————
1813.
March.
Marshal
Jourdan's
Official
correspon-
dence,
MSS.

in movement towards the northern parts, he vacillated in his resolutions, at one time thinking to
stay at Madrid, at another to march with the army
of the centre to Burgos, instead of Valladolid.
However upon the 18th of March he quitted the
capital leaving the Spanish ministers Angulo and
Almenara to govern there in conjunction with
Gazan. The army of the south then moved in two
columns, one under Couroux across the Gredos
mountains to Avila, the other under Gazan upon
Madrid to relieve the army of the centre, which
immediately marched to Aranda de Duero and
Lerma, with orders to settle at Burgos. Meanwhile
Villatte's division and all the outposts withdrawn
from La Mancha remained on the Alberche, and
the army of the south was thus concentrated between that river, Madrid, and Avila.

North of the Tagus the troops were unmolested,
save by the bands during these movements, which
were not completed before April, but in La Mancha
the retiring French posts had been followed by Del
Parque's advanced guard under Cruz Murgeon, as
far as Yebenes, and at the bridge of Algobar the
French cavalry checked the Spanish horsemen so
roughly, that Cruz Murgeon retired again towards
the Morena. At the same time on the Cuenca side,
the Empecinado having attempted to cut off a party
of French cavalry, escorting the marquis of Salices
to collect his rents previous to quitting Madrid, was
defeated with the loss of seventy troopers. Meanwhile the great dépôt at Madrid being partly removed, general Villatte marched upon Salamanca
and Gazan fixed his head-quarters at Arevalo. The
army of the south was thus cantoned between the
Tormes, the Duero, and the Adaja, with excep-

tion of six chosen regiments of infantry and four
of cavalry, in all about ten thousand men; these
remained at Madrid under Leval, who was ordered
to push advanced guards to Toledo, and the
Alberche, lest the allies should suddenly march
that way and turn the left of the French army.
But beyond the Alberche there were roads leading
from the valley of the Tagus over the Gredos mountains into the rear of the advanced positions which
the French had on the Upper Tormes, wherefore
these last were now withdrawn from Pedrahita and
Puente Congosto.

In proportion as the troops arrived in Castile
Reille sent men to the army of the north, and contracting his cantonments, concentrated his remaining
forces about Medina de Rio Seco with his cavalry
on the Esla. But the men recalled by the emperor
were now in full march, the French were in a
state of great confusion, the people urged by Wellington's emissaries and expecting great events
every where showed their dislike by withholding
provisions, and the Partida warfare became as
lively in the interior as on the coast, yet with
worse fortune. Captain Giordano, a Spaniard of
Joseph's guard killed one hundred and fifty of
Saornil's people near Arevalo, and the indefatigable
Florian defeated Morales' band, seized a dépôt in
the valley of the Tietar, beat the Medico there,
and then crossing the Gredos mountains, destroyed
near Segovia on the 28th the band of Purchas;
the king's Spanish guards also crushed some
smaller Partidas, and Renovales with his whole staff
was captured at Carvajales and carried to Valladolid. Meanwhile the Empecinado gained the
hills above Sepulveda and joining with Merino

obliged the people of the Segovia district, to abandon their houses and refuse the supplies demanded
by the army of the centre. When D'Armagnac
and Cassagne marched against them, Merino returned to his northern haunts, the Empecinado to
the Tagus, and D'Erlon then removed his head-
quarters to Cuellar.

April.
During April Leval was very much disturbed,
and gave false alarms, which extending to Valladolid caused an unseasonable concentration of the
troops and D'Erlon abandoned Cuellar and Sepul-
FrenchPa- veda. Del Parque and the Empecinado were said
to have established the bridge of Aranjuez, Elio
to be advancing in La Mancha, Hill to be in the
valley of the Tagus and moving by Mombeltran
with the intention of seizing the passes of the
Guadarama. All of this was false. It was the
Empecinado and Abuelo who were at Aranjuez,
the Partidas of Firmin, Cuesta, Rivero, and El
Medico who were collecting at Arzobispo, to mask
the march of the Spanish divisions from Estremadura, and of the reserve from Andalusia; it was
the prince of Anglona who was advancing in La
Mancha to cover the movement of Del Parque
upon Murcia. When disabused of his error, Leval
easily drove away the Empecinado who had advanced to Alcala; afterwards chasing Firmin from
Valdemoro into the valley of the Tagus, he re-
established his advanced posts in Toledo and on the
Alberche, and scoured the whole country around.
But Joseph himself was anxious to abandon Madrid
altogether, and was only restrained by the emperor's
orders and by the hope of still gathering some
contributions there to support his court at Valladolid. With reluctance also he had obeyed his

brother's reiterated orders to bring the army of the centre over the Duero to replace the detached divisions of the army of Portugal. He wished D'Erlon rather than Reille, to reinforce the north, and nothing could more clearly show how entirely the subtle spirit of Napoleon's instructions had escaped his perception. It was necessary that Madrid should be held, to watch the valley of the Tagus and if necessary to enable the French armies to fall back on Zaragoza, but principally to give force to the moral effect of the offensive movement towards Portugal. It was equally important and for the same reason, that the army of Portugal instead of the army of the centre should furnish reinforcements for the north.

In the contracted positions which the armies now occupied, the difficulty of subsisting was increased, and each general was dissatisfied with his district, disputes multiplied, and the court clashed with the army at every turn. Leval also inveighed against the conduct of the Spanish ministers and minor authorities left at Madrid, as being hurtful to both troops and people, and no doubt justly, since it appears to have been precisely like that of the Portuguese and Spanish authorities on the other side towards the allies. Joseph's letters to his brother became daily more bitter. Napoleon's regulations for the support of the troops were at variance with his, and when the king's budget shewed a deficit of many millions, the emperor so little regarded it that he reduced the French subsidy to two millions per month, and strictly forbad the application of the money to any other purpose than the pay of the soldiers. When Joseph asked, how he was to find resources? his

brother with a just sarcasm on his political and
military blindness, desired him to seek what was
necessary in those provinces of the north which
were rich enough to nourish the Partidas and the
insurrectional juntas. The king thus pushed to the
wall prevailed upon Gazan secretly to lend him fifty
thousand francs, for the support of his court, from
the chest of the army of the south; but with the
other generals he could by no means agree, and
instead of the vigour and vigilance necessary to
meet the coming campaign there was weakness,
disunion, and ill blood.

All the movements and arrangements for concentrating the French forces, as made by Joseph,
displeased Napoleon. The manner in which the
army of the centre stole away from Madrid by the
road of Lerma was, he said, only calculated to
expose his real views and draw the allies upon the
French before the communication with France was
restored. But more than all his indignation was
aroused by the conduct of the king after the concentration. The French armies were held on the
defensive and the allies might without fear for Portugal embark troops to invade France, whereas a
bold and confident offensive movement sustained
by the formation of a battering train at Burgos, as
if to besiege Ciudad Rodrigo, would have imposed
upon the English general, secured France from the
danger of such an insult, and would at the same
time have masked the necessary measures for suppressing the insurrection in the northern provinces.
To quell that insurrection was of vital importance,
but from the various circumstances already noticed
it had now existed for seven months, five of which,
the king, although at the head of ninety thousand

men, and uninterrupted by Wellington, had wasted
unprofitably, having done no more than chase a few
inferior bands of the interior while this formidable
warfare was consolidating in his rear ; and while
his great adversary was organizing the most powerful army which had yet taken the field in his front.
It is thus kingdoms are lost. I shall now trace the
progress of the northern insurrection so unaccount-
ably neglected by the king, and to the last misunderstood by him; for when Wellington was actually
in movement; when the dispersed French corps
were rushing and crowding to the rear to avoid the
ponderous mass which the English general was
pushing forward; even then, the king, who had
done every thing possible to render defeat certain,
was urging upon Napoleon the propriety of first
beating the allies and afterwards reducing the insurrection by the establishment of a Spanish civil
government beyond the Ebro !

NORTHERN INSURRECTION.

It has been already shewn how the old Partidas
had been strengthened and new corps organized on
a better footing in Biscay and Navarre; how in
the latter end of 1812 Caffarelli marched to succour
Santona, and how Longa taking advantage of his
absence captured a convoy near Burgos while other
bands menaced Logroño. All the littoral posts, with
the exception of Santona and Gueteria were then
in the possession of the Spaniards, and Mendizabel
made an attempt on Bilbao the 6th of January.
Repulsed by general Rouget he rejoined Longa and
together they captured the little fort of Salinas de
Anara, near the Ebro, and that of Cuba in the
Bureba, while the bands of Logroño invested Do-

mingo Calçada in the Rioja.   On the 26th of
January, Caffarelli, having returned from Santona,
detached Vandermaesen and Dubreton to drive the
Spaniards from Santander, and they seized many
stores there, but neglected to make any movement
to aid Santona which was again blockaded by the
Partidas ; meanwhile the convoy with all the emperor's despatches was stopped at Burgos.   Palombini re-opened the communications and enabled
the convoy to reach Madrid, but his division did
not muster more than three thousand men, and
various detachments belonging to the other armies
were now in march to the interior of Spain.   The
regiments recalled to France from all parts were
also in full movement, together with many convoys
and escorts for the marshals and generals quitting
the Peninsula ;   thus the army of the north was
reduced, as its duties increased, and the young
French soldiers died fast of a peculiar malady which
especially attacked them in small garrisons.   Meanwhile the Spaniards' forces increased.   In February
Mendizabel and Longa were again in the Bureba
intercepting the communication between Burgos and
Bilbao, and they menaced Pancorbo and Briviesca.
This brought Caffarelli from Vittoria and Palombini
from Burgos.   The latter surprised by Longa, lost
many men near Poza de Sal, and only saved himself by his courage and firmness yet he finally drove
the Spaniards away.   But now Mina returning
from Aragon after his unsuccessful action near
Huesca surprized and burned the castle of Fuenter-
rabia in a most daring manner on the 11th of March,
after which, having assembled five thousand men in
Guipuscoa, he obtained guns from the English fleet
at Motrico, invested Villa Real within a few leagues

of Vittoria, and repulsed six hundred men who
came to relieve the fort. This brought Caffarelli
back from Pancorbo. Mina then raised the siege,
and Palombini marching into the Rioja, succoured
the garrison of San Domingo Calçada and drove the
Partidas towards Soria. The communication with
Logroño was thus re-opened, and the Italians passing the Ebro marched by Vittoria towards Bilbao
where they arrived the 21st of February; but the
gens-d'armes and imperial guards immediately
moved from Bilbao to France, Caffarelli went with
them, and the Spanish chiefs remained masters of
Navarre and Biscay. The people now refused war
contributions both in money and kind, the harvest
was not ripe, and the distress of the French increased
in an alarming manner because the weather enabled
the English fleets to keep upon the coast and intercept all supplies from France by sea. The communications were all broken; in front by Longa who
was again at the defile of Pancorbo; in the rear
by Mina who was in the hills of Arlaban; on the
left by a collection of bands at Caroncal in Navarre.
Abbé, governor of Pampeluna severely checked
these last, but Mina soon restored affairs; for leaving
the volunteers of Guipuscoa to watch the defiles of
Arlaban, he assembled all the bands in Navarre,
destroyed the bridges leading to Taffalla from Pampeluna and from Puente la Reyna, and though
Abbé twice attacked him, he got stronger, and
bringing up two English guns from the coast
besieged Taffalla.

Napoleon, discontented with Caffarelli's mode of
conducting the war, now gave Clauzel the command
in the north, with discretionary power to draw as
many troops from the army of Portugal as he

judged necessary. He was to correspond directly with the emperor to avoid loss of time, but was to obey the king in all things not clashing with Napoleon's orders, which contained a complete review of what had passed and what was necessary to be done. " The Partidas," the emperor said, " were strong, organized, exercised, and seconded by the exaltation of spirit which the battle of Salamanca had produced. The insurrectional juntas had been revived, the posts on the coast abandoned by the French and seized by the Spaniards gave free intercourse with the English; the bands enjoyed all the resources of the country, and the system of warfare hitherto followed had favoured their progress. Instead of forestalling their enterprises the French had waited for their attacks, and contrived to be always behind the event; they obeyed the enemy's impulsion and the troops were fatigued without gaining their object. Clauzel was to adopt a contrary system, he was to attack suddenly, pursue rapidly, and combine his movements with reference to the features of the country. A few good strokes against the Spaniards' magazines, hospitals, or dépôts of arms would inevitably trouble their operations, and after one or two military successes some political measures would suffice to disperse the authorities, disorganise the insurrection, and bring the young men who had been enrolled by force back to their homes. All the generals recommended, and the emperor approved of the construction of block-houses on well-chosen points, especially where many roads met; the forests would furnish the materials cheaply, and these posts should support each other and form chains of communication. With respect to the

greater fortresses, Pampeluna and Santona were
the most important, and the enemy knew it, for
Mina was intent to famish the first and the English
squadron to get hold of the second. To supply
Pampeluna it was only necessary to clear the communications, the country around being rich and
fertile. Santona required combinations. The emperor wished to supply it by sea from Bayonne
and St. Sebastian, but the French marine officers
would never attempt the passage, even with favourable winds and when the English squadron were
away, unless all the intermediate ports were occupied by the land forces.

" Six months before, these ports had been in the
hands of the French, but Caffarelli had lightly
abandoned them, leaving the field open to the
insurgents in his rear while he marched with
Souham against Wellington. Since that period
the English and Spaniards held them. For four
months the emperor had unceasingly ordered the
retaking of Bermeo and Castro, but whether from
the difficulty of the operations or the necessity of
answering more pressing calls, no effort had been
made to obey, and the fine season now permitted
the English ships to aid in the defence. Castro
was said to be strongly fortified by the English,
no wonder, Caffarelli had given them sufficient
time, and they knew its value. In one month
every post on the coast from the mouth of the
Bidassoa to St. Ander should be again re-occupied
by the French, and St. Ander itself should be
garrisoned strongly. And simultaneous with the
coast operations should be Clauzel's attack on Mina
in Navarre and the chasing of the Partidas in the
interior of Biscay. The administration of the

country also demanded reform, and still more
the organization and discipline of the army of the
north should be attended to. It was the pith and
marrow of the French power in Spain, all would
fail if that failed, whereas if the north was strong,
its administration sound, its fortresses well provided
and its state tranquil, no irreparable misfortune
could happen in any other part."

Clauzel assumed the command on the 22d of
February, Abbé was then confined to Pampeluna,
Mina, master of Navarre, was besieging Taffalla;
Pastor, Longa, Campillo, Merino and others ranged
through Biscay and Castile unmolested; and the
spirit of the country was so changed that fathers
now sent their sons to join Partidas which had
hitherto been composed of robbers and deserters.
Clauzel demanded a reinforcement of twenty thousand men from the army of Portugal, but Joseph
was still in Madrid and proposed to send D'Erlon
with the army of the centre instead, an arrangement to which Clauzel would not accede. Twenty
thousand troops were, he said, wanted beyond
the Ebro. Two independent chiefs, himself and
D'Erlon, could not act together; and if the latter
was only to remain quiet at Burgos his army would
devour the resources without aiding the operations
of the army of the north. The king might choose
another commander, but the troops required must
be sent. Joseph changed his plan, yet it was the
end of March before Reille's divisions moved, three
upon Navarre, and one upon Burgos. Meanwhile
Clauzel repaired with some troops to Bilbao, where
general Rouget had eight hundred men in garrison
besides Palombini's Italians.

This place was in a manner blockaded by the

Partidas. The Pastor with three thousand men was on the right of the Durango river, in the hills of Guernica, and Navarnis, between Bilbao and the fort of Bermeo. Mendizabal with from eight to ten thousand men was on the left of the Durango in the mountains, menacing at once Santoña and Bilbao and protecting Castro. However the French had a strong garrison in the town of Durango, the construction of new works round Bilbao was in progress, and on the 22d of March Clauzel moved with the Italians and a French regiment to assault Castro. Campillo and Mendizabel immediately appeared from different sides and the garrison made a sally; the Spaniards after some sharp fighting regained the high valleys in disorder, and the design of escalading Castro was resumed, but again interrupted by the return of Mendizabel to Trucios, only seven miles from the French camp, and by intelligence that the Pastor with the volunteers of Biscay and Guipuscoa was menacing Bilbao. Clauzel immediately marched with the French regiments to the latter place, leaving Palombini to oppose Mendizabel. Finding all safe at Bilbao, he sent Rouget with two French battalions to reinforce the Italians, who then drove Mendizabel from Trucios into the hills about Valmaceda. It being now necessary to attack Castro in form, Palombini occupied the heights of Ojeba and Ramales, from whence he communicated with the garrison of Santona, introduced a convoy of money and fresh provisions there, received ammunition in return, and directed the governor Lameth to prepare a battering train of six pieces for the siege. This done, the Italians who had lost many men returned hastily to Bilbao, for the Pastor was again menacing that city.

On the evening of the 31st Palombini marched against this new enemy and finding him too strong retreated, but being promised a reinforcement of two regiments from Durango he returned; Pastor was then with three thousand men in position at Navarnis, Palombini gave him battle on the 3d and was defeated with the loss of eighty men, but on the 5th being joined by the French regiments from Durango he beat the Spaniards. They dispersed and while some collected in the· same positions behind him, and others under Pastor gained the interior, one column retired by the coast towards the Deba on the side of St. Sebastian. Palombini eagerly pursued these last, because he expected troops from that fortress to line the Deba, and hoped thus to surround the Spaniards, but the English squadron was at Lequitio and carried them off. Pastor meanwhile descending the Deba drove the French from that river to the very walls of St. Sebastian, and Palombini was forced to make for Bergara on the road to Vittoria.

At Bergara he left his wounded men with a garrison to protect them, and returning on the 9th of April attacked the volunteers of Guipuscoa at Ascoytia; repulsed in this attempt he retired again towards Bergara, and soon after took charge of a convoy of artillery going from St. Sebastian for the siege of Castro. Meanwhile Bilbao was in great danger, for the volunteers of Biscay coming from the Arlaban, made on the 10th a false attack at a bridge two miles above the entrenched camp, while Tapia, Dos Pelos, and Campillo fell on seriously from the side of Valmaceda. Mendizabel, who commanded, did not combine his movements well and was repulsed by Rouget although with difficulty ; the noise of the action reached Palombini who hastened his march, and having deposited his convoy, followed the volunteers of Biscay to Guernica and drove them upon Bermeo where they got on board the English vessels.

During these events Clauzel was at Vittoria arranging the general plan of operations. Mina had on the 1st of April defeated one of his columns near Lerin with the loss of five or six hundred men. The four divisions sent from the army of Portugal, together with some unattached regiments furnished, according to Reille, the twenty thousand men demanded, yet only seventeen thousand reached Clauzel ; and as the unattached regiments merely replaced a like number belonging to the other armies, and now recalled from the north, the French general found his expected reinforcements dwindled to thirteen thousand. Hence notwithstanding Palombini's activity, the insurrection was in the beginning of April more formidable than ever ; the line of correspondence from Torquemada to Burgos was quite unprotected for want of troops, neither was the line from Burgos to Irun so well guarded that couriers could pass without powerful escorts, nor always then. The fortifications of the castle of Burgos were to have been improved, but there was no money to pay for the works, the French, in default of transport, could not collect provisions for the magazines ordered to be formed there by the king, and two generals, La Martiniere and Rey, were disputing for the command. Nearly forty thousand irregular Spanish

troops were in the field.   The garrison of Taffalla,
five hundred strong, had yielded to Mina, and that
chief, in concert with Duran, Amor, Tabueca, the
militia men of Logroña, and some minor guerillas
occupied both sides of the Ebro, between Calahora,
Logroño, Santa Cruz de Campero, and Guardia.
They could in one day unite eighteen thousand
infantry and a thousand horsemen.   Mendizabel,
Longa, Campillo, Herrera, El Pastor, and the
volunteers of Biscay, Guipuscoa, and Alava, in
all about sixteen thousand, were on the coast
acting in conjunction with the English squadrons,
Santander, Castro, and Bermeo were still in their
hands, and maritime expeditions were preparing at
Coruña and in the Asturias.

 This Partizan war thus presented three distinct
branches, that of Navarre, that of the coast, and
that on the lines of communication.   The last
alone required above fifteen thousand men; namely
ten thousand from Irun to Burgos, and the line
between Tolosa and Pampeluna, which was destroyed, required fifteen hundred to restore it,
while four thousand were necessary between Mondragon and Bilbao, comprising the garrison of the
latter place ; even then no post would be safe
from a sudden attack.   Nearly all the army of the
north was appropriated to the garrisons and lines
of communication, but the divisions of Abbé and
Vandermaesen could be used on the side of Pampeluna, and there were besides, disposable, Palombini's Italians and the divisions sent by Reille.
But one of these, Sarrut's, was still in march, and
all the sick of the armies in Castile were now
pouring into Navarre, when, from the loss of the
contributions, there was no money to provide assist-

ance for them. Clauzel had however ameliorated
both the civil and the military administrations,
improved the works of Gueteria, commenced the
construction of block-houses between Irun and
Vittoria, and as we have seen had shaken the
bands about Bilbao. Now dividing his forces he
destined Palombini to besiege Castro, ordering
Foy and Sarrut's divisions when the latter should
arrive, to cover the operation and to oppose any
disembarkation.

The field force thus appropriated, together with
the troops in Bilbao under Rouget, was about
ten thousand men, and in the middle of April,
Clauzel, beating Mina from Taffalla and Estella,
assembled the remainder of the active army, composed of Taupin and Barbout's divisions of the
army of Portugal, Vandermaesen's and Abbé's divisions of the army of the north, in all about thirteen
thousand men, at Puenta La Reyna in Navarre. He
urged general L'Huillier, who commanded the reserve
at Bayonne, to reinforce St. Sebastian and Gueteria
and to push forward his troops of observation into
the valley of Bastan, and he also gave the commandant of Zaragoza notice of his arrival, that
he might watch Mina on that side. From Puente
la Reyna he made some excursions but he lost men
uselessly, for the Spaniards would only fight at
advantage, and to hunt Mina without first barring
all his passages of flight was to destroy the French
soldiers by fatigue. And here the king's delay was
most seriously felt because the winter season, when,
the tops of the mountains being covered with snow,
the Partidas could only move along the ordinary
roads, was most favourable for the French operations, and it had passed away. Clauzel despairing

to effect any thing with so few troops was even going to separate his forces and march to the coast, when in May Mina, who had taken post in the valley of Ronçal, furnished an occasion which did not escape the French general.

On the 13th Abbé's and Vandermaesen's divisions and the cavalry entered that valley at once by the upper and lower parts, and suddenly closing upon the Guerilla chief killed and wounded a thousand of his men and dispersed the rest; one part fled by the mountains to Navarquez, on the side of Sanguessa, with the wounded whom they dropped at different places in care of the country people. Chaplangarra, Cruchaga, and Carena, Mina's lieutenants, went off, each with a column, in the opposite direction and by different routes to the valley of the Aragon, they passed that river at St. Gilla, and made their way towards the sacred mountain of La Pena near Jacca. The French cavalry following them by Villa Real, entered that town the 14th on one side, while Mina with twelve men entered it on the other, but he escaped to Martes where another ineffectual attempt was made to surprise him. Abbé's columns then descended the smaller valleys leading towards the upper valley of the Aragon, while Vandermaesen's infantry and the cavalry entered the lower part of the same valley, and the former approaching Jacca sent his wounded men there and got fresh ammunition.

Meanwhile Mina and the insurgent junta making a push to regain Navarre by the left of the Aragon river were like to have been taken, but again escaped towards the valley of the Gallego, whither also the greater part of their troops now sought refuge. Clauzel was careful not to force them over that river, lest they should remain there and intercept the communication from Zaragoza by Jacca, which was the only free line the French now possessed and too far removed from Clauzel's true theatre of operations to be watched. Abbé therefore returned to Roncal in search of the Spanish dépôts, and Vandermaesen entered Sos at one end just as Mina, who had now one hundred and fifty horsemen and was always intent upon regaining Navarre, passed out at the other; the light cavalry pursuing overtook him at Sos Fuentes and he fled to Carcastillo, but there unexpectedly meeting some of his own squadrons which had wandered over the mountains after the action at Roncal, he gave battle, was defeated with the loss of fifty men and fled once more to Aragon, whereupon the insurrectional junta dispersed, and dissentions arose between Mina and the minor chiefs under his command. Clauzel anxious to increase this discord sent troops into all the valleys to seek out the Spanish dépôts and to attack their scattered men, and he was well served by the Aragonese, for Suchet's wise administration was still proof against the insurrectional juntas.

During these events four battalions left by Mina at Santa Cruz de Campero in the Amescoas, were chased by Taupin, who had remained at Estella when the other divisions marched up the valley of Roncal. Mina, however, reassembled at Barbastro in Aragon a strong column, crowds of deserters from the other Spanish armies were daily increasing his power, and so completely had he organized Navarre that the presence of a single soldier of his in a village sufficed to have any courier without a strong escort stopped. Many

bands also were still in the Rioja, and two French
regiments rashly foraging towards Lerim were
nearly all destroyed. In fine the losses were well
balanced, and Clauzel demanded more troops,
especially cavalry, to scour the Rioja. Nevertheless the dispersion of Mina's troops lowered the
reputation of that chief, and the French general
taking up his quarters in Pampeluna so improved
this advantage by address, that many townships
withdrew from the insurrection, and recalling their
young men from the bands commenced the formation of eight free Spanish companies to serve
on the French side. Corps of this sort were raised
with so much facility in every part of Spain, that
it would seem nations, as well as individuals,
have an idiosyncrasy, and in these changeable
warriors we again see the Mandonius and Indibilis
of ancient days.

Joseph, urged by Clauzel, now sent Maucune's
division and some light cavalry of the army of
Portugal, to occupy Pampleiga, Burgos, and
Briviesca, and to protect the great communication, which the diverging direction of Clauzel's
double operations had again exposed to the partidas. Meanwhile the French troops had not
been less successful in Biscay than in Navarre.
Foy reached Bilbao the 24th of April, and finding all things there ready for the siege of Castro
marched to Santona to hasten the preparations at
that place, and he attempted also to surprise the
chiefs Campillo and Herrera in the hills above
Santona, but was worsted in the combat. The two
battering trains then endeavoured to proceed from
Bilbao and Santona by sea to Castro, but the English vessels, coming to the mouth of the Durango,

stopped those at Bilbao, and obliged them to proceed by land, but thus gave an opportunity for those
at Santona to make the sea-run in safety.

SIEGE OF CASTRO.

This place situated on a promontory was garrisoned by twelve hundred men, under the command of Don Pedro Alvarez, three English
sloops of war commanded by the captains Bloye,
Bremen, and Tayler, were at hand, some gun-
boats were in the harbour, and twenty-seven guns
were mounted on the works. An outward wall
with towers, extended from sea to sea on the low
neck which connected the promontory with the
main land; this line of defence was strengthened by
some fortified convents, behind it came the town,
and behind the town at the extremity of the promontory stood the castle.

On the 4th of May, Foy, Sarrut, and Palombini,
took post at different points to cover the siege;
the Italian general St. Paul invested the place;
the engineer Vacani conducted the works, having twelve guns at his disposal. The defence was
lively and vigorous, and captain Tayler with
great labour landed a heavy ship-gun on a rocky
island to the right of the town, looking from the sea,
which he worked with effect against the French
counter-batteries. On the 11th a second gun was
mounted on this island, but that day the breaching
batteries opened, and in a few hours broke the
wall while the counter-batteries set fire to some
houses with shells, wherefore the English guns were
removed from the island. The assault was then
ordered but delayed by a sudden accident, for a

foraging party having been sent into the hills, came
flying back, pursued by a column of Spaniards
which had passed unperceived through the positions of the French; and the besiegers were for some
time in confusion as thinking the covering army
had been beaten; however they soon recovered,
and the assault and escalade took place in the
night.

The attack was rapid and fierce, the walls were
carried, and the garrison driven through the town
to the castle which was maintained by two companies, while the flying troops got on board the
English vessels; finally the Italians stormed the
castle, but every gun had been destroyed, and the
two companies safely rejoined their countrymen on
board the ships. The English had ten seamen
wounded, the Spaniards lost about a hundred and
eighty, and the remainder were immediately conveyed to Bermeo from whence they marched inland
to join Longa. The besiegers lost only fifty men
killed and wounded, and the Italian soldiers committed great excesses, setting fire to the town in
many places. Foy and Sarrut, separating after the
siege, marched, the former through the district of
Incartaciones to Bilbao defeating a battalion of
Biscay volunteers on his route; the latter to Orduña
with the design of destroying Longa; but that
chief crossed the Ebro at Puente Lara, and finding
the additional troops sent by Joseph were beginning to arrive in the vicinity of Burgos, recrossed
the river, and after a long chase escaped in the
mountains of Espinosa. Sarrut having captured a
few gun-carriages and one of Longa's forest dépôts of ammunition, returned towards Bilbao, and
Foy immediately marched from that place against

the two remaining battalions of Biscay volunteers,
which under the chiefs Mugartegui and Artola
were now at Villaro and Guernica.

These battalions, each a thousand strong, raised
by conscription, and officered from the best families,
were the champions of Biscay; but though brave and
well-equipped, the difficulty of crushing them and
the volunteers of Guipuscoa, was not great, because neither would leave their own peculiar provinces. The third battalion had been already dispersed in the district of Incartaciones, and Foy
having in the night of the 29th combined the march
of several columns to surround Villaro, fell at day-
break upon Mugartegui's battalion and dispersed it
with the loss of all its baggage. Two hundred of
the volunteers immediately returned to their homes,
and the French general marched rapidly, through
Durango, against Artola, who was at Guernica. The
Italians who were still at Bilbao, immediately turned
Guernica on the west by Mungia, while a French
column turned it eastward by Marquinez; then
Artola fled to Lequitio, but the column from Marquinez, coming over the mountain, fell upon his
right flank just as he was defiling by a narrow
way along the sea-coast. Artola himself escaped,
but two hundred Biscayens were killed or drowned,
more than three hundred with twenty-seven officers
were taken, and two companies which formed his
rear-guard dispersed in the mountains, and some
men finding a few boats rowed to an English vessel.
The perfect success of this action, which did not
cost the French a man killed or wounded, was
attributed to the talents and vigour of captain
Guinget, the daring officer who won the passage

of the Douro at Tordesillas in Wellington's retreat from Burgos.

When the three battalions of Biscay were thus disposed of, all their magazines, hospitals, and depôts fell into Foy's hands, the junta dispersed, the privateers quitted the coast for Santander, Pastor abandoned Guipuscoa, and the Italians recovered Bermeo from which the garrison fled to the English ships. They also destroyed the works of the little island of Isaro, which being situated three thousand yards from the shore, and having no access to the summit, save by a staircase cut in the rock, was deemed impregnable, and used as a depôt for the English stores ; but this was the last memorable exploit of Palombini's division in the north. That general himself had already gone to Italy to join Napoleon's reserves, and his troops being ordered to march by Aragon to join Suchet, were in movement, when new events caused them to remain in Guipuscoa, with the reputation of being brave and active but ferocious soldiers, barbarous and devastating, differing little from their Roman ancestors.

It has been already observed that, during these double operations of the French on the coast and in Navarre, the partidas had fallen upon the line of communication with France, thus working out the third branch of the insurrectional warfare. Their success went nigh to balance all their losses on each flank. For Mendizabel settled with Longa's partida upon the line between Burgos and Miranda de Ebro ; the volunteers of Alava and Biscay, and part of Pastor's bands concentrated on the mountains of Arlaban above the defiles of Salinas and

Descarga; Merino and Salazar came up from the
country between the Ebro and the Duero; and the
three battalions left by Mina in the Amescoa, after
escaping from Taupin, reassembled close to Vittoria.
Every convoy and every courier's escort was attacked at one or other of these points without
hindering Mendizabel from making sudden de-
scents towards the coast when occasion offered.
Thus, on the 11th of April, as we have seen, he
attacked Bilbao. On the 25th of April Longa,
who had four thousand men and several guns, was
repulsed at Armiñion, between Miranda and Trevino,
by some of the drafted men going to France; but
on the 3d of May at the same place Longa met and
obliged a large convoy, coming from Castile with
an escort of eight hundred men, to return to Miranda, and even cannonaded that place on the 5th.
Thouvenot the commandant of the government,
immediately detached twelve hundred men and
three guns from Vittoria to relieve the convoy; but
then Mina's battalions endeavoured to escalade
Salvatierra, and they were repulsed with difficulty.
Meanwhile the volunteers of Alava gathered above
the pass of Salinas to intercept the rescued convoy,
and finding that the latter would not stir from Vittoria,
they went on the 10th to aid in a fresh attack on
Salvatierra; being again repulsed they returned to
the Arlaban, where they captured a courier with a
strong escort in the pass of Descarga near Villa
Real. A French regiment sent to succour Salvatierra finally drove these volunteers towards Bilbao
where, as we have seen, Foy routed them, but
Longa continued to infest the post of Armiñion
until Sarrut arriving from the siege of Castro
chased him also.

Notwithstanding these successes Clauzel, whose troops were worn out with fatigue, declared that it would require fifty thousand men and three months' time to quell the insurrection entirely. And Napoleon more discontented than ever with the king, complained that the happy enterprizes of Clauzel, Foy, Sarrut, and Palombini, had brought no safety to his couriers and convoys; that his orders about the posts and the infantry escorts had been neglected; that the reinforcements sent to the north from Castile had gone slowly and in succession instead of at once; finally that the cautious movement of concentration by the other armies was inexcusable, since the inaction of the allies, their distance, their want of transport, their ordinary and even timid circumspection in any operation out of the ordinary course, enabled the French to act in the most convenient manner. The growing dissentions between the English and the Spaniards, the journey of Wellington to Cadiz, and the changes in his army, were, he said, all favourable circumstances for the French, but the king had taken no advantage of them; the insurrection continued, and the object of interest was now changed. Joseph defended himself with more vehemence than reason against these charges, but Wellington soon vindicated Napoleon's judgement, and the voice of controversy was smothered by the din of battle, for the English general was again abroad in his strength, and the clang of his arms resounded through the Peninsula.

CHAPTER VI.

WHILE the French power in Spain was being disorganized by the various circumstances related in
the former chapter, Lord Wellington's diligence
and energy had reorganized the allied army with
greater strength than before. Large reinforcements, especially of cavalry, had come out from
England. The efficiency and the spirit of the
Portuguese had been restored in a surprizing manner, and discipline had been vindicated, in both
services, with a rough but salutary hand; rank
had not screened offenders; some had been arrested, some tried, some dismissed for breach of
duty; the negligent were terrified, the zealous encouraged; in short every department was reformed with
vigour, and it was full time. Confidential officers
commissioned to detect abuses in the general hospitals and depôts, those asylums for malingerers,
discovered and drove so many skulkers to their
duty, that the second division alone recovered six
hundred bayonets in one month; and this salutary
scouring was rendered more efficient by the establishment of both permanent, and ambulent regimental hospitals, a wise measure, and founded on
a principle which cannot be too widely extended;
for it is certain that as the character of a battalion
depends on its fitness for service, a moral force
will always be brought to bear upon the execution

of orders under regimental controul which it is in vain to look for elsewhere.

The Douro had been rendered navigable as high up as Castillo de Alva above the confluence of the Agueda ; a pontoon train of thirty-five pieces had been formed ; carts of a peculiar construction had been built to repair the great loss of mules during the retreat from Burgos, and a recruit of these animals was also obtained by emissaries who purchased them with English merchandize, even at Madrid, under the beards of the enemy, and at the very time when Clauzel was unable for want of transport to fill the magazines of Burgos. The ponderous iron camp-kettles of the soldiers had been laid aside for lighter vessels carried by men, the mules being destined to carry tents instead; it is, however, doubtful if these tents were really useful on a march in wet weather, because when soaked they became too heavy for the animal, and seldom arrived in time for use at the end of a march. Their greatest advantage was found when the soldiers halted for a few days. Beside these amendments many other changes and improvements had taken place, and the Anglo-Portuguese troops conscious of a superior organization, were more proudly confident than ever, while the French were again depressed by intelligence of the defection of the Prussians following on the disasters in Russia. Nor had the English general failed to amend the condition of those Spanish troops which the Cortez had placed at his disposal. By a strict and jealous watch over the application of the subsidy he had kept them clothed and fed during the winter, and now reaped the benefit by having several powerful bodies fit to act in conjunction with his own forces. Wherefore being thus prepared he was anxious to strike, anxious to forestall the effects of his Portuguese political difficulties as well as to keep pace with Napoleon's efforts in Germany, and his army was ready to take the field in April, but he could not concentrate before the green forage was fit for use, and deferred the execution of his plan until May. What that plan was and what the means for executing it shall now be shewn.

The relative strength of the contending armies in the Peninsula was no longer in favour of the French. Their force which at the termination of Wellington's retreat into Portugal was above two hundred and sixty thousand men and thirty-two thousand horses, two hundred and sixteen thousand being present with the eagles, was by Appendix, No. 18. the loss in subsequent operations, and by drafts for the army in Germany reduced in March, 1813, to two hundred and thirty-one thousand men and twenty-nine thousand horses. Thirty thousand of these were in hospital, and only one hundred and ninety-seven thousand men, including the reserve at Bayonne, were present with the eagles. Of this number sixty-eight thousand including sick, were in Aragon, Catalonia, and Valencia. The remainder with the exception of the ten thousand left at Madrid, were distributed on the northern line of communication, from the Tormes to Bayonne, and it has been already shewn how scattered and how occupied.

But Wellington had so well used the five months' cessation of active operations that nearly two hundred thousand allied troops were ready to take the field, and on each flank there was a British fleet, now a more effective aid than before, because the

French lines of retreat run parallel to, and near the
sea-coast on each side of Spain, and every part
opened by the advance of the allies would furnish
a fresh depôt for the subsistence of their armies.
This mass of troops was composed in the following
manner.

The first army under Copons nominally ten
thousand, really about six thousand strong, was
in Catalonia.

The second army under Elio was in Murcia
about twenty thousand, including the divisions of
Villa Campa, Bassecour, Duran, and Empecinado.

The Anglo-Sicilian army under Murray, near
Alicant, about sixteen thousand.

The third army under Del Parque, in the Morena
about twelve thousand.

The first army of reserve under the Conde d'Abispal, in Andalusia, about fifteen thousand.

The fourth army, under Castaños, which included
the Spanish divisions in Estremadura, Julian Sanchez' Partida and the Gallicians under Giron, the
Asturians under Porlier and Barceña, together with
the Partidas of Longa and Mina, likewise belonged
to this army and were mustered amongst its divisions. This army was computed at forty thousand
men, to which may be added the minor bands and
volunteers in various parts.

Lastly there was the noble Anglo-Portuguese
army which now furnished more than seventy thousand fighting men, with ninety pieces of artillery;
and the real difference between the French and
the allies was greater than the apparent difference. The French returns included officers,
sergeants, drummers, artillery-men, engineers, and
waggoners, whereas the allies' numbers were all

sabres and bayonets. Moreover this statement of
the French number was on the 15th of March, and
as there were drafts made by Napoleon after that
period, and as Clauzel and Foy's losses, and the
reserves at Bayonne must be deducted, it would be
probably more correct to assume that the whole
number of sabres and bayonets in June, was not
more than one hundred and sixty thousand, of
which one hundred and ten thousand were on the
northern line of invasion.

The campaign of 1812 had taught the English
general the strength of the French lines of defence,
especially on the Duero, which they had since entrenched in different parts, and most of the bridges
over it, he had himself destroyed in his retreat.
But for many reasons it was not advisable to
operate in the central provinces of Spain. The
country there was exhausted, the lines of supply
would be longer and more exposed, the army further removed from the sea, the Gallicians could not
be easily brought down to co-operate, the services
of the northern Partidas would not be so advantageous, and the ultimate result would be less decisive
than operations against the great line of communication with France ; wherefore against the northern
provinces he had early resolved to direct his attack
and had well considered how to evade those lines
which he could scarcely hope to force.

All the enemy's defences on the Lower Duero
could be turned by a movement on the right, across
the Upper Tormes, and from thence skirting the
mountains towards the Upper Duero ; but that line
although most consonant to the rules of art, because
the army would thus be kept in one mass, led
through a very difficult and wasted country, the

direct aid of the Gallicians must have been dispensed with, and moreover it was there the French
looked for the allies. Hence Wellington resolved
not to operate by his right, and with great skill and
dexterity, he had by the disposition of his troops in
winter quarters, by false reports and false movements masked his real intentions. For the gathering of the Partidas in the valley of the Tagus, the
demonstrations made in Estremadura and La Mancha
by Penn'e Villemur, Morillo and Del Parque's army,
together with the presence of Hill at Coria, that general's hold of the passes of Bejar, and the magazines
formed there, all intimated a design of moving
either by the valley of the Tagus or by the district
of Avila; and the great magazines collected at
Celerico, Viseu, Penamacor, Almeida, and Ciudad
Rodrigo, in no manner belied the other indications.
But half the army widely cantoned in the interior
of Portugal, apparently for the sake of subsistence
or health, was really so placed as to be in the
direction of the true line of operations which was
by the left through the Tras os Montes.

Wellington's plan was to pass the Duero, within
the Portuguese frontier, with a part of his army; to
ascend the right bank of that river towards Zamora,
and then crossing the Esla, to unite with the
Gallician forces, while the remainder of the army,
advancing from the Agueda, forced the passage of
the Tormes. By this great movement, which he
hoped to effect so suddenly that the king would
not have time to concentrate the French armies in
opposition, the front of the allies would be changed
to their right, the Duero and the Pisuerga would
be turned, and the enemy forced in confusion over
the Carion. Then with his powerful army well in

hand the English general could march in advance without fear, strong enough to fight and strong enough to turn the right flank of any position which the French might take up; and with this advantage also, that at each step he would gain additional help by the junction of the irregular Spanish forces until he gave his hand to the insurgents in Biscay, and every port opened would furnish him a new dépôt and magazines.

But in executing this movement the army would necessarily be divided into three separate divisions each too weak to beat the whole French force singly; the march of the centre division by the Tras os Montes, upon the nice execution of which the concentration of the whole depended, would be through an extremely difficult and mountainous country, and there were three great rivers to pass. The operation was therefore one of extreme delicacy requiring nice and extensive arrangements; yet there was not much danger to be apprehended from failure; because as each separate corps had a strong country to retire upon, the probable extent of the mischief would only be the loss of time, and the disadvantage of pursuing other operations when the harvest being ripe the French could easily keep in masses. The secret then was to hide the true plan as long as possible, to gain some marches for the centre corps, and by all means to keep the French so scattered and occupied by minor combinations, that they should be unable to assemble in time to profit from their central positions. Now the bridge equipage being prepared at Abrantes in the interior of Portugal was unknown, and gave no intimation of the real design, for the bullocks which drew it came with cars from

Spain to Lamego and from thence went down to
Abrantes; the free navigation of the Douro up to
the Agueda was more conducive to a movement by
the right, and it furnished abundance of large boats
wherewith to pass that river without creating any
suspicion from their presence; the wide cantonments of the allies permitted various changes of
quarters under the pretence of sickness, and the
troops thus gradually closed upon the Douro, within
the Portuguese frontier, unobserved of the enemy
who was likewise deceived by many reports purposely spread abroad. The menacing head which
Hill, and the Spaniards in southern Estremadura
and Andalusia, carried towards the valley of the
Tagus and towards the Avila district, also contributed to draw the enemy's attention away from the
true point of danger; but more than all other things
the vigorous excitement of the insurrection in the
north occupied the French, scattered their forces,
and rendered the success of the English general's
plan nearly certain.

Neither did lord Wellington fail to give ample
employment to Suchet's forces, for his wings were
spread for a long flight even to the Pyrennees, and
he had no desire to find that marshal's army joined
with the other French forces on the Ebro. The
lynx eyes of Napoleon had scanned this point of
war also, and both the king and Clauzel had received orders to establish the shortest and most
certain line of correspondence possible with Suchet,
because the emperor's plan contemplated the arrival
of the army of Aragon in the north, but Wellington
furnished a task for it elsewhere. Sir John Murray
as we have seen, had just repulsed the French at
Castalla, and general Frere's cavalry had joined the

Andalusian reserve under Abispal, but Elio with the
third army remained near Alicant and Wellington
destined Del Parque's army to join him.   This
with the Anglo-Sicilian army made more than fifty
thousand men, including the divisions of Duran,
Villa Campa, the Empecinado, and other partizans
always lying on Suchet's right flank and rear. Now
with such a force, or even half this number of
good troops, the simplest plan would have been to
turn Suchet's right flank and bring him to action
with his back to the sea ; but the Spanish armies
were not efficient for such work and Wellington's
instructions were adapted to the actual circumstances. To win the open part of the kingdom, to
obtain a permanent footing on the coast beyond the
Ebro, and to force the enemy from the lower line
of that river by acting in conjunction with the
Catalans, these were the three objects which Wellington proposed to reach and in the following manner. Murray was to sail against Taragona, to save it
Suchet would have to weaken his army in Valencia;
Elio and Del Parque might then seize that kingdom.
If Taragona fell, good. If the French proved too
strong, Murray could return instantly by sea, and
secure possession of the country gained by the
Spanish generals. These last were however to
remain strictly on the defensive until Murray's
operations drew Suchet away, for they were not
able to fight alone, and above all things it was
necessary to avoid a defeat which would leave the
French general free to move to the aid of the
king.

The force necessary to attack Taragona Wellington judged at ten thousand, and if Murray could
not embark that number there was another mode of

operating.　Some Spanish divisions, to go by sea,
were then to reinforce Copons in Catalonia and
enable him to hold the country between Taragona,
Tortoza, and Lerida; meanwhile Murray and Elio
were to advance against Suchet in front, and Del
Parque in conjunction with the Portuguese troops
to turn his right flank by Requeña; and this operation was to be repeated until the allies communicated with Copons by their left, the partizans advancing in proportion and cutting off all communication with the northern parts of Spain.　Thus
in either case Suchet would be kept away from the
Upper Ebro, and there was no reason to expect any
interruption from that quarter.

But Wellington was not aware that the infantry of
the army of Portugal were beyond the Ebro; the spies
deceived by the multitude of detachments passing
in and out of the Peninsula supposed the divisions
which reinforced Clauzel to be fresh conscripts from
France; the arrangements for the opening of the
campaign were therefore made in the expectation
of meeting a very powerful force in Leon.　Hence
Freire's cavalry, and the Andalusian reserve
under the Conde de Abispal, received orders to
march upon Almaraz, to pass the Tagus there by a
pontoon bridge which was established for them,
and then crossing the Gredos by Bejar or Mombeltran, to march upon Valladolid while the Partidas
of that quarter should harass the march of Leval
from Madrid.　Meanwhile the Spanish troops in
Estremadura were to join those forces on the
Agueda which were destined to force the passage
of the Tormes.　The Gallicians under Giron were
to come down to the Esla, and unite with the
corps destined to pass that river and turn the line

of the Duero. Thus seventy thousand Portuguese and British, eight thousand Spaniards from Estremadura, and twelve thousand Gallicians, that is to say, ninety thousand fighting men would be suddenly placed on a new front, and marching abreast against the surprised and separated masses of the enemy would drive them refluent to the Pyrennees. A grand design and grandly it was executed! For high in heart and strong of hand Wellington's veterans marched to the encounter, the glories of twelve victories played about their bayonets, and he the leader so proud and confident, that in passing the stream which marks the frontier of Spain, he rose in his stirrups and waving his hand cried out " Farewell Portugal !"

But while straining every nerve, and eager to strike, as well to escape from the Portuguese politics as to keep pace with Napoleon's efforts in Germany, the English general was mortified by having again to discuss the question of a descent on Italy. Lord William Bentinck had relinquished his views upon that country with great reluctance, and now, thinking affairs more favourable than ever, again proposed to land at Naples, and put forward the duke of Orleans or the arch-duke Francis. He urged in favour of this project the weak state of Murat's kingdom, the favourable disposition of the inhabitants, the offer of fifteen thousand auxiliary Russians made by admiral Grieg, the shock which would be given to Napoleon's power, and the more effectual diversion in favour of Spain. He supported his opinion by an intercepted letter of the queen of Naples to Napoleon, and by other authentic documents, and thus, at the moment of execution, Wellington's vast plans were to be disarranged to meet a new scheme of war which he had already discussed and disapproved of, and which, however promising in itself, would inevitably divide the power of England and weaken the operations in both countries.

His reply was decisive.   His opinion on the state of affairs in Sicily was, he said, not changed, by the intercepted letters, as Murat evidently thought himself strong enough to attack the allies.   Lord William Bentinck should not land in Italy with less than forty thousand men of all arms perfectly equipped, since that army would have to depend upon its own means and to overcome all opposition before it could expect the people to aid or even to cease to oppose it.   The information stated that the people looked for protection from the French and they preferred England to Austria.   There could be no doubt of this, the Austrians would demand provisions and money and would insist upon governing them in return, whereas the English would as elsewhere defray their own expenses and probably give a subsidy in addition.   The south of Italy was possibly for many reasons the best place next to the Spanish Peninsula for the operations of a British army, and it remained for the government to choose whether they would adopt an attack on the former upon such a scale as he had alluded to.   But of one thing they might be certain, that if it were commenced on a smaller scale, or with any other intention than to persevere to the last, and by raising, feeding, and clothing armies of the natives, the plan would fail and the troops would re-embark with loss and disgrace.

This remonstrance at last fixed the wavering judgment of the ministers, and Wellington was

enabled to proceed with his own plans. He designed to open the campaign in the beginning of
May, and as the green forage was well advanced, on
the 21st of April, he directed Murray, Del Parque,
Elio, and Copons to commence their operations on
the eastern coast; Abispal and Freire were already
in march and expected at Almaraz on the 24th;
the Spanish divisions of Estremadura had come up
to the Coa, and the divisions of the Anglo-Portuguese force were gradually closing to the front.
But heavy rains broke up the roads, and the cum-
brous pontoon train being damaged, on its way
from the interior, did not reach Sabugal before the
13th and was not repaired before the 15th. Thus
the opening of the campaign was delayed, yet the
check proved of little consequence, for on the
French side nothing was prepared to meet the
danger.

Napoleon had urged the king to send his heavy
baggage and stores to the rear and to fix his hospitals and dépôts at Burgos, Vittoria, Pampeluna,
Tolosa, and San Sebastian. In neglect of this the
impediments remained with the armies, the sick
were poured along the communications, and in
disorder thrown upon Clauzel at the moment when
that general was scarcely able to make head against
the northern insurrection.

Napoleon had early and clearly fixed the king's
authority as generalissimo and forbad him to exercise his monarchical authority towards the French
armies. Joseph was at this moment in high dispute with all his generals upon those very points.

Napoleon had directed the king to enlarge and
strengthen the works of Burgos castle and to form
magazines in that place, and at Santona, for the

use of the armies in the field. At this time no
magazines had been formed at either place, and
although a commencement had been made to
strengthen the castle of Burgos, it was not yet
capable of sustaining four hours' bombardment and
offered no support for the armies.

Napoleon had desired that a more secure and
shorter line of correspondence than that by Zaragoza should be established with Suchet ; for his
plan embraced though it did not prescribe the
march of that general upon Zarogoza, and he had
warned the king repeatedly how dangerous it
would be to have Suchet isolated and unconnected
with the northern operations. Nevertheless the
line of correspondence remained the same and the
allies possessed the means of excising Suchet's
army from the operations in the north.

Napoleon had long and earnestly urged the king
to put down the northern insurrection in time to
make head against the allies on the Tormes. Now
when the English general was ready to act, that
insurrection was in full activity, and all the army
of the north and the greatest part of the army of
Portugal was employed to suppress it instead of
being on the lower Duero.

Napoleon had clearly explained to the king the
necessity of keeping his troops concentrated towards the Tormes in an offensive position, and he
had desired that Madrid might be held in such a
manner that it could be abandoned in a moment.
The campaign was now being opened, the French
armies were scattered, Leval was encumbered at
Madrid, with a part of the civil administration,
with large stores and parcs of artillery, and with
the care of families attached to Joseph's court,

while the other generals were stretching their imaginations to devise which of the several projects open to him Wellington would adopt. Would he force the passage of the Tormes and the Duero with his whole army, and thus turn the French right? Would he march straight upon Madrid either by the district of Avila or by the valley of the Tagus or by both; and would he then operate against the north, or upon Zaragoza, or towards the south in cooperation with the Anglo-Sicilians? Every thing was vague, uncertain, confused.

The generals complained that the king's conduct was not military, and Napoleon told him if he would command an army he must give himself up entirely to it, thinking of nothing else; but Joseph was always demanding gold when he should have trusted to iron. His skill was unequal to the arrangements and combinations for taking an initiatory and offensive position, and he could neither discover nor force his adversary to show his real design. Hence the French armies were thrown upon a timid defensive system, and every movement of the allies necessarily produced alarm, and the dislocation of troops without an object. The march of Del Parque's army towards Alcaraz, and that of the Spanish divisions from Estremadura, towards the Agueda, in the latter end of April were judged to be the commencement of a general movement against Madrid, because the first was covered by the advance of some cavalry into La Mancha, and the second by the concentration of the Partidas, in the valley of the Tagus. Thus the whole French army was shaken by the demonstration of a few horsemen, for when Leval took the alarm, Gazan marched towards the Guadarama

with three divisions, and D'Erlon gathered the
army of the centre around Segovia.

Early in May a fifth division of the army of
Portugal was employed on the line of communication at Pampliega, Burgos, and Briviesca, and
Reille remained at Valladolid with only one division
of infantry and his guns, his cavalry being on the
Esla.   D'Erlon was then at Segovia and Gazan at
Arevalo, Conroux's division was at Avila, and Leval
still at Madrid with outposts at Toledo.   The king
who was at Valladolid could not therefore concentrate more than thirty-five thousand infantry on the
Duero.   He had indeed nine thousand excellent cavalry and one hundred pieces of artillery, but with
such dispositions to concentrate for a battle in
advance was not to be thought of, and the first
decided movement of the allies was sure to roll
his scattered forces back in confusion.   The lines
of the Tormes and the Duero were effaced from
the system of operations.

About the middle of May, D'Armagnac's division
of the army of the centre came to Valladolid,
Villatte's division of the army of the south reinforced by some cavalry occupied the line of the
Tormes from Alba to Ledesma.   Daricau's, Digeon's, and D'Armagnac's divisions were at Zamora,
Toro, and other places on both sides of the Duero,
and Reille's cavalry was still on the Esla.   The
front of the French was thus defined by these
rivers, for the left was covered by the Tormes, the
centre by the Duero, the right by the Esla.   Gazan's head-quarters were at Arevalo, D'Erlon's at
Segovia, and the point of concentration was at
Valladolid ; but Conroux was at Avila, and Leval
being still at Madrid was thrown entirely out of

the circle of operations. At this moment Wellington
entered upon what has been in England called, not
very appropriately, the march to Vittoria. That
march was but one portion of the action. The concentration of the army on the banks of the Duero
was the commencement, the movement towards the
Ebro and the passage of that river was the middle,
the battle of Vittoria was the catastrophe, and the
crowning of the Pyrennees the end of the splendid
drama.

CHAPTER VII.

IN the latter part of April the Spanish troops from
Estremadura being assembled on the Tormes near
Almada, Carlos d'España's division moved to
Miranda del Castanar, and every thing was ready to
open the campaign when an unexpected and formidable danger menacing ruin arose. Some specie
sent from England had enabled the general to pay
up the British soldiers' arrears to November 1812,
but the Portuguese troops were still neglected by
their government, a whole year's pay was due
to them, a suspicion that a systematic difference
in this respect was to be established, pervaded
their minds, and at the same time many regiments
which had been raised for a limited period and
whose term of service was now expired, murmured
for their discharge, which could not be legally refused. The moment was critical, but Wellington
applied suitable remedies. He immediately threatened to intercept the British subsidy for the payment
of the troops which brought the Portuguese regency
to its senses, and he then made an appeal to the
honour and patriotism of the Portuguese soldiers
whose time had expired. Such an appeal is never
made in vain to the poorer classes of any nation;
one and all those brave men remained in the service notwithstanding the shameful treatment they

had endured from their government. This noble emotion would seem to prove that Beresford, whose system of military reform was chiefly founded upon severity, might have better attained his object in another manner; but harshness is the essence of the aristocratic principle of government, and the marshal only moved in the straight path marked out for him by the policy of the day.

When this dangerous affair was terminated Castaños returned to Gallicia, and the British cavalry, of the left wing, which had wintered about the Mondego crossed the Duero, some at Oporto some near Lamego, and entered the Tras os Montes. The Portuguese cavalry had been already quartered all the winter in that province, and the enemy supposed that Sylveira would as formerly advance from Braganza to connect the Gallicians with the allies. But Sylveira was then commanding an infantry division on the Agueda, and a very different power was menacing the French on the side of Braganza. For about the middle of May the cavalry were followed by many divisions of infantry, and by the pontoon equipage, thus forming with the horsemen and artillery a mass of more than forty thousand men under general Graham. The infantry and guns being rapidly placed on the right of the Duero by means of large boats assembled between Lamego and Castello de Alva, near the mouth of the Agueda, marched in several columns towards the lower Esla; the cavalry moved down to the same point by Braganza.

On the 20th Hill came to Bejar with the second division, and on the 22d of May, Graham being well advanced, Wellington quitted his head-quarters at Freneda and put his right wing in motion to-

wards the Tormes.   It consisted of five divisions of
Anglo-Portuguese and Spanish infantry, and five
brigades of cavalry, including Julian Sanchez'
horsemen, the whole forming with the artillery a
mass of from twenty-five to thirty thousand men.
The right under general Hill moved from Bejar
upon Alba de Tormes, the left under Wellington
himself by Matilla upon Salamanca.

On the 24th Villatte withdrew his detachment
from Ledesma, and on the 26th at ten o'clock in
the morning the heads of the allied columns with
admirable concert appeared on all the different
routes leading to the Tormes.   Morillo's and Long's
cavalry menaced Alba, Hill coming from Tamames
bent towards the fords above Salamanca, and Wellington coming from Matilla marched straight
against that city.

Villatte, a good officer, barricaded the bridge
and the streets, sent his baggage to the rear,
called in his detachment from Alba, and being
resolved to discover the real force of his enemy
waited for their approaching masses on the heights
above the ford of Santa Marta.   Too long he
waited, for the ground on the left side of the river
had enabled Wellington to conceal the movements,
and already Fane's horsemen with six guns were
passing the ford at Santa Marta in Villatte's rear,
while Victor Alten's cavalry removed the barricades
on the bridge and pushed through the town to attack
him in front.   The French general being thus suddenly pressed gained the heights of Cabrerizos,
marching towards Babila Fuente, before Fane got
over the river; but he had still to pass the defiles
of Aldea Lengua and was overtaken by both
columns of cavalry.

The guns opening upon the French squares killed thirty or forty men, and the English horsemen charged, but horsemen are no match for such infantry whose courage and discipline nothing could quell; they fell before the round shot, and nearly one hundred died in the ranks without a wound, from the intolerable heat, yet the cavalry made no impression on those dauntless soldiers, and in the face of thirty thousand enemies they made their way to Babila Fuente where they were joined by general Lefol with the troops from Alba, and finally the whole disappeared from the sight of their admiring and applauding opponents. Nevertheless two hundred had sunk dead in the ranks, a like number unable to keep up were made prisoners, and a leading gun having been overturned in the defile of Aldea Lengua, six others were retarded and the whole fell in the allies' hands together with their tumbrils.

The line of the Tormes being thus gained the allied troops were on the 27th and 28th pushed forward with their left towards Miranda and Zamora, and their right towards Toro; so placed the latter covered the communications with Ciudad Rodrigo while the former approached the point on the Duero where it was proposed to throw the bridge for communication with Graham's corps. This done Wellington left general Hill in command, and went off suddenly, for he was uneasy about his combinations on the Esla. On the 29th he passed the Duero at Miranda, by means of a basket slung on a rope which was stretched from rock to rock, the river foaming several hundred feet below. The 30th he reached Carvajales.

Graham had met with many difficulties in his

march through the rugged Tras os Montes, and
though the troops were now close to the Esla
stretching from Carvajales to Tabara, and their
left was in communication with the Gallicians who
were coming down to Benevente, the combination
had been in some measure thwarted by the difficulty of crossing the Esla. The general combination required that river to be passed on the 29th,
at which time the right wing, continuing its march
from the Tormes without halting, could have been
close to Zamora, and the passage of the Duero
would have been insured. The French armies
would then have been entirely surprised and separated, and some of their divisions overtaken and
beaten. They were indeed still ignorant that a
whole army was on the Esla, but the opposite
bank of that river was watched by picquets of
cavalry and infantry, the stream was full and rapid,
the banks steep, the fords hard to find, difficult,
and deep, with stony beds, and the alarm had
spread from the Tormes through all the cantonments.

At daybreak on the 31st some squadrons of hussars, with infantry holding by their stirrups, entered
the stream at the ford of Almendra, and at the same
time Graham approached the right bank with all
his forces. A French picquet of thirty men was
surprised in the village of Villa Perdrices by the
hussars, the pontoons were immediately laid down,
and the columns commenced passing, but several
men, even of the cavalry, had been drowned at the
fords.

On the 1st of June, while the rear was still on
the Esla, the head of the allies entered Zamora
which the French evacuated after destroying the

bridge. They retired upon Toro, and the next day

having destroyed the bridge there also, they again
fell back, but their rear-guard was overtaken near
the village of Morales by the hussar brigade under
colonel Grant. Their horsemen immediately passed
a bridge and swamp under a cannonade, and then
facing about in two lines, gave battle, whereupon
major Roberts with the tenth regiment, supported
by the fifteenth, broke both the lines with one
charge and pursued them for two miles, and they
lost above two hundred men, but finally rallied on
the infantry reserves.

The junction of the allies' wings on the Duero
was now secure, for that river was fordable, and
Wellington had also, in anticipation of failure on
one point, made arrangements for forming a boat
bridge below the confluence of the Esla; and he
could also throw his pontoons without difficulty at
Toro, and even in advance, because Julian Sanchez
had surprised a cavalry picquet at Castronuño on
the left bank, and driven the French outposts from
the fords of Pollos. But the enemy's columns were
concentrating, it might be for a battle, wherefore
the English general halted the 3d to bring the
Gallicians in conjunction on his left, and to close
up his own rear which had been retarded by the
difficulty of passing the Esla. The two divisions
of his right wing, namely, the second and light
division, passed the Duero on the morning of the
3rd, the artillery and baggage by a ford, the infantry at the bridge of Toro, which was ingeniously
repaired by the lieutenant of engineers Pringle, who
dropped ladders at each side of the broken arch, and
then laid planks from one to the other just above the

water level. Thus the English general mastered
the line of the Duero, and those who understand
war may say whether it was an effort worthy of the
man and his army.

Let them trace all the combinations, follow the
movement of Graham's columns, some of which
marched one hundred and fifty, some more than
two hundred and fifty miles, through the wild
districts of the Tras os Montes. Through those
regions, held to be nearly impracticable even for
small corps, forty thousand men, infantry, cavalry,
artillery, and pontoons, had been carried and
placed as if by a supernatural power upon the
Esla, before the enemy knew even that they were
in movement! Was it fortune or skill that pre-
sided? Not fortune, for the difficulties were such
that Graham arrived later on the Esla than Wellington intended, and yet so soon, that the enemy
could make no advantage of the delay. For had
the king even concentrated his troops behind the
Esla on the 31st, the Gallicians would still have been
at Benevente and reinforced by Penne Villemur's
cavalry which had marched with Graham's corps,
and the Asturians would have been at Leon on the
Upper Esla which was fordable. Then the final
passage of that river could have been effected by a
repetition of the same combinations on a smaller
scale, because the king's army would not have
been numerous enough to defend the Duero against
Hill, the Lower Esla against Wellington, and the
Upper Esla against the Spaniards at the same time.
Wellington had also, as we have seen, prepared
the means of bringing Hill's corps or any part of
it over the Duero below the confluence of the Esla,

and all these combinations, these surprising exertions had been made merely to gain a fair field of battle.

But if Napoleon's instructions had been ably worked out by the king during the winter, this great movement could not have succeeded, for the insurrection in the north would have been crushed in time, or at least so far quelled, that sixty thousand French infantry, ten thousand cavalry, and one hundred pieces of artillery would have been disposable, and such a force held in an offensive position on the Tormes would probably have obliged Wellington to adopt a different plan of campaign. If concentrated between the Duero and the Esla it would have baffled him on that river, because operations which would have been effectual against thirty-five thousand infantry would have been powerless against sixty thousand. Joseph indeed complained that he could not put down the insurrection in the north, that he could not feed such large armies, that a thousand obstacles arose on every side which he could not overcome, in fine that he could not execute his brother's instructions. They could have been executed notwithstanding. Activity, the taking time by the forelock, would have quelled the insurrection; and for the feeding of the troops, the boundless plains called the " *Tierras de Campos,*" where the armies were now operating, were covered with the ripening harvest; the only difficulty was to subsist that part of the French army not engaged in the northern provinces during the winter. Joseph could not find the means though Soult told him they were at hand, because the difficulties of his situation overpowered him; they would not have overpowered Napoleon, but

the difference between a common general and a
great captain is immense, the one is victorious
when the other is defeated.

The field was now clear for the shock of battle,
but the forces on either side were unequally
matched. Wellington had ninety thousand men,
with more than one hundred pieces of artillery.
Twelve thousand were cavalry, and the British and
Portuguese present with the colours, were, including
serjeants and drummers, above seventy thousand
sabres and bayonets ; the rest of the army was
Spanish. Besides this mass there were the irregulars on the wings, Sanchez' horsemen, a thousand strong, on the right beyond the Duero ; Porlier,
Barcena, Salazar and Manzo on the left between
the Upper Esla and the Carion. Saornil had moved
upon Avila, the Empecinado was hovering about
Leval. Finally the reserve of Andalusia had crossed
the Tagus at Almaraz on the 30th, and numerous
minor bands were swarming round as it advanced.
On the other hand though the French could collect
nine or ten thousand horsemen and one hundred
guns, their infantry was less than half the number
of the allies, being only thirty-five thousand strong
exclusive of Leval. Hence the way to victory was
open, and on the 4th Wellington marched forward
with a conquering violence.

The intrusive monarch was in no condition to
stem or to evade a torrent of war, the depth and
violence of which he was even now ignorant of,
and a slight sketch of his previous operations will
shew that all his dispositions were made in the
dark and only calculated to bring him into trouble.
Early in May he would have marched the army of
the centre to the Upper Duero when Leval's reports

checked the movement. On the 15th of that
month a spy sent to Bejar by D'Erlon, brought
intelligence that a great number of country carts
had been collected there and at Placentia, to follow
the troops in a march upon Talavera, but after
two days were sent back to their villages; that fifty
mules had been purchased at Bejar and sent to
Ciudad Rodrigo; that about the same time the first
and fourth divisions and the German cavalry had
moved from the interior towards the frontier, saying
they were going, the first to Zamora, and the last
to Fuente Guinaldo; that many troops were already
gathered at Ciudad Rodrigo under Wellington and
Castaños; that the divisions at Coria and Placentia
were expected there, the reserves of Andalusia were
in movement, and the pass of Baños which had
been before retrenched and broken up was now
repaired; that the English soldiers were paid their
arrears, and every body said a grand movement
would commence on the 12th. All this was extremely accurate, but with the exception of the
march to Zamora, which seemed to be only a blind,
the information obtained indicated the principal
movement as against the Tormes, and threw no light
upon the English general's real design.

On the other flank Reille's cavalry under Boyer,
having made an exploring sweep round by Astorga,
La Baneza and Benevente, brought intelligence that
a Gallician expedition was embarking for America,
that another was to follow, and that several English
divisions were also embarking in Portugal. The
23d of May a report from the same quarter gave
notice that Salazar and Manzo were with seven
hundred horsemen on the Upper Esla, that Porlier
was coming from the Asturias to join them with

two thousand five hundred men, and Giron with six thousand Gallicians had reached Astorga; but it was uncertain if Sylveira's cavalry would come from Braganza to connect the left of the English with the Gallicians as it had done the year before.

Thus on the 24th of May the French were still entirely in the dark with respect to Graham's movement, and although it was known the 26th at Valladolid, that Wellington had troops in the country beyond the Esla, it was not considered a decisive movement because the head-quarters were still at Freneda. However on the 29th Reille united his cavalry at Valderas, passed the Esla, entered Benevente and sent patroles towards Tobara and Carvajales; from their reports and other sources he understood the whole allied army was on the Esla, and as his detachments were closely followed by the British scouting parties, he recrossed the Esla and broke the bridge of Castro Gonzalo, leaving his light horsemen to watch it. But the delay in the passage of the Esla, after Graham had reached Carvajales, made Reille doubt both the strength of the allies and their inclination to cross that river. He expected the main attack on the Tormes, and proposed in conjunction with Daricau's infantry, and Digeon's dragoons, then at Toro and Zamora, to defend the Duero and the Lower Esla, leaving the Gallicians, whose force he despised, to pass the Upper Esla at their peril.

D'Armagnac's division was now at Rio Seco, and Maucune's division, which had been spread along the road to Burgos, was ordered to concentrate at Palencia on the Carion, but meanwhile Gazan on the other flank of the French position was equally deceived by the movements of the English general.

The 7th of May he heard from the Tormes that the allies' preparations indicated a movement towards that river. Leval wrote from Madrid that he had abandoned Toledo because fifteen thousand English and ten thousand Spaniards were to advance by the valley of the Tagus, that rations had been ordered at Escalona for Long's English cavalry, and that magazines were formed at Bejar. At the same time from a third quarter came news that three divisions would pass the Duero to join the Gallicians and march upon Valladolid.

Gazan rightly judging that the magazines at Bejar were to supply Hill and the Spaniards, in their movement to join Wellington, expected at first that the whole would operate by the Esla, but on the 14th fresh reports changed this opinion; he then judged Hill would advance by the Puente Congosto upon Avila, to cut Leval off from the army, while Wellington attacked Salamanca. On the 24th however his doubts vanished. Villatte told him that Wellington was over the Agueda, Graham over the Lower Douro, and at the same time Daricau, writing from Zamora, told him that Graham's cavalry had already reached Alcanizas, only one march from the Esla. Conroux was instantly directed to march from Avila to Arevalo, Tilly to move with the cavalry of the army of the south, from Madrigal towards the Trabancos, Daricau to send a brigade to Toro, and Leval to come over the Guadarama pass and join D'Erlon at Segovia.

On the 26th, Gazan thinking Wellington slow and crediting a report that he was sick and travelling in a carriage, relapsed into doubt. He now judged the passage of the Agueda a feint, thought the allies' operations would be in mass towards the Esla, and was positively assured by his emissaries that Hill would move by the Puente Congosto against Segovia. However on the 27th he heard of the passage of the Tormes and of Villatte's retreat, whereupon evacuating Arevalo he fixed his head-quarters at Rueda, and directed Conroux who was marching upon Arevalo, and so hastily that he left a moveable column behind him on the Upper Tormes, to come to the Trabancos.

Gazan at first designed to take post behind that river but there was no good position there, and the 28th he rallied Conroux's, Rey's, and Villatte's infantry and Tilly's cavalry behind the Zapardiel. Daricau's division was meanwhile concentrated at Toro, and Digeon's at Zamora; a bridge-head was commenced at Tordesillas, which was the point of retreat, and guards were placed at Pollos where the fords of the Duero were very low though as yet impracticable. These movements were made in tranquillity, for Hill had no desire by driving the French over the Duero to increase the number of their troops on the Esla. However on the 30th Gazan, hearing that Hill was advancing and that the troops on the Esla were likely to attempt the passage of that river, crossed the Duero in the night and took post at Tordesillas, intending to concentrate the whole army of the south on the right of that river; but Leval, though he had quitted Madrid on the 27th, was not yet arrived and a large artillery convoy, the ministers and Spanish families, and the pictures from the palace of Madrid were likewise on the road from that capital by the Segovia passes.

At this time the army of Portugal and D'Armagnac's division was extended from the Esla to the

Carion, the king's guards were at Valladolid, and D'Erlon was in march to the Puente Duero, from Segovia and Sepulveda, yet slowly and apparently not aware of the crisis. Meanwhile the passage of the Esla had been effected, and hence if that river had been crossed at the time fore-calculated by Wellington, and a rapid push made upon Placentia and Valladolid, while Hill marched upon Rueda, the whole French army might have been caught in what Napoleon calls " *flagrante delicto*" and destroyed. And even now it would seem that Wellington could have profited more by marching, than by halting at Toro on the 3d, for though Leval's troops and part of the army of the centre were then between the Puente Duero and Valladolid, D'Erlon had left a large division at Tudela de Duero to protect the arrival of the convoy from Madrid, which had not yet crossed the Duero ; another great convoy was still on the left bank of the lower Pisuerga, and the parcs of the armies of Portugal and of the south were waiting on the right bank of that river, until the first convoy had passed over the Carion. Nevertheless it was prudent to gather well to a head first, and the general combinations had been so profoundly made that the evil day for the French was only deferred.

On the 30th Joseph's design was to oppose Wellington's principal force with the army of the south, while the army of the centre held the rest in check, the army of Portugal to aid either as the case might be ; and such was his infatuation as to his real position, that even now, from the Duero, he was pressing upon his brother the immediate establishment of a civil Spanish administration for the provinces behind the Ebro, as the only remedy for the insurrection, and for the rendering of the army of the north disposable. He even demanded an order from the emperor to draw Clauzel's troops away from the Ebro, that he might drive the allies back to the Coa, and take the long-urged offensive position towards Portugal, Napoleon being then at Dresden and Wellington on the Duero !

On the 2d when the allies had passed the Esla, the king, who expected them at Toro the 1st, became disturbed to find his front unmolested, and concluded, as he had received no letter from Reille, that Wellington had cut his communication, turned his right, and was marching towards the Carion. His alarm was considerable and with reason, but in the evening of the 2d he heard from Reille, who had retired unmolested to Rio Seco and there rallied D'Armagnac's troops, but Maucune's division was still in march from different parts to concentrate at Palencia. The halt of the 3d was therefore to the profit of the French, for during that time they received the Madrid convoy and insured the concentration of all their troops, recovering even Conroux's moveable column which joined Leval near Olmedo. They also destroyed the bridges of Tudela and Puente Duero on the Duero, and that of Simancas and Cabeçon on the Pisuerga, and they passed their convoys over the Carion, directing them, under escort of Casa Palacios' Spanish division, upon Burgos.

The army of the south now moved upon Torre-lobaton and Penaflor, the army of the centre upon Duenas, the army of Portugal upon Palencia ; and the spirits of all were raised by intelligence of the emperor's victory at Lutzen, and by a report that the Toulon fleet had made a successful descent on

Sicily. It would appear that Napoleon certainly
contemplated an attack upon that island, and lord
William Bentinck thought it would be successful,
but it was prevented by Murat's discontent, who
instead of attacking fell off from Napoleon and
opened a negociation with the British.

The 4th Wellington moved in advance, his
bridge of communication was established at Pollos,
and considerable stores of ammunition were formed
at Valladolid; some had also been taken at Zamora,
and the cavalry flankers captured large magazines
of grain at Arevalo. Towards the Carion the
allies marched rapidly by parallel roads, and in
compact order, the Gallicians on the extreme left,
Morillo and Julian Sanchez on the extreme right,
and the English general expected the enemy would
make a stand behind that river, but the report of
the prisoners and the hasty movement of the French
columns soon convinced him that they were in full
retreat for Burgos. On the 6th all the French
armies were over the Carion, Reille had even
reached Palencia on the 4th and there rallied
Maucune's division, and a brigade of light cavalry
which had been employed on the communications.

Although the king's force was now about fifty-five
thousand fighting men, exclusive of his Spanish division, which was escorting the convoys and baggage, he did not judge the Carion a good position
and retired behind the upper Pisuerga, desiring if
possible to give battle there. He sent Jourdan to
examine the state of Burgos castle, and expedited
fresh letters, for he had already written from Valladolid on the 27th and 30th of May, to Foy, Sarrut,
and Clauzel, calling them towards the plains of
Burgos; and others to Suchet directing him to

march immediately upon Zaragoza and hoping he was already on his way there ; but Suchet was then engaged in Catalonia, Clauzel's troops were on the borders of Aragon, Foy and Palombini's Italians were on the coast of Guipuscoa, and Sarrut's division was pursuing Longa in the Montaña.

Joseph was still unacquainted with his enemy. Higher than seventy or eighty thousand he did not estimate the allied forces, and he was desirous of fighting them on the elevated plains of Burgos. But more than one hundred thousand men were before and around him. For all the Partidas of the Asturias and the Montaña were drawing together on his right, Julian Sanchez and the Partidas of Castile were closing on his left, and Abispal with the reserve and Frere's cavalry had already passed the Gredos mountains and were in full march for Valladolid. Nevertheless the king was sanguine of success if he could rally Clauzel's and Foy's divisions in time, and his despatches to the former were frequent and urgent. Come with the infantry of the army of Portugal ! Come with the army of the north and we shall drive the allies over the Duero ! Such was his cry to Clauzel, and again he urged his political schemes upon his brother; but he was not a statesman to advise Napoleon nor a general to contend with Wellington, his was not the military genius, nor were his the arrangements that could recover the initiatory movement at such a crisis and against such an adversary.

While the king was on the Pisuerga he received Jourdan's report. The castle of Burgos was untenable, there were no magazines of provisions, the new works were quite unfinished, and they commanded the old which were unable to hold

out a day; of Clauzel's and Foy's divisions nothing had been heard. It was resolved to retire
behind the Ebro. All the French outposts in the
Bureba and Montaña were immediately withdrawn,
and the great dépôt of Burgos was evacuated upon
Vittoria, which was thus encumbered with the artillery dépôts of Madrid, of Valladolid, and of
Burgos, and with the baggage and stores of so
many armies and so many fugitive families; and
at this moment also arrived from France a convoy
of treasure which had long waited for escort at
Bayonne.

Meanwhile the tide of war flowed onwards with
terrible power. The allies had crossed the Carion
on the 7th, and Joseph quitting Torquemada had
retired by the high road to Burgos with his left
wing composed of the army of the south and
centre, while Reille with that of Portugal forming
the right wing moved by Castro Xerez. But Wellington following hard, and conducting his operations continually on the same principle, pushed his
left wing and the Gallicians along bye-roads, and
passed the upper Pisuerga on the 8th, 9th, and
10th. Having thus turned the line of the Pisuerga
entirely, and outflanked Reille, he made a short
journey the 11th and halted the 12th with his left
wing, for he had outmarched his supplies, and
had to arrange the farther feeding of his troops in
a country wide of his line of communication.
Nevertheless he pushed his right wing under
general Hill along the main road to Burgos, resolved to make the French yield the castle or fight
for the possession, and meanwhile Julian Sanchez
acting beyond the Arlanzan cut off small posts
and straggling detachments.

Reille had regained the great road to Burgos on
the 9th, and was strongly posted behind the Hormaza stream, his right near Hormillas, his left on
the Arlanzan, barring the way to Burgos ; the other
two armies were in reserve behind Estepar, and in
this situation they had remained for three days and
were again cheered by intelligence of Napoleon's
victory at Bautzen and the consequent armistice.
But on the 12th Wellington's columns came up
and the light division preceded by Grant's hussars
and Ponsonby's dragoons, immediately turned the
French right, while the rest of the troops attacked
the whole range of heights from Hormillas to
Estepar. Reille, whose object was to make the
allies shew their force, seeing their horsemen in
rear of his right flank while his front was so
strongly menaced, made for the bridge of Baniel
on the Arlanzan ; then Gardiner's horse-artillery
raked his columns, and captain Milles of the fourteenth dragoons charging, took some prisoners and
one of his guns which had been disabled. Meanwhile
the right of the allies pressing forward towards the
bridge of Baniel endeavoured to cut off the retreat,
but the French repelled the minor attacks with the
utmost firmness, bore the fire of the artillery without shrinking, and evading the serious attacks by
their rapid yet orderly movement, finally passed
the river with a loss of only thirty men killed and
a few taken.

The three French armies being now covered by the
Urbel and Arlanzan rivers, which were swelled by
the rain, could not be easily attacked, and the stores
of Burgos were removed ; but in the night Joseph
again retreated along the high road by Briviesca
to Pancorbo, into which place he threw a garrison

of six hundred men. The castle of Burgos was prepared also for destruction, and whether from hurry,
or negligence, or want of skill, the mines exploded
outwards, and at the very moment when a column
of infantry was defiling under the castle. Several
streets were laid in ruins, thousands of shells and
other combustibles which had been left in the place
were ignited and driven upwards with a horrible
crash, the hills rocked above the devoted column,
and a shower of iron, timber, and stony fragments
falling on it, in an instant destroyed more than three
hundred men! Fewer deaths might have sufficed
to determine the crisis of a great battle!

But such an art is war! So fearful is the consequence of error, so terrible the responsibility of
a general. Strongly and wisely did Napoleon speak
when he told Joseph, that if he would command,
he must give himself up entirely to the business,
labouring day and night, thinking of nothing else.
Here was a noble army driven like sheep before
prowling wolves, yet in every action the inferior
generals had been prompt and skilful, the soldiers
brave, ready and daring, firm and obedient in the
most trying circumstances of battle. Infantry,
artillery, and cavalry, all were excellent and numerous, and the country strong and favourable for
defence; but that soul of armies, the mind of a
great commander was wanting, and the Esla, the
Tormes, the Duero, the Carion, the Pisuerga, the
Arlanzan, seemed to be dried up, the rocks, the
mountains, the deep ravines to be levelled. Clauzel's strong positions, Dubreton's thundering castle,
had disappeared like a dream, and sixty thousand
veteran soldiers though willing to fight at every
step, were hurried with all the tumult and con-

fusion of defeat across the Ebro. Nor was that
barrier found of more avail to mitigate the rushing
violence of their formidable enemy.

Joseph having possession of the impregnable
rocks, and the defile and forts of Pancorbo, now
thought he could safely await for his reinforcements, and extended his wings for the sake of
subsistence. On the 16th D'Erlon marched to Aro
on the left, leaving small posts of communication
between that place and Miranda, and sending detachments towards Domingo Calçada to watch the
road leading from Burgos to Logroño. Gazan
remained in the centre with a strong advanced
guard beyond Pancorbo, for as the king's hope
was to retake the offensive, he retained the power
of issuing beyond the defiles, and his scouting
parties were pushed forward towards Briviesca in
front, to Zerezo on the left and to Poya do Sal on
the right. The rest of the army of the south was
cantoned by divisions as far as Armiñion behind
the Ebro, and Reille, who had occupied Busto
marched to Espejo, also behind the Ebro and on
the great road to Bilbao. There being joined by
Sarrut's division from Orduña he took post, placing
Maucune at Frias, Sarrut at Osma, and La Martiniere at Espejo ; guarding also the Puente Lara,
and sending strong scouting parties towards Medina de Pomar and Villarcayo on one side and
towards Orduña on the other.

While these movements were in progress, all the
encumbrances of the armies were assembled in the
basin of Vittoria, and many small garrisons of the
army of the north came in ; for Clauzel having
received the king's first letter on the 15th of June
had stopped the pursuit of Mina, and proceeded

to gather up his scattered columns, intending to
move by the way of Logroño to the Ebro. He
had with him Taupin's and Barbout's divisions of
the army of Portugal, but after providing for his
garrisons, only five thousand men of the army of
the north were disposable, so that he could not
bring more than fourteen thousand men to aid
the king; nevertheless the latter confident in the
strength of his front was still buoyant with the hope
of assembling an army powerful enough to retake the
offensive. His dream was short-lived.

The 13th, while the echoes of the explosion at
Burgos were still ringing in the hills, Wellington's
whole army was in motion by its left towards the
country about the sources of the Ebro. The Gallicians moved from Aguilar de Campo high up on
the Pisuerga, Graham with the British left wing
moved from Villa Diego, and in one march
reaching the river, passed it on the 14th at the
bridges of Rocamunde and San Martin. The
centre of the army followed on the 15th, and the
same day the right wing under Hill marched
through the Bureba and crossed at the Puente
Arenas. This general movement was masked by
the cavalry and by the Spanish irregulars who infested the rear of the French on the roads to Briviesca and Domingo Calçada, and the allies being
thus suddenly placed between the sources of the
Ebro and the great mountains of Reynosa, cut
the French entirely off from the sea-coast. All the
ports except Santona and Bilbao, were immediately
evacuated by the enemy; Santona was invested by
Mendizabel, Porlier, Barcena, and Campillo, and
the English vessels entered Sant Andero, where a
dépôt and hospital station was established, because

the royal road from thence through Reynosa to
Burgos furnished a free communication with the
army. This single blow severed the connection
of the English force with Portugal. That country
was cast off by the army as a heavy tender is cast
from its towing rope, and all the British military
establishments were broken up and transferred by
sea to the coast of Biscay.

The English general had now his choice oftwo
modes of action. The one to march bodily down
the left bank of the Ebro, and fall upon the enemy
wherever he could meet with them; the other to
advance, still turning the king's right, and by
entering Guipuscoa, to place the army on the great
communication with France, while the fleet keeping pace with this movement furnished fresh dépôts
at Bilbao and other ports. The first plan was a
delicate and uncertain operation, because of the
many narrow and dangerous defiles which were to
be passed, but the second which could scarcely be
contravened, was secure even if the first should
fail; both were compatible to a certain point,
inasmuch as to gain the great road leading from
Burgos by Orduña to Bilbao, was a good step for
either, and failing in that the road leading by Valmaceda to Bilbao was still in reserve. Wherefore
with an eagle's sweep Wellington brought his left
wing round, and pouring his numerous columns
through all the deep narrow valleys and rugged
defiles descended towards the great road of Bilbao
between Frias and Orduña. At Modina de Pomar
a central point, he left the sixth division to guard
his stores and supplies, but the march of the other
divisions was unmitigated; neither the winter
gullies nor the ravines, nor the precipitate passes

amongst the rocks, retarded the march even of the CHAP.
VII.
artillery; where horses could not draw men hauled, —
and when the wheels would not roll the guns were 1813.
June.
let down or lifted up with ropes; and strongly did
the rough veteran infantry work their way through
those wild but beautiful regions; six days they
toiled unceasingly; on the seventh, swelled by the
junction of Longa's division and all the smaller
bands which came trickling from the mountains,
they burst like raging streams from every defile,
and went foaming into the basin of Vittoria.

During this time many reports reached the General
Thouve-
not's Cor-
respon-
dence,
MSS.
French, some absurdly exaggerated, as that Wel-
lington had one hundred aud ninety thousand men,
but all indicating more or less distinctly the true
line and direction of his march. As early as the Marshal
Jourdan's
correspon-
dence,
MSS.
15th Jourdan had warned Joseph that the allies
would probably turn his right, and as the reports
of Maucune's scouts told of the presence of English troops, that day, on the side of Puente Arenas,
he pressed the king to send the army of Portugal to
Valmaceda, and to close the other armies towards
the same quarter. Joseph yielded so far, that Reille
was ordered to concentrate his troops at Osma on
the morning of the 18th, with the view of gaining
Valmaceda by Orduña, if it was still possible; if
not he was to descend rapidly from Lodio upon
Bilbao, and to rally Foy's division and the garrisons
of Biscay upon the army of Portugal. At the
same time Gazan was directed to send a division
of infantry and a regiment of dragoons from the
army of the south, to relieve Reille's troops at
Puente Lara and Espejo, but no general and decided dispositions were made.

Reille immediately ordered Maucune to quit

Frias, and join him at Osma with his division, yet having some fears for his safety gave him the choice of coming by the direct road across the hills, or by the circuitous route of Puente Lara. Maucune started late in the night of the 17th by the direct road, and when Reille himself reached Osma, with La Martiniere's and Sarrut's divisions, on the morning of the 18th, he found a strong English column issuing from the defiles in his front, and the head of it was already at Barbarena in possession of the high road to Orduña. This was general Graham with the first, third, and fifth divisions, and a considerable body of cavalry. The French general who had about eight thousand infantry and fourteen guns, at first made a demonstration with Sarrut's division in the view of forcing the British to shew their whole force, and a sharp skirmish and heavy cannonade ensued, wherein fifty men fell on the side of the allies, above a hundred on that of the enemy. But at half past two o'clock, Maucune had not arrived, and beyond the mountains, on the left of the French, the sound of a battle arose which seemed to advance along the valley of Boveda into the rear of Osma ; Reille, suspecting what had happened, instantly retired fighting, towards Espejo, where the mouths of the valleys opened on each other, and from that of Boveda, and the hills on the left, Maucune's troops rushed forth begrimed with dust and powder, breathless, and broken into confused masses.

Official
Journal of
the chief of
the staff,
General
Boyer,
MSS.

That general, proverbially daring, marched over the Araçena ridge instead of going by the Puente Lara, and his leading brigade, after clearing the defiles, had halted on the bank of a rivulet near the village of San Millan in the valley of

Boveda. In this situation, without planting picquets, they were waiting for their other brigade and the baggage, when suddenly the light division which had been moving by a line parallel with Graham's march, appeared on some rising ground in their front; the surprise was equal on both sides, but the British riflemen instantly dashed down the hill with loud cries and a bickering fire, the fifty-second followed in support, and the French retreated fighting as they best could. The rest of the English regiments having remained in reserve, were watching this combat and thinking all their enemies were before them, when the second French brigade, followed by the baggage, came hastily out from a narrow cleft in some perpendicular rocks on the right hand. A very confused action now commenced, for the reserve scrambled over some rough intervening ground to attack this new enemy, and the French to avoid them made for a hill a little way in their front, whereupon the fifty-second, whose rear was thus menaced, wheeled round and running at full speed up the hill met them on the summit. However, the French soldiers without losing their presence of mind threw off their packs, and half flying, half fighting, escaped along the side of the mountains towards Miranda, while the first brigade still retreating on the road towards Espejo were pursued by the riflemen. Meanwhile the sumpter animals being affrighted, run wildly about the rocks with a wonderful clamour, and though the escort huddled together fought desperately, all the baggage became the spoil of the victors, and four hundred of the French fell or were taken; the rest, thanks to their unyielding resolution and activity, escaped, though pursued through the

mountains by some Spanish irregulars, and Reille
being still pressed by Graham then retreated behind
Salinas de Añara.

A knowledge of these events reached the king
that night, yet neither Reille nor the few prisoners
he had made could account for more than six
Anglo-Portuguese divisions at the defiles; hence as
no troops had been felt on the great road from
Burgos, it was judged that Hill was marching with
the others by Valmaceda into Guipuscoa, to menace the great communication with France. However it was clear that six divisions were concentrated on the right and rear of the French armies,
and no time was to be lost in extricating the latter
from its critical situation; wherefore Gazan and
D'Erlon marched in the night to unite at Armiñon,
a central point behind the Zadora river, up the left
bank of which it was necessary to file in order to
gain the basin of Vittoria. But the latter could only
be entered, at that side, through the pass of Puebla de
Arganzan which was two miles long, and so narrow
as scarcely to furnish room for the great road; Reille
therefore, to cover this dangerous movement, fell
back during the night to Subijana Morillas, on the
Bayas river. His orders were to dispute the
ground vigorously, for by that route Wellington
could enter the basin before Gazan, and D'Erlon
could thread the pass of Puebla; he could also
send a corps from Frias to attack their rear on the
Miranda side, while they were engaged in the
defile. One of these things by all means he
should have endeavoured to accomplish, but the
troops had made very long marches on the 18th,
and it was dark before the fourth division had
reached Espejo. D'Erlon and Gazan, therefore,

united at Armiñon without difficulty about ten o'clock in the morning of the 19th, and immediately commenced the passage of the defile of Puebla, and the head of their column appeared on the other side at the moment when Wellington was driving Reille back upon the Zadora.

The allies had reached Bayas before mid-day of the 19th, and if they could have forced the passage at once, the armies of the centre and of the south would have been cut off from Vittoria and destroyed; but the army of Portugal was strongly posted, the front covered by the river, the right by the village of Subijana de Morillas, which was occupied as a bridge-head, and the left secured by some very rugged heights opposite the village of Pobes. This position was turned by the light division while the fourth division attacked it in front, and after a skirmish in which about eighty of the French fell, Reille was forced over the Zadora; but the army of the centre had then passed the defile of Puebla and was in position behind that river, the army of the south was coming rapidly into second line, the crisis had passed, the combat ceased, and the allies pitched their tents on the Bayas. The French armies now formed three lines behind the Zadora, and the king hearing that Clauzel was at Logroño, eleven leagues distant, expedited orders to him to march upon Vittoria; general Foy also, who was in march for Bilbao, was directed to halt at Durango, to rally all the garrisons of Biscay and Guipuscoa there, and then to come down on Vittoria. These orders were received too late.

CHAPTER VIII.

THE basin into which the king had now poured all his troops, his parcs, convoys, and encumbrances of every kind, was about eight miles broad by ten in length, Vittoria being at the further end. The river Zadora, narrow and with rugged banks, after passing very near that town, runs towards the Ebro with many windings and divides the basin unequally, the largest portion being on the right bank. A traveller coming from Miranda by the royal Madrid road, would enter the basin by the pass of Puebla, through which the Zadora flows between two very high and rough mountain ridges, the one on his right hand being called the heights of Puebla, that on his left hand the heights of Morillas. The road leads up the left bank of the river, and on emerging from the pass, on the left hand at the distance of about six miles would be seen the village of Subijana de Morillas, furnishing that opening into the basin which Reille defended while the other armies passed the defile of Puebla. The spires of Vittoria would appear about eight miles distant, and from that town the road to Logroño goes off on the right hand, the road to Bilbao by Murgia and Orduña on the left hand crossing the Zadora at a bridge near the village of Ariaga; further on, the roads to Estella and to Pampeluna branch off on the right, a road to Durango on the

left, and between them the royal causeway leads
over the great Arlaban ridge into the mountains of
Guipuscoa by the formidable defiles of Salinas.
But of all these roads, though several were practicable for guns, especially that to Pampeluna, the
royal causeway alone could suffice for the retreat
of such an encumbered army. And as the allies
were behind the hills forming the basin on the
right bank of the Zadora, their line being parallel
to the great causeway, it followed that by prolong-
ing their left they would infallibly cut off the
French from that route.

Joseph felt the danger and his first thought was
to march by Salinas to Durango, with a view to
cover his communications with France, and to rally
Foy's troops and the garrisons of Guipuscoa and
Biscay. But in that rough country, neither his artillery nor his cavalry, on which he greatly depended,
though the cavalry and artillery of the allies were
scarcely less powerful, could act or subsist, and
he would have to send them into France; and if
pressed by Wellington in front and surrounded by
all the bands in a mountainous region, favourable
for those irregulars, he could not long remain in
Spain. It was then proposed if forced from the
basin of Vittoria, to retire by Salvatierra to Pampeluna and bring Suchet's army up to Zaragoza;
but Joseph feared thus to lose the great communication with France, because the Spanish regular
army, aided by all the bands, could seize Tolosa
while Wellington operated against him on the side
of Navarre. It was replied that troops detached
from the army of the north and from that of Portugal might oppose them; still the king hesitated,
for though the road to Pampeluna was called

BOOK
XX.
————
1813.
June.

practicable for wheels, it required something more for the enormous mass of guns and carriages of all kinds now heaped around Vittoria.

One large convoy had already marched on the 19th by the royal causeway for France, another, still larger was to move on the 21st under escort of Maucune's division; the fighting men in front of the enemy were thus diminished and yet the plain was still covered with artillery parcs and equipages of all kinds, and Joseph shut up in the basin of Vittoria, vacillating and infirm of purpose, continued to waste time in vain conjectures about his adversary's movements. Hence on the 19th nothing was done, but the 20th some infantry and cavalry of the army of Portugal passed the Zadora to feel for the allies towards Murguia, and being encountered by Longa's Spaniards at the distance of six miles, after some successful skirmishing recrossed the Zadora with the loss of twenty men. On the 21st at three o'clock in the morning Maucune's division, more than three thousand good soldiers, marched with the second convoy, and the king took up a new line of battle.

Reille's army reinforced by a Franco-Spanish brigade of infantry, and by Digeon's division of dragoons from the army of the south, now formed the extreme right, having to defend the passage of the Zadora, where the Bilbao and Durango roads crossed it by the bridges of Gamara Mayor and Ariaga. The French division defended the bridge; the Franco-Spanish brigade was pushed forward to See plan 8. Durana on the royal road, and was supported by a French battalion and a brigade of light horsemen; Digeon's dragoons and a second brigade of light cavalry were in reserve behind the Zadora, near Zuazo de Alava and Hermandad. The centre of the king's army, distant six or eight miles from Gamara, following the course of the Zadora, was on another front, because the stream, turning suddenly to the left round the heights of Margarita descends to the defile of Puebla, nearly at right angles with its previous course. Here covered by the river and on an easy open range of heights, for the basin of Vittoria is broken by a variety of ground, Gazan's right extended from the royal road to an isolated hill in front of the village of Margarita. His centre was astride the royal road, in front of the village of Arinez; his left occupied more rugged ground, being placed behind Subijana de Alava on the roots of the Puebla mountain facing the defile of that name, and to cover this wing a brigade under general Maransin was posted on the Puebla mountain. D'Erlon's army was in second line. The principal mass of the cavalry with many guns, and the king's guards formed a reserve, behind the centre, about the village of Gomecha, and fifty pieces of artillery were massed in the front, pointing to the bridges of Mendoza, Tres Puentes, Villodas, and Nanclares.

While the king was making conjectures, Wellington was making various dispositions for the different operations which might occur. He knew that the Andalusian reserve would be at Burgos in a few days, and thinking that Joseph would not fight on the Zadora, detached Giron with the Gallicians on the 19th to seize Orduña. Graham's corps was at first destined to follow Giron but finally penetrated through difficult mountain ways to Murguia, thus cutting the enemy off from Bilbao and menacing his communications with France. However the rear of the army had been so much

scattered in the previous marches that Wellington
halted on the 20th to rally his columns, and taking
that opportunity to examine the position of the
French armies, observed that they seemed steadfast
to fight; whereupon immediately changing his own
dispositions, he gave Graham fresh orders and
hastily recalled Giron from Orduña.

The long expected battle was now at hand, and
on neither side were the numbers and courage of the
troops of mean account. The allies had lost about
two hundred killed and wounded in the previous
operations, and the sixth division, six thousand five
hundred strong, was left at Medina de Pomar; hence
only sixty thousand Anglo-Portuguese sabres and
bayonets, with ninety pieces of cannon, were actually
in the field, but the Spanish auxiliaries were above
twenty thousand, and the whole army, including
serjeants and artillery-men, exceeded eighty thousand combatants. For the French side, as the
regular muster-roll of their troops was lost with
the battle, an approximation to their strength must
suffice. The number killed and taken in different
combats, from the Esla and Tormes to the Zadora,
was about two thousand men, and some five thousand had marched to France with the two convoys.
On the other hand Sarrut's division, the garrison
of Vittoria, and the many smaller posts relinquished
by the army of the north, had increased the king's
forces, and hence, by a comparison with former
returns, it would appear, that in the gross, about
seventy thousand men were present. Wherefore
deducting the officers, the artillery-men, sappers,
miners, and non-combatants, which are always borne
on the French muster-rolls, the sabres and bayonets
would scarcely reach sixty thousand, but in the

number and size of their guns the French had the advantage.

The defects of the king's position were apparent both in the general arrangement and in the details. His best line of retreat was on the prolongation of his right flank, which being at Gamara Mayor, close to Vittoria, was too distant to be supported by the main body of the army; and yet the safety of the latter depended upon the preservation of Reille's position   Instead of having the rear clear, and the field of battle free, many thousand carriages and impediments of all kinds were heaped about Vittoria, blocking all the roads, and creating confusion amongst the artillery parcs.   Maransin's brigade placed on the heights above Puebla was isolated and too weak to hold that ground.   The centre indeed occupied an easy range of hills, its front was open, with a slope to the river, and powerful batteries seemed to bar all access by the bridges; nevertheless many of the guns being pushed with an advanced post into a deep loop of the Zadora, were within musket-shot of a wood on the right bank, which was steep and rugged, so that the allies found good cover close to the river.

There were seven bridges within the scheme of the operations, namely, the bridge of La Puebla on the French left beyond the defile; the bridge of Nanclares, facing Subijana de Alava and the French end of the defile of Puebla; then three bridges which, placed around the deep loop of the river before mentioned, opened altogether upon the right of the French centre, that of Mendoza being highest up the stream, that of Vellodas lowest down the stream, and that of Tres Puentes in the centre; lastly the bridges of Gamara Mayor and Ariaga

on the Upper Zadora, opposite Vittoria, which were
guarded by Reille, completed the number, and none
of the seven were either broken or entrenched.

Wellington having well observed these things
formed his army for three distinct battles.

Sir Thomas Graham moving from Murguia, by
the Bilbao road, was to fall on Reille, and if possible
to force the passage of the river at Gamara Mayor
and Ariaga; by this movement the French would be
completely turned and the greatest part of their
forces shut up between the Puebla mountains on one
side and the Zadora on the other.   The first and fifth
Anglo-Portuguese divisions, Bradford's and Pack's
independent Portuguese brigades, Longa's Spanish
division, and Anson's and Bock's cavalry, in all
near twenty thousand men with eighteen pieces of
cannon, were destined for this attack, and Giron's
Gallicians, recalled from Orduña, came up by a
forced march in support.

Sir Rowland Hill was to attack the enemy's left,
and his corps, also about twenty thousand strong,
was composed of Morillo's Spaniards, Sylveira's
Portuguese, and the second British division together with some cavalry and guns. It was collected on the southern slope of the ridge of Morillas, between the Bayas and the Lower Zadora,
pointing to the village of Puebla, and was destined
to force the passage of the river at that point, to
assail the French troops on the heights beyond, to
thread the defile of La Puebla and to enter the
basin of Vittoria, thus turning and menacing all
the French left and securing the passage of the
Zadora at the bridge of Nanclares.

The centre attack, directed by Wellington in
person, consisted of the third, fourth, seventh,

and light divisions of infantry, the great mass of
the artillery, the heavy cavalry and D'Urban's Portuguese horsemen, in all nearly thirty thousand
combatants.   They were encamped along the Bayas
from Subijana Morillas to Ulivarre, and had
only to march across the ridges which formed the
basin of Vittoria on that side, to come down to
their different points of attack on the Zadora, that
is to say, the bridges of Mendoza, Tres Puentes,
Villodas and Nanclares.   But so rugged was the
country and the communications between the different columns so difficult, that no exact concert could
be expected and each general of division was in
some degree master of his movements.

BATTLE OF VITTORIA.

At day-break on the 21st the weather being
rainy, with a thick vapour, the troops moved from
their camps on the Bayas, and the centre of the
army, advancing by columns from the right and
left of the line, passed the ridges in front, and entering the basin of Vittoria slowly approached the
Zadora. The left-hand column pointed to Mendoza,
the right-hand column skirted the ridge of Morillas
on the other side of which Hill was marching, and
that general, having seized the village of Puebla
about ten o'clock, commenced passing the river
there.   Morillo's Spaniards led and their first
brigade moving on a bye way assailed the mountain
to the right of the great road; the ascent was so steep
that the soldiers appeared to climb rather than to
walk up, and the second Spanish brigade, being to
connect the first with the British troops below,
ascended only half way ; little or no opposition was
made until the first brigade was near the summit

when a sharp skirmishing commenced, and Morillo was wounded but would not quit the field; his second brigade joined him, and the French, feeling the importance of the height, reinforced Maransin with a fresh regiment. Then Hill succoured Morillo with the seventy-first regiment, and a battalion of light infantry, both under colonel Cadogan, yet the fight was doubtful, for though the British secured the summit, and gained ground along the side of the mountain, Cadogan, a brave officer and of high promise, fell, and Gazan calling Villatte's division from behind Ariñez, sent it to the succour of his side; and so strongly did these troops fight that the battle remained stationary, the allies being scarcely able to hold their ground. Hill however again sent fresh troops to their assistance, and with the remainder of his corps passing the Zadora, threaded the long defile of Puebla and fiercely issuing forth on the other side won the village of Subijana de Alava in front of Gazan's line; he thus connected his own right with the troops on the mountain, and maintained this forward position in despite of the enemy's vigorous efforts to dislodge him.

Meanwhile Wellington had brought the fourth and light divisions, the heavy cavalry, the hussars and D'Urban's Portuguese horsemen, from Subijana Morillas, and Montevite, down by Olabarre to the Zadora. The fourth division was placed opposite the bridge of Nanclares, the light division opposite the bridge of Villodas, both well covered by rugged ground and woods; and the light division was so close to the water, that their skirmishers could with ease have killed the French gunners of the advanced post in the loop of the river at Villodas. The weather had cleared up, and when Hill's battle

began, the riflemen of the light division, spreading
along the bank, exchanged a biting fire with the
enemy's skirmishers, but no serious effort was made,
because the third and seventh divisions, meeting
with rough ground, had not reached their point
of attack; and it would have been imprudent to
push the fourth division and the cavalry over the
bridge of Nanclares, and thus crowd a great body
of troops in front of the Puebla defile before the
other divisions were ready to attack the right and
centre of the enemy.

While thus waiting, a Spanish peasant told
Wellington that the bridge of Tres Puentes on the
left of the light division, was unguarded, and
offered to guide the troops over it. Kempt's
brigade of the light division was instantly directed
towards this point, and being concealed by some
rocks from the French, and well led by the brave
peasant, they passed the narrow bridge at a running
pace, mounted a steep curving rise of ground, and
halted close under the crest on the enemy's side of
the river, being then actually behind the king's
advanced post, and within a few hundred yards of
his line of battle. Some French cavalry immediately
approached and two round shots were fired by the
enemy, one of which killed the poor peasant to whose
courage and intelligence the allies were so much
indebted; but as no movement of attack was made,
Kempt called the fifteenth hussars over the river,
and they came at a gallop, crossing the narrow
bridge one by one, horseman after horseman, and
still the French remained torpid, shewing that there
was an army there but no general.

It was now one o'clock, Hill's assault on the
village of Subijana de Alava was developed, and

a curling smoke, faintly seen far up the Zadora on
the enemy's extreme right, being followed by the
dull sound of distant guns shewed that Graham's
attack had also commenced. Then the king finding
both his flanks in danger caused his reserve about
Gomecha to file off towards Vittoria, and gave
Gazan orders to retire by successive masses with
the army of the south. But at that moment the
third and seventh divisions having reached their
ground were seen moving rapidly down to the
bridge of Mendoza, the enemy's artillery opened
upon them, a body of cavalry drew near the bridge,
and the French light troops which were very strong
there commenced a vigorous musketry. Some
British guns replied to the French cannon from the
opposite bank, and the value of Kempt's forward
position was instantly made manifest; for colonel
Andrew Barnard springing forward, led the riflemen of the light division, in the most daring
manner, between the French cavalry and the river,
taking their light troops and gunners in flank, and
engaging them so closely that the English artillery-
men, thinking his darkly clothed troops were
enemies, played upon both alike.

This singular attack enabled a brigade of the
third division to pass the bridge of Mendoza without opposition; the other brigade forded the
river higher up, and the seventh division and Vandeleur's brigade of the light division followed.
The French advanced post immediately abandoned
the ground in front of Villodas, and the battle
which had before somewhat slackened revived with
extreme violence. Hill pressed the enemy harder,
the fourth division passed the bridge of Nanclares,
the smoke and sound of Graham's attack became

more distinct, and the banks of the Zadora presented a continuous line of fire. However the French,
weakened in the centre by the draft made of Villatte's division and having their confidence shaken
by the king's order to retreat, were in evident per-
plexity, and no regular retrograde movement could
be made, the allies were too close.

The seventh division, and Colville's brigade of
the third division which had forded the river,
formed the left of the British, and they were immediately engaged with the French right in front
of Margarita and Hermandad. Almost at the same
time lord Wellington, seeing the hill in front of
Arinez nearly denuded of troops by the withdrawal
of Villatte's troops, carried Picton and the rest of
the third division in close columns of regiments at
a running pace diagonally across the front of both
armies towards that central point; this attack was
headed by Barnard's riflemen, and followed by the
remainder of Kempt's brigade and the hussars, but
the other brigade of the light division acted in
support of the seventh division. At the same
time general Cole advanced with the fourth division from the bridge of Nanclares, and the heavy
cavalry, a splendid body, also passing the river,
galloped up, squadron after squadron, into the
plain ground between Cole's right and Hill's left.

The French thus caught in the midst of their
dispositions for retreat, threw out a prodigious
number of skirmishers, and fifty pieces of artillery
played with astonishing activity. To answer this
fire Wellington brought over several brigades of
British guns, and both sides were shrouded by a
dense cloud of smoke and dust, under cover of
which the French retired by degrees to the second

range of heights, in front of Gomecha, on which
their reserve had been posted, but they still held
the village of Arinez on the main road. Picton's
troops headed by the riflemen, plunged into
that village amidst a heavy fire of muskets and
artillery, and in an instant three guns were captured ; but the post was important, fresh French
troops came down, and for some time the smoke
and dust and clamour, the flashing of the fire-arms,
and the shouts and cries of the combatants, mixed
with the thundering of the guns, were terrible,
yet finally the British troops issued forth victorious
on the other side. During this conflict the seventh
division, reinforced by Vandeleur's brigade of the
light division, was heavily raked by a battery at
the village of Margarita, until the fifty-second
regiment, led by colonel Gibbs, with an impetuous
charge drove the French guns away and carried
the village, and at the same time the eighty-seventh
under colonel Gcugh won the village of Hermandad. Then the whole advanced fighting on the
left of Picton's attack, and on the right hand of that
general the fourth division also made way, though
more slowly because of the rugged ground.

When Picton and Kempt's brigades had carried
the village of Arinez and gained the main road,
the French troops near Subijana de Alava were
turned, and being hard-pressed on their front, and
on their left flank by the troops on the summit of
the mountain, fell back for two miles in a disordered
mass, striving to regain the great line of retreat
to Vittoria. It was thought that some cavalry
launched against them at the moment would have
totally disorganized the whole French battle and
secured several thousand prisoners, but this was

not done, the confused multitude shooting ahead
of the advancing British lines recovered order,
and as the ground was exceedingly diversified,
being in some places wooded, in others open, here
covered with high corn, there broken by ditches
vineyards and hamlets, the action for six miles resolved itself into a running fight and cannonade,
the dust and smoke and tumult of which filled all
the basin, passing onwards towards Vittoria.

Many guns were taken as the army advanced,
and at six o'clock the French reached the last defensible height, one mile in front of Vittoria.
Behind them was the plain in which the city
stood, and beyond the city, thousands of carriages
and animals and non-combatants, men women and
children, were crowding together, in all the madness
of terror, and as the English shot went booming over
head the vast crowd started and swerved with a con-
vulsive movement, while a dull and horrid sound of
distress arose ; but there was no hope, no stay for
army or multitude. It was the wreck of a nation.
However the courage of the French soldier was
not yet quelled, Reille on whom every thing now
depended, maintained his post on the Upper Zadora,
and the armies of the south and centre drawing up
on their last heights, between the villages of Ali
and Armentia, made their muskets flash like lightning, while more than eighty pieces of artillery,
massed together, pealed with such a horrid uproar,
that the hills laboured and shook, and streamed
with fire and smoke, amidst which the dark figures
of the French gunners were seen, bounding with
a frantic energy.

This terrible cannonade and musketry kept the
allies in check, and scarcely could the third divi-

sion, which was still the foremost and bore the
brunt of this storm, maintain its advanced position.
Again the battle became stationary, and the French
generals had commenced drawing off their infantry
in succession from the right wing, when suddenly
the fourth division rushing forward carried the hill
on the French left, and the heights were at once
abandoned. It was at this very moment that Joseph,
finding the royal road so completely blocked by carriages that the artillery could not pass, indicated
the road of Salvatierra as the line of retreat, and the
army went off in a confused yet compact body on
that side, leaving Vittoria on its left. The British
infantry followed hard, and the light cavalry galloped through the town to intercept the new line of
retreat, which was through a marsh, but this road
also was choked with carriages and fugitive people,
while on each side there were deep drains. Thus
all became disorder and mischief, the guns were
left on the edge of the marsh, the artillery-men
and drivers fled with the horses, and, breaking
through the miserable multitude, the vanquished
troops went off by Metauco towards Salvatierra;
however their cavalry still covered the retreat with
some vigour, and many of those generous horsemen
were seen taking up children and women to carry
off from the dreadful scene.

The result of the last attack had placed Reille, of
whose battle it is now time to treat, in great
danger. His advanced troops under Sarrut had been
placed at the village of Aranguis, and they also
occupied some heights on their right which covered
both the bridges of Ariaga and Gamara Mayor,
but they had been driven from both the village and
the height a little after twelve o'clock, by general

Oswald, who commanded the head of Graham's
column, consisting of the fifth division, Longa's
Spaniards, and Pack's Portuguese. Longa then
seized Gamara Menor on the Durango road, while
another detachment gained the royal road still
further on the left, and forced the Franco-Spaniards
to retire from Durana. Thus the first blow on this
side had deprived the king of his best line of retreat
and confined him to the road of Pampeluna. However Sarrut recrossed the river in good order and
a new disposition was made by Reille. One of
Sarrut's brigades defended the bridge of Ariaga
and the village of Abechuco beyond it; the other
was in reserve, equally supporting Sarrut and La
Martiniere who defended the bridge of Gamara
Mayor and the village of that name beyond the
river. Digeon's dragoons were formed behind the
village of Ariaga, and Reille's own dragoons being
called up from Hermandad and Zuazo, took post
behind the bridge of Gamara; a brigade of light
cavalry was placed on the extreme right to sustain
the Franco-Spanish troops, which were now on the
Upper Zadora in front of Betonio, and the remainder
of the light cavalry under general Curto was on the
French left extending down the Zadora between
Ariaga and Govea.

Oswald commenced the attack at Gamara with
some guns and Robinson's brigade of the fifth
division. Longa's Spaniards were to have led and
at an early hour when Gamara was feebly occupied, but they did not stir, and the village was
meanwhile reinforced. However Robinson's brigade
being formed in three columns made the assault
at a running pace. At first the fire of artillery
and musketry was so heavy that the British troops

stopped and commenced firing also, and the three
columns got intermixed, yet encouraged by their
officers, and especially by the example of general
Robinson an inexperienced man but of a high and
daring spirit, they renewed the charge, broke
through the village and even crossed the bridge.
One gun was captured, and the passage seemed to
be won, when Reille suddenly turned twelve pieces
upon the village, and La Martiniere rallying his
division under cover of this cannonade, retook the
bridge; it was with difficulty the allied troops could
even hold the village until they were reinforced.
Then a second British brigade came down, and,
the royals leading, the bridge was again carried, but
again these new troops were driven back in the same
manner as the others had been. Thus the bridge
remained forbidden ground. Graham had meanwhile attacked the village of Abechuco which
covered the bridge of Ariaga, and it was carried at
once by colonel Halkett's Germans, who were supported by Bradford's Portuguese and by the fire
of twelve guns; yet here as at Gamara the French
maintained the bridge, and at both places the
troops on each side remained stationary under a
reciprocal fire of artillery and small arms.

Reille, though considerably inferior in numbers,
continued to interdict the passage of the river, until
the tumult of Wellington's battle, coming up the Zadora, reached Vittoria itself, and a part of the British
horsemen rode out of that city upon Sarrut's rear.
Digeon's dragoons kept this cavalry in check for the
moment, and some time before, Reille, seeing the retro-
gade movement of the king, had formed a reserve of
infantry under general Fririon at Betonia which
now proved his safety. For Sarrut was killed at the

bridge of Ariaga, and general Menne the next in
command, could scarcely draw off his troops while
Digeon's dragoons held the British cavalry at
point, but with the aid of Fririon's reserve Reille
covered the movement and rallied all his troops at
Betonio. He had now to make head on several
sides, because the allies were coming down from
Ariaga from Durana and from Vittoria, yet he
fought his way to Metauco on the Salvatierra road
covering the general retreat with some degree of
order. Vehemently and closely did the British
pursue, and neither the resolute demeanour of the
French cavalry, which was covered on the flanks
by some light troops and made several vigorous
charges, nor the night, which now fell, could stop
their victorious career until the flying masses of the
enemy had cleared all obstacles, and passing Metauco got beyond the reach of further injury.
Thus ended the battle of Vittoria; the French
escaped indeed with comparatively little loss of
men, but to use Gazan's words, " they lost all
their equipages, all their guns, all their treasure,
all their stores, all their papers, so that no man
could prove how much pay was due to him;
generals and subordinate officers alike were reduced to the clothes on their backs, and most of
them were barefooted."

Never was an army more hardly used by its
commander, for the soldiers were not half beaten,
and never was a victory more complete. The trophies were innumerable. The French carried off
but two pieces of artillery from the battle. Jourdan's baton of command, a stand of colours, one
hundred and forty-three brass pieces, one hundred
of which had been used in the fight, all the
parcs and dépôts from Madrid, Valladolid, and

Burgos, carriages, ammunition, treasure, every
thing fell into the hands of the victors. The loss
in men did not however exceed six thousand,
exclusive of some hundreds of prisoners; the
loss of the allies was nearly as great, the gross
numbers being five thousand one hundred and
seventy-six, killed wounded and missing. Of
these one thousand and forty-nine were Portuguese
and five hundred and fifty-three were Spanish;
hence the loss of the English was more than double
that of the Portuguese and Spaniards together,
and yet both fought well, and especially the Portuguese, but British troops are the soldiers of
battle. Marshal Jourdan's baton was taken by the
eighty-seventh regiment, and the spoil was immense; but to such extent was plunder carried
principally by the followers and non-combatants,
for with some exceptions the fighting troops may
be said to have marched upon gold and silver without stooping to pick it up, that of five millions and
a half of dollars indicated by the French accounts
to be in the money-chests, not one dollar came to
the public, and Wellington sent fifteen officers with
power to stop and examine all loaded animals passing the Ebro and the Duero in hopes to recover the
sums so shamefully carried off. Neither was this
disgraceful conduct confined to ignorant and vulgar
people. Some officers were seen mixed up with the
mob and contending for the disgraceful gain.

On the 22d the allies followed the retreating
enemy, and Giron and Longa entered Guipuscoa,
by the royal road, in pursuit of the convoy which
had moved under Maucune on the morning of the
battle; the heavy cavalry and D'Urban's Portuguese
remained at Vittoria, and general Pakenham with
the sixth division came up from Medina Pomar;

the remainder of the army pursued Joseph towards
Pampeluna, for he had continued his retreat up
the Borundia and Araquil valleys all night. The
weather was rainy, the roads heavy, and the French
rear-guard having neither time nor materials to
destroy the bridges set fire to the villages behind
them to delay the pursuit. At five o'clock in the
morning of the 22d Reille had rallied his two
divisions and all his cavalry in front of Salvatierra,
where he halted until he was assured that all the
French had passed, and then continued his march
to Huerta in the valley of Araquil, thirty miles
from the field of battle. Joseph was that day at
Yrursun, a town, situated behind one of the sources
of the Arga, and from which roads branched off to
Pampeluna on one side, and to Tolosa and St.
Esteban on the other. At this place he remained
all the 23d sending orders to different points on
the French frontier to prepare provisions and succours for his suffering army, and he directed Reille
to proceed rapidly by St. Estevan to the Bidassoa
with the infantry, six hundred select cavalry, the
artillery-men and horses of the army of Portugal; meanwhile Gazan's and D'Erlon's army
marched upon Pampeluna intending to cross the
frontier at St. Jean Pied de Port. Joseph reached
Pampeluna the 24th, but the army bivouacked on
the glacis of the fortress, and in such a state of destitution and insubordination that the governor would
not suffer them to enter the town. The magazines
were indeed reduced very low by Mina's long Jones's Sieges.
blockade, and some writers assert that it was even
proposed to blow up the works and abandon the
place; however by great exertions additional provisions were obtained from the vicinity, the garri-

son was encreased to three thousand men, and the
army marched towards France leaving a rear-guard
at a strong pass about two leagues off.

The 23d Wellington having detached Graham's
corps to Guipuscoa by the pass of Adrian, left the
fifth division at Salvatierra, and pursued the king
with the rest of the army.

On the 24th the light division and Victor Alten's
cavalry came up with the French rear-guard; two
battalions of the riflemen immediately pushed the
infantry back though the pass, and then Ross's
horse artillery galloping forward, killed several
men and dismounted one of the only two pieces
of cannon carried off from Vittoria.

The 25th the enemy covered by the fortress of
Pampeluna went up the valley of Roncevalles.
He was followed by the light division which turned
the town as far as Vilalba, and he was harassed by
the Spanish irregular troops now swarming on
every side.

Meanwhile Foy and Clauzel were placed in very
difficult positions. The former had reached Bergara the 21st, and the garrison of Bilbao and the
Italian division of St. Paul, formerly Palombini's,
had reached Durango; the first convoy from Vittoria was that day at Bergara, and Maucune was
with the second at Montdragon. The 22d the garrison of Castro went off to Santona; the same day
the fugitives from the battle spread such an alarm
through the country that the forts of Arlaban,
Montdragon, and Salinas, which commanded the
passes into Guipuscoa were abandoned, and Longa
and Giron penetrated them without hindrance.

Foy who had only one battalion of his division
in hand, immediately rallied the fugitive garrisons,

and marching upon Montdragon, made some prisoners and acquired exact intelligence of the battle.
Then he ordered the convoy to move day and night,
towards France; the troops at Durango to march
upon Bergara, and the troops from all the other posts
to unite at Tolosa, to which place the artillery, baggage, and sick men were now hastening from every
side; and to cover their concentration Foy, reinforcing himself with Maucune's troops, gave battle to
Giron and Longa, though three times his numbers,
at Montdragon; the Spaniards had the advantage
and the French fell back, yet slowly and fighting,
to Bergara, but they lost two hundred and fifty men
and six guns.

On the 23d Foy marched to Villa Real de Guipuscoa, and that evening the head of Graham's
column having crossed the Mutiol mountain by the
pass of Adrian, descended upon Segura. It was then
as near to Tolosa as Foy was, and the latter's situation became critical; yet such were the difficulties
of passing the mountain, that it was late on the
24th ere Graham, who had then only collected
Anson's light cavalry, two Portuguese brigades of
infantry, and Halket's Germans, could move towards Villa Franca. The Italians and Maucune's
divisions which composed the French rear, were
just entering Villa Franca as Graham came in sight,
and to cover that town they took post at the village
of Veasaya on the right bank of the Orio river.
Halket's Germans, aided by Pack's Portuguese, immediately drove Maucune's people from the village
with the loss of two hundred men, and Bradford's brigade having engaged the Italians on the French right,
killed or wounded eighty, yet the Italians claimed
the advantage; and the whole position was so

CHAP.
VIII.

1813.
June.

Graham's
despatch.

General
Boyer's
official
Journal,
MSS.

strong, that Graham had recourse to flank operations, whereupon Foy retired to Tolosa.   Giron
and Longa now came up by the great road, and
Mendizabel, having quitted the blockade of Santona, arrived at Aspeytia on the Deba.

The 25th Foy again offered battle in front of Tolosa,
but Graham turned his left with Longa's division
and Mendizabel turned his right from Aspeytia;
while they were in march, colonel Williams, with
the grenadiers of the first regiment and three companies of Pack's Portuguese, dislodged him from an
advantageous hill in front, and the fight was then
purposely prolonged by skirmishing, until six
o'clock in the evening, when the Spaniards having
reached their destination on the flanks, a general
attack was made on all sides.   The French being
cannonaded on the causeway, and strongly pushed
by the infantry in front, while Longa with equal
vigour drove their left from the heights, were soon
forced beyond Tolosa on the flanks; but that town
was strongly entrenched as a field-post and they
maintained it until Graham brought up his guns
and bursting one of the gates opened a passage
for his troops; nevertheless Foy profiting from the
darkness made his retreat good with a loss of only
four hundred men killed and wounded, and some
prisoners who were taken by Mendizabel and
Longa.   These actions were very severe ; the loss
of the Spaniards was not known, but the Anglo-
Portuguese had more than four hundred killed and
wounded in the two days' operations, and Graham
himself was hurt.

The 26th and 27th the allies halted to hear of
lord Wellington's progress, the enemy's convoys
entered France in safety, and Foy occupied a

position between Tolosa and Ernani behind the
Anezo. His force was now encreased by the
successive arrival of the smaller garrisons to sixteen thousand bayonets, four hundred sabres, and
ten pieces of artillery, and the 28th he threw a
garrison of two thousand six hundred good troops
into St. Sebastian and passed the Urumia. The
29th he passed the Oyarsun, and halted the 30th,
leaving a small garrison at Passages, which however surrendered the next day to Longa.

On the 1st of July the garrison of Gueteria
escaped by sea to St. Sebastian, and Foy passed
the Bidassoa, his rear-guard fighting with Giron's
Gallicians ; but Reille's troops were now at Vera
and Viriatu, they had received ammunition and
artillery from Bayonne, and thus twenty-five thousand men of the army of Portugal occupied a
defensive line from Vera to the bridge of Behobie,
the approaches to which last were defended by a
block-house. Graham immediately invested St.
Sebastian, and Giron concentrating the fire of his
own artillery and that of a British battery upon
the block-house of Behobie obliged the French to
blow it up and destroy the bridge.

While these events were passing in Guipuscoa,
Clauzel was in more imminent danger. On the
evening of the 22d he had approached the field
of battle at the head of fourteen thousand men, by
a way which falls into the Estella road, at Aracete
and not far from Salvatierra. Pakenham with the
sixth division was then at Vittoria, and the French
general, learning the state of affairs soon retired to
Logroño, where he halted until the evening of the
25th. This delay was like to have proved fatal,
for on that day, Wellington who before thought he

was at Tudela, discovered his real position, and leaving general Hill with the second division to form the siege of Pampeluna, marched himself by Tafalla with two brigades of light cavalry and the third, fourth, seventh, and light divisions of infantry. The fifth and sixth divisions and the heavy cavalry and D'Urban's Portuguese marched at the same time from Salvatierra and Vittoria upon Logroño; and Mina also, who had now collected all his scattered battalions near Estella, and was there joined by Julian Sanchez' cavalry, followed hard on Clauzel's rear.

The French general moving by Calahorra, reached Tudela on the evening of the 27th, and thinking that by this forced march of sixty miles in forty hours with scarcely a halt, he had outstripped all pursuers, would have made for France by Olite and Tafalla. Wellington was already in possession of those places expecting him, but an alcalde gave Clauzel notice of the danger, whereupon recrossing the Ebro he marched upon Zaragoza in all haste, and arriving the 1st of July, took post on the Gallego, gave out that he would there wait until Suchet, or the king, if the latter retook the offensive, should come up. Wellington immediately made a flank movement to his own left as far as Caseda, and could still with an exertion have intercepted Clauzel by the route of Jacca, but he feared to drive him back upon Suchet and contented himself with letting Mina press the French general. That chief acted with great ability; for he took three hundred prisoners, and having every where declared that the whole allied army were close at hand in pursuit he imposed upon Clauzel, who, being thus deceived, destroyed some of his

artillery and heavy baggage, and leaving the rest
at Zaragoza retired to Jacca.

During this time Joseph, not being pressed, had
sent the army of the south again into Spain to take
possession of the valley of Bastan, which was
very fertile and full of strong positions. But
O'Donnel, count of Abispal, had now reduced the
forts at Pancorbo, partly by capitulation, partly
by force, and was marching towards Pampeluna;
wherefore general Hill, without abandoning the
siege of that place, moved two British and two Portuguese brigades into the valley of Bastan, and on
the 4th, 5th, 6th, and 7th, vigorously driving Gazan
from all his positions, cleared the valley with a
loss of only one hundred and twenty men. The
whole line of the Spanish frontier from Ronscevalles
to the mouth of the Bidassoa river was thus occupied by the victorious allies, and Pampeluna and St.
Sebastian were invested. Joseph's reign was over,
the crown had fallen from his head, and after
years of toils, and combats which had been rather
admired than understood, the English general,
emerging from the chaos of the Peninsula struggle,
stood on the summit of the Pyrennees a recognised
conqueror. On those lofty pinnacles the clangor
of his trumpets pealed clear and loud, and the
splendour of his genius appeared as a flaming bea-
con to warring nations.

OBSERVATIONS.

1°. In this campaign of six weeks, Wellington,
with one hundred thousand men, marched six hundred miles, passed six great rivers, gained one
decisive battle, invested two fortresses, and drove

a hundred and twenty thousand veteran troops from
Spain. This immense result could not have been
attained if Joseph had followed Napoleon's instructions; Wellington could not then have turned
the line of the Duero. It could not have been
attained if Joseph had acted with ordinary skill
after the line of the Duero was passed. Time was
to him most precious, yet when contrary to his
expectations he had concentrated his scattered
armies behind the Carion, he made no effort to
delay his enemy on that river. He judged it an
unfit position, that is, unfit for a great battle; but
he could have obliged Wellington to lose a day
there, perhaps two or three, and behind the Upper
Pisuerga he might have saved a day or two more.
Reille who was with the army of Portugal on the
right of the king's line complained that he could
find no officers of that army who knew the Pisuerga
sufficiently to place the troops in position; the
king then had cause to remember Napoleon's
dictum, namely, that " to command an army well
a general must think of nothing else." For why
was the course of the Pisuerga unknown when the
king's head-quarters had been for several months
within a day's journey of it?

King's
correspon-
dence,
MSS.

2⁰. The Carion and the Pisuerga being given up,
the country about the Hormaza was occupied and
the three French armies were in mass between that
stream and Burgos; yet Wellington's right wing
only, that is to say, only twenty-three thousand infantry, and three brigades of cavalry, drove Reille's
troops over the Arlanzan, and the castle of Burgos
was abandoned. This was on the 12th, the three
French armies, not less than fifty thousand fighting
men, had been in position since the 9th, and the

king's letters prove that he desired to fight in
that country, which was favourable for all arms.
Nothing then could be more opportune than Wellington's advance on the 12th, because a retrograde
defensive sytem is unsuited to French soldiers,
whose impatient courage leads them always to
attack, and the news of Napoleon's victory at
Bautzen had just arrived to excite their ardour.
Wherefore Joseph should have retaken the offensive
on the 12th at the moment when Wellington approached the Hormaza, and as the left and centre
of the allies were at Villa Diego and Castroxerez,
the greatest part at the former, that is to say, one
march distant, the twenty-six thousand men immediately under Wellington, would probably have
been forced back over the Pisuerga, and the king
would have gained time for Sarrut, Foy and Clauzel
to join him. Did the English general then owe his
success to fortune, to his adversary's fault rather
than to his own skill? Not so. He had judged
the king's military capacity, he had seen the haste,
the confusion, the trouble of the enemy, and knowing well the moral power of rapidity and boldness
in such circumstances, had acted, daringly indeed,
but wisely, for such daring is admirable, it is the
highest part of war.

3°. The manner in which Wellington turned the
line of the Ebro was a fine strategic illustration.
It was by no means certain of success, yet failure
would have still left great advantages. He was
certain of gaining Santander and fixing a new base
of operations on the coast, and he would still have
had the power of continually turning the king's
right by operating between him and the coast;
the errors of his adversary only gave him additional

advantages which he expected, and seized with promptness. But if Joseph, instead of spreading his army from Espejo on his right to the Logroño road on his left, had kept only cavalry on the latter route and on the main road in front of Pancorbo; if he had massed his army to his right pivoting upon Miranda, or Frias, and had scoured all the roads towards the sources of the Ebro with the utmost diligence, the allies could never have passed the defiles and descended upon Vittoria. They would have marched then by Valmaceda upon Bilbao, but Joseph could by the road of Orduña have met them there, and with his force increased by Foy's and Sarrut's divisions and the Italians. Meanwhile Clauzel would have come down to Vittoria, and the heaped convoys could have made their way to France in safety.

4°. Having finally resolved to fight at Vittoria, the king should, on the 19th and 20th, have broken some of the bridges on the Zadora, and covered others with field-works to enable him to sally forth upon the attacking army; he should have entrenched the defile of Puebla, and occupied the heights above in strength; his position on the Lower Zadora would then have been formidable. But his greatest fault was in the choice of his line of operation. His reasons for avoiding Guipuscoa were valid, his true line was on the other side, down the Ebro. Zaragoza should have been his base, since Aragon was fertile and more friendly than any other province of Spain. It is true that by taking this new line of operations he would have abandoned Foy; but that general, reinforced with the reserve from Bayonne, would have had twenty thousand men and the fortress of St. Sebas-

tian as a support, and Wellington must have left a
strong corps of observation to watch him. The
king's army would have been immediately increased
by Clauzel's troops, and ultimately by Suchet's, which
would have given him one hundred thousand men
to oppose the allied army, weakened as that would
have been by the detachment left to watch Foy.
And there were political reasons, to be told hereafter, for the reader must not imagine Wellington
had got thus far without such trammels, which
would have probably rendered this plan so efficacious as to oblige the British army to abandon
Spain altogether. Then new combinations would
have been made all over Europe which it is useless
to speculate upon.

5°. In the battle the operations of the French,
with the exception of Reille's defence of the
bridges of Gamara and Ariaga, were a series of
errors, the most extraordinary being the suffering
Kempt's brigade of the light division, and the
hussars, to pass the bridge of Tres Puentes and
establish themselves close to the king's line of
battle, and upon the flank of his advanced posts at
the bridges of Mendoza and Villodas. It is quite
clear from this alone that he decided upon retreating the moment Graham's attack commenced
against his right flank, and his position was therefore in his own view untenable. The fitting thing
then was to have occupied the heights of Puebla
strongly, but to have placed the bulk of his infantry by corps, in succession, the right refused,
towards Vittoria, while his cavalry and guns
watched the bridges and the mouth of the Puebla
defile ; in this situation he could have succoured
Reille, or marched to his front, according to cir-

cumstances, and his retreat would have been secure.

6°. The enormous fault of heaping up the baggage and convoys and parcs behind Vittoria requires no comment, but the king added another and more extraordinary error, namely the remaining to the last moment undecided as to his line of retreat. Nothing but misfortunes could attend upon such bad dispositions; and that the catastrophe was not more terrible is owing entirely to an error which Wellington and Graham seem alike to have fallen into, namely, that Reille had two divisions in reserve behind the bridges on the Upper Zadora. They knew not that Maucune's division had marched with the convoy, and thought Clauzel had only one division of the army of Portugal with him, whereas he had two, Taupin's and Barbout's. Reille's reserves were composed not of divisions but of brigades drawn from La Martiniere's and Sarrut's divisions, which were defending the bridges; and his whole force, including the French-Spaniards who were driven back from Durana, did not exceed ten thousand infantry and two thousand five hundred cavalry. Now Graham had, exclusive of Giron's Gallicians, nearly twenty thousand of all arms, and it is said that the river might have been passed both above and below the points of attack; it is certain also that Longa's delay gave the French time to occupy Gamara Mayor in force, which was not the case at first. Had the passage been won in time, very few of the French army could have escaped from the field; but the truth is Reille fought most vigorously.

7°. As the third and seventh divisions did not

See Wellington's despatch.

come to the point of attack at the time calculated
upon, the battle was probably not fought after the
original conception of lord Wellington; it is likely
that his first project was to force the passage of the
bridges, to break the right centre of the enemy
from Arinez to Margarita, and then to envelope the
left centre with the second, fourth, and light divisions and the cavalry, while the third and seventh
divisions pursued the others. But notwithstanding
the unavoidable delay, which gave the French
time to commence their retreat, it is not easy to
understand how Gazan's left escaped from Subijana
de Alava, seeing that when Picton broke the centre
at Arinez, he was considerably nearer to Vittoria
than the French left, which was cut off from the
main road and assailed in front by Hill and Cole.
The having no cavalry in hand to launch at this
time and point of the battle has been already
noticed; lord Wellington says, that the country Despatch.
was generally unfavourable for the action of that
arm, and it is certain that neither side used it
with much effect at any period of the battle;
nevertheless there are always some suitable openings, some happy moments to make a charge, and
this seems to have been one which was
neglected.

8°. Picton's sudden rush from the bridge of
Tres Puentes to the village of Arinez, with one
brigade, has been much praised, and certainly
nothing could be more prompt and daring, but the
merit of the conception belongs to the general in
chief, who directed it in person. It was suggested
to him by the denuded state of the hill in front
of that village, and viewed as a stroke for the occasion it is to be admired. Yet it had its disadvan-

tages. For the brigade which thus crossed a part
of the front of both armies to place itself in advance, not only drew a flank fire from the enemy,
but was exposed if the French cavalry had been
prompt and daring, to a charge in flank; it also
prevented the advance of the other troops in their
proper arrangement, and thus crowded the centre
for the rest of the action. However these sudden
movements cannot be judged by rules, they are
good or bad according to the result. This was
entirely successful, and the hill thus carried was
called the Englishmen's hill, not, as some recent
writers have supposed, in commemoration of a
victory gained by the Black Prince, but because of
a disaster which there befel a part of his army.
His battle was fought between Navarrette and
Najera, many leagues from Vittoria, and beyond
the Ebro ; but on this hill the two gallant knights
sir Thomas and sir William Felton took post with
two hundred companions, and being surrounded
by Don Tello with six thousand, all died or were
taken after a long, desperate, and heroic resistance.

9°. It has been observed by French writers, and
the opinion has been also entertained by many
English officers, that after the battle Wellington
should have passed the frontier in mass, and
marched upon Bayonne instead of chasing Clauzel
and Foy on the right and left; and if, as the
same authors assert, Bayonne was not in a state
of defence and must have fallen, there can be little
question that the criticism is just, because the
fugitive French army having lost all its guns and
being without musket ammunition, could not have
faced its pursuers for a moment. But if Bayonne

had resisted, and it was impossible for Wellington
to suspect its real condition, much mischief might
have accrued from such a hasty advance. Foy
and Clauzel coming down upon the field of Vittoria
would have driven away if they did not destroy
the sixth division; they would have recovered
all the trophies; the king's army returning by
Jacca into Aragon, would have reorganized itself
from Suchet's dépôts, and that marshal was actually coming up with his army from Valencia;
little would then have been gained by the battle.
This question can however be more profitably discussed when the great events which followed the
battle of Vittoria have been described.

Explanatory Sketch
of the
SURPRISE OF ALMARAZ.
May, 1812.
The Scene of Action Enlarged.

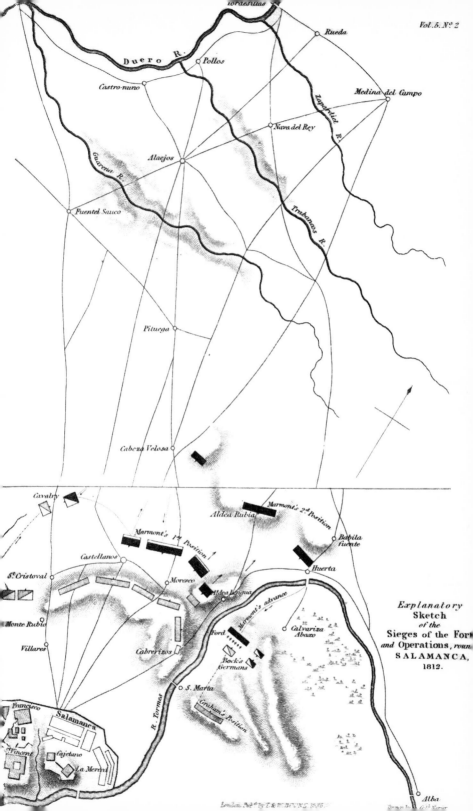

Iordesillas

Rueda

Duero R.

Pollos

Castro-nuno

Medina del Campo

Zapardiel R.

Nava del Rey

Alaejos

Guareña R.

Fuentel Sauco

Trabancos R.

PitueJga

Cabeza Velosa

Cavalry

Marmont's 2.ᵈ Position

Aldea Rubia

Marmont's 1.ˢᵗ Position

Babila fuente

Castellanos

Huerta

S.ᵗ Cristoval

Moresco

Monte Rubio

Aldea lengua

Marmont's advance

Villares

Ford

Galvariza Abaxo

Cabrerizos

Bock's Germans

Explanatory
Sketch
of the
Sieges of the Fort
and Operations, roun
SALAMANCA,
1812.

S.ᵗ Marta

R. Tormes

Graham's Position

Francisco

Salamanca

S.ᵗ Vincent

Cajetano

La Merced

Alba

London, Pub.ᵈ by T. & W. BOONE 1845

Drawn by G.ᵈˡ Xavier

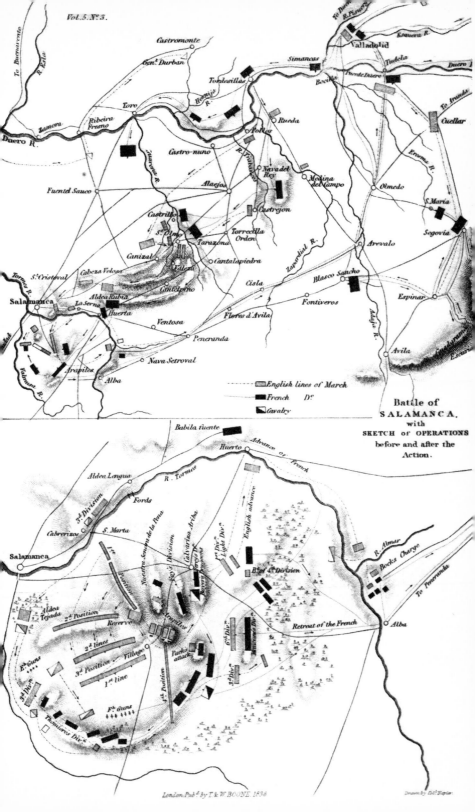

Battle of
SALAMANCA.
with
SKETCH of OPERATIONS
before and after the
Action.

Drawn by Col.l Napier.

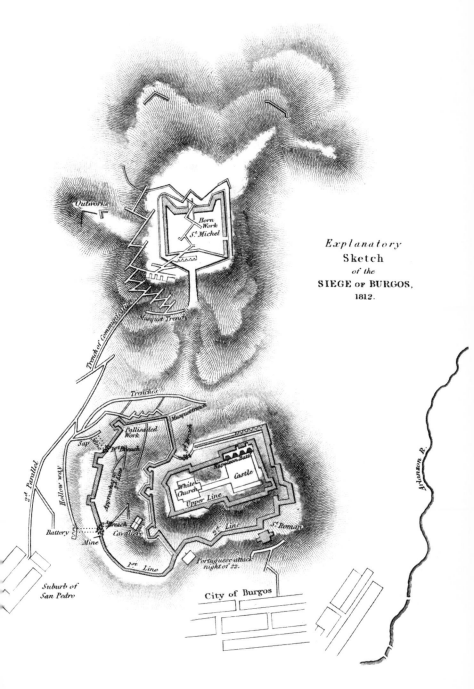

Outworks

Horn Work Sₜ Michel

Explanatory
Sketch
of the
SIEGE of BURGOS,
1812.

Sanjuie Trench

Trench of Communication

Trenches

Pallisaded Work

Sap

Napoleon Bat.

White Church

Castle

Upper Line

2ᵈ Line

Sₜ Roman

Breach Cavalier

Battery

Mine

1ˢᵗ Line

Portuguese attack
night of 22.

Suburb of
San Pedro

City of Burgos

Arlanzon R.

London, Pub.ᵈ by T. & W. BOONE, 1836.

Drawn by Colₗ Napier.

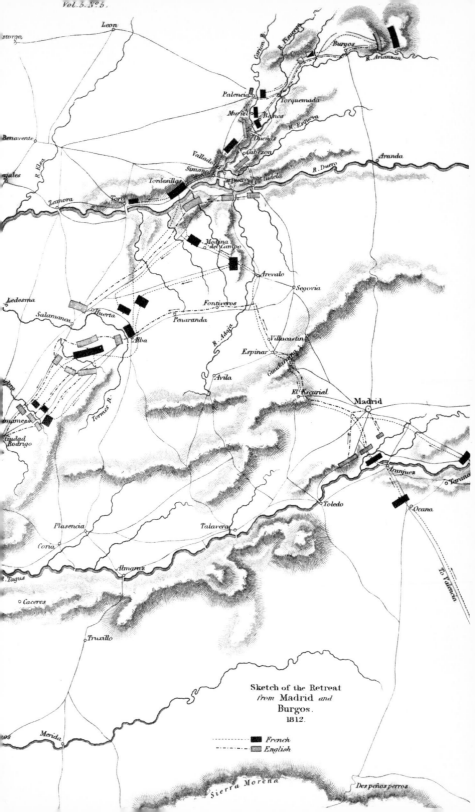

Sketch of the Retreat
from Madrid *and*
Burgos.
1812.

- - - - - French
━━━━ English

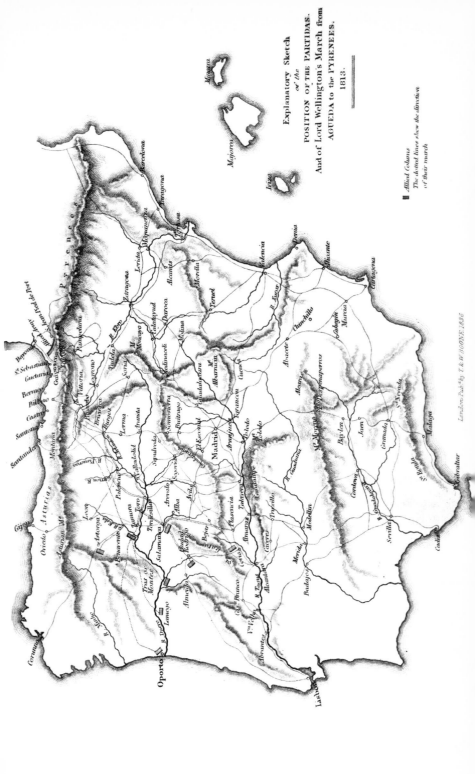

Explanatory Sketch
of the
POSITION of the PARTIDAS.
And of Lord Wellington's March from
AGUEDA to the PYRENEES.
1813.

■ Allied Colums
The dotted lines shew the direction
of their march

London. Pub.d by T. & W. BOONE 1836.

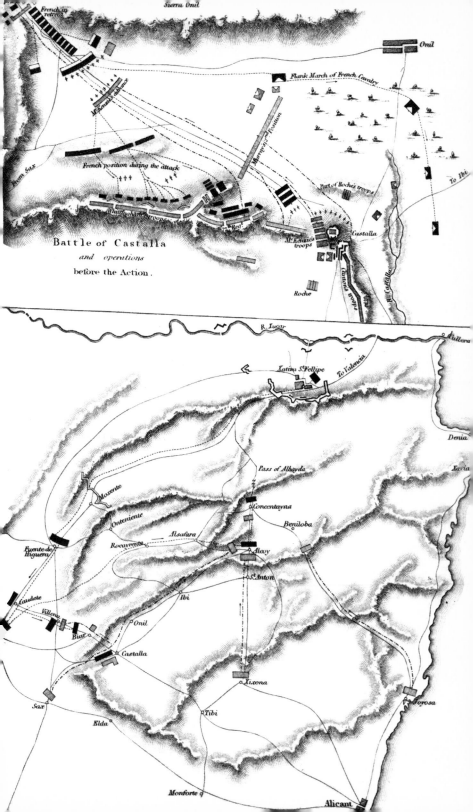

Sierra Onil

French in retreat

Onil

Flank March of French Cavalry

M⁹Kenzie's advance

To Ibi

Marquesize's Position

From Sax

French position during the attack

Part of Roche's troops

To Ibi

Whittingham's troops

M⁹Kenzie's troops

Castalla

Batle of Castalla

and operations

before the Action.

Roche

R. de Castalla

R. Iucar

Sullera

Xativa S⁹ Fellipe

To Valencia

Denia

Pass of Albayda

Maxente

Xavia

S⁹ Concentayna

Onteniente

Beniloba

Alsafara

Recayredes

Alcoy

Fuente de Higuera

S⁹ Anton

Ibi

Caudete

Villena

Onil

Biar

Castalla

Xixona

Sax

Jorosa

Tibi

Elda

Monforte

Alicant

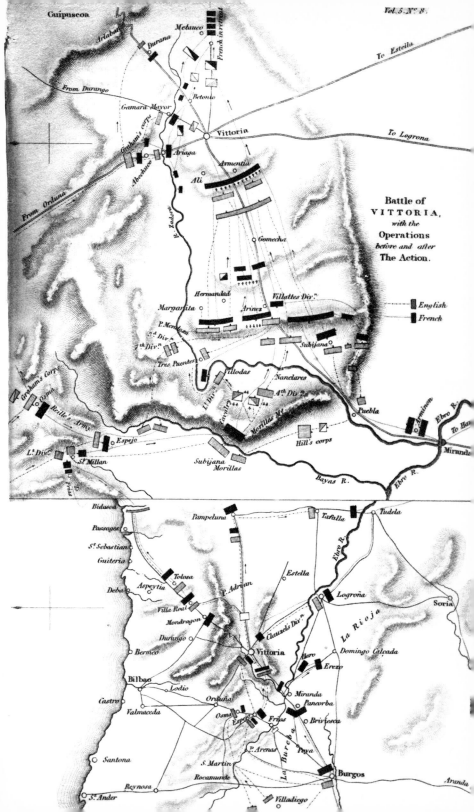

Battle of
VITTORIA,
with the
Operations
before and after
The Action.

English
French

Guipuscoa

To Estella

To Logrona

From Durango

From Orduna

Metauco

French in retreat

Durana

Arlaban

Betonio

Gamara Mayor

Graham's corps

Ariaga

Abechuco

Ali

Armentia

Vittoria

Gomecha

R. Zadora

Hermandad

Margarita

Arinez

Villattes Div.ⁿ

P. Mendoza

3.ᵈ Div.ⁿ

7.ᵗʰ Div.ⁿ

Tres Puentes

Tillodas

Nanclares

Subijana

L.ᵗ Div.ⁿ

Cavalry

4.ᵗʰ Div.ⁿ

Morillas M.ᵗ

Puebla

Graham's Corps

Osma

Reille's Army

Espejo

Hill's corps

Armines

L.ᵗ Div.ⁿ

St. Millan

Subijana
Morillas

Bayas R.

Ebre R.

Ebre R.

Miranda

To Haro

Bidasoa

Passages

St. Sebastian

Guiteria

Tolosa

Aspeytia

Deba

Villa Real

Mondragon

Durango

Bermeo

Bilbao

Lodio

Castro

Valmaceda

Santona

St. Ander

Reynosa

Pampeluna

P. Adrian

Estella

Clausels Div.ⁿ

Vittoria

Orduña

Osma

Espejo

Frias

S. Martin

Rocamunde

Villadiego

P. Arenas

Poza

Tafalla

Tudela

Ebre R.

Logroña

Soria

La Rioja

Haro

Erezo

Domingo Calcada

Miranda

Pancorba

Briviesca

La Bureba

Burgos

Aranda

APPENDIX.

APPENDIX.

No. I.

THE following extracts of letters are published to avoid any future cavils upon the points they refer to, and also to shew how difficult it is for the historian to obtain certain and accurate details, when eye-witnesses, having no wish to mislead, differ so much.

BATTLE OF SALAMANCA.

Extract of a memoir by Sir Charles Dalbiac, who was one of Le Marchant's brigade of heavy cavalry.

" Throughout these charges upon the enemy, *the heavy brigade was unsupported by any other portion of the cavalry whatever;* but was followed, as rapidly as it was possible for infantry to follow, by the third division which had so gloriously led the attack in the first instance and had so effectually turned the enemy's extreme left."

Extract from a memoir by colonel Money, who was one of general Anson's brigade of light cavalry.

" The third division moved to the right, and *the cavalry, Le Marchand's and Anson's,* were ordered to charge as soon as the tirailleurs of the third division began to ascend the right flank of the hill."—" The rapid movement of the cavalry which now began to gallop, and the third division pressing them (the French), they run into the wood, which separated them from the army; *we (Anson's light cavalry) charged them under a heavy fire of musketry and artillery from another height*; near two thousand threw down their arms in different parts of the wood, and we continued our charge through the wood until our brigade came into an open plain of ploughed fields, where the dust was so great we could see nothing, and halted; when it cleared away, we found ourselves within three hundred yards of a large body of French infantry and artillery, formed on the declivity of a hill. A tremendous battle was heard on the other side, which prevented the enemy from perceiving us. At last they opened a fire of musketry and grape-shot, and we retired in good order and without any loss."

Extract of a letter from sir Henry Watson, commanding the first regiment of Portuguese cavalry under general D'Urban.

" When Marmont, at the battle of Salamanca, advanced his left, lord Wellington ordered down the reserve, of which the first and tenth Portuguese cavalry and two squadrons of the British cavalry under captain Townsend, now lieutenant-colonel Townsend, formed a part under Sir B. D'Urban. The cavalry was pushed forward in contiguous columns, and were protected from the enemy by a small rising ground, which, as soon as I had passed, I was ordered to wheel up, and charge the front in line. *The enemy had formed a square*, and gave us a volley as we advanced, the eleventh and fourteenth remained en potence. *In this charge we completely succeeded*, and the enemy appeared panic-struck, and made no attempt to prevent our cutting and thrusting at them in all directions until the moment I was about to withdraw; then a soldier, at not more than six or eight paces, levelled his musquet at me, and shot me through the shoulder, which knocked me off my horse, where I continued to lie till the whole of our infantry had passed over."

Extract from a letter of colonel Townsend, 14th Dragoons.

" At the battle of Salamanca I perfectly recollect seeing D'Urban's cavalry advance up the hill, and charge the French infantry. *They were repulsed*, and left Watson (now sir Henry), who led his regiment, the first Portuguese, badly wounded on the field."—" *I am almost positive the French were not in square,*

*but in line, waiting to receive the attack of the leading brigade
of the third division,* which gallantly carried every thing before
it."

No. II.

*Copies de deux dépêches de l'empereur au ministre de la guerre
relatives au duc de Raguse.*

Dresde, le 28 Mai, 1812.

MONSIEUR LE DUC DE FELTRE,

Je vous renvois la correspondance d'Espagne.   Ecrivez au duc
de Raguse que c'est le roi qui doit lui donner des directions, que
je suppose qu'il s'est retiré devant lord Wellington selon les règles
de la guerre, en l'obligéant à se masser, et non en se reployant
devant sa cavalerie légère ; qu'il aura conservé des têtes de pont
sur l'Agueda, ce qui peut seul lui permettre d'avoir des nouvelles
de l'ennemi tous les jours, et de le tenir en respect.   Que si au
contraire il a mis trente lieues d'intervalle entre lui et l'ennemi,
comme il l'a déjà fait deux fois contre tous les principes de la
guerre, il laisse le général Anglais maître de se porter où il veut,
il perd constamment l'initiative, et n'est plus d'aucun poids dans
les affaires d'Espagne, que la Biscaye et le nord sont dans des
dispositions facheuses par les suites de l'évacuation des Asturias
par la division Bonnet, que la réoccupation de cette province n'a
pas encore eu lieu, que le nord est exposé à de grands malheurs,
que Santona et St. Sebastian sont compromis, que les libres communications des guerillas avec la Galice et les Asturies par la mer
les rendront formidables, que s'il ne fait pas réoccuper promptement les Asturies, sa position ne peut s'ameliorer.

Recommandez au général Caffarelli de réunir davantage ses
troupes, et d'avoir toujours une colonne dans la main.

Ecrivez au général L'Huillier d'avoir l'œil sur St. Sebastian, et
d'avoir toujours 3000 hommes dans la main pour les diriger sur
cette place si elle avoit besoin d'être secourue.

En général pour parer à la mauvaise manœuvre et à la mauvaise
direction que le duc de Raguse donne à nos affaires il est nécessaire d'avoir beaucoup de monde à Bayonne.   Activez la marche
du 3ᵉ et du 106ᵐᵉ et de la 5ᵉ demi brigade provisoire sur cette

place. Tenez y deux généraux de brigade afin que le général L'Huillier puisse toujours disposer des forces pour être en mesure d'agir selon les circonstances.

Réunissez un millier d'hommes des dépôts de cavalerie de l'armée d'Espagne, et dirigez les en régimens de marche sur Bayonne.

Prescrivez au général L'Huillier de tenir ses troupes dans la vallée de Bastan, à Bayonne, St. Jean de Luz, et Irun, en les munissant bien, les barraquant, les exerçant, et les formant. Ce sera au moyen de cette ressource que si le duc de Raguse continue à faire des bévues on pourra empêcher le mal de devenir extrême.

Sur ce, je prie Dieu, &c.

(Signé)   NAPOLEON.

[*For second despatch*, see Appendix No. VII.]

No. III.

Lettre de M. le duc de Dalmatie au roi.

Seville, 12 *Août,* 1812.

Je n'avais reçu aucune nouvelle de V. M. depuis les lettres qu'elle m'a fait l'honneur m'écrire des 6 et 7 Juillet dernier. Enfin je viens de récevoir celle datée de Segovie le 29 du même mois. Les rapports publiés par les ennemis m'avaient déjà instruit des évènemens survenus en Castille lesquels étaient naturellement exagérés ; V. M. a bien voulu en quelque sorte fixer à ce sujet mes idées. Je déplore les pertes que l'armée de Portugal a éprouvées. Dans l'état ou étaient les affaires d'Espagne une bataille ne devait se donner qu'à la dernière extrémité, mais tout n'est pas perdu. V. M. après m'avoir communiqué les dispositions qu'elle a faites depuis le 6 (date de la dernière lettre) au 19 Juillet m'ordonne comme une ressource d'évacuer l'Andalousie et de me diriger sur Tolêde. Je ne puis dissimuler que cette disposition me parait fort extraordinaire. J'étais loin de penser que V. M. s'y serait déterminée. Le sort de l'Espagne est il donc décidé ? V. M. veut elle sacrifier le royaume à la capitale ? et a-t-elle la certitude de la conserver en prenant ce parti ? Enfin l'évacuation de l'Andalousie et ma marche sur Tolêde sont elles l'unique ressource qui nous reste ? Je vais me préparer à cette disposition que je regarde comme des plus funestes pour l'honneur des armes impériales, le bien du service de l'empereur et l'intérêt de V. M.

dans l'espoir qu'avant qu'elle s'exécute V. M. l'aura changée ou modifiée suivant les propositions que j'ai eu l'honneur de lui faire le 19 Juillet, le 8 de ce mois, et par M. le colonel Desprez.

J'ai l'honneur d'adresser à votre Majesté triplicata de ma lettre du 8 de ce mois. En me référant aux observations et propositions qu'elle renferme, si V. M. ne prend pas des dispositions en conséquence, je considére que l'évacuation de toute l'Espagne est decidée, car il faut que V. M. se persuade que du moment que mon mouvement sera commencé je serai suivi par soixante mille ennemis lesquels ne me donneront pas le tems ni la liberté de prendre la direction que V. M. m'indique et qui se réuniront à ceux qui ont pénétré en Castille et m'empécheront de séjourner sur le Tage encore moins d'arriver à Madrid. Il n'y a qu'un moyen pour rétablir les affaires : que V. M. vienne en Andalousie et qu'elle y améne toutes les troupes de l'armée du centre, de l'armée de Portugal, de.l'armée d'Arragon auxquelles ses ordres pourront parvenir, quand bien même tout le royaume de Valence devrait être évacué. Qu'importe à V. M. de conserver Madrid si elle perd le royaume ? Philippe V. en sortit trois fois et y rentra en souverain. Du moment que nous aurons 70 ou 80 mille Français réunis dans le midi de l'Espagne, le théâtre de la guerre est changé ; l'armée de Portugal se trouve dégagée et elle peut se reporter successivement jusqu'au Tage. D'ailleurs ce serait sans inconvénient qu'elle gardât Burgos et la rive gauche de l'Ebre et que tout l'espace compris entre elle et le Sierra Morena fut à la disposition des ennemis jusqu'à ce que des renforts vinssent de France et que l'empereur eût pu prendre des dispositions. Le sacrifice une fois fait il n'y a plus de moyen d'y remédier. Les armées impériales en Espagne repassent l'Ebre d'ou peut-être la famine les chassera, les affaires de l'empereur dans le nord de l'Europe peuvent s'en ressentir, l'Amerique qui vient de déclarer la guerre à l'Angleterre fera peut-être la paix. V. M. a sans doute refléchi à toutes les conséquences d'un pareil changement ; la perte momentanée de Madrid et des Castilles est nulle pour la politique de l'empereur, elle peut se réparer en plus ou moins de tems. La perte d'une bataille par l'armée de Portugal n'est qu'un grand duel qui se répare également, mais la perte de l'Andalousie et la levée du siége de Cadiz sont des évènemens dont les effets seront ressentis dans toute l'Europe et dans le nouveau monde. Enfin en fidèle sujet de l'empereur je dois déclarer à V. M. que je ne crois pas les affaires d'Espagne assez désespérées pour prendre un parti aussi violent. J'entrevois encore du remède si V. M. veut prendre les dispositions que j'ai proposées; tout en me préparant à l'exécution de ses ordres je me permets de lui demander de nouvelles instructions. J'ai surtout l'honneur de prier V. M. d'ordonner que les communications de l'Andalousie avec Toléde soient rétablies et quelque évènement qui survienne de vouloir bien faire prendre à l'armée du centre, la direction de Despeña Perros ou d'Almaden pour se joindre à l'armée du midi. Alors je réponds de tout, et j'exécuterai les dispositions que j'ai énoncées dans ma lettre du 8 de ce mois.

Je, &c. &c. &c.

No. IV.

Lettre de M. le maréchal duc de Dalmatie à M. le Ministre de la guerre à Paris.

Monsieur le Duc,

Toute communication de l'Andalousie avec la France étant interrompue et n'ayant rien réçu depuis les premiers jours de Mai; depuis un mois le roi ayant même retiré les troupes qui étoient dans la Manche et ne pouvant communiquer avec Madrid, j'entreprens de faire parvenir mes rapports à votre excellence par la voie de mer. Si le bâtiment que je fais à cet effet partir de Malaga peut arriver à Marseille, l'empereur sera plutôt instruit de ce qui se passe dans le midi de l'Espagne et de la position de son armée.

A ce sujet j'ai l'honneur d'adresser à votre excellence copie des derniers rapports que j'ai faits au roi, lesquels contiennent les représentations que j'ai cru devoir soumettre à sa majesté pour le bien du service de l'empereur, la conservation des conquêtes et l'honneur des armées impériales.

Je ne suis instruit des malheurs que l'armée de Portugal a éprouvés que par les bruits populaires et les rapports de l'ennemi; car le roi en m'écrivant le 29 Juillet de Ségovie ne m'en a donné aucun détail. Je dois donc m'imaginer que les pertes que nous avons faites en Castile sont beaucoup exagérées et j'en tire la conséquence que les affaires de l'empereur en Espagne ne sont pas aussi desespérées que le roi parait en être persuadé. Cependant sa majesté après être resté 23 jours sans m'écrire, lorsque les ennemis étoient en plein mouvement et que sa majesté se portoit avec 14,000 hommes de l'armée du centre à la rencontre du duc de Raguse qui sans l'attendre s'etoit engagé precipitamment et éprouvait une défaite ; le roi dis-je en me faisant part le 29 Juillet de ses mouvemens me donna l'ordre formel d'évacuer l'Andalousie et me diriger sur Tolede, et il me dit expressément que c'est l'unique ressource qui nous reste.

Je suis loin de partager l'avis de sa majesté, je crois fermement qu'il est possible de mieux faire et que tout peut s'arranger en attendant que d'après les ordres de l'empereur V. E. ait pû mettre les armées qui sont dans le nord de l'Espagne à même de reprendre les opérations, ainsi que j'en fais la proposition à sa majesté dans les lettres dont je mets ci-joint copies. Mais mon devoir est d'obéïr et je me chargerais d'une trop grande responsibilité si j'éludais l'exécution de l'ordre formel d'évacuer que le roi m'a donné.

Je vais donc me préparer à exécuter cette disposition que je regarde comme funeste, puisqu'elle me force à livrer aux ennemis des places de guerre susceptibles d'une bonne défense tout aprovisionnées, les établissemens et un matériel d'artillerie immense et de laisser dans les hôpitaux beaucoup de malades que leur situation et le manque de transport ne permettent point d'emmener. Je ne ferai cependant mon mouvement que progressivement et je ne négligerai aucun soin pour qu'il ne reste en arrière rien de ce qui peut être utile à l'armée.

Je ne puis encore assurer que je ne ferai ce mouvement par Tolede, car du moment qu'il sera entrepris je serai suivi par 60,000 ennemis qui se joindront aux divisions que lord Wellington aura déjà portées sur le Tage. Ainsi il est possible que je me dirige par Murcie sur Valence suivant ce que j'apprendrai ou les nouveaux ordres que je recevrai du roi.

Dans cet état de choses, je ne puis dissimuler à V. E. que je regarde l'évacuation de l'Espagne au moins jusqu'à l'Ebre comme décidée du moment que le roi m'ordonna d'évacuer l'Andalousie et de me diriger sur Toléde, car il est bien certain qu'il ne sera pas possible de rester en position sur le Tage ni dans les Castilles et que dès-lors les conquêtes des armes impériales en Espagne dont l'empereur avait ordonné la conservation, sont sacrifiées.

A ce sujet je ne puis me défendre de réflechir sur d'autres évènemens qui se passent. J'ai lu dans les journaux de Cadiz, que l'ambassadeur du roi en Russie avait joint l'armée Russe, que le roi avait fait des insinuations au gouvernement insurgent de Cadiz, que la Suéde avait fait un traité avec l'Angleterre, et que le prince héréditaire avait demandé à la regence de Cadiz 250 Espagnols pour sa garde personelle. (Avant hier un parlementaire que le général Semélé avait envoyé à l'escadre Anglaise pour réclamer des prisonniers resta pendant quelques instans à bord de l'amiral, lequel lui montra une frégate, qui, dit il, est destinée à porter en Angleterre et ensuite en Suéde les 250 Espagnols que le prince Bernadotte demande pour sa garde personelle.) Enfin j'ai vu dans les mêmes journaux que Moreau et Blucher étaient arrivés à Stockholm, et que Rapatel, aide-de-camp de Moreau, était à Londres. Je ne tire aucune conséquence de tous ces faits, mais j'en serai plus attentif. Cependant j'ai cru devoir déposer mes craintes entre les mains de six généraux de l'armée, après avoir exigé d'eux le serment qu'ils ne révéleront ce que je leur ai dit qu'à l'empereur lui-même ou aux personnes que S. M. aura specialement déléguées pour en reçevoir la déclaration, si auparavant je ne puis moi-même en rendre compte. Il est pourtant de mon devoir de manifester à V. E. que je crains que le bût de toutes les fausses dispositions que l'on a prises et celui des intrigues qui ont lieu ne soient de forcer les armées impériales qui sont en Espagne à repasser au moins l'Ebre et ensuite de présenter cet évènement comme l'unique ressource (expression du roi, lettre du 20 Juillet) dans l'espérance d'en profiter par quelque arrangement.

Mes craintes sont peut-être mal fondées, mais en pareille situation il vaut mieux les pousser à l'extrémité que d'être négligent, d'autant plus que ces craintes et ma sollicitude tournent au bien du service de l'empereur et à la sureté de l'armée dont le commandement m'est confié.

J'ai l'honneur de prier V. E. de vouloir bien si ma lettre lui parvient, la mettre le plutôt possible sous les yeux de l'empereur et d'assurer S. M. que moi et son armée du midi serons toujours dignes de sa suprême confiance. Je désire bien vivement que V. E. puisse me faire savoir que mes dépêches lui sont parvenues et surtout recevoir par elle les ordres de sa majesté.

J'ai l'honneur, &c.
(Signé)   DALMATIE.

Seville, 12 *Août*, 1812.

No. V.

SIRE,

Je suis arrivé à Paris hier 21 du courant. Je me suis sur le champ présenté chez le ministre de la guerre et je lui ai remis la lettre de V. M. ainsi que celles de M. le maréchal Jourdan. S. E. m'a questionné sur les affaires d'Espagne, mais sans me demander mes dépêches pour l'empereur. Elle m'a, suivant les intentions de V. M., pourvu des ordres dont j'ai besoin pour poursuivre ma route avec célérité.

Ce matin le ministre m'a fait appéler et j'ai eu avec lui une longue conférence. Il m'a pressé de m'expliquer avec franchise sur ce que j'avais pu remarquer pendant mon séjour en Andalousie, m'a témoigné quelque inquiétude sur l'influence que pouvoit exercer le maréchal tant sur l'armée que sur les autorités civiles. Il a rappelé les intrigues de Portugal et a conclu en me disant qu'il dépouillait devant moi le caractère de ministre pour causer avec un homme de votre confiance, et que les services que vous lui aviez rendus à l'époque de sa disgrâce devaient être pour V. M. une garantie du désir qu'il avait d'agir suivant ses intentions. Quelque franches que m'aient parus ces ouvertures, je n'ai pas cru devoir parler de la partie la plus délicate de ma mission. J'ai seulement répondu que l'armée du midi serait toujours celle de l'empereur, que lorsque S. M. enverrait ses ordres déterminés, elle serait obéie, et que tout ce que j'avais entendu en Andalousie ne me laissait à ce sujet aucun doute. Au reste ma conversation avec le duc de Feltre m'a prouvé qu'aucune lettre de la nature de celle dont je suis porteur ne lui etait encore parvenue et cela est pour ma mission une circonstance favorable.

J'ai causé avec S. E. de la résistance que les chefs de l'armée francaise en Espagne avaient toujours opposée aux ordres de V. M. Il a declaré que tous avaient été mis sous vos ordres et sans aucune restriction, qu'avant son départ l'empereur avait témoigné son étonnement sur les doutes que manifestaient à cet égard les lettres de V. M. et qu'il avait ordonné que l'on fit connaître ses intentions d'une manière encore plus positive. J'ai cité la lettre ou le maréchal Suchet s'autorise d'une phrase du Prince de Neufchatel, celles du général Dorsenne et du général Caffarelli, il parait que tous les obstacles qui pouvaient entraver l'exécution de vos ordres ont été levés par des instructions adressées postérieurement aux généraux en chef. Quant à la désobeissance formelle du maréchal Soult S. E. a dit d'abord que V. M. avait le droit de lui ôter le commandement, mais elle est convenue ensuite qu'une démarche semblable ne pouvait être faite que par l'ordre exprès de l'empereur.

Le ministre est aussi entré dans quelques détails sur les affaires militaires, les ordres donnés par V. M. et par le maréchal Jourdan aux diverses époques de la campagne, ont eu, m'a-t-il dit, l'approbation générale et ce qu'a écrit l'empereur depuis qu'il a appris la bataille de Salamanque prouve qu'il donne entièrement droit à V. M. l'opinion publique à cet égard est encore plus prononcée que celle des hommes en place, et je ne puis exprimer à V. M. avec quelle rigueur sont jugés en France les maréchaux Soult et Marmont.

Le duc de Feltre m'a parlé du mouvement sur Blasco Sancho. Peut-être a-t-il dit, l'empereur reprochera un peu d'hésitation ; exécuté deux jours plutôt il aurait produit les plus heureux effets. V. M. se rappelle que j'avais prévu cette objection et je ne serai point embarrassé pour y répondre.

S. E. a cru que j'allais auprès de l'empereur pour solliciter de nouveaux renforts; elle m'a dit que la guerre de Russie avait jusqu'à présent absorbé tous les moyens, qu'il était loin de pouvoir envoyer les troupes sur lesquelles paraissait compter M. le maréchal Jourdan, que l'on pourrait seulement pourvoir à la perte matérielle faite par l'armée de Portugal, il parait que les nouvelles troupes envoyées en Espagne ne s'élèvent pas au-delà de vingt mille hommes, au reste la grande victoire remportée par l'empereur fera probablement prendre des dispositions plus favorables aux affaires de la Peninsule.

Le duc de Feltre à reçu des nouvelles du général Clauzel. Ce général annonce que l'armée anglaise marche vers le nord, que lord Wellington s'est de sa personne porté vers le Duero, que l'armée de Portugal s'est ralliée, que ses pertes sont beaucoup moindres qu'on ne l'avait cru, que le général Foy avait fait un mouvement pour délivrer Astorga et Tordesillas, mais que déja ces deux places s'étaient rendues que l'on pourrait accuser de faiblesse les deux gouverneurs et que peut-être la conduite de celui de Tordesillas devait être jugée plus sévèrement encore.

J'ai parlé au ministre de la position embarrassante dans laquelle me mettait le décret du 26 Août, il a répondu que je pouvais sans inconvénient me présenter à l'empereur avec les décorations du grade que m'a donné V. M. que ce n'était point contre les officiers à votre service que le décret avait été dirigé et qu'il serait modifié en leur faveur.

J'ai l'honneur de prévenir V. M. que je partirai ce soir de Paris, je poursuivrai sans m'arrêter ma route jusqu'au quartier général de l'empereur.

J'ai l'honneur de mettre aux pieds de V. M. l'hommage de mon profond respect et de mon entier dévouement.

(Signé)   Le Colonel Despres.

Paris, 22 Septembre, 1812.

No. VI. A.

Lettre confidentielle écrite au roi par monsieur le duc de Feltre.

Paris, 10 Novembre, 1812.

Sire,

La lettre chiffrée que V. M. m'a écrite de Requeña le 18 Octobre, m'est parvenue il y a quelques jours, et je l'ai sur le champ transmise à l'empereur qui ne la recevra toute fois que 19 jours après le départ de cette même lettre de Paris. A la distance ou l'empereur se trouve de sa capitale, il est des choses sur lesquelles la politique force à fermer les yeux : du moins momentanement. Si la conduite de monsieur le maréchal duc de Dalmatie est équivoque et cauteleuse ; si ses démarches présentent le même aspect que celles qu'il paroît avoir faites et qui ont précédé l'abandon du Portugal après la prise d'Oporto, il viendra un moment ou l'empereur pourra l'en punir s'il le juge convenable, et peut-être est-il moins dangereux où il est qu'il ne le serait ici où quelques factieux ont pu du sein même des prisons qui les renfermaient méditer en l'absence de l'empereur, une révolution contre l'empereur et sa dynastie, et presque l'exécuter, le 2 et 3 Octobre dernier. Je pense donc, sire, qu'il est prudent de ne pas pousser à bout le maréchal duc de Dalmatie tout en contrariant sous main les démarches ambitieuses qu'il pourrait tenter, et en s'assurant de la fidelité des principaux officiers de l'armée du midi envers l'empereur et même de celle des Espagnols qu'il traine à sa suite. L'arme du ridicule qu'il est facile de manier en cette occasion suffira, ce me semble, pour déjouer ses coupables projets s'ils existent, et le ramener à son devoir, sauf à faire prendre par la suite des précautions pour qu'il ne s'en écarte jamais.

Quoiqu'il en soit je suis incontestablement dans la nécessité d'attendre les ordres de l'empereur sur le contenu de la lettre de V. M. datée de Requena le 18 Oct. Elle voit par la présente que je partage ses sentimens sur l'objet dont elle traite ; je viens d'être assez heureux pour donner à l'empereur et à sa famille de nouvelles preuves de ma fidelité et de mon attachement, et je suis assuré que si V. M. connaît les détails de ma conduite le 2 et 3 Octobre, elle la trouvera conforme aux sentimens que je me suis fait un plaisir de lui exprimer en faveur de l'empereur et de sa famille au moment ou j'ai pris congé de V. M. à Luneville il y a quelques années, &c. &c.

Note.—It is only necessary to add to this letter that notwithstanding the duke of Feltre's professions of attachment he was soon afterwards one of the most zealous courtiers of the Bourbons and the most bitter enemy of the emperor.

The constancy with which the duke of Dalmatia served that great man is well known.

No. VI. B.

Colonel Desprez to the King.

Paris, 3 Janvier, 1813.

SIRE,

J'ai eu l'honneur d'annoncer à V. M. mon arrivée à Paris. Mais j'ai dû en me servant de la voie de l'estafette user d'une extrême discrétion. La reine m'ayant conseillé de vous écrire avec quelque détail et ayant daigné m'offrir de faire partir ma lettre par le premier courier qu'elle expédierait, j'en profite pour rendre compte à V. M. de ma mission et lui faire connaître une partie des évènemens dont j'ai été témoin.

Je suis arrivé à Moscou le 18 Octobre au soir. L'empereur venait d'apprendre que l'avant garde commandée par le roi de

Naples avait été attaquée et forcée à la retraite avec une partie de son artillerie. Déja le départ était résolu et les troupes se mettaient en mouvement. On m'annonça à S. M. qui répondit d'abord d'une manière peu favorable. Cependant au milieu de la nuit on me fit appeler. Je remis à l'empereur les dépêches dont V. M. m'avait chargé, et sans les ouvrir, il me questionna sur leur contenu. Puis il fit sur les opérations de la campagne une partie des objections qu'avait prévues V. M.

Il dit que le mouvement en faveur de l'armée de Portugal avait été commencé trop tard, qu'il aurait pu être fait un mois plutôt, que lui-même avait daté la conduite à tenir dans cette circonstance lorsqu'en 1808 il avait sans hésiter quitté Madrid pour marcher aux Anglais qui s'étaient avancés jusqu'à Valladolid. Je répondis que V. M. s'était mise en marche peu d'heures après la division Palombini, qu'elle avait dû attendre cette division pour conduire vers l'armée de Portugal un renfort tel que le succès ne pût être douteux ; qu'elle avait d'autant moins cru devoir précipiter son mouvement, que M. le maréchal Marmont avait écrit plusieurs fois qu'il se croyait trop faible pour lutter seul contre l'armée Anglaise, que ce maréchal avait été maître du tems, qu'il n'avait point été battu dans sa position sur le Duero, mais bien sur un champ de bataille dans lequel rien ne l'avait forcé de s'engager. L'empereur prétendit ensuite que V. M. après avoir appris la perte de la bataille de Salamanque aurait dû se porter sur le Duero et rallier l'armée de Portugal. Je rappelai alors le mouvement fait du Guadarama vers Ségovie et la position critique dans laquelle vous avez laissé la duc de Raguse qui avait lui-même proposé ce mouvement. L'empereur dit qu'il connaissait très bien tous les reproches qu'à cet égard on pouvait faire au maréchal Marmont. Il ajouta que l'armée du centre ayant fait sa retraite sur Madrid elle aurait du garder plus longtems les défilés du Guadarama, qu'on avait trop tôt passé le Tage, que du moins ce mouvement ayant été resolu, il fallait ne point laisser de garnison au Retiro, briser tous les affuts, emporter les aigles et bruler les effets d'habillement ; qu'il n'avait jamais considéré ce poste que comme propre à contenir la population de Madrid, que l'ennemi étant maître de la campagne, on devait l'abandonner et que de toutes les fautes de la campagne c'était celle qu'il avait le moins conçue. Je répondis à cette objection ainsi que j'en étais convenu avec V. M. L'empereur en venant ensuite à la lettre du duc de Dalmatie me dit qu'elle lui était déja parvenue par une autre voie, mais qu'il n'y avait attaché aucune importance ; que le

maréchal Soult s'était trompé, qu'il ne pouvait s'occuper de sem-
blables *pauvretés* dans un moment où il *était à la tête de cinq
cent mille hommes et faisait des choses immenses.* Ce sont ses
expressions, qu'au reste les soupçons du duc de Dalmatie ne l'éton-
naient que faiblement; que beaucoup de généraux de l'armée
d'Espagne les partageaient et pensaient que V. M. préférait
l'Espagne à la France; qu'il savait parfaitement qu'elle avait le
cœur françois mais que ceux qui la jugeaient par ses discours
devaient avoir une autre opinion. Il ajouta que le maréchal
Soult était la seule tête militaire qu'il eut en Espagne, qu'il
ne pouvait l'en retirer sans compromettre l'armée, que d'ailleurs il devait être parfaitement tranquille sur ses intentions
puisqu'il venait d'apprendre par les journaux anglais qu'il
évacuait l'Andalousie et se réunissait aux armées du centre et
d'Aragon, que cette réunion opérée on devait être assez en force
pour reprendre l'offensive; que d'ailleurs il n'avait point d'ordres
à envoyer, qu'il ne savait point en donner de si loin, qu'il ne se
dissimulait point l'étendue du mal et qu'il regrettait plus que
amais que V. M. n'ait point suivi le conseil qu'il lui avait donné
de ne pas retourner en Espagne; qu'il était inutile que je repar-
tisse, que je resterai à l'armée ou l'on m'emploieroit. J'insistai
alors pour être renvoyé à V. M. d'une manière qui parut faire
sur l'empereur quelque impression, et il finit par me dire que je
serai expédié mais que je ne pouvais l'être dans ce moment,
qu'ayant besoin de repos je resterais à Moscou, et que puisque
j'étais officier du génie, je serais chargé de diriger sous les ordres
du duc de Trevise les travaux et la défense du Kremlin. Je
reçus en conséquence un ordre écrit du Prince de Neufchatel.
Lorsqu'après l'entière évacuation de Moscou le corps de M. le M.
Mortier eut rejoint l'armée, je demandai et j'obtins d'y rester
attaché jusqu'à ce que je fusse expédié. Je craignais que si je
restais au quartier général on ne m'y désignât des fonctions qui
seraient un nouvel obstacle à mon retour. Je pensai que peut-être
on éviterait d'envoyer à V. M. un témoin des évènemens qui se
passaient, et je préférai attendre qu'une occasion favorable se pré-
sentât. Etant arrivé à Wilna peu de tems après le départ de
l'empereur, je demandai au duc de Bassano, et il me donna
l'autorisation de venir attendre des ordres à Paris. J'ai eu l'honneur d'annoncer à V. M. dans un autre lettre que l'altération de
ma santé me forçait à suspendre mon retour en Espagne.

L'armée au moment où je la quittai était dans la plus affreuse
détresse. Depuis longtems déjà la désorganisation et les pertes

étaient effrayantes, l'artillerie et la cavalerie n'existaient plus.
Tous les corps étaient confondus. Les soldats marchaient pêle-
mêle et ne songaient qu'à prolonger machinalement leur existence ; quoique l'ennemi fut sur nos flancs, chaque jour des
milliers d'hommes isolés se répandaient dans les villages voisins
de la route et tombaient dans les mains des Cosaques. Cependant
quelque grand que soit le nombre des prisonniers, celui des morts
l'est incomparablement davantage. Il est impossible de peindre
jusqu'à quel point la disette s'est fait sentir pendant plus d'un
mois ; il n'y eut point de distributions ; les chevaux morts étaient
la seule ressource, et bien souvent les maréchaux mêmes manquaient
de pain. La rigueur du climat rendait la disette plus meurtrière,
chaque nuit nous laissions au bivouac plusieurs centaines de morts.
Je crois pouvoir sans exagérer porter à cent mille le nombre qu'on
a perdu ainsi, et peindre avec assez de vérité la situation des
choses en disant que l'armée est morte : la jeune garde qui faisait
partie du corps auquel j'étais attaché était forte de 8000 hommes
lorsque nous avons quitté Moscou, à Wilna elle en comptait à
peine quatre cents. Tous les autres corps d'armée sont réduits
dans la même proportion, et la retraite ayant dû se prolonger au-
delà du Niemen, je suis convaincu que vingt mille hommes
n'auront pas atteints la Vistule. On croyait à l'armée que beaucoup de soldats avaient pris les devants et qu'ils se rallieraient
lorsqu'on pourrait suspendre le mouvement rétrograde. Je me
suis assuré du contraire ; à cinq lieues du quartier général, je ne
rencontrai plus d'hommes isolés et je connus bien alors la profon-
deur de la plaie. Une phrase pourrait donner à V. M. une idée
de l'état des choses, depuis le passage du Niemen un corps de
800 Napolitains, le seul corps qui eût conservé quelque consistance,
faisait l'arrière garde d'une armée française, forte n'aguère
de trois cents mille hommes. Il est impossible d'exprimer
jusqu'à quel point le désordre était contagieux ; les corps réunis
des ducs de Bellune et de Reggio comptaient 30,000 hommes
au passage de la Beresina, deux jours après ils étaient dissous
comme le reste de l'armée. Envoyer des renforts c'était aug-
menter les pertes et l'on reconnut enfin qu'il fallait empêcher les
troupes neuves de se mettre en contact avec cette multitude en
désordre à laquelle on ne peut plus donner le nom d'armée. Le
roi de Naples disait hautement qu'en lui laissant le commandement l'empereur avait exigé le plus grand sacrifice qu'il pût
attendre de son dévouement. Les forces physiques et morales
du prince de Neufchâtel étaient entièrement épuisées. Si main-

tenant V. M. me demandait quel doit être le terme du mouvement rétrograde, je lui répondrais que l'ennemi est maître de le
fixer. Je ne crois pas que les Prussiens fassent de grands efforts
pour défendre leur territoire. M. de Narbonne que j'ai vu à
Berlin et qui était chargé de lettres de l'empereur pour le roi de
Prusse, m'a dit que les dispositions de ce prince et de son premier
ministre étaient favorables, mais il ne se dissimulait pas que celles
de la nation ne sont pas les mêmes. Déjà plusieurs rixes s'étaient
engagées entre les habitans de Berlin et des soldats de la garnison
française; et en traversant la Prusse j'ai eu lieu de m'assurer
que l'on ne pouvait guère compter sur cette alliée de nouvelle
date.

Il parait aussi que dans l'armée autrichienne les officiers décla-
maient publiquement contre la guerre.

Quel triste que soit ce tableau, je crois l'avoir peint sans exa-
gération et l'avoir observé de sang froid. Mon opinion sur l'étendue du mal est la même que lorsque j'étais plus voisin du théâtre.

No. VII.

Ghiart, le 2 Septembre, 1812.

MONSIEUR LE DUC DE FELTRE,

J'ai reçu le rapport du duc de Raguse sur la bataille du 22. Il
est impossible de rien lire de plus insignifiant : il y a plus de
fatras et plus de rouages que dans une horloge, et pas un mot qui
fasse connaître l'état réel des choses. Voici ma manière de voir
sur cette affaire, et la conduite que vous devez tenir. Vous
attendrez que le duc de Raguse soit arrivé, qu'il soit remis de sa
blessure, et à-peu-près entièrement rétabli. Vous lui demanderez
alors de répondre catégoriquement à ces questions. Pourquoi
a-t-il livré bataille sans les ordres de son général-en-chef ? Pourquoi n'a-t-il pas pris des ordres sur le parti qu'il devoit suivre,
subordonné au système général sur mes armées d'Espagne ? Il
y a là *un crime d'insubordination* qui est la cause de tous les malheurs de cette affaire, et quand même il n'eut pas été dans l'obli-
gation de se mettre en communication avec son général-en-chef
pour exécuter les ordres qu'il en recevrait, comment a-t-il pu
sortir de sa défensive sur le Duero, lorsque, sans un grand effort
d'imagination, il étoit facile de concevoir qu'il pouvoit être secouru

par l'arrivée de la division de dragons, d'une trentaine de pièces de canon, et de plus de 15 mille hommes de troupes Françaises que le roi avoit dans la main ? Et comment pouvoit il sortir de la défensive pour prendre l'offensive sans attendre la réunion et le secours d'un corps de 15 à 17 mille hommes ?

Le roi avoit ordonné à l'armée du nord d'envoyer sa cavalerie à son secours ; elle étoit en marche. Le duc de Raguse ne pouvoit l'ignorer, puisque cette cavalerie est arrivée le soir de la bataille. De Salamanque à Burgos il y a bien des marches. Pourquoi n'a-t-il pas retardé de deux jours pour avoir le secours de cette cavalerie, qui lui étoit si importante ? Il faudroit avoir une explication sur les raisons qui ont porté le duc de Raguse à ne pas attendre les ordres de son général-en-chef pour livrer bataille sans attendre les renforts que le roi, comme commandant supérieur de mes armées en Espagne, pouvoit retirer de l'armée du centre, de l'armée de Valence et de l'Andalousie. Le seul fonds de l'armée du centre fournissoit 15 mille hommes de pied, et 2500 chevaux, lesquels pouvoient être rendus dans le même temps que le duc de Raguse faisoit battre son corps, et en prenant dans ses deux armées, le roi pouvoit lui amener 40 mille hommes. Enfin le duc de Raguse sachant que 1500 chevaux étoient partis de Burgos pour le rejoindre, comment ne les a-t-il pas attendus ?

En faisant coïncider ces deux circonstances d'avoir pris l'offensive sans l'ordre de son général-en-chef et de ne pas avoir retardé la bataille de deux jours pour ne pas recevoir 15,000 hommes d'infanterie que lui amenoit le roi, et 1500 chevaux de l'armée du nord, on est fondé à penser que ce maréchal a craint que le roi ne participe au succès de la bataille, et qu'il a sacrifié à la vanité la gloire de la patrie et l'avantage de mon service.

Donnez ordre aux généraux divisionnaires d'envoyer les états de leurs pertes. Il est intolérable qu'on rende des comptes faux et qu'on me dissimule la vérité.

Prescrivez au général Clausel, qui commande l'armée, d'envoyer la situation avant et après la bataille. Demandez également aux chefs de corps des situations exactes. Finalement, vous ferez connoître au duc de Raguse en temps opportun combien je suis indigné de la conduite inexplicable qu'il a tenue, en n'attendant pas deux jours que les secours de l'armée du centre et de l'armée du nord le rejoignissent. J'attends avec impatience l'arrivée du général aide-de-camp du roi pour avoir des renseignemens précis. Ce qu'il a écrit ne signifie pas grande chose.

(Signé) NAPOLEON.

No. VIII. A.

Extract from general Souham's despatch to the minister of war, Briviesca, 2d October, 1812.

Par votre lettre du 6 Octobre vous m'annoncez que le duc de Dalmatie venait de réunir son armée à Grenade et à Jaen, et que le roi alloit se mettre incessamment en communication avec ce maréchal pour marcher de concert sur Madrid. En consequence de ces mouvemens je resolus de marcher à la rencontre de l'ennemi, et de le forcer à lever le siège de Burgos. Le 18 toute mon armée se mit en mouvement sur trois colonnes, et le 19 elle occupait les positions ainsi qu'il suit. La droite à Termino, le centre sur les hauteurs de Monasterio, et la gauche à Villa Escuso la Solano et Villa Escuso la Sombria. La journée du 20 devait être celle du combat, lorsque je reçus à l'instant, à deux heures du matin, par un aide-de-camp, une lettre de S. M. C. qui m'ordonne de ne point engager d'affaire générale, et d'attendre que par ses manœuvres lord Wellington soit forcé d'évacuer sa position de Burgos ; ainsi il me faut renoncer à tous mes projets, et non sans un violent chagrin, car je puis assurer V. E. que mon armée était parfaitement disposée, et que j'aurais pu combattre l'ennemi avec avantage. Cependant l'armée n'a des vivres que pour quatre jours, et à cette epoque, si lord Wellington n'est point en retraite, je serai forcé de l'attaquer. J'entrevois moins de peril de marcher en avant que de rétrograder. Dans un instant où le moral du soldat commence à se raffermir tout mouvement en arrière produit le plus mauvais effet.

(Signé)　　　　Comte Souham.

No. VIII. B.

Extracts from two letters written by the duke of Feltre to King Joseph, dated Paris, 8th Oct. and 19th Nov., 1812.

On one of the letters is the following note, in pencil, by the duke of Wellington. " *Advantage of English newspapers.*"

" Sire,—J'ai l'honneur d'adresser ci-joint à votre majesté

quelques extraits des journaux Anglais les plus récents dont j'ai choisi ce qui pourrait être de quelque intérêt dans les circonstances actuels."

" Sire,—J'ai l'honneur d'adresser ci-joint à V. M. plusieurs extraits des journaux Anglais contenant quelques faits utiles ou intéressans à connaître."

These extracts taken from the Courier, Morning Post, Times, Alfred, Statesman, and Morning Chronicle, contained minute details upon the numbers, situation, and destination of the Sicilian, Spanish, and Anglo-Portuguese armies, and the most exact account of the reinforcements sent from England. In fine a complete system of intelligence for the enemy.

No. IX.

Extract of a letter from marshal Jourdan to colonel Napier.

Soisy sous Etiole, 14 *Janvier*, 1829.

" Le 10 Novembre, 1812. Les armées du midi, du Portugal, et du centre se trouvaient réunies sur la Tormes. Vous connaissez la position qu'occupait l'armée des alliés. Cette position ayant été bien reconnue, dans la journée du 11, par le roi, accompagné du duc de Dalmatie, de plusieurs généraux, et de moi, je proposai de passer la Tormes, guéable prèsque partout entre Villa-Gonzala et Huerta, et de nous porter rapidement sur Calvarissa de Ariba, qui se trouvait au centre de la ligne des ennemis. J'esperais que lord Wellington ne pourrait éviter la bataille ; et j'étais d'avis que nous devions faire tous nos efforts pour le forcer à l'accepter ; me flattant qu'avec une armée de 80 milles hommes, dont 10 milles de cavalerie et 120 pièces de canon,* nous étions en état de remporter un brilliant succès, sur le même champ de bataille où quelques mois avant nous avions essuyé un revers.

---

* These numbers are somewhat below those I have assigned to the French army ; my calculation was made from the imperial muster-rolls, but the difference may be easily accounted for by the length of time which elapsed when marshal Jourdan wrote this letter. His numbers are evidently from memory, and probably he did not mean to include the king's guards and Spaniards.

Le duc de Dalmatie, n'étant pas de mon avis, proposa d'aller passer la Tormes, à des guès qu'il avait reconnus à deux lieues au-dessus d'Alba ; ce parti était sans doute plus prudent ; mais il avoit, suivant moi, l'inconvenient que je voulais éviter, c'est-à-dire, qu'il laissait à nos adversaires la facilité de se retirer sans combattre. Cependant comme je n'étais revêtu d'aucun commandement, tandis que le duc de Dalmatie avait sous ses ordres les deux tiers de l'armée, le roi jugea convenable d'adopter son plan, et lui en confia l'exécution ; vous en connaissez le resultat : il fut tel que je l'avais prévu.

Permettez moi, Monsieur, d'ajouter une reflexion. Il me semble que lord Wellington decidé à battre en retraite, aurait dû commencer à l'opérer le 14ème jour, où nous franchîmes la Tormes. En ne se mettant en mouvement que le 15, il se trouva dans la nécessité de défiler devant nous pendant une partie de la journée ; et sans les mauvais tems, et surtout sans beaucoup trop de circonspection de notre côté il eût peut-être couru quelque danger.

On a publié que pendant leur retraite les alliés ne perdirent que 50 ou 60 tués, 150 blessés, 170 prisonniers. Il est, cependant, certain que le nombre de prisonniers Anglais, Portugais, et Espagnols, conduits au quartier général à Salamanque, étoit, le 20 Novembre, de 3520."

The justice of the marshal's opinion as to lord Wellington having staid too long on the Tormes is confirmed by the following note of a conversation held with the duke of Wellington on the subject.

" Lord Wellington would have fought the French on the old position of the Arapiles in 1812 notwithstanding their superior numbers, but he staid too long at Salamanca."

No. X.

The duke of Feltre, minister of war, to the king of Spain.

Paris, le 29 *Janvier*, 1813.

SIRE,

J'ai eu l'honneur d'écrire à V. M. le 4 de ce mois pour lui faire connaître les intentions de l'empereur au sujet des affaires d'Espagne, et la necessité de transporter le quartier général de Madrid à Valladolid. Cette dépêche a été expediée par duplicate et triplicate, et j'ignore encore si elle est parvenue à V. M. Depuis sa dépêche de Madrid du 4 Decembre je suis privé de ses lettres, et ce long silence me prouve que les communications de Madrid à Vittoria restent constamment *interceptées*. Il est vrai que les opérations du général Caffarelli qui s'est porté avec toutes ses troupes disponibles sur la côte de Biscaye pour dégager Santona fortement menacé par l'ennemi et parcourir la côte, a donné aux bandes de la Castille une facilité entière d'intercepter la route de Burgos à Vittoria. Les dernières nouvelles que je reçois à l'instant de l'armée de Portugal sont du 5 Janvier. A cette époque tout y était tranquille, mais je vois toujours la même difficulté pour communiquer. Cet état de choses rend toujours plus nécessaire de s'occuper très sérieusement et très instamment de balayer les provinces du nord, et de les délivrer enfin de ces bandes qui ont augmentés en forces et en consistance à un point qui exige indispensablement toute notre attention et tous nos efforts. Cette pensée a tellement attiré l'attention de l'empereur que S. M. I. m'a réitéré quatre fois successivement l'ordre exprès de renouveller encore l'expression de ses intentions que j'ai déjà adressée à V. M. par ma lettre du 4 Janvier pour l'engager à revenir à Valladolid, à garder Madrid par une division seulement, et à concentrer ses forces de manière à pouvoir envoyer des troupes de l'armée de Portugal vers le nord, en Navarre, et en Biscaye, afin de délivrer ces provinces, et d'y rétablir la tranquillité. Le général Reille également frappé de l'état des choses dans le nord de l'Espagne a bien compris la nécessité de prendre un parti decisif à cet égard. Il m'a transmis à cette occasion la lettre qu'il a eu l'honneur d'écrire à V. M. le 13 Octobre dernier, et j'ai vu qu'il lui a présenté un tableau frappant et vrai de la situation des affaires qui vient entièrement à l'appui de ma dépêche du 4 courant. Quant à l'occupation de Madrid, l'empereur m'ordonne de mettre sous les yeux de V. M. le danger qu'il y aurait dans l'état actuel des affaires de vouloir occuper cette capitale comme point central, et d'y avoir encore des hôpitaux et établissemens qu'il faudrait abandonner à l'ennemi au premier mouvement prononcé qu'il ferait vers le nord. Cette considération seule doit l'emporter sur toute autre, et je n'y ajouterai que le dernier mot de l'empereur à ce sujet; c'est que toutes les convenances dans la position de l'Europe veulent que V. M. occupe Valladolid, et pacifie le nord. Le premier objet rempli facilitera beaucoup le second, et pour y contribuer par tous les moyens comme pour économiser un tems précieux, et mettre à profit l'inaction des Anglais, je transmets directement aux généraux commandant en chef les armées du nord et de Portugal, les ordres de l'Empereur pour que leur exécution ne souffre aucun retard, et que ceux de V. M. pour appuyer et consolider leurs opérations n'éprouvent ni lenteur ni difficulté lorsqu'ils parviendront à ces généraux. Je joins ici copie de mes lettres, sur lesquelles j'ai toujours reservé les ordres que V. M. jugera à-propos de donner pour l'entière exécution de ceux de l'empereur. Ma lettre était terminée lorsqu'un aide-de-camp de M. le maréchal Jourdan est arrivé avec plusieurs dépêches, dont la dernière est du 24 Decembre. J'ai eu soin de les mettre sous les yeux de l'empereur, mais leur contenu ne saurait rien changer aux intentions de S. M. I. et ne peut que confirmer les observations qui se trouvent dans ma lettre. J'aurai l'honneur d'écrire encore à V. M. par le retour de l'officier porteur des dépêches de M. le maréchal Jourdan. Je suis avec respect, Sire, de votre majesté, le très humble et très obéissant serviteur,

Le ministre de la guerre,

DUC DE FELTRE.

No. XI.

The duke of Feltre to the king of Spain.

SIRE,

Depuis la lettre que j'ai eu l'honneur d'écrire à votre majesté le 29 Janvier, l'empereur, après avoir pris connoissance des dépêches apportées par l'aide-de-camp de monsieur le maréchal Jourdan, me charge encore de réitérer son intention formelle et déjà deux fois transmise à votre majesté, qu'elle porte son quartier général à Valladolid afin de pouvoir s'occuper efficacement de soumettre et pacifier le nord ; par une conséquence nécessaire de ce changement, Madrid ne doit être occupé que par l'extremité de la gauche de manière à ne plus faire partie essentielle de la position générale et à pouvoir être abandonné sans inconvénient, au cas qu'il soit nécessaire de se réunir sur un autre point. Cette nouvelle disposition procure à votre majesté les moyens de faire réfluer des forces considérables dans le nord et jusqu'à l'Arragon pour y détruire les rassemblemens qui existent, occuper en force tous les points importans, interdire l'accès des côtes aux Anglais, et opérer la soumission entière du pays. Il est donc d'une importance extrême pour parvenir à ce bût, de profiter de l'inaction des Anglais, qui permet en ce moment l'emploi de tous nos moyens contre les insurgés et doit amener promptement leur entière destruction, si les opérations entreprises pour cette effet sont conduites avec l'activité, l'energie et la suite qu'elles exigent. Votre majesté a pu se convaincre par la longue et constante interruption des communications autant que par les rapports qui lui sont parvenus de toute l'étendue du mal, et de la nécessité d'y porter remède. On ne peut donc mettre en doute son empressement à remplir les intentions de l'empereur sur ces points importans des changemens, qui ont eu lieu pour le commandement en chef des armées du midi, du nord, et de Portugal, me font espérer que votre majesté n'éprouvera plus de difficultés pour l'exécution de ses ordres et que tout marchera au même bût sans contradiction, et sans obstacle. Ces nouvelles dispositions me dispensent de répondre à différentes observations contenues dans les lettres de votre majesté, et m'engagent à attendre qu'elle me fasse connoître les résultats des changemens ordonnés par l'empereur. Je ne dois pas oublier de prévenir votre majesté d'un ordre que sa majesté impériale m'a chargé de transmettre directement à monsieur le général Reille pour lui faire envoyer une division de son armée en Navarre dont la situation exige impérieusement des secours prompts et efficaces. Cette disposition ne peut contrarier aucune de celles que votre majesté sera dans le cas d'ordonner à l'armée de Portugal pour concourir au même bût et amener la soumission des provinces du nord de l'Espagne.

Je suis avec respect, Sire, de votre majesté

Le très humble et très obéïssant serviteur

Le Ministre de la Guerre,

Duc de Feltre.

No. XII.

Duke of Feltre to the king of Spain.

Paris, le 12 Fevrier.(No. 2.) 1813.

SIRE,

Par ma lettre de ce jour No. 1, j'ai eu l'honneur de faire connaître à V. M. les intentions de l'empereur sur les opérations à suivre en Espagne. La présente aura pour bût de répondre plus particulièrement à la lettre dont V. M. m'a honoré en date du 8 Janvier et que j'ai eu soin de mettre sous les yeux de l'empereur. Les plaintes qu'elle contient sur la conduite du maréchal duc de Dalmatie et du général Caffarelli deviennent aujourd'hui sans objet par l'éloignement de ces deux généraux en chef. Je dois cependant prévenir V. M. qu'ayant fait connaître au général Caffarelli qu'on se plaignait à Madrid de ne point recevoir de comptes de l'armée du nord, ce général me répond sous la date du 27 Janvier qu'il a eu l'honneur de rendre à V. M. des comptes extrêmement frequens, qu'il lui a envoyé la situation de l'armée et des doubles des rapports qui me sont adressés. La général Caffarelli ajoute qu'il avait demandé à V. M. d'ordonner que deux divisions de l'armée de Portugal vinssent appuyer les opérations de l'armée du nord, et il pense que ces lettres se seront croisées avec les dépêches de Madrid parceque les courriers ont éprouvé beaucoup de retard, mais il y a lieu de présumer que tout ce qui a été adressé de l'armée du nord a du parvenir à Madrid avant la fin de Janvier. V. M. réitère dans sa lettre du 8 Janvier ses demandes relativement aux besoins de l'armée. Toutes ont été mises sous les yeux de l'empereur. S. M. I. m'ordonne de répondre au sujet des fonds dont la demande se retrouve dans plusieurs dépêches précédentes que l'argent nécessaire aux armées d'Espagne se serait trouvé dans ces riches et fertiles provinces dévastées par les bandes et par les juntes insurrectionelles, qu'en s'occupant avec l'activité et la vigueur convenables pour rétablir l'ordre et la tranquillité, on y gagnera toutes les ressources qu'elles peuvent encore offrir, et que le tems ramènera dans toute leur étendue. C'est donc un motif de plus pour V. M. d'employer tous les moyens dont elle dispose pour mettre fin à cette guerre interne qui trouble le repos des habitans paisibles, ruine le pays, fatigue nos armées et les prive de tous les avantages qu'elles trouveraient dans l'occupation tranquille de ces belles contrées. L'Arragon et la Navarre aujourd'hui sous les loix de Mina alimentent de leurs productions et de leur revenus cette lutte désastreuse, il est tems de mettre un terme à cet état de choses et de faire rentrer dans les mains du gouvernement légitime les ressources d'un pays florissant lorsqu'il est paisible, mais qui ne servent aujourd'hui qu'à son détriment.

Je suis avec respect, Sire, de votre majesté, le très humble et très obéïssant serviteur,

Le ministre de la guerre,

DUC DE FELTRE.

No. XIII.

The duke of Feltre to the king of Spain.

Paris, le 12 *Fevrier,* 1813.

SIRE,

J'ai eu l'honneur d'écrire trois fois à V. M. dans le courant de Janvier, pour lui transmettre les intentions de l'empereur sur la conduite des affaires en Espagne, et j'ai eu soin de faire expedier toutes mes dépêches au moins par triplicata, tellement que je puis et dois espérer aujourd'hui qu'elles sont parvenues à leur destination. Je reçois en ce moment le dup^ta d'une lettre de V. M. en date du 8 Janvier, dont le primata n'est point arrivé et j'y vois une nouvelle preuve de la difficulté toujours subsistante de communication, les inconveniens de cet état de choses deviennent plus sensibles dans les circonstances actuelles, où il étoit d'une haute importance que les ordres de l'empereur reçussent une prompte exécution. S. M. I. pénétrée de cette idée, attend avec une véritable impatience de savoir ce qui s'est opéré à Madrid, d'après ses instructions, et cette attente, journellement deçue lui fait craindre qu'on n'ait perdu un temps précieux, les Anglais étant depuis plus de deux mois dans l'impuissance de rien faire. L'empereur espère du moins que lorsque V. M. aura eu connaisance du 29me bulletin, elle aura été frappée de la nécessité de se mettre promptement en communication avec la France et de l'assurer par tous les moyens possibles. On ne peut parvenir à ce bût qu'en faisant refluer successivement les forces dont V. M. peut disposer sur la ligne de communication de Valladolid à Bayonne, et en portant en outre des forces suffisantes en Navarre et en Aragon pour combattre avec avantage et détruire les bandes qui dévastent ces provinces.

L'armée de Portugal combinée avec celle du nord est bien suffisante pour remplir cet objet tandisque les armées du centre et du midi, occupant Salamanque et Valladolid, présentent assez de forces pour tenir les Anglais en échec en attendant les évènements. L'empereur m'ordonne de réitérer à V. M. que l'occupation de *Valladolid* comme quartier général et résidence pour la personne, est un préliminaire indispensable, à toute operation. C'est de-là qu'il faut diriger sur la route de Burgos et successivement sur tous les points convenables les forces disponibles qui doivent renforcer ou seconder l'armée du nord. Madrid et même Valence ne peuvent être considérés dans ce système que comme des points à occuper par l'extremité gauche de la ligne, et nullement comme lieux à maintenir exclusivement par une concentration de forces. Valladolid et Salamanque deviennent aujourd'hui les points essentiels entre lesquels doivent être réparties des forces prêtes à prendre l'offensive contre les Anglais et à faire échouer leurs projets. L'empereur est instruit qu'ils se renforcent en Portugal, et qu'ils paraissent avoir le double projet ou de pousser en Espagne ou de partir du port de Lisbonne pour faire une expédition de 25 mille hommes, partie Anglais partie Espagnols, sur un point quelconque des côtes de France pendant que la lutte sera engagée dans le nord. Pour empêcher l'exécution de ce plan il faut être toujours en mésure de se porter en avant et ménacer de marcher sur Lisbonne ou de conquerir le Portugal. En même tems il faut conserver des communications aussi sûres que faciles avec la France pour être promptement instruits de tout ce qui s'y passe, et le seul moyen d'y parvenir est d'employer le tems ou les Anglais sont dans l'inaction pour pacifier la Biscaye et la Navarre comme j'ai eu soin de le faire connaître à V. M. dans mes précédentes. La sollicitude de l'empereur pour les affaires d'Espagne lui ayant fait réitérer à plusieurs reprises et reproduire sous toutes les formes ses intentions à cet égard je ne puis achever mieux de les remplir qu'en récapitulant les idées principales que j'ai eu l'ordre de faire connaître à V. M. Occuper Valladolid et Salamanque, employer avec la plus grande activité possible tous les moyens de pacifier la Navarre et l'Aragon, maintenir des communications très rapides et très sûres avec la France, rester toujours en mésure de prendre l'offensive au besoin, voilà ce que l'empereur me prescrit de faire considérer à V. M. comme instruction générale pour toute la campagne et qui doit faire la base de ses operations. J'ai à peine besoin d'ajouter que si les armées Francaises en Espagne restaient oisives et laissaient les Anglais maîtres de faire des expeditions sur nos côtes, la tranquillité de la France serait compromise et la décadence de nos affaires en Espagne en serait l'infaillible résultat. Je suis avec respect,

Sire, de votre majesté,
le très humble et très obéïssant serviteur
Le Ministre de la Guerre,
Duc de Feltre.

No. XIV.

The duke of Feltre to the king of Spain.

Paris, le 12 Mars, 1813.

Sire,

La difficulté toujours subsistante des communications a apporté dans ma correspondance avec V. M. des retards considérables et de longues interruptions dont les résultats ne peuvent être que très préjudiciables au service de l'empereur. Depuis plus de deux mois j'expédie sans cesse et par tous les moyens possibles ordre sur ordre pour faire exécuter les dispositions prescrites par S. M. I. et je n'ai aucune certitude que ces ordres soient parvenus à leur destination. L'empereur extrêmement mécontent de cet état de choses renouvelle sans cesse l'injonction la plus précise de le faire cesser, et j'ignore encore en ce moment si les mouvemens prescrits se préparent ou s'exécutent, mais je vois toujours d'avantage que si des ordres relatifs à cette mesure doivent partir de Madrid cela entrainerait une grande perte de tems. L'empereur en a été frappé. Il devient donc tout-à-fait indispensable de s'écarter un moment de la voie ordinaire et des dispositions par lesquelles tout devroit emaner de V. M. au moins pour ce qui concerne le nord et l'armée de Portugal. Je prends pour cet effet le parti d'adresser directement aux généraux commandant de ces armées les ordres d'exécution qui dans d'autres circonstances devraient leur parvenir de Madrid, et j'ai l'honneur d'adresser ci-joint à V. M. copies des lettres que j'ai écrites au général Reille et au général Clauzel pour déterminer enfin l'arrivée des renforts abso-

lument nécessaires pour soumettre l'Aragon, la Navarre et la
Biscaye ; les details contenus dans ma lettre au général Clauzel
me dispensent de m'étendre d'avantage sur cet objet important.
V. M. y verra surtout qu'en prescrivant l'exécution prompte et
entière des ordres de l'empereur j'ai toujours reservé l'exercise de
l'autorité supérieure remise entre les mains de V. M. et qu'elle
conserve également la direction ultérieure des opérations des
qu'elle pourra les conduire par elle-même.

Toutes mes précédentes dépêches sont d'allieurs assez précises
sur ce point pour ne de laisser pas doute à cet egard.

The duke of Feltre to the king.

Paris, 18 *Mars*, 1813.

SIRE,

Parmi les lettres dont V.M. m'a honoré, la plus récente de celles
qui me sont parvenues jusqu'à ce jour est du 1 Fevrier, et je vois
qu'à cette epoque V. M. n'avait point encore reçu celle que j'ai
eu l'honneur de lui adresser par ordre de l'empereur le 4 Janvier
pour l'engager à transferer son quartier général à Valladolid.
Cette disposition a été renouvellée dans toutes mes dépêches pos-
térieures sous les dates de 14, 29 Janvier, 3, 12, 25 Fevrier,
1, 11 et 12 Mars, sans avoir eu jusqu'à present de certitude que
mes lettres fussent arrivées à leur destination. Enfin une lettre de
M. le duc d'Albufera en date 4 Mars me transmit copie de celle
que V. M. lui a adressée le 23 Fevrier pour le prevenir que
ma lettre du 4 Janvier est arrivée à Madrid, et qu'on s'y préparait
à exécuter les dispositions prescrites par l'empereur. Ainsi c'est
de Valence que j'ai reçu la première nouvelle positive à cet égard,
et cette circonstance qui dévoile entièrement nôtre situation dans
le nord d'Espagne est une nouvelle preuve de l'extrême urgence
des mesures prescrites par l'empereur et de tout le mal que d'in-
explicables retards ont causé. S. M. I. vient à cette occasion de
me réitérer l'injonction de faire sentir à V. M. la fausse direction
qu'ont prise les affaires d'Espagne par le peu de soin qu'on a
apporté à maintenir les communications avec les frontières. L'empereur est etonné qu'on ait si peu compris à Madrid l'extrême
importance de conserver des communications sûres et rapides avec

la France. Le defaut constant de nouvelles était un avertisse-
ment assez clair et assez positif de l'impuissance ou se trouvait
l'armée du nord de proteger la route de Madrid à Bayonne.
L'état des affaires dans le nord de l'Europe devait plus que jamais
faire sentir la nécessité de recevoir des nouvelles de Paris et de
prendre enfin des mesures décisives pour ne pas rester si longue-
ment dans un état d'isolement et d'ignorance absolu sur les vues
et l'intention de l'empereur. V. M. avoit trois armées à sa disposition pour rétablir les communications avec l'armée du nord, et
l'on ne voit pas un mouvement de l'armée de Portugal ou de celle
du centre qui soit approprié aux circonstances, tandis que l'inaction des Anglais permettait de profiter de notre supériorité pour
chasser les bandes, nettoyer la route, assurer la tranquillité dans
le pays. L'empereur m'a ordonné de faire connaître sa façon de
penser sur cet objet au général Reille, auquel j'ai adressé directement les ordres de S. M. I. pour les forces qu'il a dû mettre
sans retard sous les ordres du général Clauzel ainsi que j'ai eu l'honneur d'en prévenir V. M. par mes lettres du 29 Janvier, 3 Fevrier
et 12 Mars. En effet les circonstances rendent cette mesure d'une
extrême urgence. L'inaction où l'on est resté pendant l'hiver a
encouragé et propagé l'insurrection. Elle s'etend maintenant de la
Biscaye, en Catalogne, et l'Aragon exige, pour ainsi dire, le même
emploi des forces pour la pacifier, que la Biscaye et la Navarre.
Il est donc de la plus haute importance que V. M. etende ses soins
sur l'Aragon comme sur les autres provinces du nord de l'Espagne,
et les évènemens qui se préparent rendront ce soin toujours plus
nécessaire. D'un côté toutes les bandes chassées de la Biscaye
et de la Navarre se trouveront bientôt forcées à refluer dans l'Aragon, et d'autre part l'évacuation de Cuenca, par résultat du mouvement général des armées du centre et du midi priverait le général
Suchet de toute communication avec V. M. dans un moment ou
les ennemis se renforcent devant lui d'une manière assez *inquié-
tante.* Il est donc très important de se procurer une autre ligne
de communication avec Valence et cette ligne ne peut s'établir
que par l'Aragon. C'est à votre majesté qu'il appartient de donner à cet égard les ordres nécessaires. Il suffira sans doute de lui
avoir fait connaître l'état de choses et la position du maréchal
Suchet pour lui faire prendre les déterminations que les circonstances rendraient les plus convenables. Il me tarde beaucoup
d'apprendre enfin de V. M. elle-même l'exécution des ordres de
l'empereur et de pouvoir satisfaire sur ce point la juste impatience
de S. M. I.

No. XV.

Joseph O'Donnel to general Donkin.

Malaga, the 6th December, 1812.

DEAR SIR,

The letter you did me the honour to adress to me on the 6th of September has been mislaid all this long time on account of my being separated from the armie since the moment I gave up the command of it, and it was only last night I had the pleasure of receiving it. I feel a great comfort in seingh an officer of your reputation affected so kindly with the sorrows which so unlucky as undeservedly (I believe) fell upon me as a consequence of my shamefull defaite at Castalla. But I beg to be excused if I continue this letter in French. I kno you understand it very well and I can not explain my toughts so well in English. Je crois, M. le général, que tout militaire, instruit des faits, et à la vue du malheureux champ de bataille de Castalla, ou du plan qui le représente, doit faire le même raisonement que vous avez fait, à moins qu'il ne soit épris des petites passions et des prejugés qui ne dominent que trop souvent les hommes. Je crois l'avoir demontré à l'evidence dans mon rapport officiel au gouvernement (que vous devez avoir vu imprimmé) accompagné de la carte des environs et des copies de toutes les ordres que je donnai la veille du combat. J'aurois certainement été vainquer si l'officier qui commandoit les 760 chevaux, avec deux pièces de 8 à mon aile gauche eut obéi mes ordres, on eut seulement tâché de se laisser voir de loin par la cavallerie enemie, qui au nombre de 400 chevaux étoit stationée dans le village de Viar ; mais point du tout, cet officier, au lieu de se trouver sur Viar au point du jour de la bataille, pour tenir en échec la cavallerie ennemie, pour la battre s'il en trouvoit une occasion probable, ou pour la suivre en tout cas, et l'empêcher de tomber sur Castalla impunément, comme il lui était très expressément ordonné par des ordres écrites qu'il avoue, cet officier alla se cacher derrière Villena, et quoiqu'il entendit le canon de Castalla, et qu'il fut instruit de la marche des dragons de Viar par la route d'Onil, il resta tranquilement en position de l'autre côté de Villena jusqu'à passé huit heures du matin. Nous étions déjà battus, et trois malheureux bataillons hachés en pièces (quoiqu'ayant repoussé la première charge) quand M. le brigadier

Santistevan se mit en marche de Villena pour venir à mon secours. Jugez donc, Mons. le général, si j'ay pû empêcher ce désastre. Cependant, le public, qui ne peut juger que par les resultats, se dechaina d'abord contre moi, et je ne m'en plains pas, car cela étoit fort naturel ; c'est un malheur attaché à notre profession, et que les généraux Espagnols doivent resentir sur touts les autres, puisqu'ils font la guerre sans resources, et manquant de tout contre un ennimi aguerri qui ne manque de rien ; mais je me plains des *Cortes* de la nation, je me plains de ces pères de la patrie, qui sachant que j'avois demandé moimême à être jugé par un conseille de guerre, ont cependant donné le ton à l'opinion publique se rependant en invectives contre moi, et même contre mon frère le régent, avant de scavoir si je suis en effet coupable. Après un pareile traitement, et dans l'ètât de misère et de détresse où se trouvent nos armées, ou trouvera t'on de généraux qui veuillent exposer leur honneur, et en accepter le commandement ? Quant à moi je servirai ma patrie par devoir et par inclination jusqu'au dernier soupir, mais je n'accepterai jamais aucun commandement, supposant qu'il me fut offert. Les informations que l'on prend relativement à l'affaire en question ne sont pas encore finies, car tout va doucement chez nous. J'en attends le resultat ici avec l'aveu du gouvernement, et aussitôt que l'on aura prononcé en justice j'irai me présenter comme simple volontaire dans une de nos armées si l'on ne veut pas m'employer dans ma calité de général subalterne. Je vous ay trop ennuyé de mes peines ; c'est que j'en ay le cœur navré, et que votre bonté m'a excité à m'en soulager en vous les racontant. Il me reste encore un espoir flatteur, c'est le jugement de touts mes camarades qui ont vû de près mes dispositions à l'affaire de Castalla, et les efforts que j'avois fait pendant sept mois, luttant toujours contre la detresse et le désordre, pour préparer à la victoire une armée qui étoit tout-à-fait nulle quand je fus obligé a en prendre, malgré moi, le commandement. Je m'estimerai heureux, Monsieur le général, de mériter aussi le sufrage d'un officier aussi distingué que vous l'êtes, et je vous prie d'agréér le temoignage du sincère attachement de votre très humble et très obéissant serviteur,

JOSEF O'DONELL.

Monsieur le général Donkin,
    &c. &c.

No. XVI.

Freneda, February 25th, 1813.

Sir,

I have received your letter of the 12th instant, regarding the conduct of the second Italian regiment, and I entirely concur in all the measures you have adopted, and applaud the decision and firmness of your conduct. I am prepared likewise to approve of whatever you shall determine upon deliberation regarding the future state of the men of the regiment, whether to be formed into a regiment again, or not; or if so formed, whether to be kept as part of the army or sent back to Sicily.

The foreign troops are so much addicted to desertion that they are very unfit for our armies, of which they necessarily form too large a proportion to the native troops. The evil is aggravated by the practice which prevails of enlisting prisoners as well as deserters, and Frenchmen as well as other foreigners, notwithstanding the repeated orders of government upon the subject. The consequence is therefore that a foreign regiment cannot be placed in a situation in which the soldiers can desert from it, that they do not go off in hundreds; and in the Peninsula they convey to the enemy the only intelligence which he can acquire.

With this knowledge I seldom if ever use the foreign British troops of this army on the duty of outposts; and whatever you may determine regarding the second Italian regiment, I recommend the same practice to your consideration.

There is nothing new on this side of the Peninsula. The armies are nearly in the stations which they took up in the end of November.

I have the honour to be,

Sir,

Your most obedient Servant,

WELLINGTON.

Major-General Campbell,
&c. &c. &c.

No. XVII.

*Extract of a letter from the marquis of Wellington to lieute-
nant-general sir John Murray, dated Freneda, April 6th,
1813.*

" In regard to feeding the Spanish troops in Spain, I have invariably set my face against it and have never consented to it or
done it, even for a day in any instance. My reasons are, first
that it entails upon Great Britain an expense which the country
is unable to bear ; secondly, that it entails upon the department
of the army which undertakes it a detail of business, and a burthen in respect to transport, and other means to which the departments if formed upon any moderate scale must be quite unequal ;
thirdly, I know from experience that if we don't interfere, the
Spanish troops, particularly if paid as yours are, and in limited
numbers, will not want food in any part of Spain, whereas the
best and most experienced of our departments would not be able
to draw from the country resources for them. I have already
consented to the formation of a magazine for the use of general
Whittingham and general Roche's corps for a certain number of
days, if it should be found necessary to give them assistance of
this description. I can go no farther, and I earnestly recommend
to you if you give assistance to all, to give over a magazine to
last a given time, but not to take upon yourself to supply the
Spanish troops engaged in operations. If, however, you should
notwithstanding this recommendation take upon yourself to give
such supplies, I must object, as commander-in-chief of the
Spanish army, to your giving more than bread to the troops who
receive pay, as that is positively contrary to the regulations and
customs of the Spanish army. I recommend to you also to attend with caution to the demands of both general Whittingham
and general Roche, and to observe that in proportion as you will
comply with their demands, demands will be made upon you by
general Elio and others, and you will involve yourself in a scale of
expense and difficulty, which will cramp all your operations, and
which is quite inconsistent with the views of government on the
eastern coast of the Peninsula."

No. XVIII.

General state of the French army, April 15, 1812.

Extracted from the Imperial Muster-rolls.

	Present under Arms.		Detached.		Hospitals.	Total.	
	Men.	Horses.	Men.	Horses.		Men.	Horses.
Armée de Midi	55,797	11,014	2,498	700	6,065	64,360	11,714
Centre....	19,148	3,993	144	51	624	19,916	4,044
Portugal..	56,937	8,108	4,394	2,278	7,706	69,037	10,386
Ebre	16,830	1,873	21	6	3,425	20,276	1,879
Arragon ..	14,786	3,269	2,695	658	1,467	18,948	3,927
Catalogne	28,924	1,259	1,163	49	5,540	35,627	1,308
Nord	48,232	7,074	1,309	72	8,677	58,276	7,213
Total......	240,654	36,590	12,224	3,814	33,504	286,440	40,471
Reserve de Bayonne	4,038	157	36	35	865	4,939	192
General Total	244,692	36,747	12,260	3,849	34,369	291,370	40,663
Civic guards attached to the army of the south...............	6,497	1,655	,,	,,	258	6,755	1,497
Troupes Espagnols..	33,952	525	,,	,,	,,	33,952	525
Total Espagnols	40,449	2,180	,,	,,	258	40,707	2,022

General state, May 15, 1812.

	Present under Arms.		Detached.		Hospitals.	Total.		
	Men.	Horses.	Men.	Horses		Men.	Cavalry.	Artillery.
Armée de Midi	56,031	12,101	2,787	660	4,652	63,470	7,311	4,340
Centre	17,395	4,208	158	37	766	19,203	3,332	420
Portugal ..	52,618	7,244	9,750	1,538	8,332	70,700	4,481	3,448
Arragon ..	27,218	4,768	4,458	605	3,701	35,377	2,976	1,980
Catalonia	33,677	1,577	1,844	267	6,009	41,530	1,376	279
Nord	38,771	6,031	2,560	271	7,767	49,098	4,443	1,163
Total...............	225,710	35,929	21,557	3,378	31,227	279,378	23,919	11,630
Old Reserve at Bayonne	3,894	221	1,642	,,	964	6,500	207	,,
New Reserve at Bayonne	2,598	116	3,176	,,	5	5,769	103	,,
General Total ..	232,202	36,266	26,375	3,378	32,196	291,647	24,229	11,630

General state of the French Armies, March 15, 1813.

	Present under Arms.		Detached.		Hospitals.	Total.		
	Men.	Horses.	Men.	Horses.	Men.		Cavalry.	Train.
Armée de Midi	36,605	6,602	2,060	1,617	7,144	45,809	8,650	2,601
Centre	16,227	1,966	940	76	2,401	19,568	2,790	451
Portugal..	34,825	3,654	157	,,	7,731	42,713	6,726	2,149
Arragon ..	36,315	3,852	55	,,	2,442	38,812	6,123	1,799
Catalonia	27,323	1,109	110	,,	2,013	29,446	1,884	635
Nord	40,476	1,978	41	,,	8,030	48,547	3,171	830
Reserve de Bayonne	5,877	55	80	,,	634	6,591	78	21
Total...............	197,648	19,216	3,443	1,693	30,395	231,486	29,422	8,486

The operations and misfortunes of the French prevented any general states being sent home between the 15th of March and the 15th of August, when a new organization of the armies took place ; but the numbers given in the narrative of this History are the result of calculations founded on the comparison of a variety of documents, and are believed to be a very close approximation to the real strength of the armies.

No. XIX.

Especial state of the army of Portugal, June 15, 1812.

Head-quarters, Tordesillas.

	Present under arms.		Detached.	Hospital.	Total.	Horses.		
	Men.	Horses.	Men.	Horses.		Men.	Cavalry.	Train.
1st Division.... Foy	5,138	,,	319	,,	516	5,973	,,	,,
2d do. ...... Clausel	7,405	,,	678	,,	613	8,696	,,	,,
3d do. ...... Ferey	5,547	,,	12	,,	926	6,485	,,	,,
4th do. ...... Sarrut........	5,056	,,	214	,,	862	6,132	,,	,,
5th do. ...... Maucune....	5,269	,,	588	,,	1,513	7,370	,,	,,
6th do. ...... Brennier	5,021	,,	124	,,	720	5,865	,,	,,
7th do. ...... Thomieres ..	6,352	61	,,	,,	1,905	8,257	61	,,
8th do. ...... Bonnet	6,681	139	66	,,	685	7,432	139	,,
LightCavalry, Curto... ...... 13 escadrons	1,386	1,398	1,073	324	246	2,705 ·	1,722	,,
Dragoons ...... Boyer	1,389	1,378	479	358	86	1,954	1,736	,,
Artillery	3,612	2,339	513	258	220	4,345	347	2,148
Genie...........................	414	9	67	7	84	565	,,	12
Equipage..........................	955	1,107	51	44	242	1,251	,,	1,084
Gendarmes et Infirmerie..	325	75	,,	,,	15	340	54	,,
Total	54,550	6,506	4,184	991	8,633	67,370	4,059	3,244

From these 54,550 men, present under arms, must be deducted the
artillery, engineers, equipages, and garrisons, the officers and sergeants,
and the losses sustained between the siege of the forts and the battle of
Salamanca, the result will be about 42,000 sabres and bayonets in the
battle.

Reinforcements en marche de l'armée du nord **1,370**
Do.   de Bayonne **12,676**

Note.—These troops did not join before the battle of Salamanca.

Artillery of the army of Portugal, June 15, 1812, Materiel.

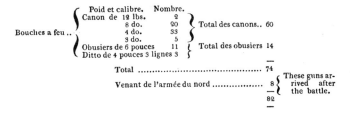

	Poid et calibre.	Nombre.	
	Canon de 12 lbs.	2	
	8 do.	20	Total des canons.. 60
Bouches a feu ..	4 do.	33	
	3 do.	5	
	Obusiers de 6 pouces	11	Total des obusiers 14
	Ditto de 4 pouces 3 lignes	3	

Total 74

Venant de l'armée du nord 8   These guns ar-
                                           —   rived after
                                           82   the battle.

Total loss of the army of Portugal from 10th July to 10th of August, 1812, including the battle of Salamanca. Extracted from the Imperial Muster-rolls.

		Tués.	Blessés.
Officiers superieurs.............. {	Duke de Raguse	,,	1
	General Clauzel	,,	1
	General Bonnet..................	,,	1
	General Ferrey	1	,,
	General Thomieres..............	1	,,
	General Desgravier Bertholet..	1	,,
	General Carrie..................	,,	1 Prisoner.
	General Menne	,,	1
Aide-de-camp du duc de Raguse	Colonel Richemont	,,	1
	Le Clerc de Montpree	1	,,
	Darel	,,	1

Total .... Tués 4   Blessés 7

Officiers inferieurs et soldats.	Tués ou Pris.	Blessés.	Traineurs.
Officiers.............................	162	232	,,
Soldats	3,867	7,529	645
Grande Total........	4,029	7,761	645

Officiers et Soldats 12,435
Chevaux 1,190
Canons 12
Deux aigles de 22eme et 101eme Regt. de ligne.

No. XX.

Strength of the Anglo-Portuguese army under Lord Viscount Wellington, on the morning of the 22d of July, 1812. Extracted from the original morning state.

Note.—The numbers are exclusive of officers, sergeants, trumpeters, artillery-men, and staff, shewing merely the sabres and bayonets in the field.

British cavalry, one division, present under arms .... 3,314 men 3,388 horses.
British infantry, seven divisions   do.   .... 22,067 ,,   ,,   ,,

Total British... 25,381
D'Urban's Portuguese cavalry, three regi-
    ments, about .... 1,500 These troops not in the state
Portuguese infantry, seven divisions, and two
    independent brigades 16,017

17,517

Total Anglo-Portuguese.......... 42,898
Carlos d'Espana's Spanish division, about .. 3,000
    Julian Sanchez' cavalry 500

3,500

Sabres and bayonets...... 46,398

No. of British, German, Portuguese, and Spanish guns at the battle of Salamanca.

		Weight of calibre.	Number of guns.
British horse artillery		6 lbs.	18
Foot	do.	9 lbs.	12
Do.	do.	12 lbs.	12
German	do.	9 lbs.	6
Portuguese and British brigaded together		24 lb. howitzers	6
			54
One Spanish battery			6

General total .... 60 pieces.

No. XXI.

Official report of the loss of the allies on the Trabancos and Guarena rivers, 18th July, 1812.

	Officers.	Sergeants.	Rank and file.	Horses.		Men.
British	3	3	56	59	Killed........	
	16	7	274	65	Wounded ..	
	,,	,,	27	21	Missing	543
Portuguese......	1	2	31	,,	Killed........	
	6	3	87	,,	Wounded ..	
	,,	,,	27	,,	Missing......	
Total............	26	15	502	145		

Loss of the allies in the battle of Salamanca.

British	28	24	336	96	Killed........	
	188	136	2,400	120	Wounded ..	
	,,	,,	74	37	Missing	5,224
Portuguese......	13	4	287	18	Killed........	
	74	42	1,436	13	Wounded ..	
	1	1	180	7	Missing......	
Total	304	207	4,713	291		

Loss of the German cavalry on the Almar Stream, July 23.

Men and Officers.	Horses.	
117	117	117

The British loss by infantry divisions and cavalry brigades.

Cavalry	Le Marchant's brigade,	lost	Men and officers		105	
	Anson's	do.	do.		5	
	Vr. Alten's	do.	do.		31	
Infantry..	1st Division	General Campbell	lost	Men and officers	69	
	3d do.	General Pakenham	do.	do.	456	
	4th do.	General Cole	do.	do.	537	
	5th do.	General Leith	do.	do.	464	
	6th do.	General Clinton	do.	do.	1,198	
	7th do.	General S. Hope	do.	do.	119	
	Light do.	General C. Alten	do.	do.	29	
	Artillery	General Framingham	do.	do.	14	

3,027

No. XXII.

Strength of the Anglo-Portuguese army at Vittoria.   Extracted from the
morning state of the 19th June, 1813.

	Present under arms.	On command.	Total. Present.	On command.
British Cavalry 7,791		851		
Portuguese do. 1,452		225		
Total cavalry			9,243	1,076
British infantry 33,658		1,771		
Portuguese do. 23,905		1,038		
Total infantry...			57,563	2,809
Sabres and bayonets......			66,806	3,885
Deduct the 6th division left at Medina de Pomar			6,320	
Sabres and bayonets......			60,486	

	Spanish Auxiliaries.		
Infantry .... {	Morillo's division	about	3,000
	Giron's do.	do.	12,000
	Carlos d'Espagna's do.	do.	3,000
	Longa's do.	do.	3,200
Cavalry	Penne Villemur	do.	1,000
	Julian Sanchez	do.	1,000
			23,000

Grand Total 83,486

No. of Anglo-Portuguese guns at the battle of Vittoria.

Colonel A. Dickson commanding.

British horse artillery .... 9 lbs.			45
Do. do. .... 6 lbs.			30
Do. do. .... 5½ inch howitzers			15
Total			90

No Spanish guns set down in the return.   Number unknown.

END OF VOL. V.